To our good friend Shari.

PEOPLE + ME

We have had many great times together.

I hope you enjoy reading about my early years and the many people I have enjoyed.

Jim Frederick
March 13, 2025

People + Me

A Thank You To The Many People
In My Life And Those Who
May Have Influenced It

Joseph B. Frederick

Volume 1

Copyright © 2015 by Joseph B. Frederick.

Library of Congress Control Number:	2015904876
ISBN: Hardcover	978-1-5035-5802-1
Softcover	978-1-5035-5800-7
eBook	978-1-5035-5801-4

All rights reserved. No part of this book may be reproduced or transmitted in any form or by any means, electronic or mechanical, including photocopying, recording, or by any information storage and retrieval system, without permission in writing from the copyright owner.

Any people depicted in stock imagery provided by Thinkstock are models, and such images are being used for illustrative purposes only. Certain stock imagery © Thinkstock.

Print information available on the last page.

Rev. date: 07/20/2015

To order additional copies of this book, contact:
Xlibris
1-888-795-4274
www.Xlibris.com
Orders@Xlibris.com
540090

Contents

Preface ix
Acknowledgments xi
Introduction and Overview xiii

Part I: My Parents and Their Parents

Chapter 1   The Frederick Family 1
Chapter 2   The Schlotterer Family 9
Chapter 3   My Parents 22

Part II: The Formative Years

Chapter 4   God Gave One Twin and Kept the Other 59
Chapter 5   My Supportive Siblings in the Early Years 76
Chapter 6   Grade School Days and Before 120
Chapter 7   Other Memories of My Grade School Years 163

Part III: Approaching Adulthood

Chapter 8   Willard High School..241
Chapter 9   My High School Neighbors, Community
                 Activities, Family, and Work..290

Part IV: On My Own

Chapter 10   My First Years at John Carroll University.......................335
Chapter 11   The Last Years at John Carroll University......................388

Part V: Really on My Own

Chapter 12   Bowling Green State University and Kathy 449
Chapter 13   Engagement, Marriage, and our First Year.....................477

Bibliography I...503

To my family: my lovely wife, Kathy; my two sons, Joe II and Mark; Joe's wife, Tara; and their two sons, Zachary and Joshua.

Preface

Each of us lives our life in a different manner. After all, each is a unique person with different heredity, living circumstances, and exposure to other people.

My background was a small railroad town in Northern Ohio named Willard. From the beginning, I was destined to be a very active person in a world that provided me with many interesting experiences. I was to find that my family, friends, profession, and community provided me with many challenges and, for the most part, enjoyment.

As I neared the end of my professional career, I began to review all the boxes of information collected in my life. The material was too good not to use. The experiences inspired me to write about my life. As ideas came to me, I continued to write and enter them into my manuscript. I found that there was one setting that jogged my memory and raised more ideas for the book than any other. That would be my weekly church service at Blessed John XXIII Parish in Perrysburg, Ohio. While I was praying in church, I found the purpose of the book. It was in a true sense a thank you to God for the life He had given me and a thank you to many people for the support, experiences, and influences on my life.

The book is filled with events that I think others will find interesting. There is a great deal of variety and, at times, entertainment in the happenings. There are writings that may be useful for others in living their lives. As I reread the text, I questioned who else was inspiring me as I wrote, for it seems as if forces assisted me in this process. I found many answers about my support system. I still search for answers with God and my twin who died in utero at three months. I thank you for entering into my world and trust you will find enjoyment in your reading.

Acknowledgments

With the writing of this book, I hope I have not neglected my wife, Kathy; my two sons, Joe II and Mark; my daughter-in-law, Tara; and my grandsons, Zachary and Joshua. They have supported me in this task. My goal of giving time to my family and others is more important than the priority of my book and is consistent with my principles of life and love.

God's gift to me of life is the supreme acknowledgment. My life is really God's life, and my goal has been to use the blessings and gifts He has given me to His honor and glory in this book.

My parents taught that other people's influence through love and giving cannot be ignored. Following the example of my parents, I have been fortunate to be involved in several community, educational, and church-related organizations. My parents encouraged me to "give back" or "leave the world a better place than I found it"; it has been my guiding light. This guiding light tells me that giving back to God is essential, and this book is an opportunity to do that.

My mother; my father; my sister, Mary Lu; and my namesake Uncle Joe Schlotterer, PhD, who have left this world have given me support in many ways. Other support for this book came from my friend Dr. Ted Sipes, who has tirelessly reviewed my draft copies and helped develop my ability to express my ideas through the written word before his passing. My wife, Kathy, filled a difficult role of supporting my writing and at the same time giving me constructive suggestions on the content. My neighbor Sue Welty journeyed with me page by page through the final draft to make sure it was the best possible product. I wish to recognize Jamie Welty for his excellent skills in accomplishing the comprehensive review of the book. Good Job Jamie! My cousin George Schlotterer and high school friend Bob Bauerle have encouraged me throughout the process. Tom Hickey produced the descendants family trees, which allowed my family to be identified by sight and demographic data. Each played their part at the proper time and with the appropriate support. Without all of their support, this book would not have materialized.

In addition, I need to acknowledge the many people who have shared and contributed a part of their lives, their intellect, and their skills with me so that I could be a part of their rich lives as they were to be a part of mine. The living persons who were identified in these pages were kind enough to give me permission to include some of their personal stories. Also, several publications gave me permission to use their copyright documents.

The following acknowledgment for the use of the New American Bible for numerous and probably the most copyright permissions in this book is gratefully included. Scripture texts in this work are taken from the New American Bible with revised New Testament © 1986, 1970 Confraternity of Christian Doctrine, Washington, D.C. and are used by permission of the copyright owner. All rights reserved. No part of the New American Bible may be reproduced in any form without permission in writing from the copyright owner. Mary Elizabeth Sperry, associate director for the New American Bible, has been my competent contact over the past several years. Thank you, Mary Beth, for enabling me to share God's words.

This book would not have been possible if it had not been for my publisher Xlibris. The several submissions representatives, especially Kris Alberto, who labored with me throughout the several years' process, and Marie Giles and Mary Flores. A special thank you to Lindsey Mattel for the essential final touches. The staff supported my every need to make this book the best it could be.

Introduction and Overview

About the Direction and Title

During the first few years I was writing this book, I spent time trying to sharpen its direction. On July 20, 2008, I did receive a great deal of help when I was attending ten-thirty morning Mass at Blessed John XXIII (now Saint John XXIII) Parish near Perrysburg, Ohio. I was listening to Fr. Herb Weber, our parish priest, introduce Sr. Pat McClain, a member of our parish. In fact, Sr. Pat, principal of Lial Catholic School in Whitehouse, Ohio, was celebrating that very day her twenty-fifth anniversary in the religious order of the Notre Dame. Sister Pat was sitting in front of my wife, Kathy, and me with her natural family and religious community of other Notre Dame Sisters.

At a point in the Mass near the homily, Sister Pat renewed her vows and said a few words to the congregation. I was immediately taken in by her words. It was as if she was talking directly to and for me about my book as she thanked everyone present for "the opportunity to experience many wonderful people." I had been struggling with the title of my book and knew at that moment that the struggle had ended.

The thought hit me very clearly that the intent of my book was the privilege of sharing stories about other people in my life and also about me. In this process of sharing, a mutual giving between others and myself was taking place. I knew that writing about these experiences would in a sense be a form of thanking everyone for having been a part and in many cases an influence in my life by telling their stories. I took out my small Swiss Army knife with a pen and wrote Sister Pat's words; I knew they would influence the words in my new title and the direction of the book. Her words helped guide my story, and the book title became *People + Me*. Thanks, Sister Pat, for helping me crystallize my direction.

The Influence of Others and Me

As time passed, another thought about the title of my book struck me. I am but a product of all my experiences, which include all other people, if I am open to them. It works another way. Other people who are open to me would have the capability of showing reflections of me in their lives. We are all more like others than different when we analyze their influence on our lives and ours on theirs. While the book was about me, I wanted it to be as much as possible about other people.

Our influences on others and theirs on us are at times recognized. Often influences are not recognized, but they do take place. The importance of influences is that they do take place and are often helpful to others, not that people get credit. In these writings, recognition for helpful actions is many times an incomplete act.

Goals

Knowing and getting to where one wishes to be in life is of paramount importance. That is why my life has been driven by goals. I would speculate that some of my major goals are similar to many of your goals: to obtain an education, to love God, to have meaningful relationships, perhaps to fall in love, to marry, to have children, and to be successful at one's profession. In the end, we hope to find sources of fulfillment and happiness. One other more unusual goal for me is to write this book based on my experiences. All of these goals have one common denominator: to help me live a worthwhile existence and if possible in the process help other people on their life journeys.

Support

In pursuing my goals, I have realized that other people often supported me even when I thought I was trying to help them. Over the years, I have found, and it will be evident as you read, that the greatest help I have received was from God. I feel my twin who died at three months in utero has been another important influence to me.

Writing the Book

As I have grown older and experienced various events, I made it a practice to constantly document and share the many good and not so positive times in my life. The passing of persons, particularly my father, mother, sister, many friends, and neighbors, has always caused me to think about life's journey. My hope is that I can pay homage to many people and to the most influential being in my life, God. When I have a potentially memorable experience, either in the present or past, I try to quickly evaluate the happening to see if it is one that I can document and share. It is exciting for me to have the opportunity to share my life and the people in my life with others. It is actually more than exciting; it is a major driving force in my life to develop this book for others' enjoyment and benefit. While it is impossible to sum up one's life in a book, it is possible to leave behind stories about many other wonderful people and myself.

It is never my intention to embarrass, make fun of, or in any way put down anyone in my writings. If I made an error in judgment and hurt someone, I am sorry. You see, writing this book is a risk. The risk is that, at times, I may not convey the information in the best possible manner, and it would be offensive. To guard against this possibility, I have obtained permission from others, when appropriate. I would be remiss if I do not acknowledge the unsought encouragement that frequently accompanied many of the permissions that I received from people I was privileged to include in the book. In writing this book, I have striven to make the text interesting, the contents related to reader's needs, something entertaining yet not dragging, and one that can be read in either short or longer periods with the use of vignettes. It is important that the text be understood by the intended audience and that the content have some commonality with the readers' lives. A constant concern I have is that the script be free of errors. While reviews have been done to eliminate misspellings, incorrect verb tenses, and other such errors, it probably won't be perfect. Please know that I and others have done their best on the manuscript. I ask you to enjoy the readings and forgive any unintentional errors in the text.

Experiences in our lives are unique to each of us. No other person can go through them as we have. Yet our experiences do usually have similarities with other people's experiences. For example, when we were into the Halloween holiday, we had the anticipation of obtaining lots of candy. We were also into choosing the right costume and going with our siblings or friends door to door in the neighborhood. When we hear, see, think, or read about Halloween, we identify with these memories. As you read this book, my hope is that you can identify with many of the experiences I have gone through and enjoy parts of your life again.

One Book Becomes Two

I invite you to join me in reliving my life's experiences and important lessons I have learned from them. As I began writing the book, the number of pages dictated that two books must be the end result. The first volume covers my life from the beginning up to and including my first year of marriage and is titled *People + Me*. The second volume covers my professional career and exemplifies, as the title states, that *God Keeps on Giving* to me professionally and personally. *People + Me* will be covered in this text.

Influence of Others

Many people have made a difference in my life. I have seen that everyone I have known or will meet may potentially affect my life in some way. A poem sent to me for Christmas in 2007 by Maxine Mobley, grandmother to my daughter-in-law Tara, written by an unknown author, captured my sentiments on the influence of other people affecting my life very accurately. Part of the poem went like this:

For I am but a total of the many folks I've met
And you happen to be one of those I prefer never to forget,
And whether I have known you for many years or few,
In some way you have had a part of shaping things I do.

Everyone's life is shaped by others; please enjoy how mine has been shaped—possibly by you.

Part I

My Parents and Their Parents

Chapter 1

The Frederick Family

My grandfather Charles Frederick and stepgrandmother Marguerite were the grandparents I knew well on the Frederick side of the family despite the fact that my grandfather was married three times. My grandfather was in his late sixties when I remember visiting him in his home on 414 Park Street, Willard, Ohio. Grandma and Grandpa were located one block and a few houses from our residence on 519 Clark Street. The age of my

The Frederick homestead on 414 Park Street

grandfather and his challenged ability to ambulate did not help him enjoy his later years. I always believed that the relationship between my father and grandfather could have been better and heard my father say that his beliefs about life and his father's were very different.

While I never knew my grandfather's first wife, Clara, I vaguely remember his second wife, Mary Ann. His third wife, Marguerite, was a very hardworking lady and spent a great deal of her time taking care of the house and my grandfather. She was always kind to me and my family. I am in the middle of this First Communion picture. From left to right, we have my grandparents Lucille Schlotterer, Charles and Marguerite Frederick, and Karl Schlotterer. The abbreviated family tree titled Descendants of Charles Heffner Frederick is contained in this next image.

My First Communion day

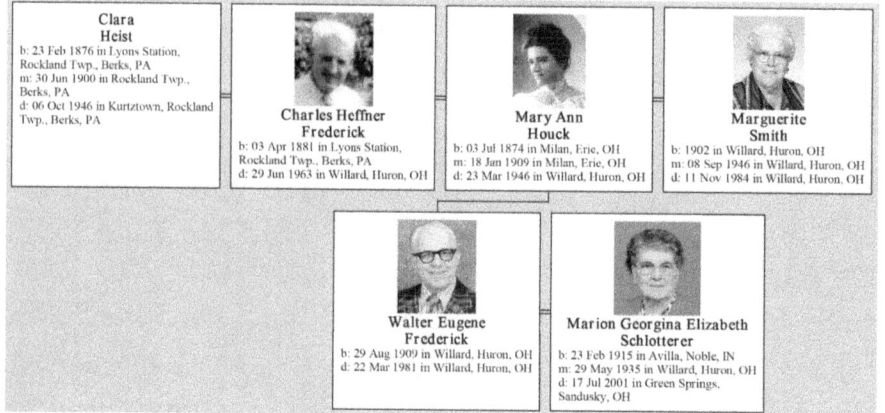

Descendants of Charles Heffner Frederick

Grandpa Charles Frederick

Grandpa Frederick was my father's father. Grandpa Frederick was from Reading, Pennsylvania, and was born on April, 3, 1881, in Lyons Station, Pennsylvania. Pennsylvania Dutch or German was his lineage, and being the head of the family was a strong trait of the men. There were two brothers, Oscar and Joseph; four sisters, Ellen, Ida, Emma, and Lizzie; six stepsisters; and two stepbrothers.

Three of these stepsisters were well-known to our family: Aunt Cora, Aunt Agnes, and Aunt Elsie. We would often take family vacations to Pennsylvania when I was young. The family would stay with Aunt Cora and Aunt Agnes. They had a large tourist home and reserved the rooms for us when we visited.

The Hose

It was in Pennsylvania at the tourist home that the following event happened. One afternoon, my brothers and sisters were playing with the hose in the backyard. I was young and remember well that I had control of the garden hose and was probably spraying at them. It was great fun until I remember Aunt Agnes coming into the backyard. She didn't move too fast because she was up in years. Aunt Agnes was about twenty feet behind me when she told me to give her the hose. Without thinking, I turned and gave Aunt Agnes the hose square in her face. I can still see her drying her glasses with her apron. That was the last time we had access to the garden hose or touched it.

The Ranch

Another memorable time in Pennsylvania was visiting the ranch owned by Walter Knoll, a relative of ours. The ranch was several acres and located in the country. Included were a two-story building, a swimming pool, and a large concrete fish-and-frog pond. When we swam, we had the best time. It was like owning one's own pool.

On the first floor of the building, there was a keg of birch beer (like root beer). The birch beer was extremely cold and had a great taste. It seemed like the supply was endless. In addition to owning the ranch, Mr. Knoll was also the owner of a car distributorship. My brother Walt traveled from Willard to Western Pennsylvania to drive home the 1950 Ford he bought from Mr. Knoll.

More on Grandpa Frederick

My grandfather originally worked in Pennsylvania on the railroad and transferred to Willard and a very good job as engineer on the B&O (Baltimore and Ohio Railroad). Since my grandfather was from Pennsylvania Dutch background (German stock), the nickname "Dutch" followed him in his life. He married his first wife, Clara Heist, on June 30, 1900, in Western Pennsylvania. When he left Pennsylvania, he also left his children and his first wife, a woman he never saw after that day.

In Willard, on January 18, 1909, Grandpa married Mary Ann Houck, who was born on January 3, 1874, in Milan, Ohio. They had two sons, my father, Walter, and my uncle Charles. My father and Charles were to be lifelong friends. Mary Ann was interested in my father's activities, which often involved music. When Mary Ann passed on March 23, 1946, later that year, Charles married Marguerite. There were no children from this third marriage.

I never knew my grandfather to be anything but an elderly man. His gait was slow, and he rarely left his easy chair. He loved to smoke cigars and occasionally liked a sip of rock and rye whiskey. After Grandpa was finished with a cigar box, Grandma Marguerite would give it to us grandchildren as a toy. I felt my grandfather could have been a happier person. When my family would visit with Grandmother and Grandfather Frederick, the setting was pretty uneventful. My grandfather would sit in his chair while my mother, father, and grandmother did most of the talking. I don't ever remember seeing Grandfather smile or say more than a few words to the kids. When my family visited our grandparents, the children usually played in the kitchen or on the front porch with the door closed, as noise from the children would bother my grandfather.

My father's brother was Charles. Charles and his wife, Mary, lived next to Grandpa and Grandma. Charles drove truck. Mary was a friendly person who talked with a laugh. She was well-known in the African violet circles and had the distinction of having an African violet named after her. Charles and Mary had a daughter, Patti, who was a speech therapist.

My Height

One of my greatest challenges up to and including high school was my height (5'2") and size. I was always small, and the older I became, the more it bothered me. When entering a room of my peers or adults, I would look around and think, *Who is shorter than me?* If I wasn't the shortest, I felt a bit better about my height. If I was the shortest, my inferiority complex would surface. I would frequently read the ads on the Charles Atlas bodybuilding courses advertised at that time in many magazines. I did work out with weights in my father's workshop. I would do anything to increase my height or body size.

It was from Aunt Mary that I received the best advice on my size and height when I was in high school. She was a dearly loved aunt. As we were sitting down to supper once at Grandfather Frederick's house, Aunt Mary, who was also short in stature, asked me how I was doing. I mentioned to her I hated being short. With her traditional laughing voice, she told me how she also had my concern when she was younger. I asked her what she did about this concern. She told me that she had found out in her life that height or size of the body did not matter as much as she thought. What did matter was the type of person one was, especially when it came to how one treated other people. While my complex on height and size did not vanish immediately, I soon developed a better outlook on it. The few times that a girl would not dance with me or date me because of what I perceived as my size seemed to become less important.

Water

My grandfather had a cistern at his house, which collected rainwater from the roof of his large home. Every few weeks, either my sister Ann or my brother Mike and I would pull our red wagon with five or six one-gallon glass jugs to my grandparents and fill them up with rainwater for my dad's tropical-fish aquariums. I can remember on one or two occasions that the jugs hit each other and broke. We never got in trouble for those breakages.

Backyard

I also remember there was a large grape arbor in the backyard in addition to the many fruit trees. The grape arbor was old and would not support our small bodies. We usually climbed cautiously, so we didn't break the arbor or the grapevines. As we climbed what we were not to be climbing, we always kept one eye on the house.

There was an outbuilding behind the residence that housed chickens which produced eggs. Mike, Ann, and I loved to venture into the chicken coop and chase the chickens. My grandmother would hear the chickens cackling, and she would escort us out of the coop. She said the chickens would not lay eggs if they were excited. Behind the chicken coop was a single-car garage that always housed a new Studebaker. I remember one of the Studebakers was bright yellow in color and reminded me of a new car color I recently saw. The garage was so small that I never understood how anyone could drive the car in or get out of the car once it was in the garage.

Grandma Clara (Heist) Frederick

I knew little about Grandma Clara who was born February 23, 1876, in Berks County, Pennsylvania. She married my grandfather at the age of twenty-five and bore him three children before the separation. She worked at a shoe factory. When my grandfather left his first wife, Clara, it is said that she was not able to see him. In later years, my grandfather would go to visit his children and other relatives in Pennsylvania. Clara is buried in Mertz Church Cemetery, Rockland Township, in Berks County, Pennsylvania.

Grandma Mary Ann (Houck) Frederick

Grandma Mary Ann was my biological grandmother. She was born on July 3, 1874. When my father played musical instruments in a barn dance, my mother reported to me that Grandma Mary Ann would go with them. Usually, my grandfather was working on the railroad and was unable to attend these social events. Grandma Mary Ann was employed at the L. E. Simmons Clothing in downtown Willard. My mother and father both spoke highly of her. Her nickname was Mame, the same nickname as my mother. Grandma Mary Ann died on March 23, 1946, in Willard, when I was one year and almost six months old.

Grandma Marguerite Frederick

Grandma Marguerite was the Grandma Frederick I remember. She was a very nice person and always took time for us children. When I was a young boy, I would go down to my grandparents in the summer to pick the Queen Anne cherries by the bucketful. Queen Anne cherries are sweet large white cherries. Grandma would have someone put up the ladders, and we would climb to the top of the tree to pick the sweetest and biggest cherries. There were two cherry trees; one was very large, and the other was one-third the size of the big one. The sweetest and largest cherries came from the smaller tree. Grandma was always at the bottom of the steps because she would help us if we needed it. Boy, were those cherries good!

Marguerite was a faithful church-going person, which probably contributed to her giving spirit and enjoyment of life. My grandmother was one of the best cooks I knew. Her gift for cooking wild game for my brother and me has never been forgotten. My brother Mike and I would hunt or trap woodchuck, squirrel, rabbit, muskrat, and raccoon. The meat was great, but the mashed potatoes and gravy were beyond description.

Kathy, my wife, and I helped Grandma to move from her house on Park Street to a smaller house on Dale Avenue in Willard. Grandma gave us some of the items she would no longer need, such as canning jars. I remember those large crocks and other antiques she wanted us to take, but we had no place to store them. I wish I had those items today. We always enjoyed talking to Grandma Marguerite and sharing our lives with her.

Chapter 2

The Schlotterer Family

A very strong Catholic faith of both my Schlotterer grandparents probably contributed to their happy lives and constant giving to their sixteen children, many grandchildren, and others in their lives. Examples of their giving to others as well as many overtones of their happy lives will be addressed. The abbreviated Schlotterer family tree showing only Marion Schlotterer is the next image. A picture of Lucille and Karl Schlotterer, parents of sixteen children, follows.

Descendants of Karl Francis Schlotterer

Karl Francis Schlotterer
b: 16 Jan 1891 in Avilla, Noble, IN
d: 04 Sep 1970 in Willard, Huron, OH

Lucille Augusta Helena Samuelson
b: 27 Jan 1896 in Brooklyn, Kings, NY
m: 08 Aug 1914 in Fort Hancock, Monmouth, NJ
d: 05 Mar 1996 in Lexington, Richland, OH

Marion Georgina Elizabeth Schlotterer
b: 23 Feb 1915 in Avilla, Noble, IN
d: 17 Jul 2001 in Green Springs, Sandusky, OH

Walter Eugene Frederick
b: 29 Aug 1909 in Willard, Huron, OH
m: 29 May 1935 in Willard, Huron, OH
d: 22 Mar 1981 in Willard, Huron, OH

Lucille and Karl Schlotterer

Grandpa Karl Schlotterer

Grandpa Schlotterer was my mother's father. He was born in Avilla, Indiana, on January 16, 1891. He was raised in Avilla, a small town of about 500 residents. There is a bar, a restaurant, a church, and a cemetery, as well as several residences. Another bar (which doesn't exist as a bar today) was owned and operated by my great-grandfather Charles Schlotterer. I recently visited Avilla with Kathy and cousins George, Betty, Leo, and Deb Schlotterer. We briefly visited the bar and also ate at a very nice restaurant, St. James.

Why Is the Schlotterer Family in America?

A story I heard was about my great-great-grandfather Joseph Schlotterer. Joseph had a brother named Charles Schlotterer, and the reason that Joseph and his brother moved to America was one of them had killed someone. Their father, a high-ranking officer in the German Army, sent them to America because of this killing. I have no more information available on the circumstances and truth of this story. If some or all parts of this story were true, it could shed light on why the Schlotterer family is in America.

My grandfather had ten brothers and sisters. The brothers were Florence, Urban, John, Frederick, Godfrey, and Victor. The sisters were Emma, Josephine, Rose, and Eda. Grandfather grew up on a farm owned by his grandparents.

More about Grandpa Schlotterer

My grandfather served from 1912 to January 1915 in the U.S. Coastal Artillery and was stationed at Fort Hancock, Sandy Hook, New Jersey. It was here that my grandfather and grandmother met. They were married on August 8, 1914. He was of average stature. Grandpa worked many different jobs. He was a bartender, a glassworker, a plasterer, an undertaker assistant, a farmer, a painter, and a lumber company employee, in addition to holding various jobs on the B&O Railroad, such as fireman and watering the passenger cars and engines. Passenger trains were common when I was a boy, and I used them as a college student at John Carroll University. After Grandpa retired from the railroad, he was a security guard at Midwest Industries and at Pioneer Rubber Company, both in Willard. Grandpa Schlotterer was known for his infectious laugh and contagious smile.

I knew that my grandfather worked third shift because I always needed to be quiet if I visited his house during the day. Grandpa Schlotterer, unlike Grandfather Frederick, was a very jovial person. He was frequently laughing and rarely refused a bottle of beer, especially an Old Dutch. I was around him when I was a very young boy.

Grandpa Schlotterer and me

Being with My Grandfather

My grandfather was an easygoing person and would allow his grandchildren to explore various areas in the house and garage. I remember two instances when I was given the privilege of being allowed to experiment by my grandfather. One was when my grandpa was whitewashing the cellar in the house on 119 Spring Street, one of eight homes in Willard the family lived. I was sure that I

The Schlotterer home on 119 Spring Street

created a big mess, but my grandfather said, "Joey has to learn how to paint someday." I guess I didn't create as large a mess as I thought I would. This experience was probably my first exposure to painting.

The second experience was at the second Schlotterer home on Woodbine Street, also in Willard. My sister Ann and I were sitting on the front porch. It was in the afternoon one summer when I was about to enter Willard High School. I asked my grandpa, "How do you chew tobacco?" Grandpa took his Mail Pouch Tobacco out of his pocket and put a slug into his mouth and said, "I don't swallow the tobacco juice, or I will get dizzy and sick." I went into the house for a drink and saw a pouch of chewing tobacco. I took a smaller amount of tobacco out of the pouch, put it in my mouth, and went out on the porch and chewed the tobacco in a spot where my grandfather wouldn't see me. Ann was a little smarter than me; she took a piece of the tobacco, touched it to her tongue, and immediately threw it away because it burned her tongue.

To this day, I can remember chewing the tobacco and telling myself that I was not going to get dizzy or sick from the tobacco juice. I closed off the entrance to my throat by placing my tongue as tightly against the roof of my mouth and the throat to avoid swallowing the juice. I chewed and chewed for a while. All at once, I could feel myself getting dizzy. I thought, *This cannot be. I haven't swallowed any of the tobacco juice.* At that time, I remember seeing the mother of one of my friends walk by. She asked me how I was doing, and I told her, "Fine." What a fibber I was!

I ran into the house and spit out the tobacco into the wastebasket. I saw a glass of milk, which turned out to be warm milk, and I drank it. I was really getting sick after the warm milk. I don't know which was worse, the warm milk or the tobacco. As I sat down on the front porch, it didn't take long for me to realize that the tobacco was to date one of the worst experiences in my life because I was becoming dizzier after each breath I took. I really needed some help from some source: God, my twin, or both. I did not get "throw-up sick," but I surely wished I would have because that chewing tobacco continued to cast its spell of dizziness on my body. I never tried chewing tobacco after that. I have thought many times that my grandfather, whether he knew it or not, taught me a good lesson about tobacco.

Each time I glanced at my grandpa after that day, he had a smile on his face, maybe thinking of the time I was dizzy from the Mail Pouch Tobacco. On the other hand, my grandfather usually had a smile on his face, so the smile could have meant anything. Grandpa Schlotterer died on September 4, 1970.

A Trip to Avilla, Location of Grandpa Schlotterer's Early Years

I always had an interest in knowing more about where people grew up and what the buildings, such as their church, restaurants, and stores, looked like. A road trip to Avilla allowed me to learn more about the town and my grandfather. On September 5, 2008, my cousin George Schlotterer of Dayton, Ohio and his wife, Betty, as well as my brother Walt and his wife, Judy, from North Carolina met at our house so we could have an early start the next morning for Auburn and Avilla, Indiana. Originally, my brother Walt was to bring his Winnebago, and everyone going to Indiana was to travel in the motor home. Unfortunately, Walt and Judy only made it to Hilliard, Ohio, near Columbus, and their vehicle had a mechanical problem. They had pulled another vehicle behind their motor home, and they used it to travel to our home in New Rochester, Ohio.

After supper at our house on Friday and an early breakfast at the nearby Edgewood Restaurant, the five travelers departed for Indiana. The first stop in Indiana was to see some of my relatives on Grandfather Schlotterer's side. I had not known any of the family we were to meet that day, but we were hoping for some good information from some relatives we were able to meet.

We entered the small town of Kendallville, Indiana. The town was very inviting and clean. The older buildings were well maintained, and the downtown area was vibrant. It was a successful downtown shopping area.

We arrived at Timothy's Jewelry in the morning and met Tim, our cousin, who was our contact person for the relatives. Tim's shop was a jewelry store in the front and a shop in the back. Since Tim makes custom jewelry and clocks as well as repairs them, I began to understand why he had so many different machines in the shop. He was finishing a ring when we arrived. As he made last adjustments to the ring, I was amazed at the manner in which he moved from machine to machine. He was smooth, accurate, and precise in his movements while he seemed to be in sync with music I did not hear. Tim was very helpful in assisting me to develop a plan to repair my 400-day clock.

A few minutes later, the daughters of Godfrey Schlotter entered the back of the jewelry shop. They are Sharon, Cheryl, and Rebecca. At some point in time, I found that some of the Schlotterers had adopted a new spelling of the name to Schlotter. We began to talk about various descendants of Charles Schlotterer. Tim was the son of Richard Schlotter who was the son of Godfrey Schlotter. Godfrey was a brother to my grandfather Karl Schlotterer. Cheryl shared that their grandson Jordan and his wife, Casey, were married on national television that year on *Live with Regis and Kelly*. During the conversation, an interesting fact was discussed. Urban, the oldest brother of Karl Schlotterer, had a somewhat unusual relationship in his marriage. Urban Schlotterer married Edith M. Sprague Good who was the mother of Berdena. Berdena Belle Good was the wife of Victor "Johnnie" Hugo Schlotter. Thus, a mother and her daughter married brothers.

Mary-Catherine Manuel, wife of Tim, came into the shop after delivering jewelry in the community. She had made two large platters of appetizers for those in attendance. As a token to remember the day, Tim had made Schlotter's coins, which he had crafted from one of the original coins used in Great-grandfather Charles Schlotterer's bar. The coins were good for a beer or a game of cards. A discussion and viewing of the family websites offered new information on how to keep up with the Schlotterer/ Schlotter families.

We said our goodbyes, and the remainder of the day was spent at the Auburn Cord Duesenberg Museum in Auburn. Time was also spent in the St. Mary's Church and Cemetery in Avilla. My grandparents and mother's elder brothers and sisters attended the church. The evening meal was there in St. James Restaurant. Charles Schlotterer was at one time the owner of St. James Restaurant. Across the street from the restaurant is the building that probably was the former bar owned by Charles.

On Saturday evening, we stayed with George's daughter and son-in-law Amy and Ron Sarrazine in Fort Wayne. On Sunday, we attended the Immaculate Conception Church food festival. With a full stomach of very good food, we were on our way to my house in Ohio for a light supper to finish the weekend of the family heritage tour. It was a warm and enjoyable feeling to look at one's roots.

Grandma Lucille (Samuelson) Schlotterer

My grandmother was a tiny lady born on January 27, 1896, in Brooklyn, New York. Her religious belief was Episcopalian. She had three brothers, Anton, Victor, George, and five sisters, Anne, Rachael, Marie, Pauline, and Esther. When I was young, my family had visited Uncle George and Aunt Esther in New York and Marie in Connecticut.

The Bottle

In later years, Grandma had a favorite story about Aunt Esther's husband and how it pays to watch your trash. As the story goes, Aunt Esther's husband came home one day from work. He had stopped that day at the liquor store and purchased a bottle of whiskey. As he was climbing the back steps to their Brooklyn apartment, he had a heart attack, died, and fell down the steps. The bottle broke and covered the body of Aunt Esther's husband with whiskey.

The life insurance company was called to settle the life insurance claim. Much to Aunt Esther's dismay, the insurance company came to the apartment to investigate and said they couldn't pay off the insurance policy, as Esther's husband had been drinking, fell down the steps, and died because of the intoxication. Being the analytical person she was, Esther told the insurance man to come with her because the trash would not be picked up until the next day. Sure enough, the broken bottle of whiskey was in the trash, along with an unbroken seal on the cap. The insurance claim was paid.

More about Grandma Schlotterer

When Grandma and Grandpa met, she was a maid for a captain at Fort Hancock, New Jersey, while Grandpa was a serviceman. Grandma converted to Catholicism around her wedding date, a change in her life that would have a profound and lasting influence on her and the lives of her children and hundreds of grandchildren. Grandma came to Avilla around 1915 and lived most of her early years with Grandpa there until approximately 1930 when they moved to Willard. Grandma Schlotterer was always an active person. She loved tea ("One sugar cube, please") and loved to play cards and other games. She loved to win! She was a whiz with math, attended church regularly, sorted and counted sales tax redemption stamps for St. Joseph's Church in Plymouth, Ohio, visited the sisters at Madonna Hall in Willard, and talked often with her family and friends. She loved to travel and would be ready to go on a five minutes' notice. If you gave her the map, she could direct the driver almost anywhere.

She was a devoted Christian and, with her husband, raised their sixteen children on a limited budget. Twenty-four-seven were her hours. The Blessed Mary was very important to Grandma. She enrolled each of her children in the Immaculate Heart of Mary, also known as the Sacred Heart of Mary, and asked each of her children to recite their decade of the rosary every day.

She was asked one day, "What are you going to do when you meet Jesus?" She answered with a big smile, "What do we do when we greet each other? I will give Him a big hug and kiss." She was 100 years old when she died on March 5, 1996.

Schlotterer Family Prayer

Grandma had been a member of the Episcopalian faith before marrying Grandpa. Her conversion to the Catholic faith encouraged her actions in prayer. It is reported that every one of her children was taught to pray, and one of the prayers learned was a prayer called the Schlotterer Family Prayer. This prayer was said every night before bed and at reunions, funerals, and other family gatherings. Research has shown that the words from the prayer were nearly the same as a hymn titled *"Jesus, tender Shepherd, hear me"* written by Mary Lundie Duncan in 1839. The Schlotterer Family Prayer had a first line not in the hymn and ended with an Amen not in the original hymn. The hymn talked about a little lamb, and the prayer talked about a little child.[1]

This is the prayer:

Schlotterer Family Prayer

Lord, let us be, no one ere lost a family in heaven
Jesus, tender Shepherd, hear me
Bless thy little child tonight

> Through the darkness be thou with me
> Keep me safe till morning light
> All this day, thy hand has lead me.
> And I thank thee for thy care
> Thou has warmed and clothed and fed me
> Listen to my evening prayer
> Let my sins be all forgiven
> Bless the friends I love so well
> Take me when I die to heaven
> Happy there with thee to dwell
> Amen.

I must report that as I was examining the use of this prayer near the end of writing this book, my first inclination was to not use it. There could be much work in clearing the copyright to use the prayer, and I needed to finish the book. Some force told me to pick up the prayer and try to use it. I am convinced that my mother had something to do with the inclusion of this prayer.

I also am convinced that my grandmother may have come in contact with this hymn as she was Episcopalian, and this hymn was published in the Episcopal Hymn Book in 1871.[2] It would seem logical that this could have led to the Schlotterer Family Prayer.

Regardless of the origin of this prayer, its effect upon the Schlotterer family has been most positive, seeing the attention to, the reverence of, and the continued practice with points to an ongoing belief and trust in God.

The Schlotterer Family

Grandpa and Grandma Schlotterer moved to Avilla around 1915. They left for a short period to live in New York but returned to Avilla. Being a city girl, Grandma was not used to living in a small town. Seven children were born in the Avilla area. After moving to Willard, she was to give birth to nine more children. They had seven sons and nine daughters. At Grandma's death, she had eighty-five grandchildren, 165 great grandchildren, and thirty-seven great-great-grandchildren. Religion was very important to the Schlotterer family. The boys were servers, and the girls cleaned the Catholic church. As adults, they continued their service to the church, being active in the various church organizations, such as the Women's Altar and Rosary Society and the Men's Knights of Columbus to name a few.

Three of their sons served in the military during World War II, and one of her daughters served in the Waves. During the 1950s, three other sons were in the Navy. They had grandchildren who served in the Vietnam War, in the Desert Storm War, and in Afghanistan. Several military awards were earned by their children and grandchildren. After their children's marriages, many were to leave the state to pursue their various life dreams.

Family get-togethers were frequent throughout their lives. With the offspring of sixteen, there were many reasons for a party. Parties were very active and fun-filled, as the many relatives enjoyed being together. There were always parties for Baptisms, First Communions, Confirmations, high school graduations, wedding showers, weddings, baby showers, and New Year's Eve.

Grandma and Grandpa never owned a car and walked to church in town. They sponsored a young man from Kenya through the priesthood. This priest became a bishop of Kenya. They loved to dance, and when they did, the dance floor cleared for all to enjoy watching.

Their lives were based on faith, hope, and love, and they did their best to instill these traits in each of their children. The children continue to instill these values in their family's lives. The Schlotterer family is said to be the largest family with roots in Willard.

Conclusion

There were many wonderful contributions to my life from both of my parents' families. The families were very different, but the value of hard work and continued family ties was always present. Both families received their major income from the B & O Railroad. The railroad was a major economic influence in my families. Both families were active in their religion, and that factor is most important in my life. I thank my grandparents and their families for what I have been able to accomplish because of their influence.

---

[1] Anonymous, *"Jesus, tender Shepherd, hear me,"* accessed 4/10/2015, http://www.hymntime.com/tch/htm/j/t/e/jtenders.htm.

[2] Anonymous, *"Jesus, tender Shepherd, hear me,"* accessed 4/10/2015, http://www.hymnary.org/text/jesus_tender_shepherd_hear_me.

Chapter 3

My Parents

Support from my brothers, sisters, mother, and father has been a constant in my life. With the deaths of my father, my mom, and my elder sister, Mary Lu, I lost much of their support. As life has progressed, the influence of these three family members has remained active even though they have passed on.

I believe my living brothers and sister would echo my comments about these family members. My family was a happy family, and religion was at the center of the reasons we existed. Today even though two of my brothers live out of state, and one brother and a sister live miles apart in Ohio, we try to meet around Christmastime, the Fourth of July, and any other times we are able to do so.

The Frederick family initially lived on 519 Clark Street in Willard. After Dad's heart attack and most of the children had left home, Mom, Dad, and the youngest brother, Bob, moved to 584 Butte Street to enjoy their newly built ranch home.

Walter E. and Marion G. Frederick

Family life was very important to the six children and their parents, Walter and Marion Frederick. Each Sunday after Mass, we had a family outing to a place of interest. Visits to shrines and churches were common, and attendance at weekly devotions was a necessity. Looking back, it is easy to see a family who cherished life and each other. A male family tradition was the frequent summer trips to the Willard Conservation League to catch bluegill and, once in a while, bass using lures, worms, crickets, maggots, and grasshoppers as bait. Catching turtles in the fishnet provided pets to enhance the wildlife community in the Fredericks' backyard.

The age span of the siblings was seventeen and a half years from the oldest, Mary Lu, to the youngest child, Bob. Rumor has it that since Bob was the youngest, his ability to claim the favorite-child position was a predestined fact. Helping out in the family was expected, as each had their own assigned tasks to do on a daily or weekly basis. Mopping the kitchen floor on my hands and knees was a Saturday morning tradition for me. Catching a small stone in my knee was not a favorite part of this routine. I am still a floor mopper.

Here are my parents with some examples of their cares, laughs, disappointments, and love of life.

Walter E. Frederick Sr.

The Early Years

My father was born in Willard on August 29, 1909. He had one brother, Charles. Except for a brief time in his early employment, he lived in Willard his entire life. He was an honors graduate of Willard High School in 1927 and Tiffin (Ohio) Business University in 1929. My father received only As and one B on his high school report cards. This achievement was one I could never hope to attain.

Dad knew a priest when he graduated from high school. In those days, appointments to access West Point were through influential people. The priest that Dad knew had access to an appointment to West Point. Unfortunately, the priest gave back the appointment a week before he knew Dad would be interested in it. This lost opportunity for a four-year college degree meant his dream would be limited to a two-year college degree.

My dad was employed at the B & O Railroad, at the Akron Goodyear Company, and for forty-five years at the former Pioneer Rubber Company, where he become the vice president and comptroller of the company's holdings. As an accountant, he could be termed a "bean counter." During his early years, he also was employed as a musician. He played piano and accordion at what was termed "barn dances." I never heard much about this interesting experience other than that my mother would attend with my father. Mom and Dad were married on May 29, 1935. Grandfather Frederick did not attend the wedding because he had some objection to the marriage.

When my father was courting my mother, he came and left by the front door. Then he would go to the side door to visit with his future mother and father-in-law. In essence, he had two dates in one night.

Religion and service to the community were important cornerstones of his life. He was a member of the Girl Scout Finance Committee. For twenty years, he served the Boy Scouts of America and received its St. George Award. Two of his sons received the Eagle Scout Award, Mike and me. Were it not for Dad, I would not have passed the signaling requirement for first class, which cleared me to carry on requirements for the Eagle Scout Award. If it needed to be done, Dad would do it.

His associations with the Catholic Church were exemplary. He was past president of the National Council of Catholic Men, Toledo Diocese and Sandusky Deanery. In this capacity, he was involved in instituting the family pilgrimage each summer in Carey, Ohio, at Our Lady of Consolation Shrine. He also wrote a prayer that was used at this event. He was a perpetual member of St. Francis Home Auxiliary in Tiffin; Sacred Heart MSC Center in Shelby, Ohio; and the Propagation of the Faith. He was an honorary Third Degree member of Rosecrans Council K of C in Willard and he held all offices. In addition, he was a member of the Fourth Degree assembly of the K of C, Archbishop Schrembs, Tiffin; a member of the Holy Name Society, Willard; a member of the third order of St. Francis, Carey; and a lay distributor and lector at St. Francis Xavier Catholic Church, Willard. Dad was past chairman of the Willard Area Hospital Board Finance Committee and a member of the Eagles Lodge 550.

Professionally he was in the 1955 *Who's Who in Commerce and Industry* book and a member of the National Association of Credit Men. He was a recipient of the Distinguished Serviceman's Award as Man of the Year through the Willard Jaycees.

Recently I was reading a remarkable book titled *Tuesdays with Morrie*. Morrie Schwartz, a retired college professor, is near the end of his life. Mitch Albom was a student of Morrie and wrote a book about his visits with his former professor. As I read this next quote from Morrie, I thought of my father.

"So many people walk around with a meaningless life. They seem half asleep, even when they're busy doing things they think are important. This is because they're chasing the wrong things. The way you get meaning in life is to devote yourself to loving others, devote yourself to your community around you, and devote yourself to creating something that gives you purpose and meaning."[3]

The many organizations to which my father and my mother gave service showed that they had purpose and meaning in their lives. Service to the community is important, and I hope that all generations see the importance of this venture for their and others' sake.

Dad was not only a smarthead but also very skilled with his hands. He built the garage attached to our home on Clark Street, the back patio, and the kitchen extension. He was always performing woodwork, plumbing, and electrical or cement work around the house. He loved crafts and made miniature ships, plastic animal and bird kits, totem poles, model airplanes, and more kits. He would paint the many parts as needed.

Dad had tropical-fish aquariums, African violets, and other plants, such as cacti. He made wine and frequently barbequed food. Occasionally he would pull out his accordion and play it with or without sheet music. In this picture, he is playing his accordion in our backyard near the grape arbor. Dad also played the piano, and he and Mom encouraged their children to study music.

Dad playing the accordion

He read many types of books and enjoyed watching television until the wee hours of the morning. He read books about the origins of the earth or any other topic that fascinated him. It has been said that the children inherited their brains from their father and their ability to work hard from their mother; we were lucky our parents possessed both of these skills.

The Barbeque

Dad was a person who was always trying to give special gifts to his family. Some of these gifts were immediate while others required time. Once my father was given a special present by the family called a barbeque grill. He decided it was time for him to use the new grill, charcoal, lighter, utensils, and an apron. It was in the 1950s, and barbequing food was a fairly new trend. Dad wanted to make sure the coals were hot, so he heavily doused them in charcoal lighter fluid. The fire had begun to slow down, and Dad felt that the coals were ready. Steaks were put on the grill, and they began to get a little hot over the partially started coals and flames from the lighter fluid. However, the steaks were not cooking well because the coals were not hot enough. It was getting time to eat, and the steaks still were not done.

My mother decided that she would finish the steaks on the broiler in her range. She broiled the steaks in no time but began to complain that there was a funny smell in her kitchen. She served the meal, we said our prayers, and the eating began. It wasn't too long before everyone knew that the peculiar smell and taste was charcoal lighter fluid. The steaks were a total loss, and my mother found some ground beef for our supper. By the way, my father became one of the best barbeque chefs for miles around once he learned how to start the charcoal. He was living out the lesson we all learned when we were very young. That lesson was not to give up when things do not go as planned.

Tropical Fish

Another event gone sour was the purchase of tropical fish. My dad had located a tropical-fish supplier in Sandusky. The pet shop was operated out of what looked like a large garage. The owner was knowledgeable about tropical fish.

On our first trip to the pet shop, Dad bought a modest-size fish tank with all the accessories: cleaning apparatus, food, a liquid to beautify the back section of the glass, an aeration system, a thermostat, gravel, and some tropical fish. The tropical fish were of a common and hearty variety, such as black mollies, red swordtails, and guppies. When we reached home, Dad applied the liquid paint to the back inside section of the glass so it could dry and become an attractive covering. The solution dried in a short period as planned, and the fish could be placed; it was time to ready the tank. My father filled the tank with water from the tap—first mistake. He placed the thermostat on the side of the tank and set it on the desired temperature. It was time to put in the fish. With great anticipation, the kids all watched the fish go into the water.

All was well for a few minutes until the fish started swimming in funny patterns and began dying. We took the cover off the tank and noticed the beautiful blue coloring or paint had separated from the back inside section of the aquarium. We quickly surmised that the coloring was creating a catastrophe for our tropical fish. Painting the tank's back on the inside rather than on the outside was the problem. Dad thought he had followed the directions. The directions had in fact said, "Paint the back section of the tank." Nothing was mentioned about painting the outside of the glass.

Dad experienced the painful task of doing it all over again. As we were discussing with the owner the process we had used, she also informed us that it was best to use rainwater to avoid all the chemicals in city water. The second time was a charm. Soon we were the proud owners of baby guppies and baby black mollies.

We visited the shop several times over the years to purchase additional fish for our thriving aquarium. Two other interesting events followed during these visits. As we came into Sandusky by the New Departure

Company, we noticed an ice cream shop. We found the hot dogs they served were the best we had tasted, and we named these hot dogs "Scrumptious" to fit their taste. The other incident happened because there was a monkey in the tropical-fish store. One of my siblings put a finger into the cage to pet the monkey. The only touching that was done was to my sibling's finger by the screeching monkey. Minor first aid was applied, and we found that the monkey could have caused a lot more damage than he did to the finger and hand of my sibling. If the monkey had caught my sibling off guard and pulled the finger and hand into the cage, it would have been very possible that a severe bite could have resulted. The lesson learned from the fish tank episode was to ask questions before attempting a new task. The lesson learned from the monkey was to keep your fingers out of strange places, especially cages.

At this time, my brother Bob had not been born. Here we see Walt on the left, Mary Lu holding Mike, me, and Ann.

The Frederick family around 1950

Sayings

Over the years, there have been many sayings from my parents and others that have guided me. These sayings have been guideposts in my private and public life. One of my dad's original sayings was "Refrain from perching in the cherry tree unless you intend to eat the cherries." The interpretation was not to be involved in something unless you are serious about your involvement. Another application of this saying referred to involvement with the opposite sex. While my father gave me guidelines for my life, he was not always telling me how to live my life.

My father was always concerned about timing and making sure that action was taken at the right time. The right time would usually equal success. Also important in taking action is being positive. Dad had two sayings in this regard. The first was that he had a problem "with talk that was negative," and he "would rather hear nothing than something negative." The second was "Gossip hurts people." I cannot remember my father saying many negative or gossipy statements, as he was usually smiling and was kind in his communication and action.

There was one phrase that was used more frequently than others. My father used the term "Judas Priest" when he was slightly upset about a happening. The use of the term went back to my young age. If he was working on a woodworking project, and he cut the board wrong, "Judas Priest" would be heard everywhere in the room. If a drink were to spill, you would hear "Judas Priest." I don't remember hearing my dad's explanation of "Judas Priest," but mine is that Judas was a disciple who had betrayed Christ, and the use of his name said something had gone wrong. It made sense; "Judas Priest" held a negative connotation when used by my father. Dad's language could have been much worse than an occasional "Judas Priest." Dad had some stronger phrases, but he rarely used them.

Having Fun

Some of the most memorable times my brothers and sisters had with our dad involved church or fishing. The family was always going to church. Fishing trips to the Willard Conservation League were almost nightly in the summer. The kids would spend the day finding worms, grasshoppers, or crickets, and when Dad came home, we were ready to go fishing. We almost always caught fish.

Dad was a master at accomplishing more than one task at a time or multitasking. A trip to fish was on many occasions also a trip to educate. For example, education could involve learning new techniques to improve our fishing, knowing various birds, and understanding the birds and bees. Let me explain the last learning. There was an island at the Willard Conservation League, and the rabbits on the island were good props for my father to do a little sex education with his children. The talk was so well-known that the brothers would periodically ask each other if they had received the talk about the rabbits on the island yet. Yes, fishing took place as the education lesson was delivered by my father.

When we were older, especially in college, the country bar called the Havana Tavern in the town of Havana, Ohio, provided many evenings of entertainment. A trip home to see Mom and Dad frequently was cause to go to the Havana Tavern. Food, drinks, the jukebox, a pool table, cards, and shuffleboard provided enough diversity for an evening's entertainment.

A major trademark of my father was being a social creature. My dad could have been a double for Will Rogers. Will's quote that "I never met a man I didn't like"[4] described my dad to a T. Whenever he would enter a public building, the family would brace itself for a long wait. It was impossible for my father to leave any social setting quickly. There was always someone he would know and with whom to converse. It was said that my father was always capable of meeting his "newest best friend." His family, without even trying, would emulate his ability to talk to and enjoy people. In fact, it could easily be said about me that "if you knew me, you knew my father."

A good example of how my father was held in high esteem by others occurred during the later years of his employment at the Pioneer Rubber Company when there was a workers strike. My father was one, if not the only, management employee escorted into the plant. This action caused both negative and positive challenges for him.

Good-Bye

The last three months of my dad's life progressed quickly and produced many memories. In December of 1980, before my father's death in March of 1981, he had broken his arm while climbing a stepladder. The family had noticed that his thinking was not as good as it had been. Dad had gone to Cleveland to complete my brother's income tax, a yearly task he did for all his kids and many of his family and friends. My brother Mike called me and said Dad could not make out his income tax, and he was taking him to the Cleveland Clinic for tests. Almost immediately, they found brain cancer and scheduled for surgery a few days later.

The family was there early on the morning of surgery. Concern and fear were visible on the faces of everyone. Our prayers were said, and the long surgery was begun. A few minutes after the start of the surgery, the surgeon came out announcing that there would be no surgery, as the cancerous tumor had spread from a quarter to half of the brain in two days. The surgeon told us how the cancer would progress over the next few months. Unfortunately, his predictions were correct. Dad went downhill very quickly. The process went from walking and talking to sitting and not talking and finally to being bedridden. All day and through the night, my mother and usually one member of the family were there to give the medication, especially the medication that should help shrink the tumor. I felt good that I was able to on occasion be with my Mom and Dad and still make it to work after a night of helping Dad. Dad died peacefully at the age of seventy-one.

Many of my father's associates were made out of the same fabric as Dad. A monsignor was a longtime friend of my father and one of the priests that my mother requested to officiate at the funeral. The monsignor was based in some desolate place in Michigan where a plane was his only way of getting to the funeral. Monsignor had purchased his plane ticket and was waiting in line to board the plane. A sick child also was in need of airplane transportation. The monsignor missed his plane, but the young child did not. There was one less priest at the funeral.

A Franciscan priest and close friend of the family conducted the funeral Mass and with his sermon helped us and the congregation to be better able to handle their grief. His ability to show concern and embrace the life of our wonderful father was a great comfort to a grieving family and a church full of people.

There was one consolation that we had with Dad as he neared death and died. Years before when he was about to retire, he had a heart attack and a near-death experience. Dad told us about the bright light and seeing his close friends and relatives ready to greet him in heaven. They didn't get to follow through on the greetings, as Dad came back to this world instead of being with God. From that point on, Dad said he was not afraid of death because he knew how great heaven was going to be.

Marion Georgina (Schlotterer) Frederick

The Young Girl and Lady

My mother was born in Avilla, on February 23, 1913. She lived there and in Long Island, New York. When she was in seventh grade, her family moved to Willard, but she stayed in Avilla to finish the school year. Mom stayed with friends of the family and worked in the residence and on the farm for her room and board. On weekends, she would travel on the train to Willard from Garrett, Indiana, for 25¢. Coincidentally, the conductor on the train was Dale Williams, a family friend, who was always helpful to my mom when she traveled. She graduated from Willard High School in 1933, where she was a member of the women's basketball team; her coach was Verna Williams, wife of Dale Williams.

There were sixteen children in Mom's family, and there were nine daughters: Marion Frederick (the eldest), Eda Briggs, Bertha Bapst, Pauline "Peg" Strauss, Rita Schlotterer, Rose Kleinhans, Theresa Prendergast, Lucille King, and Carol Shriner.

There were seven sons: George, Karl, Louis "Louie," Joseph "Joe," James "Jim," William "Bill," and Richard "Dick," all with the last name of Schlotterer.

During her school days, Walter Frederick was someone she "always kept an eye on." Mom was thirteen years old and Dad nineteen when they first became interested in each other. She would see him, his brother Charles, and two friends at the railroad station coming from Tiffin Business University. Mom always liked to go to daily Mass, especially on Saturday and Sunday. This gave Mom a chance to see my dad who was a server.

In an interview with my mother on February 5, 1994, she relayed a story to me about my deceased father. She was walking down the street, and the heel on her shoe broke off. A friend and my dad were sitting on the front step of a house when the friend offered to have Walter fix the shoe. My mother consented to the repair, and this was the rekindling of their relationship.

Since my mother was the oldest in a family of sixteen, she was able to cook, can, sew, administer first aid, and do anything else needed to keep the household going. Later these skills were handed down to her brothers and sisters, as well as her own children, and were often used in and outside the family. I will never forget those summer days when Mother pulled out bushels of tomatoes or peaches. It wasn't hard to figure that our day was going to be spent preparing them for canning or freezing.

Her Active Life

Mom was employed at numerous businesses in town. A few places of employment were Beviers Clothing Store, Hagerman Jewelry Store, Schriner's Law Office, Staph's Drug Store, Willard Credit Union, Sharick's Jewelry, Western Auto Toy Department, and Ben Franklin. She also owned and operated the Frederick-Elchert Religious Gift Shop in the basement of our home. She loved retail business, and everyone seemed to like her. Mom was into customer relations before it was popular.

She was active in Cub Scouts, Boy Scouts, and Girl Scouts. For eleven years, Mom organized many trips for the Girl Scouts, including ones to Cleveland, Ohio, Washington, D.C., and the 1962 New York World's Fair. Religion was very important to Mom, and she was active in the Altar Rosary Society, Parish Council, and Liturgy Committee. She was a sacristan, usher, lector, eucharistic minister, and RCIA and catechism instructor. She often took her children with her when she was a migrant program leader. Mom took several years of Spanish lessons so she could better help the many migrants who worked on the Celeryville, Ohio vegetable farms. We have many fond memories of being with my mom as she ministered to the migrants spiritually and physically by distributing food and clothing. I remember a story about a former migrant child, now a married woman, who was hospitalized in the Willard Area Hospital. She asked a sister from St. Francis Church about a Mrs. Frederick who had been so good to her by not only preparing her spiritually but also helping her meet many of her physical needs.

Mom graduated from the Toledo Diocese Lay Ministry Program and was active in the Third Order of St. Francis at Carey. She was a member of the Propagation of Faith; a member of the Catholic Ladies of Columbia; a member of the Sacred Heart MSC Seminary Auxiliary in Shelby, and a board member and past president of the St. Francis Home Auxiliary in Tiffin.

Other associations of honor she had been part of were the Red Cross Bloodmobile and the election board. She volunteered 11,860 hours during her twenty-eight years at the Willard Hospital. She received several awards, such as Mother of the Year in 1960 by the Willard Eagles Lodge, the Special Services Award by the Ohio Special Olympics, and the distinguished Roger J. Seibert Shared Responsibility Award by the Diocese of Toledo.

Interesting stories

I remember many interesting experiences with my mom probably because she was around the house more often than Dad. Here are a few of those stories.

The Fire

An unfortunate experience was when Mom was preparing the skillet to fry some meat, and the grease in the frying pan caught fire. The fire was leaping several feet from the frying pan toward the ceiling. In my mind, I was afraid that the house was going to catch fire. Since Dad was not home, my brother Walt, in his true-to-form quick-action mode, picked up a towel and quickly carried the flaming pan outside, thereby saving the day and the house. I can still see the yellow kitchen walls covered with black smoke after the fans had cleared the smoke out the windows. I was very happy to have a bed to sleep on that evening. My respect for Walt's gift of quick action remains with me to this day.

The Clubhouse

One night when I was a small boy, maybe ten years old, my mother was going to the back of our property to burn some papers in the fireplace my father had made. The fireplace was made of beautifully colored red brick. The fireplace was located in the middle of the back property on the inside of a five to six-foot fence. To the left of the fireplace in the inside corner of the lot was our "lean to" clubhouse. I was happy to see my mother light the papers in the fireplace, as it was very dark, and this would give some light to the backyard. As Mom lit the papers, I clearly heard something move in our clubhouse. I whispered to my mom, "There is someone in our clubhouse."

My mother made sure the fire was burning well and said, "Come on, Joey, we are done with the papers. We need to go to the house."

After we were in the house, I repeated myself, "Mom, I told you outside that there was someone in the clubhouse, and all you said was 'Let's go to the house.'"

My mother wisely said, "Yes, I heard you and the noise, but I didn't want whoever it was to know we heard them and possibly have them hurt us." Early the next morning, Ann, Mike, and I checked out our clubhouse. The previous day, we had placed new straw in the clubhouse, and when we checked, the straw had the imprint of what looked like a human being on it. Since none of us had been on the straw after we placed it into the clubhouse the day before, we thought it safe to guess that it was a hobo traveling through town on the B&O Railroad. Mom was a smart mom.

The Peeper

My mom had my dad build an addition to the kitchen so the family would have more room to eat, play, and study. Located in the back of this room overlooking the backyard was a large picture window. One evening after dark, my mother decided to open the blinds of the window so the sun could shine in the following morning. I happened to be in the kitchen on this occasion and looked up as my mother opened the blinds and simultaneously screamed. I quickly looked out the window and saw the face of a man staring at my mother. As fast as the "peeping Tom" appeared, he left, leaving two shocked people.

Mom's Sayings

My mother had many favorite sayings she frequently used. These are a few of her favorite sayings:

1. "You cannot play unless your jobs and homework are done."
2. "Make sure your hands are clean before you come to the dinner table."
3. "You must clean your plate before you can leave the table or have dessert."
4. "You must wear clean clothes to church."
5. "Say your prayers at meals and at night."
6. "Remember to sleep on your side of the bed."
7. "Self-praise stinks" is still quoted in many of her children's households. My mother's use of this saying had a biblical basis. I was surprised to find that Proverbs 27:2 stated, "Let another praise you—not your own mouth; someone else—not your own lips."[5]

I wonder if she or Dad knew where this saying originated. Mom certainly used it often to keep her children from praising themselves.

My mother also had a pet saying she used. This saying was "Jesus, Mary, and Joseph," which denotes the Holy Family. This phrase was a short prayer for Mom. If one of the kids would act up or she received bad news, she would say, "Jesus, Mary, and Joseph." I believe this phrase invoked the Holy Family to be with her in her time of need. At times, my family would find a JMJ (Jesus, Mary, and Joseph) on a letter or note to us. This again was asking the blessing of the Holy Family in a written communication.

Another location for the JMJ was above the doorways in our home. This must have been an activation of a blessing on all who passed into the room. I often wish I had the ability to pray as often as my mother did.

Mom had another cute saying that has stuck with me. When I was hungry, vegetables were not my favorite food. When my mother was trying to convince me that I should eat my peas, she had a poem that would ease my mind and helped me eat the peas.

The anonymous poem went like this:

I eat my peas with honey;

I ate them all my life.

It makes the peas taste funny,

But it keeps them on the knife.[6]

When the topic of peas comes up, I still enjoy reciting my mother's poem. Surprisingly enough, I had not found any other family who knows this poem.

An Extremely Busy Person

Throughout her life, Mom was constantly busy and communicative. It has been said that she gave much of her active lifestyle to her family and the rest to the community. In her younger years, Mom was close to and helped her mother and father and siblings. Likewise, as a mother and wife, she would spend much time with my brothers, sisters, and dad. She made sure that she would always be fair with her time to her family. An example would be to write or call them on the phone. She usually had a blessing in her correspondence and in her phone calls. When I was in college, I would receive letters each week from Mom. Many times this was the only correspondence I had, and Mom's letters and cards were always upbeat and supportive. I have kept a few of them.

While my mother was always busy, she was bothered with headaches a good part of her life. The headaches were so severe that medical attention in the home often was necessary. My mother believed in praying the rosary and asking God to help her through those trying times. My parents often told us to enjoy every day of our life. When my mother was sick, she must have tried to make the best of it by praying. She was very organized and kept the house going by teaching us children how to help. I don't think she enjoyed the pain of being sick, but she enjoyed being close to God in prayer. I learned as, I believe, the other children did that the tough times in our lives were the ones that we most remember and were the times we most needed the skills and talents that God had given us.

The Later Years

When Mom was in her eighties, we began to notice that her thinking was not as sharp, and her moods seemed to vary more. Mom began to live with each of her children for periods. She was traveling from Chicago to Pemberville, Ohio to Willard to Norwalk, Ohio to Raleigh and to Cleveland. One day, she was to come home from my elder sister's home when, according to Mom, Mary Lu didn't get in the car fast enough to leave. At that point, Mom left Mary Lu's house on her own and walked a few miles down the long county road with her suitcase and entered a main highway before being picked up in the car. The danger in this situation was great.

On another occasion, she was to go to a doctor's appointment in Willard, and my brother Mike, who was to take her, didn't put away the tools fast enough for Mom. Again, she started walking from her house to her doctor's office across town. Mike had to walk with her as he couldn't persuade her to get into his car. These two situations presented questions for discussion with her doctor.

A trip to her doctor proved our fears; Mom had Alzheimer's disease. My elder brother Walt, from North Carolina, arranged for Mom to have tests to confirm her doctor's diagnosis at Duke University. The tests at Duke confirmed the diagnosis of Alzheimer's. Mom's behavior continued to deteriorate, so arrangements were made for her to go to a local nursing home, as none of our children's homes could give her the secure environment or twenty-four-hour care she needed. Mary Lu, Mike, and I arranged for and took her to a center for care, but she did not want to go in; she wanted to go back to her home. This was to be one of the hardest days in our lives. After several trips around the block, we finally were able, with the assistance of the nursing home personnel, to help her into the nursing home.

She stayed there for a few weeks and then moved to a facility closer to my home. One Friday evening shortly after her admission, I was driving by the home and noticed that an ambulance was in front of the facility. I said to Kathy, "I hope it isn't for Mom." Less than a minute later, I received a call on my cell phone; it was the facility, and they said, "Could you please meet your mother at the hospital, as she has fallen."

As a result of the fall, Kathy and I had a few days to find another placement since the present facility was no longer appropriate. How were we going to find a facility in such a short notice? We had visited many facilities, and we were not comfortable with any of them. We had no good options.

I remembered a friend of mine talking about an excellent facility in the area that they had used. We called our friends Jerry and Linda Johnson. They cleared their calendar for the next evening, and we met for dinner. As we talked, Jerry and Linda's description of the facility and its programs sounded like the right place. The next day, we visited the facility and liked what we saw. There was a single room open. We called our brothers and sisters and explained the options. It fell into place almost immediately. It sounded too good to be true.

Mom stayed in Green Springs, Ohio for the rest of her life. The family was involved in all facets of her treatment, and we were always notified of every unusual incident. When she passed on July 17, 2001, the nurse called about her passing and informed us they would keep the body there for a few hours if we wished to spend time with her. All my brothers and sisters who lived within two hours of the facility came. We cleaned out her belongings, and the nurse asked if they could keep a photograph of my mother so that they could have a memorial service. Then the residents would be able to know for sure with the picture who had passed on. We were flattered and gladly left the photo.

My mother had every detail of her funeral on paper. She even specified which family member was to bring which gift during the offertory of the Mass. She was a woman of great energy, organization, and commitment. She lived to be eighty-six years old.

The Frederick Family

The union of Marion and Walter, my mom and dad, took place May 29, 1935, at the St. Francis Xavier Catholic Church in Willard. Standing in my parents' wedding picture are Marion's sister, Bertha, the maid of honor, and Walter's brother, Charles, the best man. Marion, bride, and Walter, groom, are seated in this picture.

How We Were Raised

My parents raised our family by word and example. While there were many words they imparted to us, there were three particular ones that stand out in my mind. The first one was that we are all children of God, and we are all equal. We are not

Wedding picture of Walter and Marion Frederick

better nor less than any other person in the world. These words have stayed with me. When I was with people whose clothes were worn, who went to a private school, whose parents had an expensive car, or who were of a different race, I had been taught to treat them all the same. While at times it was hard to think this way, it was the only way I had been taught to treat others, and I have felt comfortable with this belief. This belief influenced the manner in which I looked at people, talked to people, and acted with people. I know my life has been more fruitful trying to practice this belief.

The second one my parents used to guide us originated from Matthew 6:1, which was translated into "Give to others, and expect nothing in return."[7] Since God is an all-giving God, it made sense that imitating Him in giving while expecting nothing in return was the desirable way to live one's life. A review of my parents' activities in the community would verify their commitment to giving.

The third guide was to live our lives for God by enjoying each day while not looking back more than what is necessary. In regard to looking back in one's life, my father used the adage "You can't plow a straight furrow looking backward." I still use that phrase when a past happening is concerning me.

I saw the application of these words by my parents' giving. Giving to others was very important to my parents and a guiding force from our Catholic religion and the patron saint Francis of Assisi. The Prayer of St. Francis was as follows:

> Lord, make me an instrument of your peace;
> Where there is hatred, let me sow love;
> Where there is injury, pardon;
> Where there is doubt, faith;
> Where there is despair, hope;
> Where there is darkness, light;
> Where there is sadness, joy.
>
> O Divine Master, grant that I may not so much seek To be consoled as to console;
> To be understood as to understand;
> To be loved as to love. For it is in giving that we receive;
> It is in pardoning that we are pardoned;
> And it is in dying that we are born to eternal life.[8]

My family always lived by the Prayer of St. Francis. His prayer was familiar ground in my everyday actions and a constant reminder of my parents' guidance through St. Francis. Before and after my parents' deaths, this prayer was constantly alive in guiding my deeds. How happy they must be with our pope Francis.

The Family

There were six children in the Frederick family: Mary Lu (Frederick) Eldred, Walter "Walt" E. Frederick II, Joseph "Joe" B. Frederick, Ann H. (Frederick) Herner, Michael "Mike" J. Frederick, and Robert "Bob" J. Frederick. All of the brothers and sisters attended college, and three graduated from John Carroll University in Cleveland. John Carroll is a Jesuit school, and the young men who attended this university had the advantage of having great teachers and an excellent education. Walt was the son who served his country in the military. Walt worked hard to be a successful Marine.

In Willard, there were a couple of well-known facts about the Frederick family. One was that they were Catholics, and the other is that they had a station wagon. At that time, there were several Protestant churches in the town. Catholics dating Protestants was not always a desirable arrangement. Sunday morning, we went to church, and Sunday afternoon was traditionally a time to go for a drive in the country or to a nearby shrine. When the children became young adults and wished to have a date on a Sunday afternoon, they were reminded that Sunday was our family day. Eventually a date on Sunday afternoon became acceptable.

Many of our recreational activities were associated with religion. The Knights of Columbus periodically held dances in the K of C Hall located over Sternbaum's grocery store in downtown Willard. Religious-type activities, such as plays or breakfasts, were held in Madonna Hall on the east side of town. The block rosary was held at private homes, and the event moved from house to house with a social time after the rosary.

The Frederick family was close-knit. We prayed together before and after meals and either together or individually at night. Everyone was expected to be at the meals. After homework was completed, we often played board games and other games. We also had fun watching Dad's fish aquariums and playing with the family dog. Each child had their own toys, and they were expected to share them.

When each of the sons and daughters left home, they continued to practice their Catholic faith. Each of the spouses was or became Catholic. Mom and Dad's example of Christian love and marriage was celebrated here on their thirty-fifth anniversary.

Marion and Walter Frederick

Clark Street was a close-knit neighborhood. Some neighbors were closer than others, but there were seldom ill feelings in the neighborhood.

More Guiding Principles of Walter and Marion Frederick

A closer look at the guiding principles of my parents should give readers a better understanding of their influences on the family. Research has easily shown that the Bible is the most purchased book in the world.

This fact coupled with the importance of the Catholic religion made the lessons of the Bible commonplace in the guidance my parents gave to me and my siblings. Some of these influences were living our life for God, not wasting time or physical resources, money is the root of all evil, respect one's body and other people's bodies, a good education is a worthy goal, and others. While each of these is important, there was one principle, which we have touched on, I feel could be related to many others, and that was loving or the act of giving to others.

Love or Giving to Others

An oft-quoted verse on love is from 1 Corinthians 13:13. "So faith, hope, love remain, these three; but the greatest of these is love."[9] Yes, there is even more that we can remember on this subject.

Verses on the importance of love, which is a closely related form of giving, are emphasized in the Gospel of Matthew 22:34–40. Consistent application of these principles can develop into a habit.

The following is an abbreviated version of the famous story:

A scholar of the law tested [Jesus] by asking, "Teacher, which commandment in the law is the greatest?"

He said to him, "You shall love the Lord, your God, with all your heart, with all your soul, and with all your mind. This is the greatest and the first commandment. The second is like it: You shall love your neighbor as yourself. The whole law and the prophets depend on these two commandments."[10]

This quotation is as important as any Bible verse. It gave the law of the land; God must be loved first, and then one's neighbor must be loved as oneself. Since religion was so important in the Frederick family, the love of God and giving to God was paramount. We knew that when you give to others, you give to God.

Morrie Schwartz, subject of the book, *Tuesdays with Morrie*, had an interesting way of talking about love. He stated, "Love is when you are as concerned about someone else's situation as you are about your own."[11] As a family, it was the goal while we were at home, and it was expected that when we left home, we would always love and respect other members of the family and other people in the world. Getting along with others was the only option, and we also were to love our enemies, even if our enemies didn't wish to return the favor. It was the only way that there would be peace at home and in the world.

My parents' approach became more pointed in this and other areas of concern as we were instructed that our actions were rarely going to be stagnate. We were going to improve the situation we were in or make it worse; staying the same would not happen. We were intelligent enough to know the difference and to do the right thing by following the lead of our parents.

You Are an Example to Others

Being a good example also contributed to a growth process of love. We see in Matthew 5:16 Jesus emphasizing to the disciples the importance of being an example when He said, "Just so, your light must shine before others, that they may see your good deeds and glorify your heavenly Father."[12]

Having goodness seen in one's acts is a first step for others to see one's example. Praising God for all His divine giving, which makes it possible for us to do and show one's good acts, is important. Showing off one's good acts for one's own benefit is not the emphasis in this process. Having positive examples available to others is essential for us to continue forward in praising our Father. While showing a good example is important, we shall see shortly that we need to temper recognition of our good deeds so that we may receive rewards in our next life for our actions on earth.

Principles of Giving

The principles taught to us by our parents were simply to give our gifts, possessions, and ourselves to others. Our parents instilled in us that it is easy to be concerned about ourselves and our needs. It is much more important to be concerned about other people's needs. In giving, we should expect nothing in return because otherwise, our giving has strings, and we have been rewarded for our giving. The ultimate giver is God since He has created the world and has given us everything that exists. God's giving is based on the principle that giving for recognition is not a worthy form of giving.

In Matthew 6:1, it states, "[But] take care not to perform righteous deeds in order that people may see them; otherwise, you have no recompense from your heavenly father."[13] It is important to note that if one does not believe in God, the principles of giving and receiving graciously would still seem applicable. Without receiving, there would be no giving. Without giving, there is no receiving. Giving and receiving are dependent on each other for productive actions. Giving and receiving must be interdependent. While giving is easy for me, I find I must work on receiving from others.

The key in giving is to trust God when we give. God will take care of us if we are good givers. I try to let life flow, and I try not to look for rewards from any good deeds I do. I had been told that when given a compliment or recognition, offer it up to and thank God for giving me my skills that foster any of my good acts I do. It also can be seen as a prayer when we thank God or offer our acts of kindness to Him. It has always been a pleasure for me to share the glory with other deserving people. Rarely are any of us totally responsible for good deeds. I see everyday people showing these values of giving and loving. These people appear to be very happy and inspiring for others.

Opportunity

My parents taught us not to miss the chance to give when opportunity knocks. If one receives something in return, thank that person for the gift, and realize that when others give, it is a part of their joy to give. Human beings are social creatures, and giving makes us charitable persons. Love is a powerful emotion and a basis for living, which develops over time. Love is manifested by giving. Giving following giving can become a habit, which will lead to feeling more comfortable in being able to love and give to others. The opposite of giving is being selfish or keeping one's gifts to oneself. It is good to look for opportunities to give to others.

You had previously been introduced to Morrie Schwartz, professor, and Mitch Albom, his former student, in *Tuesdays with Morrie*. In this discussion, sports cars and big houses were named as things not needed by Morrie. He went on to say, "The truth is you don't get satisfaction from these things. You know what really gives you satisfaction?"

Mitch says, "What?"

Morrie says, "Offering others what you have to give."

"You sound like a Boy Scout," Mitch comments.

Morrie replies, "I don't mean money, Mitch. I mean your time."[14]

If we go a little deeper into this concept, Morrie adds, "This is how you start to get respect, by offering something that you have."[15] As I thought about this discussion, it really makes sense.

This discussion makes it so simple, and one thing that can be offered by everyone is time. Yes, my parents agreed with Morrie; you can get satisfaction by giving to others something that you have and are free to give, your time. What a beautiful way to be satisfied. You give what costs you nothing, and you receive satisfaction.

Morrie goes on to be even clearer when he says to Mitch, "Remember what I said about finding a meaningful life? I wrote it down, but now I can recite it: Devote yourself to loving others, devote yourself to your community around you, and devote yourself to creating something that gives you purpose and meaning."[16] The opportunity to give is everywhere, and a meaningful-life opportunity is presented to us every day of our life. My parents realized, understood, and took advantage of these opportunities and consequently found a meaningful life. As Morrie said, "Do the kinds of things that come from the heart . . . You'll be overwhelmed with what comes back."[17]

My Parents' Example

The purpose of this section is to reexamine the examples my parents gave. A look at the type of organizations in which they were involved should give direction to their ideas of giving. Examples of organizations in which they gave or gave to others and then received were many. My father was active in many Catholic-related groups, such as the Knights of Columbus, Council of Catholic Men, and Holy Name Society, and in being a lay distributor and lector in his church. Organizations that received Dad's time other than church were Cub, Boy, and Girl Scouts and the Willard Hospital. Mother was also active in church-related groups, such as the Rosary Altar Society, Parish Council, Migrant Program, and the Catholic Ladies of Columbia. Other nonreligious organizations of Mom's were Cub, Boy, and Girl Scouts; the Red Cross; and Special Olympics. A benefit of giving now is that one is blessed through our giving in this or our next life.

Communion and Giving

One of the most important parts of my parents' existence was the celebration of the Mass. During the Mass, participation in the reception of Jesus Christ's body and blood through Holy Communion was the most central activity. On June of 2013, I saw a connection to giving that I had not yet fully realized. Fr. Herb Weber, pastor at Blessed John XXIII Parish, was giving a homily on Corpus Christi or the body of Christ. In his homily, he talked about the concept that when Jesus comes to us in Communion, He is transforming our bodies as we receive Jesus. Essentially, "we are being fed in Communion. . . We become the body of Christ. . . With Christ's presence in us, we feed people any way we can."[18] Therefore, as we have been fed by Christ, we have the opportunity to give to others. I find this a real and most powerful opportunity for any of us to receive and to give.

Saving

My parents were strong believers in saving that which had been received especially if it could be useful for the future. One never knew when something could be useful. For example, I had learned at a young age that collecting newspaper clippings, various papers I had written, and papers from events in my field of work was important. I treasured scrapbooks my mother compiled for me containing photographs to help me remember the early events from 519 Clark Street.

Likewise, I collected and my mother compiled yearbooks from Willard High School and John Carroll University. The many photos Kathy and I collected from our years living in Mansfield, Ohio and Pemberville were taken by me and organized by Kathy. As I reviewed all these materials, it became clear to me that these values from my parents now have become the central resources for this book. Were it not for the preservation of these many resources, this book would not have been written. Another big help would be the sharing and reviewing of memories with family and friends. Ordinary experiences have the capacity of being of extraordinary significance.

The Influence of Mom and Dad

My life was profoundly influenced by my parents. The influence of my parents went far beyond my life to other people. In looking at how giving and receiving have influenced my life, one wouldn't need to look far, as religion and community service hold many good examples. These areas are related closely to the ultimate goal of living a good spiritual and community life that ends in eternal salvation and gives human beings the chance to be with God forever.

A review of my parents' examples of positive virtues and our own will help us better understand our life's direction. A positive life helps make a positive world. While I try to lead my life according to these fairly simple principles, I may not always be successful, but we strive for improvement.

One of the variables that needs to be addressed is how could my parents give so much to the community and at the same time give to the family. It was expressed often by our parents that it is not the amount of time that is spent; it is the quality of time that matters. So if my parents were in the community or with us, they were giving their undivided attention wherever they were and making the most of the time they had in their life. I have found that it is a juggling act in that wherever the time is spent, it must be assessed and given in a fair manner.

People Influence Others

It also is important to note that the book title *People + Me* is about the influence of people on me and my influence on them. Human beings tend to enjoy being around people who share their same interests. You will observe that many of the people I associate with tend to share the same interests and values I have. I feel I have been blessed with many interesting people and experiences.

A powerful homily by Fr. Herb Weber, made at a funeral Mass in 2011 is that people tend to want to be near goodness. Good people and good actions tend to draw people. Goodness is infectious and will call many people to being good to others. The growth of goodness involves self-perpetuating acts that make a better world.[19] Desirable acts tend to produce more desirable acts or become habits.

There are influences that can work the opposite way if people hurt other people. Some people do not understand or accept goodness. The daily newspaper attests to this fact. A big challenge is to make goodness more available to all people in all our daily lives.

After reflecting on Father Herb's homily, a few thoughts came to mind about my parents and others. My mother and father were good people, and my siblings and I were near them and their goodness by the luck of the draw. While we children did not choose them as parents, I believe each of us would have wanted no one other than the parents we were given. The goodness we have seen exhibited by good people has an excellent chance of being emulated by us and others.

3   Mitch Albom, *Tuesdays with Morrie*, (New York: Broadway Books, 1997), 43.

4   Will Rogers, "*I never met a man I didn't like*," accessed 4/10/2015, en.wikiquote.org/wiki/Will_Rogers.

5   Patrick Cardinal O'Boyle, Imprimatur, *The New American Bible, Saint Joseph Edition*, (New York, Catholic Book Publishing Co., Old Testament, 1970), 728.

6   Anonymous, "I Eat My Peas with Honey," *Poetry Foundation*, accessed 1/21/2013, http://www.poetryfoundation.org/poem/171639.

7   James A. Hickey, Imprimatur, *The New American Bible, Saint Joseph Edition, Revised Edition* (New Jersey, Catholic Book Publishing Corp., New Testament, 1986), 18-19.

8   Anonymous, *Novena to St. Francis*, (New York, Gerffert-Hirten Publisher, 2005), 20.

9   Hickey, op. cit., 259.

10   Ibid., 51.

11   Albom, op. cit., 178.

12   Hickey, op. cit., 16.

13   Ibid., 18.

14   Albom, op. cit., 126.

15   Ibid., 127.

16   Ibid.

17   Ibid., 128.

18   Fr. Herb Weber, "*Speech given at Blessed John XXIII Parish*," Perrysburg, Ohio, June 2, 2013.

19   Fr. Herb Weber, "*Speech given at Blessed John XXIII Parish*," Perrysburg, Ohio, February 5, 2011.

Part II

The Formative Years

Chapter 4

God Gave One Twin and Kept the Other

I was to live with the knowledge that my mother had a miscarriage at three months, and I was born six months later. This fact was to be of special significance to me and provided me with lifelong questions about my twin.

My Beliefs

The end of life—death—comes in different ways. My twin died, and the true realization of this loss came to me eight years after the passing. My wombmate remains a mystery to me.

I have three guiding principles in my life regarding my twin. The first is a belief in God. I believe that God is the Supreme Being who is all-knowing and loving. The next belief I have is that life begins at conception. My twin's passing at three months left me to understand that my twin did exist, did die, had a soul, and somehow has an influence on my life, and I have a responsibility to my twin. Finally, God leads me into the last of the three beliefs, that is, our actions on earth determine everyone's destiny after death. My twin's destiny is with God since my twin could not have done any wrong.

A Quick Overview of My Life

Before discussing my twin, I need you to be somewhat aware of my life so you have a background to begin to understand me and my twin. Some of the experiences in my life that you will become familiar with start in my infancy and a disease called whooping cough. I had the trademark rapid coughing that produced "whooping" sounds between coughs. I was only a few days old when I contracted the disease. The coughing was so severe that I ruptured my belly button, and I almost died from the disease and its complications. Yes, my twin died, and I almost died in infancy.

I was part of a blessed family, and the Catholic faith was central to our life. A challenge for me in school was my size. I remember being the smallest (or near smallest) male student from grade school through high school. In a height-conscious world, it required a lot of energy to deal with the negative attitude I had developed. I needed to seek some solution to what I saw as at least a physical limitation.

At age eight, I realized that my twin, who had died at three months in utero, provided me with some new ways of thinking about others. As I obviously lived after my twin died, I felt a responsibility to be successful in my life for both me and my twin. I see no reason to think differently.

Additional challenges to my thinking and living were presented through adapting to my physically challenging work years on the farm, my private college education, and my graduate education leading to a PhD. My adult work experiences with challenging job situations and life-altering experiences all required time, energy, and some help from my God and I believe involved influence from my twin, who is with God. In addition, receiving support and help was essential, and giving support and help to other people still is for me essential in making progress in life. I was fortunate to have a supportive Christian family, friends, neighbors, and community to aid me throughout my life.

Twins

Let's begin with an unusual start to life—the death of a sibling or the death of a twin before my birth. Birth and life in this world is influenced by many factors. Two of the most common are heredity and environment. The influence of these factors affects birth in all individuals' lives.

I lost my twin in the first trimester of my mother's pregnancy. Six months later, I was born. After I realized the loss of my twin, I grew up wondering about the influence of my deceased twin in my life or if my unborn twin was simply out of the picture. I have explored this question, as have other people in this situation, throughout my life and still am in the process. Since I do not know the sex of the fetus, I will substitute the words *twinless*, *sibling*, *wombmate*, or the generic *he* or derivatives when I talk about my twin.

A Trip to the Cemetery

We celebrate our birth; however, to me, conception is the start of life. In hindsight, I see my life being strongly influenced by the death of my twin, which was six months before my birth. While I had previously heard my parents talk about my deceased twin, it really did not register until the day my father took me to the St. Joseph Cemetery in Willard. Now there is a beautiful stone marking the cemetery at the entrance.

St. Joseph Catholic Cemetery

I was eight years old when my father asked me to go with him to the cemetery. As I later considered the impact of this trip to the cemetery and this newfound knowledge about the death of my twin, I knew it was impossible for a baby to be aware of the death of a twin at birth since a baby cannot comprehend death. Therefore, time is needed by parents to judge when it is best to share the information with the surviving twin. I feel it would be unfair for a parent not to share the knowledge of the death of a twin with the surviving or twinless twin at the appropriate time. Yes, there should be a time that the surviving child is told of this loss. I know it was traumatic for me, and I would assume it would be traumatic for others. The realization at age eight and after made me wonder how do I deal with this situation in my life. The awareness of my lost twin has both a painful and joyful part in my life. It was not to be the only part of my life containing a mystery of the unknown.

I was the one child my father asked to go with him to the cemetery that day though our family usually traveled as one. I was very curious about where we were going. My father pulled into the cemetery and drove to the rear right side of it. He stopped the car and told me, "We are going to get out of the car here because I have something to show you." I looked around as we left the car, and I saw several tombstones. The one that caught my eye had a small lamb lying on the top of the stone. My father noticed me staring at the tombstone with the lamb and explained that a lamb on a tombstone usually means that there is a baby buried in that grave.

My father then pointed at a large bush. He told me, "Six months before you were born, I buried your twin under that bush." I can remember my body froze, and I could not think. I was shocked!

I composed myself and said to my father, "You mean I had a twin, and he died?"

My father said, "You had a twin, and we do not know if it was a boy or a girl, but yes, your twin died." My mother verified the same story that day. I noticed that she would look at me with a mixture of happiness and sadness when she talked about my twin. Being a "twinless twin" was a struggle in my life—to understand the influence on my life and to know if and how I could ever directly know him.

When my father informed me that day about my twin dying three months after conception, I instantly began to develop more questions, many of which I feel will last a lifetime. One of the questions was what would he look like. Another was would he have been my closest friend. What would my sibling's occupation have been? One of the most important ongoing questions was how would all of this affect my life. Why had my twin died? Will I ever see or meet him? Very early in my life, I began to wonder that since my sibling had died, and not lived his life, would he be with me and how. Just because he was dead did not mean there was no identity because from the biological view at eight weeks, the embryo is a fetus, is alive, and is a somewhat recognizable human. The twin would have had a soul, a presence, and energy. The idea that my twin and I will somehow be together has never left me.

The important question was do I have a greater responsibility in living my life since my twin has died, and I have survived. As I ask these questions and others, the world almost stands still. I knew so little about him and wondered if I would ever have a better understanding.

That day at the cemetery has become the most important experience associated with my twin. Until this writing, I had shared with only a few people the fact that I had a twin who died. I kept to myself my feelings and beliefs about him until I began to write this book and pushed myself to express any feelings and knowledge I possess. Yes, I do not remember talking much about my twin when I was younger. Remember, I would be talking about the death of my twin; death was not a sought-after topic of discussion. I found it very unsettling yet at the same time very exciting to begin talking about my wombmate in recent years. Why unsettling, you might ask. Well, if you continue to have questions and the answers didn't come, came hard, or were hard to prove, that is unsettling. How does it sound if someone says their twin has died, and they are really unsure of their relationship with the twin, but the feelings are there that the twin has a strong influence on their life? The importance of my wombmate has never left me. Although the bush is gone, the location in the cemetery is of course still there where he was buried, and there are many questions and fewer answers.

Previously my parents had told me about a twin that had died. It really didn't register until I saw the place where my twin was buried. I knew I would never forget that day and the bush that was the marker for his grave. It is still embedded in my memory, and it is now in an adult rather than in a child's brain. I have mixed emotions of joy and sorrow when I think of my sibling. I have had the feeling that since my twin died, there is no one to live his life. The responsibility to live my life as best I can for myself and my twin is present. The feeling is real, though not constant. If I did or didn't receive energy (inspiration) from my twin, I still needed to accomplish and be successful for us. Since he is not on this earth, he will not be accomplishing good tasks as a human being. It is therefore my task for my God, for my twin, and for me to make accomplishments.

Yes, my life has definitely been influenced by a lost twin. In order to understand him and some of the feelings I have about him, it seems important to briefly review some basic information on twins, how they interact as well as how they are viewed by society. It is a common fact that when one child is born, it is truly a miracle. It is truly more unusual that two persons are born as twins.

Some information on twins will be presented now. Some might say since my twin died in the first trimester, I could say there is nothing to discuss—I can't make this statement. So we will proceed to examine twins and the relationship between them.

What Are Twins

Twins are either fraternal or identical. Identical twins share one egg in conception while fraternal twins come from separate eggs at conception or eggs that are fertilized separately. Identical twins are more alike than are fraternal twins or siblings. There are many fascinating factors about twins living apart or together. I was fortunate to interview two identical twins reared together.

Twins Raised Together

I had searched for a set of twins who had for a long time lived in close or separate proximity. I became aware of a set of twins locally; I was to find more than I expected from these twins. When I read the account of identical twins in the local paper, the *Daily Sentinel-Tribune*,[20] I knew my search was over. I was sure that a firsthand look at twins raised together and living in close proximity for seventy-five years should give me and others a better understanding about this interesting and intriguing phenomenon. I was right.

An interview was arranged in November of 2012 with identical twins Karol Heckman and Karen Fahle. The near-two-hour interview produced a desired understanding of twins.

Our story begins on August 12, 1937, on a cold and rainy day in Pemberville, a small community thirty minutes from Toledo. Karol and Karen were born six weeks early to Dennis and Lois Dewyre, parents who were expecting a single birth. Karol weighed three and a half pounds with a distinct dark skin color. Karen arrived in a breech birth at four pounds fifteen minutes later. As the babies were born six weeks early, an improvised incubator housed them in a large lined basket covered with hot water bottles constructed by Dr. Vincent Stephenson, the attending physician.

At the twins' party for their fiftieth birthday, Dr. Stephenson shared with them that they were the only set of twins he had ever delivered where both babies survived. Life was made even more precious to the twins as they learned how infrequent survival was for twins at that time.

What was life like for them as children? We are about to learn some interesting happenings. For example, when their family took a walk, people would often stop and comment on how much the two looked alike. When the girls dressed for school each morning, they never had a disagreement on what matching outfits would be worn that day.

Both ladies married their high school sweethearts. They were married a month apart in 1956 with first Karen to Dale Fahle and then Karol to Dick Heckman. The sisters still live near each other. They talk on the phone about four times a day. The calls range from a minute to around an hour. According to the twins, their husbands decided early in the relationship not to fight the twin thing. But while the twin relationship still is important, the husbands and children always came before their twin.

Sometime after the sisters were married, they went shopping for draperies separately. They found they had each purchased drapes and wanted to see the other's purchase. They met to compare their choices and found both had made their purchase at the same store. Both had bought the same design with only the color being different. On another occasion, they both had bought new blouses. When they met at a social event, they both had the same style of blouse, but one was purple, and the other was green.

The twins are able to confide in each other. The trust they have is so great that telling each other anything is like telling themselves. It is that comfortable. There is little judgment or challenge involved in their talk or actions. Jealousy is foreign to the twins, and their biggest concern is what is important to the other.

The twins admit that they have never fought. One way they have avoided confrontations is to not criticize each other. As I listened to them talk, it became evident that their thoughts were nearly identical, and they were able to finish each other's sentences. If I were to close my eyes, I would have thought that there was only one person talking. Not only could they finish each other's thoughts with the same voice but they also did so without interrupting each other or caring if that happened.

A question arises: How identical are they? Both of the twins worked at Bowling Green State University. Karen started there first in the personnel department. There was an opening in the education department, so Karol wanted to apply. On the day of Karol's interview, Karen had just been in her boss's office and left. Her twin Karol came in to say hi before her interview. Karen asked Karol to put her head into her boss's office to see his reaction. As Karol did so, her boss said, "Karen, do you need something?" At that moment, Karen walked in. Then the boss realized the switch.

Karol then had walked in the education department supervisor's office. The supervisor said, "Karen, I never thought you would leave the personnel department for the education department." Karen walked in to join Karol, and the supervisor realized the switch. Karol got the job in the education department and stayed for four years. She then transferred to the same department as Karen's. The twins retired together. A picture of the identical twins from the left follows.

Karen Fahle and Karol Heckman

One of the differences between the twins is that they do not practice the same religious belief. They solve that difference by not talking about it. When the ladies were adults, they were often asked, "What does it feel like to be a twin?" The response the twins developed was "What does it feel like not to be a twin?"

Many stories I have read about twins raised apart or together seem impossible to believe. The stories about twins raised together in most cases contain experiences based on their genetic and environmental similarities. In considering my twin, I wondered if he would have had some of my characteristics, such as being a person with strong work ethics, an abundance of energy, an inquisitive mind, and similar looks. As I began to write this chapter, I thought about my trip to the cemetery with my father and at that moment remembered that I had a feeling that my twin was close somehow. I began to rethink the responsibility I have to my unborn twin's life since he could not humanly live it. While I felt a closeness to him, I felt this relationship was very minute in comparison to what it could have been if I really had known him. Once I knew I had a twin, I have felt a great loss of what could have been a close and fulfilling relationship with a person probably much like me.

The Surviving Twin

There can be emotional and psychological overlays for a surviving twin who has lost his twin in death. Dr. Thomas Stuttaford addressed this issue when he said,

> Coupled with the feeling that he or she is guilty, the twin who lives may also sense that they have been deserted by the dead sibling, who has left them with an immense obligation to make it up to the parents for the family loss. Thereafter they believe that they have to do better, and be better, because of the death—emotions which can put a great burden on shoulders, which are not always strong enough to carry them.[21]

This quote is the most useful to me of all the numerous ones I have read. This quote was a missing piece to the puzzle of trying to understand me and my twin that day at the cemetery. While it didn't give me the whole answer, it did give me a direction of better understanding. It hit home with my feelings, experiences, and beliefs about my twin. I felt left alone but knew it was not done purposefully. Another factor presented with the loss is that a surviving twin feels he or she needs to do something—better. It is very important to note that since my twin had passed, I did have a feeling that I should do better and be better. Since he was not alive, I felt it was up to me. I remember feeling some responsibility to him from the first visit at the cemetery. I was motivated by the responsibility I felt, and while it is usually unconscious, it was in the back of my mind to do better, to be better, and not to fail. These factors are a source of inspiration or energy for me.

So how does it work? The guideline to do better and be better can come from more than one source. To do better meant I was to constantly improve and to be better, doing the best I could. One goal that my parents instilled in me and my siblings was to give to other people, which could be measured to do better and be better. Being a good role model was an expectation from my parents. Since my parents were giving people, I saw this as an important area to develop. At the cemetery, I felt a direction, which was to do the best I could for him. While my twin never told me how to do better and be better, the feeling I had was that my twin was gone, and I was the one left to do what I could for my twin. If my twin were alive, it would have been important to him to follow my parents' directions as it was to me and all my other siblings. I believe my direction came initially from my parents and started at birth, and that is the direction I felt I needed to take for my twin.

Another contributing factor is that this feeling that I should do better and be better stems from the responsibility of using the gifts or skills I had been given and each of us had been given by God. My parents often would remind us children that we had the responsibility to use God's unique gifts as best we could. This prompting rested on the belief that God gave us certain gifts, and we must develop and use them. At the last judgment, our eternal happiness will be decided on how well we have accomplished this. While being able to do my best with the skills God had given me already had meaning, I now felt that whatever responsibility I had for my twin would also be seen as important. My siblings all used their skills well, so the use of my skills would also follow my parents' expectations. This approach seemed to me to be the only and safest guideline for my life and for my twin.

These beliefs would require an ongoing predisposition of being ready to use the skills and gifts at all times. This predisposition to do better and be better may or may not be common for other people, but I feel it is right for me because of my parents and my twin. This strong belief makes me feel like I am being truthful about my twin who is not alive in this world today. I am the only person in the world who can and will in some way carry on for him. Yes, this meant I had to be better and do better since my twin could not do so in this world. I feel I am a doer, and I strive to be better; my life in this regard is an open book.

Knowing Others Who Lost Their Twin

Before looking at other factors between my twin and me, it seemed important to examine other persons who were in a similar circumstance of losing a twin. In my life, I felt fortunate to have had three acquaintances who were involved with having a twin die in utero and then having a live birth of the surviving twin within the same nine-month period.

The first was years ago in college with a passing acquaintance whose mother had a twin miscarriage and his birth within the same nine months. The second was a niece of mine by marriage, Hilary Crawford with her second child, Cary, over sixteen years ago. Hilary told me she was not aware that she was having twins and that the loss came at eight weeks into her pregnancy. Since she had a previous miscarriage, she felt she was mentally and physically prepared for the loss. From a mother's viewpoint, she was pleased to have her oldest son, Cody, and daughter Cary. She was concerned about the possibility, after the fact, that if Cary and her twin had both lived, she probably would not have had her present youngest daughter, Caty. Hilary and her husband, Jim, had hoped to have three children. Hilary has not dwelled upon the loss of her other child.

On the other hand, Cary shared that she had known most of her life that she had a twin. She felt her mother was always open about the lost twin, and it wasn't until her preteens that it really hit her. I had reviewed with Cary the quote from Dr. Stuttaford when he talked about the influence on a surviving twin that "Thereafter they believe that they have to do better, and be better, because of the death—emotions which can put a great burden on shoulders, which are not always strong enough to carry them."[22] Cary had a similar response to this quote as I did in that it helped her realize that she did believe that she worked harder in areas such as music. She also felt that she was more motivated to do well but did not know why. After further reflection, she felt her twin is looking after her and keeping her out of danger, like a guardian angel. An example of her twin helping her was when she and her sister, Caty, were in a car wreck, and neither of them was hurt.

Cary relayed to me that she really never thought a great deal about her twin before we talked and was glad that we did because she now has the chance to think about him/her. After reflection, she expressed the thought that her twin is still in her life, as he/she makes sure she does well in everything she does. Some days she wishes that her twin was alive and with her. She does know in her heart that he/she is looking after her. Seeing Cary come closer to her twin was a positive experience for me.

The third instance of a person who lost a twin in utero is Richard "Dick" Edwards. Dick and I both were employees of Wood County. I was attending a play with my wife at one of the local churches in Bowling Green. During the break, I began talking with Dick, and he asked me how things were going. I mentioned to him that I had begun writing a book, and one of the major influences in my life had been a twin who had died in utero at three months. Dick looked at me and immediately said that he could understand that circumstance, as his twin sister had died at six months, and he was born three months later. The intermission was over, so our talk stopped temporarily.

A short while later, Dick related more specifics on his life and the influence of his twin on him. His birth occurred in the small Bellevue Hospital in Bellevue, Ohio. During delivery, there were some complications. A very wise and skilled country "doc" made the birth successful. He was informed of his sister's death in his teens. While his mother talked about this lost twin periodically, his father rarely talked about the premature death of his sister and his survival.

Dick oftentimes wondered about his twin sister's physical appearance and whether or not she would have pursued the same interests and shared the same kinds of talents. But such thoughts have only been fleeting and nothing in depth. As a result of his twin's death, throughout his life, Dick has felt a special sense of appreciation for the sanctity of life and all its many blessings. A particular closeness to his mother and his younger sister by two years has lasted. Dick has spent his professional life serving others and now is doing so as the mayor of Bowling Green.

Addressing My Beliefs

Addressing my thoughts about my twin in a comprehensive manner is challenging. Yes, the first meaningful interaction about my twin came when I was eight years old at the cemetery where he was buried. I have already addressed how I, as a surviving twin, perceived the ideas of doing better and being better. We have already established that I will substitute the words *twinless, sibling, wombmate,* or the generic *he* or derivatives when I talk about my twin.

The remaining beliefs need more attention. My memory is going back sixty years. Nothing was placed on paper then; those are the memories of a small boy. There have been sixty years of additional knowledge, thought, and varying degrees of certainty about my present beliefs.

What I Believe to Be True

Ever since the cemetery experience with my father, there have been various feelings about my twin. Every time I hear the word *twin* or see twins, I instantly think of my twin. On the other hand, the strength of this bond varies. My life exists because I believe that God gives each of us this life and a chance to be happy hereafter. I do believe my ability to be successful in this life has been influenced by my wombmate. While I have never seen my twin, I like to think there is a connection between us.

Understanding my twin and how he would influence me has been a factor in my mind. While I can't promise a resolution to all the questions, I will present a truthful, brief analysis of the influences I see from him.

My twin did exist in my mother's womb for a trimester but was never born. I feel an identical twin might have given me more physical information than the fraternal twin I was told was conceived.

My twin has led me in two directions: one is surprise and the other adventure. Many events in my life have been surprising as was the news about his existence and death. Living a life without knowing much about him yet living my life the best I can for him is an adventure.

There is a simple link behind understanding God and my twin. While I was looking for a face-to-face encounter, it didn't happen. On several occasions, hindsight gave me direction. I had the strongest feeling about my twin when I visited the cemetery and learned about him. Although I was a small boy, I had the thought that I was to act in some way on behalf of my twin. I knew I could not live his life, but I knew that as a result of his death, I was the one person who could act somehow on his behalf. I had sixty years of growth before I saw the quote of "doing better and being better" for my twin. I can't say that at eight years of age, those were my exact thoughts, but after living sixty years and seeing that quote, it made sense. Doing better and being better is a reflection that best reflects my bond with him.

I have close connections with God through prayer. I obtain some peace in understanding how I had discovered God, my twin, my mother, my father, my deceased sister, or others in prayer and my life experience through looking back.

There have been instances other than the cemetery experience from where I would not have had trouble saying my twin influenced me. The day I went to the cemetery was the strongest link to understanding. Another was in Washington, D.C., as a college student. Late at night I went to the bar area by myself, got lost, and ultimately was chased by many people down a dark street. Another was the support I received in writing my dissertation, a feat that took many months and required much energy, time, and little sleep. These instances point out to me that it was possible for my God with my twin to positively influence my life with their support. Yes, there are others.

While writing this book, occasionally I have felt that I am not completely responsible for the direction of the content. In writing difficult sections, I have felt I received help in my writings, particularly in this chapter. At times ideas and resources for this book have come out of the blue as I type this manuscript and analyze my life. I become completely drained trying to understand and explain my twin and my life. Somehow I receive energy and go on. Yet I can't explain these happenings other than God being the source and at times possibly my twin or the influence of my parents.

A Conclusion

My responsibility is to use my energy to do better and be better particularly in supporting others. While my twin comes and goes, I think he is somehow involved.

In utero, we were close. This was our closest physical relationship. I might add that I accept the existence of my twin as a comfortable feeling. The uncomfortable feeling is understanding my twin in this world when he is in another world.

I have presented the best information and understanding I possess on my twin. I believe any additional proof of my twin's influence will have to wait until the next world.

---

[20] Jan Larson McLaughlin, "Pemberville twins are very identical," *Sentinel-Tribune*, August 4, 2012, 1 and 5.

[21] Thomas Stuttaford, "Ghost of the Missing Twin; Body and Mind," *The Times*, August 8, 1996, 14.

[22] Ibid.

Chapter 5

My Supportive Siblings in the Early Years

Each of the six Frederick children was born in Willard Municipal Hospital and attended and received their sacraments from St. Francis Xavier Church in Willard. All of the children attended and graduated from Willard public schools. The family home was located at 519 Clark Street until a new home was built in 1972 at 584 Butte Avenue in Willard.

As adults, two of the children, Mary Lu and Ann, lived within thirty minutes of Willard while the rest lived at least an hour or more away. Occupations, offspring, and other information will be given with each child's section. A look at each of the children and their families from oldest to youngest will afford a view of each person and a look at the home environment that fostered a rich, caring love for others. While my brothers and sisters will be involved in future chapters, this chapter is meant to be a brief overview of each sibling and some happenings about their lives at home and in some cases their lives as adults so that the reader will have a better understanding of each personality. All of the information listed in this and other sections of my brothers' and sisters' families is correct at the time of writing. It is obvious that my mother and father are held in high regard and as most unforgettable people. Each of my brothers and sisters also holds that honor. The Walter and Marion Frederick family is shown as adults.

Descendants of Walter Eugene Frederick

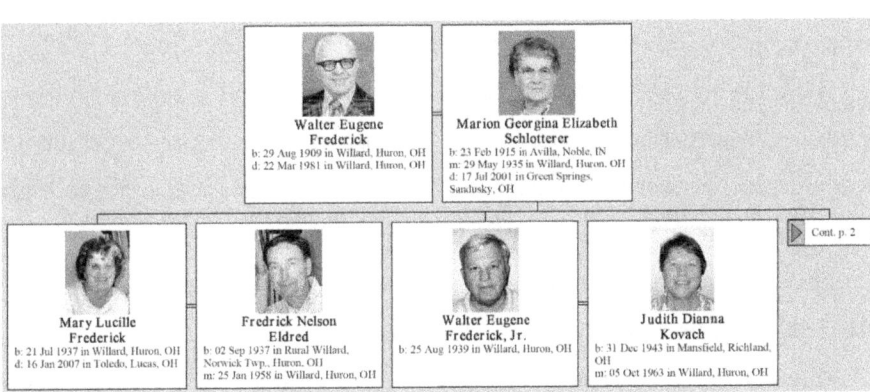

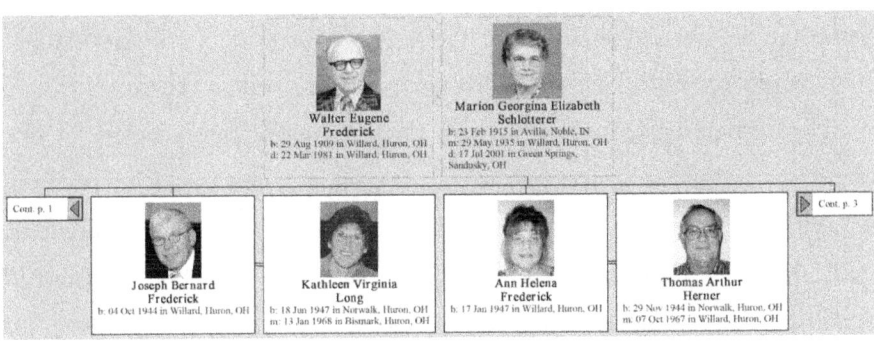

Mary Lucille (Frederick) Eldred

Mary Lu or Lu was the eldest of the six children. She was often called to care for her siblings and others. In the family, Mary Lu's position was, like our mother's, a matriarchal one. At that time, parents and elder siblings were respected. Mary Lu was seven years my senior, born July 21, 1937.

In high school, Mary Lu was a popular girl, and I believe she was a freshman attendant to the queen. One of her jobs during high school was working for our family dentist Dr. Pillar. After graduating from high school, she attended Mary Manse College in Toledo. She was much more interested in a handsome young man named Fred Eldred than college. Mary Lu and Fred dated a few years before they were married.

I remember the wedding well and the reception held at the local Eagles Hall. In Willard, the Eagles Hall was one of the largest halls in town. My dad was a member, so that may be why we used the Eagles. I also remember that there were both alcoholic and nonalcoholic drinks at the reception.

As I entered the men's restroom the evening of the reception, I saw some young men who were attacking the paper dispenser. One of them would hit it with his fist and then check to see if it was tight against the wall. Another would hit it and also test to see if the metal on the front of the dispenser was against the wall. I remember one of the guys saying, "If you can make that metal move a fraction of an inch, I will see that it moves another foot." They gave up shortly thereafter on the paper dispenser. I bet my dad paid for the dispenser.

As we left the hall that evening, I remember that there was a snowstorm that January day; however, it was not comparable to the one that Kathy and I had on our wedding day.

Mary Lu was initially employed at the Pioneer Rubber Company, a company where our father and two brothers, Walt and I, were to be employed. Fred was employed as a machinist at the B & O Railroad (now

CSX Transportation). Mary Lu and Fred have one daughter, Deborah. Deb married Pat Fritz. They have two sons, Jason and Evan. Mary Lu possessed and proudly displayed large collections of Hummel figurines and American Fostoria glass. I have memories of the farm that include several summers of working and living there with Lu and Fred. Those memories include learning to work hard from early morning until late at night and of good home-cooked meals that Lu made for Fred, Deb, and me. Mary Lu was the baker in the family. She would always bring pies to family events. Lemon, butterscotch, and pumpkin were my favorites. She could bake about any kind of pie she wished, and she was also a great cookie baker. Mary Lu was the family genealogist and coordinated genealogy for the Schlotterer family of sixteen children.

Mary Lu and Fred lived on the same farm their entire married life. She used her accounting and financial skills in the family farm business. Corn, beans, wheat, and hay were their principal crops. Mary Lu would work the fields when help was short. They maintained a social relationship with classmates from high school, neighbors, and church friends. A favorite pastime was cards.

Mary Lu had been sick for two weeks before she was transported to St. Vincent Hospital in Toledo in January of 2007 to have her condition diagnosed. The day she went to St. Vincent was one of the most memorable days of my life. Her sickness turned out to be an intestinal infection, which resulted in a septic infection. She had intestinal surgery within a few hours of the diagnosis. I was so happy that she had made it through the surgery, and there was hope that she would recover. We couldn't see her following the operation.

Since we lived a short distance from the hospital in Toledo, that evening Fred stayed at our house. I remember Fred lying down to sleep that evening. He had not slept for a few days, so he went to sleep almost immediately after his face hit the pillow. Little did we know that we were headed into one of the longest and saddest evenings of our lives. Just as Fred fell asleep, the hospital called and said they thought it would be wise for the family to come to the hospital. I gave the phone to Fred, and he talked to the nurse. I knew things must not be good. All my brothers and sisters who were at the hospital had gone home. We traveled rapidly to the hospital, and Fred, Kathy, and I were not prepared for the next few hours. The staff did what they could do for Mary Lu. When the doctor told us that we could each have a few private minutes with her, I knew I was not prepared for this occasion. There was nothing positive in my mind. As I approached Mary Lu, I could see that she was very sick. I made a general request for help from God and anyone else who could help us through that seemingly hopeless time. The energy to make it through such a challenging occasion required prayers, inner strength, and help from many sources. The end came very fast, and I was completely stunned by the happenings of the evening.

I had gone through the death of my parents and father-in-law, but I was not present at the actual time of death. This was the first time I had been with a person I knew well when they passed on. Lu had been very close to me throughout my life. A few years before, she had handled all of my mother's finances as I had handled all of my mother's medical needs. I had lived with Lu and Fred when I was younger, working on the farm. Mary Lu had been the lead person, with Ann and me supporting her for all the burial arrangements for my mother. Now we were working with Fred on the arrangements.

The funeral Mass was a beautiful ceremony. The pallbearers were her nephews. As her brothers and sister came into the church with the casket and spread the pall or covering over it, an opening prayer was recited. As the prayer was being said and my brothers and sister stood around the casket, each of us was drawn to the casket and each other. All five of us held hands over Lu's casket during the prayer. It was one of the closest times I ever experienced with my siblings. While it was my pleasure to say a few words about my sister during the service, I was never sure that I would make it through the presentation and keep my composure, but somehow I did. Testing the skills that God has given us can be risky but also fulfilling.

There are several memories I have of Lu and Fred when I worked on the farm as a junior high and high school student. Here are a few of those.

Shooting the .22 Rifle

My family will never forget the time I was about to attend Willard High School, and I tried to unload a pump .22 rifle in Mary Lu's laundry room. The rifle was used on the farm for hunting. It was tricky to unload. I should have unloaded the gun outside, but I was in a hurry. The rifle discharged as I attempted to unload it, and it scared me to the point of losing speech. Lu called me and asked what had happened. I couldn't talk, and I didn't know at the time that Lu was thinking I had shot myself. It took her only a few seconds to come to the back room and see me alive staring at the hole I had put in the floor. Fred wasn't around at this time of day, and I decided I didn't want to be around when he came home. I thought that the safest place on the farm for me was anywhere but the house. I went out to the barn to shoot rats and tried to figure out how I was going to pay for the hole in the back room floor. About an hour after I was in the barn, Fred came in and sat down beside me not saying one word. After a few minutes, he calmly asked me if I was going to come in and eat supper. He never did ask me to pay for the damages. I gained a lot of respect for and knowledge from Mary Lu and Fred for the way they handled the hole in the floor. I reasoned that they thought I had learned my lesson.

The Whirlwind (Small Cyclone)

I was always very proud of my Marlin Model 99 semiautomatic .22 rifle that I had bought with my own money. One windy summer day, I was on lunch break from farming and decided to do some bird hunting. Bird hunting was a favorite pastime on the farm, and I enjoyed shooting guns. There were several birds around, and sparrows were a particular nuisance. There were only two inhabited houses located on this section of the road. Fred's parents lived on one side and Mary Lu and Fred on the other side. Other than those houses, there were a few barns and some outbuildings; the rest was farmland.

I was hunting behind Mary Lu and Fred's house in a fencerow when high in the sky I noticed a large paper feed bag coming straight toward me. As the bag came closer, I noticed the wind was picking up speed. Something told me to shoot the bag as it came in close enough for me to have a decent shot. I took a couple of shots and saw the bag turn to my right around a series of small sheds and a large barn. I looked on the other side of the barn to my far right and saw a pigpen made of very large beams with a tin roof being lifted into the air. As I watched the debris from the pigpen travel high into the air, I saw a car traveling down the road that barely missed a large piece of tin from the roof of the pigpen. I knew that something wasn't right and have been very happy to this day that I have never again been close to such a sight nor been picked up by the high, swirling wind. I think that I had turned away the whirlwind as I was shooting at the paper feed bag. Another thought was that God or my twin was responsible.

The Tarred Road

One of the summers that I stayed with my sister Mary Lu and her husband, Fred, I had a day off work on the farm, as there had been a heavy rain, and we could not get into the wet fields. On this particular day, Fred's Grandpa Swartz (father to Fred's mother, Rosie) wanted me to drive him around the countryside so he could visit his relatives and other friends. Grandpa Swartz lived with Rosie or Rose and Russel Eldred, Fred's parents. This driving job was an easy task, and I said I would be more than happy to be his driver. Grandpa had been a very successful farmer and businessman and had a beautiful big yellow Buick to cap off his success. I got into the big Buick and began to take Grandpa to his first destination. As I was going down the road in front of a house, Grandpa shouted to me to slow down and to run the car in the grass, as the road had just been tarred. I looked at the road and thought if I go fast, the tar would never catch me. I had the wheel in my hand, and I had control over the car.

After we passed a few more houses and a few more tarrings, Grandpa Swartz's car was not the beautiful car we had started with earlier in the day. The yellow Buick was a black Buick from the middle of the door down. I admitted to Grandpa that I had made a slight mistake, and his decision was better than mine. I asked him how I could make it right to him by restoring the Buick to its original color. He said he knew of one way to make everything right, and that was simply by finding a solution called tar remover and applying it to the affected areas on the car. Grandpa's tar remover was none other than a liquid called gasoline. Well, I didn't have any protective covering for my hands or arms, so I applied the tar remover to a rag and wiped the tar off with my bare hands and a rag. After a few hours of elbow grease, the yellow was coming back. With several applications and cleanings, the car was beginning to look better. The gasoline felt cool on my skin that hot summer day. I finally had the car in a presentable condition when it was time to go to the fields as the sun had come out and dried the soil. I hopped on my trusty Allis-Chalmers tractor and began to prepare the ground for planting. After the first half hour in the sun, my skin began to feel uncomfortable; it itched and burned unbearably. After an hour and a half, I could stand it no more. I went to the farmhouse and began to wash my hands and arms with a mild soap. I then went back to work and finished my day.

The next morning, I awoke at around seven o'clock and went to the bathroom to wash up. As I looked at myself in the mirror, I noticed that I was beginning to lose skin on my arms and hands, and my beautiful tan was rapidly disappearing. I continued losing several layers of my beautiful tan for days thereafter. I discovered that gasoline on my skin and the sun did not mix. I never went to the field after that with fresh gasoline on my skin. This was one of many lessons I definitely learned the hard way!

The Neighbor's New Tractor

While living with my sister and brother-in-law, one of the most delightful experiences I had was to meet and talk to neighbors. One of the most interesting and enjoyable neighbor families lived a short distance up the road. The neighbors were farmers, and one also worked on the railroad. The neighbor and his wife and my brother-in-law's parents, Rose and Russel, were all very good friends. I often heard them talking about going down to the lake together.

This neighbor was always trying to pull pranks on me and had been successful on a few occasions. On this particular day, he had brought a new tractor to our farm for us to see. The neighbor was driving the tractor around the barnyard, stopping it and making it go forward. Soon he drove over to where Rosie, Russel, and I were standing. He was explaining to Rosie and Russel all the new features of his purchase. As they were talking,

I walked around to the carburetor and turned off the gas. I then quickly went around to the other side of the tractor and, knowing my timing had to be perfect, yelled to the neighbor, "This bucket of bolts will be lucky to get out of the barnyard."

He looked at me, squinted his eyes, and said, "I will show you how this tractor works." He gave the engine some gas, popped out the clutch, and heard the motor sputter and promptly go dead. He looked at me and said, "You little smarty. You turned off the carburetor." By this time, I was rolling in the barnyard having one of the best laughs of my life. I had finally caught the neighbor at his own game.

The Blacksmith

A metal piece from one of the tractors had broken. Russel told me that the only way to fix it fast was to go to the blacksmith. As we traveled to the blacksmith's shop, I tried to picture the appearance of a blacksmith. I was to find out shortly what that would be as the shop was located near our farm.

As I left the truck, the smell of something burning was very clear. We walked into the shop, and the blacksmith was working. He was short and had a beard, a hat on his head, clothing that had the appearance of being close to a fire, a hammer in one hand, and a piece of hot metal held in large pliers in the other. Everything in the room had soot on it from the fire. This was nothing like I had imagined. A large anvil and hot coals were close to him. He would place the metal into the fire, wait for it to get red-hot (looked yellow to me being color blind), and then take the hot metal out of the fire and pound it into the desired shape on the anvil. He asked us what we needed to be fixed, and Russel told him. It wasn't too long before he worked on our metal and had successfully fixed it. A blacksmith was common in the rural fifties but isn't very common today.

Walter Eugene Frederick Jr.

My elder brother is Walt. He was born August 25, 1939, and was five years older than me. Since he was older, I looked up to him. Walt was always on the move, so I had to pay attention so I didn't miss his advice. I always wondered who had guided him since he had no elder brother. I guess he guided himself. Walt was born two years after Mary Lu. He probably guided himself at times too much because I can remember my father and him talking about whose rules were to be followed around the house. Walt was active in high school with his car and sports. He was nicknamed Sonny Frederick. I don't know what that nickname meant, but I do remember that his senior name card said "I am Sonny Frederick. Who the (a picture of a devil inserted) are you?"

Walt had a 1950 Ford he bought on a family trip to Reading, Pennsylvania. One of our uncles had an automobile dealership, and this car appealed to Walt when he saw it on the lot. Walt was a member of a "car club" whose reason for existence was to rent a garage so its members could fix up their cars. On occasion, Walt would take me to the garage, and I was always fascinated seeing the motors of various automobiles lying open to be repaired. I knew I couldn't put them back together. Walt completely restored the inside and outside of the 1950 Ford, spending many hours and dollars on the motor and body. It was truly a beautiful car when completed. I remember our neighbor Butch Rothschild coming over to our house to see and talk about that car. It was hard to say who between Butch and Walt was prouder of it.

Walt began his professional career at the Pioneer Rubber Company as an engineer. At the same time, he was attending classes at Bowling Green State University. He later married Judy Kovach from Mansfield. Kovach was Judy's nickname for years to come. Walt was then employed with IBM starting in Mansfield. IBM is an abbreviation for International

Business Machines. It was informally referred to as "I've Been Moved" because of the frequent reassignment of many of its employees. Walt's family moves included Mansfield; Lima, Ohio; Pittsburgh, Pennsylvania; Philadelphia, Pennsylvania; Cincinnati, Ohio; Cary, North Carolina; and Middlesex, North Carolina. The visits to North Carolina were like all our visits to Walt and Judy—memorable. Holidays, birthdays, religious events, graduations, and weddings were some of the reasons to travel to their home to celebrate.

The home in Cary was large like their other homes. The Cary home in addition to having a great entertainment room also had a large outdoor pool. The children were young and loved to play a tag game called Marco Polo. Marco Polo is a hider and seeker game. The seeker closes his eyes and says, "Marco." The person to be caught would say, "Polo" so the seeker would have some idea where the person to be caught was located. The person to be caught would usually dive to another location to avoid being caught as the seeker came close. If caught, the seeker and the one caught would switch spots while the other players would remain hiders. The game would last for hours and be enjoyed by all, and rarely would a player leave the game. Volleyball was another favorite game in the pool, especially as the children grew older.

A feature of the entertainment room was a large jukebox. When our son Mark was five years old, he fell in love with the song "Elvira" while visiting North Carolina. If we heard the record once, we heard it near continuously that week.

After retiring from IBM, Walt and Judy started an interior wood plantation shutters business. The business is called Shutterworks, and the process starts with large boards and ends with shutters. Large machines mill the rough wood into the pieces to be custom cut, assembled, and painted or stained into the beautiful final product. The last step is the installation. My sons, Mark and Joe, and I worked on the construction of the buildings that house the milling and assembly of the shutters. Both Joe and Mark have gone on some of the shutter installation jobs when we have vacationed in North Carolina. We had Shutterworks install interior shutters in our house's windows.

Walt and Judy have six children; all but Jackie lived around Raleigh. Walt and Judy's eldest son is Walter Frederick III or Trace, who married Renee Johnson. Renee and Trace have one son and three daughters. Stephanie is married to Chris Mize. They have a baby girl named Callie. Their second daughter, Kristal, is married to Chris Norris. They have two small children, Christian and Caleb. Their only son is Walter E. Frederick IV or "Dutch." Their youngest daughter is Kaitlin.

Jackie is the oldest daughter and the second oldest offspring and lives with her husband, Carlos Suarez, in Sandpoint, Idaho. Another daughter is Denise Willet, and she has two sons, Tommy or T. J. and Nicholas or Nick, and a daughter, Heather.

Peter was the next son and is married to Julie Bramble. They have two children, Peter and Hannah. Becky is next and is married to Kenneth Munday. They have a blended family with her two children, Ryan and Ashley, and Kenny's two children, Seth and Cassie. Angela is Walt and Judy's youngest.

The following are a few incidents about my brother Walt.

The $1 Bill

Homemade go-karts were a big thing with my brother Walt and me when we were kids. Cars of any kind would be an especially big interest of Walt. When he was a teenager, he was on the top of the world when he was able to drive cars and customize them as he did with his 1950 Ford. On this particular day, Walt and I had our red wagon and were pulling it down Tiffin Street toward the Willard Lumber Company. We were able to walk in the street because it was the early fifties, and there were not that many cars on the road.

Any scrap wood left at the lumber company after building or selling lumber was kept in one storage place and was given away free. We had a set of wheels and a steering wheel for our kart, so the lumberyard was the place to find wood. Any nails, screws, or other hardware as well as tools were borrowed from my father's workshop. Supplies such as nails were usually "a permanent borrow."

On this particular day, we were headed down Tiffin Avenue and were about a half block away from Myrtle Avenue, the Main Street in town, when Walt yelled out, "Wait a minute. I think I see money." Well, we would stop for any amount of money whether it was a 50¢ piece, a quarter, a dime, a nickel, or even a penny. In those days, a penny would get you a piece of gum from the penny machine or maybe a prize from the same machine. I loved penny gum and trinket machines. The prize I most wanted was a miniature cigarette lighter.

Walt got down on his hands and knees and put his head near the side of the curb, which opened into a sewer where water from the street was collected. In those days, not all receptacles on a catch basin had top grates. This sewer opening had no grate, so it was possible, but dangerous, to put part of your body into the catch basin. Walt said, "I think there is a dollar bill on top of the water, but it is dark, and I can't see too well. I'm too big for the opening and cannot reach the money." I thought a dollar bill was a lot of money. I had never thought about finding a dollar bill. The more I thought, the more excited I got because I could easily spend my share of a $1 bill.

I wanted to look good to my brother, and I wanted the money, so I said, "If you hold my legs, I can go into the sewer opening, and if I go far enough, I can reach the dollar bill if it's floating on the sewer water."

Another thought hit me: we needed to get that dollar fast before it sank in the water.

Walt said that I had a good plan and that he would hold my legs very tight. There would be no way that he would let me loose, so I went into the sewer water. I was feeling pretty good that Walt liked my plan, and then I began to get a little scared because I had thought about Walt losing the grip on my legs and me falling into the water. I did not know how deep the water was, and I wasn't sure how good a swimmer I would be if I fell into the catch basin.

Walt must have known that I was starting to get cold feet because he immediately laid down next to the four-foot opening into the catch basin. I got on my stomach and began to put my head into the opening in the curb. Walt firmly grabbed my feet and said, "I've got you." Well, that made me feel better, and I was now in a position to see the dollar bill. I yelled out, "It is a dollar." Walt said, "Pick it up." I was deep in the hole almost past my ribs, and the dollar was just out of my reach. I wiggled my legs a few times and finally my hand touched the money. Although it was a hot summer day, I was starting to get chilled in the sewer hole. I yelled to Walt, "I got it. Pull me out!" Walt began to pull me out, but I had stopped moving. I could feel Walt pulling, but I wasn't moving. I told Walt, "Check my clothes. They may be stuck." Walt tugged on my pants, and I was on my way out. When I came out, I had a nice dollar bill.

We both were very happy and congratulated each other on our good fortune and our ability to work together to get the dollar. The lumberyard could wait; we had money to spend. We walked to Rager's Grocery Store, which was a short distance from the catch basin. I got 50¢ as did Walt. I don't remember how Walt spent his money, but I spent mine on an essential commodity for someone my age—candy. Every time I would think of risking my life in that sewer opening, I would start to think about what could have happened to me if Walt had lost his hold on my legs. Then I would think Walt is my big brother, and he always has been there for me then and now. I also think about the fact that Walt and I were not very good at saving money. We didn't have the money in our hands more than twenty minutes.

Caught in the Railroad Tracks

In my youth, St. Francis Xavier Catholic Church was on the east side of town. In order to get to catechism classes, we had to walk through town and across two sets of railroad tracks. Crossing the tracks was not a big deal as long as there was no train coming. In October of 1954, my brother Walt and sister Ann and I were about to cross the second set of railroad tracks when we noticed a train was coming down the tracks. You couldn't miss it because it was big, and the engineer was laying on his whistle.

We knew we were going to be late for our religion classes unless we crossed ahead of the train. As we approached the tracks, Walt was first in line followed by Ann and then me. I watched as Walt and Ann crossed over the tracks, and since I had lagged behind, I was running as fast as I could to cross. As I touched the tracks, something pulled on my left leg, and I could not move it. I looked up and saw the train closing in on me. I looked down and saw that my sandal was caught in the rails. By this time, the train was only twenty-five feet away from me. All I could see was the large train engine as tall as a building coming toward me. The engineer was motioning to me to get off the tracks. I was so petrified that I couldn't look at the train anymore.

I didn't know what to do other than to continue pulling my foot out of its trap. The train was now within a few feet of me. Everything was a blur as I kept pulling on the sandal and saw the train coming closer. I know I should have prayed, but there wasn't much time, and I wasn't thinking well. I thought I was going to die. My instincts took over and I yelled, "Help!"

My brother Walt came out of nowhere. He quickly loosened the sandal strap, pulled out my foot, and pushed me to safety while he retrieved the sandal from between the tracks. As the train neared us, he rolled himself to safety. Walt, Ann, and I looked up at the train, seeing its monstrous body pass by us. There was no award for my elder brother other than knowing he had saved my leg and foot and, probably, my life. I never forgot Walt's help and have since shared this story publicly. I knew I was very lucky not to have lost my leg or my life.

Junior G-Man

You have probably already seen that my elder brother was a person who prided himself in being a man of action as well as a constant role model for his younger siblings. Walt's ability to be a role model was ingrained in him by our parents and faithfully practiced by him. Here is another look at his ability to take actions into his own hands. In Walt's junior year, he took his written driving permit exam on his sixteenth birthday. He was in Norwalk as soon as the office opened. Once Walt had his permit, it was difficult for anyone else to get driving rights to the family car. Interestingly enough, Walt then passed his driver's license exam soon after he received his permit.

One day in the spring of 1957, Walt had asked our dad if he could take the family car to the Willard Conservation League to go fishing in our boat. Shortly before, Walt and his close friend George had been out at the Conservation League fishing when one of the trustees approached the pair and asked for their junior membership card. The Conservation League is a private club and anyone on site was to be a card-carrying member.

After showing their card, the trustees said, "Would you two gentlemen be willing to seek out anyone you see on site who isn't a member? Anyone you see who isn't carrying a membership card is to be reported to the authorities, and they will take it from there." It seems there had been some trespassers on the grounds and some damage done, and this was not to be tolerated.

A few days later, Walt and George decided to go fishing there. They arrived at the lake and were transporting their equipment to our boat located down a hill near the lake. As they were walking down the hill, they looked toward the clubhouse and saw two young men. They swung into action and began to approach them so they could do their duty of checking their membership cards. As they came close to the pair, they began running in different directions. Walt and George were not sure what was going on, so Walt said he would take the one on the right and told George to take the one on the left. As my brother caught up with the young man, he saw him throw a pistol on the ground. This was not exactly what my brother had in mind when he had said he would check membership cards, but he was into the situation much deeper than he wished to be, and now he needed to follow through with action. George also had caught his man, so they made arrangements for the police to pick up the trespassers. The police chief asked George and Walt for a detailed description of what had happened. You must understand that the police chief was a huge man, and with his uniform on, he could be quite intimidating. If I had been Walt or George making out a report for Chief Carlton Riddle, I would have made out the reports exactly as directed, and that is exactly what they did.

Walt and George didn't hear anything else about the case after they made out their report until they heard that people were calling them Junior GMen as they had captured thieves. They also found out that the night before they caught the trespassers, the men had robbed Ott's Sporting Goods in downtown Willard. It was an exciting time in Willard, as robberies were not common in those days. It was an exciting time for Walt or Sonny, as Dad was a little more lenient in allowing him to use the family car after this incident. After all, Walt was a Junior GMan!

The Robber

There were four bedrooms and seven people who lived in our house on 519 Clark Street. At this time, Mary Lu was married and no longer living at home. In December of 1958, Walt was home, on leave from the Marines. In the middle of the night, I heard somebody downstairs, and they seemed to be in my mother's silverware. I immediately thought it must be a burglar. I woke Walt and told him about the noises I had heard. He always kept his .22 caliber pistol next to the bed. He quickly loaded the gun and told me to crawl down the steps, and he would follow with the pistol. I was to grab the intruder, and he would hold the robber at bay until the police came. Our steps were a little steep and descended about ten steps to a landing and then made a right turn followed by six more steps to the main floor.

I began to crawl down the steps on my stomach with Walt and his gun following behind me. Just as I was reaching the landing before the steps turned to the right, my mother came out of her bedroom and stood in the middle of the upstairs hallway looking at me on my stomach and Walt with a gun.

Mom said loudly, "What are you boys doing?" Hearing these words caused me to jump up and at the same time my brother Walt to come down the steps so fast he ran into me. We both went rolling down the rest of the steps. When we reached the main floor, we put on the lights, and there was no one to be seen. We must have been too noisy and taken too much time to catch the burglar. Right?

The Pheasant

One day in 1961, my brother and a friend were out in Walt's car riding around in the country. They stopped at a stop sign and saw a pheasant in the field. My brother was driving, so he pulled over and parked his car. My brother always kept his hunting gun with him during hunting season, so he went to the trunk, pulled out the gun, and loaded it. By this time, the pheasant had gone deeper into the field. He followed the pheasant and took a shot. As he finished the shot, he saw a car coming down the road. In the car was Father Mehling, his parish priest at St. Francis Xavier Parish. He waved to Father as he went by, and Father waved back. He ran over and picked up the dead cockbird and put it and his unloaded gun in the trunk.

When he arrived home, he told our mother that he had shot a pheasant. Walt wanted to make things a little interesting, so he told Mom he was pretty sure pheasant season was open. My mother told him not to bring the pheasant on to our property until he knew for sure the season was in. He informed her that the pheasant was in the garage, and he wanted her to clean it. My mother finally agreed to clean the bird, but she wanted the garage doors and windows closed so no one could look in the garage and see the pheasant. She also wanted it clear that she was cleaning the bird so that it didn't go to waste, and it must be given to charity if it had been shot out of season.

My mother had worked on the farm when she was younger, so she had learned how to clean birds. As my mother was plucking the feathers, I secretly went around the garage to the back door. I could hear my mother inside the garage telling Walt never to shoot a pheasant out of season. I felt that Mom was uncomfortable about this whole affair. I knocked as hard as I could on the back garage door. As I opened the door, I could see the fear in her eyes. I could see that everyone saw the humor in my and Mom's actions, except her. She had to be convinced to continue cleaning the pheasant. Walt then told me that Mom threw the pheasant into the air as soon as I knocked on the door. It didn't help much when Walt again told Mom that pheasant *was* in season. She never did see anything funny about this incident.

Mom and the Boat

Walt almost always had some type of a boat after he moved to North Carolina. All of Walt's children were grown up when my mother, wife, and sons, Joey and Mark, decided to visit Walt and Judy's family. On this particular summer day in the 1980s, we had decided to go to Kerr Lake with the pontoon. After a while, we were getting hot. We decided to take the boat close to shore, and everyone, except my mom, went swimming. We were having a great time, and most everyone had gone to the shore to rest.

Someone looked up at the boat and saw that the pontoon was drifting out toward the middle of the lake. My mother was on the pontoon and seemed content to crochet and look at the water. We yelled out to mom, but she was too far out to understand us. She just waved when we called out to her. Walt said someone needed to bring Grandma back to shore, or she would continue to go out to points unknown on the large lake. Walt's son Peter volunteered to swim to the runaway boat and bring her and the pontoon back to safety. This was the plan, and this is what happened. Mom never seemed upset by this incident, but everyone else present certainly was extremely concerned.

Ann Helena (Frederick) Herner

Ann was the fourth offspring and the last daughter born after me. Throughout our younger years, Ann and I were close in not only age but also as friends. Ann always had a beautiful smiling face and attractive blond hair. As a young girl, her hair was wrapped in strings of cloth so that it would end up being long and wavy blond when it was combed. Years later, she used large curlers so that her hair would once again be wavy.

At this particular time, Ann, Mike, and I formed a secret club called the Owl Club. This club met irregularly or when we felt like meeting. The insignia was a ring with an owl on it. The ring was shown at the beginning of each meeting, and that is about the extent of what happened with this secret club. The owl call was the signal used if one of us was in trouble and needed help.

Ann attended Willard High School as did all my brothers and sisters. She was a popular girl and thus had many girl friends. Since I was her brother and many of the girls in Ann's class would come over to our house, I had an excellent chance to meet different girls without leaving home. One of Ann's friends was to be my future wife, Kathleen Long. One nice thing about Ann was that she was always willing to introduce me to her friends.

Ann attended St. Mary of the Springs College (Ohio Dominican) in Columbus. That year, she began dating Thomas "Tom" Herner, and they were to soon marry. Tom is a dump truck driver, and Ann works in sales and is in charge of several departments related to health and beauty. They have four children. The oldest is Michelle "Shell" Saiter who in 1999 had a rare disease, which only three people in the world were known to have contracted. Michelle almost died from it, but it is now successfully being treated by her physicians. Michelle has a friend, Brian Kinnard. Their blended family is her children, Rachael Brock and Dustin Brock, and his kids, Eddie and Magnum. Rachael's friend is Steve Ebinger, and their son is Chase William Ebinger. Dustin's son is Wyatt James Brock, and his friend is Ashleigh DeCaprio.

Ann's next child is Thomas II or Tommy. Tommy is married to April Ortner. Tommy and April have a blended family of his children, Nicholas and Vincent, and her daughter, Micah.

Jeffrey or Jeff comes next, and his friend is Gina Francisco. Jeff and Gina's blended family is his daughters, Chayla, Kelsey, and Chloee, and her children, Cassi and Logan. Cassi is married to Mark Brown, and they have a son named Carson. Cassi's daughter is Paige Sterns.

Ann's youngest child is Kristine or Kris who is married to Jim Weinert. They have three children, Jordan, Logan, and Braydan.

The following are a few of the memories I have about Ann, which should be helpful in understanding our relationship:

Under the Bed

When we were in our early grade school years, one of my favorite tricks I played on Ann was I would crawl under her bed before she was in her room and just before she got into bed. Since she was ready for bed, she would turn off her light then go to bed. At just the right moment, I would grab her leg as she was getting into her bed. She would let out a loud bloodcurdling scream. This made Ann the center of attention in the house, and everyone in the house would come running to her room. I would try to leave the room before the light was turned on so I would not be caught. This was not a frequent happening because if I were to attempt this prank too often, Ann would remember to look under the bed and catch me red-handed. But it was always worth a laugh for me.

Tom the Neighbor

Tom and his wife lived behind our family house and across the alley. We never knew the name of Tom's wife. All we knew is that she had white hair and frequently sat in a chair near a rear window from which she was able to protect her vast flower garden from the Frederick children. Tom, on the other hand, was often out working in the garden wearing his straw hat. I cannot ever remember myself or a member of my family talking to Tom or his wife. My father must have talked to them, as he talked to about everyone. We kids knew one sure fact about Tom: he would chase us if we went into his vegetable or flower garden to retrieve one of our balls.

Due to the age span, it was not unusual for Ann, Mike or me to play ball together in the back yard. The children in our family loved to play baseball. In order to play baseball we only had one direction to hit the ball. That was toward Tom's yard. No matter how hard we tried, it was near impossible to hit a ball well and have it stop before going into Tom's garden. Another important point that must be made crystal clear is that there was a fence surrounding Tom's yard that we could climb over, but it was high enough that once we got into the yard it was challenging to get out. For some reason the fence rarely stopped our balls from going into Tom's yard. Once in the yard it seemed especially hard to get out if Tom or his wife saw us in their yard trying to retrieve a ball; fear was then a big factor.

Once a ball went into Tom's yard, we had to get it back right away, or Tom would find the ball and keep it. I do not remember Tom ever throwing our balls back into our yard. When Tom found our balls, he must have taken them into his garage for storage. The more balls in storage, the less balls for the Frederick kids to hit into their backyard. It didn't do any good to tell Dad or Mom about a lost ball, as they had already put us in a Catch22 situation. They told us, "You can play ball, but don't allow the balls to go into Tom's yard."

One afternoon, I had asked Ann and Mike to play some ball. I was playing in the field so it had to be either Ann or Mike who hit the new ball so hard that it went out of our property, over the alley, and over Tom and his wife's fence into one of the flower gardens. It was very important to follow the ball closely if it went into Tom's yard because we had to get in fast and out fast; there was no time for locating the ball. We could not get out fast if we did not know where the ball was laying. Nobody had ever been caught by Tom for being in the garden, and no one wanted to be the first to experience such a terrible event. All I could think was that being caught by Tom was a fate worse than death.

Since the ball was hit hard over my head into Tom's yard, guess who had to retrieve the ball? Yes, I was the one to go after the ball because I was closest to it when it went in the flower garden. I saw where it went, and I as the fielder was the closest. I carefully looked around the yard to make sure that I didn't see either Tom or his wife before jumping over the fence. On this particular day, I saw no one in the backyard. It even looked like Tom and his wife were not home because the back window where Tom's wife would look out over her flowers was closed. I went back a few steps, ran toward the fence, and jumped over it. I was in safe. I hadn't gotten my clothes caught on the wire fence. A feeling of relief was experienced in my entire body since there was no sign of Tom or his wife. I went directly to the spot where I last saw the ball and found it was not there. I frantically looked for the ball. I should be on my way out by now, but I hadn't found the ball. I smiled to myself. Why was I worried? Tom or his wife was nowhere to be seen. I turned around just to be safe and looked up at the gate by the house, and I couldn't believe my eyes.

I saw the worst possible option to this ball rescue mission; Tom was on his way into the garden and was now coming directly toward me. I felt like Peter Rabbit in Mr. McGregor's cabbage patch. My goose was coming close to being cooked. I heard Ann and Mike both screaming to me, telling me to forget about the new ball and get out before I got caught. Tom was now about twenty feet from me and moving fast. I frantically looked for the ball because I knew where our new ball was going if Tom got his hands on it. I was sweating and could hardly see because I was so afraid; no, I was petrified. Tom was now ten feet away from me, and I had to abort the project without saving the ball. I could see Tom closing in on me, so I darted for the fence. I had taken four steps toward the fence and looked down and saw the new ball at my feet. I reached down, grabbed the ball as I ran to the fence, and took what I thought was the best leap I had ever taken to cross the fence. The leap must not have been my best because I got caught on the fence. With Tom just a few steps behind me, I was about ready to give up. Ann and Mike had other plans because both grabbed my pants and pulled them and me loose from the fence. I was out of Tom's backyard and safe.

From that point forward, I was sure that Ann and Mike were truly great friends, in addition to being a good sister and brother. I was congratulated by my siblings on a great ball save. I accepted the praise, as it was probably the most challenging ball save in my life. I would never forget this adventure. I know now that God was with us and perhaps extra help may have been present from my twin. To this day, I am not sure if I ever tried another ball rescue over Tom's fence.

Years later, I came to the conclusion that Tom and his wife were not the most horrible people in the world. After all, they had never snitched on us kids to our parents about entering their property to retrieve the balls, and they never caught us. I also wondered if Tom and his wife would have given the balls back to us if we had asked for them. I came to the conclusion that jumping the fence and almost getting caught contributed a lot of excitement and mystery to our youth. I should have asked Tom and his wife for our balls. I would have at least had a chance to get them back.

The Wreck

This story is one of the all-time terrible, embarrassing, and unfortunately most quoted family story about my driving. Ann was present for the entire incident and has never shied away from reminding me of the details of this wreck. I have wished this incident had never happened on more than one occasion. Without success, I have tried to make the incident a bit more positive from my perspective. It all began when Ann, Mike, and some friends and I went to evening catechism, which are instructions in the Catholic faith. I was in high school. There had been a snowstorm, and the streets were very slippery. I was driving without supervision in my first winter storm. Also, I had borrowed my brother-in-law Fred's 1957 Ford Fairlane 500.

As I came around the corner heading on to Laurel Street, the car began to slip on the ice and snow. It was a new experience and was fun fishtailing on the ice that had covered the road. Before I knew what happened, a telephone pole must have come out of the ground. I had not seen the telephone pole, but it appeared and embedded itself into the exact center of the front bumper and hood. I was scared out of my skin. I had no idea how the telephone pole made it into the hood of the car. It was then I realized I had wrecked a car that wasn't mine. At first, I told Ann and Mike not to tell anyone. The car was making loud screeching noises, so I turned off the key. I was having visions of policemen taking me to jail. Quickly I realized I had no money to repair the damages.

I told Ann I would run home for help. Luckily, it was only four blocks to our home. When I reached home, I banged on the door, for this was truly an emergency, and I had no key. I was half hysterical and crying as I relayed to my parents how I had hit the telephone pole. The only phrase I remember saying was trying to deny the truth and the same phrase I had used with Ann after the wreck: "Tell me this wreck didn't happen." Ann will never let me forget the phrase nor me saying it.

My brother-in-law Fred Eldred, the owner of the wrecked car, happened to be at my house. After he was informed of the wreck, he said calmly that he would look over the wreck to see what needed to be done. His calmness made me feel a little better. As Fred arrived at the scene and started the car, we again heard that terrible screeching noise. Since Fred was both a diesel machinist and knew car mechanics, he knew he had to cut the fan belt. The noise stopped because the fan had been pushed into the motor and couldn't turn. The car now could be driven a few blocks to my house.

Yes, Fred was cool about the whole thing. I was to work off any cost not covered by Grange Insurance by cleaning their newly remodeled bathroom. I also learned to drive safely on ice. By the way, since that wreck, I made sure I had Grange Insurance on my cars. I was more than impressed with the manner they handled this claim. Grange is still my insurance company largely because of the treatment I received under Fred's policy.

Rosemary

My mother was not home for supper one evening, and she delegated the job of fixing supper to my younger sister, Ann. Ann was a very good cook and a very good baker, so I thought this meal would be a done deal. The meal was to be spaghetti, one of my favorites.

The plan was that Ann would make the meal, and the family members who were home that evening would eat it. It sounded like a good plan. So everyone didn't have the wrong impression of my contribution to supper. I was willing to contribute to the meal by washing the dishes, only if needed.

I smelled spaghetti sauce, and I smelled spaghetti boiling in hot water. Ann told us supper was ready, and I knew I was both ready and hungry. We prayed, and everyone began to eat. The first mouthful that everyone took produced the same result.

That result made everyone say, "What is in the spaghetti?" Everyone was now looking at their spaghetti to see if they could solve the riddle of why it tasted different than usual. Ann admitted that she had put a small amount of spice called rosemary in the spaghetti to improve the taste. Everyone began to inspect the spaghetti and to pull out the long thin pieces of rosemary. Soon there was a rather large pile of rosemary that we had extracted from the spaghetti.

At this point, Ann asked everyone to continue pulling out some of the rosemary, as it looked as if she must have put in a bit more rosemary than she had intended. She was surprised that the taste was greatly affected with the amount of rosemary she had put in it.

Everyone continued to pick out the rosemary so they could eat their spaghetti. After that experience, anytime I see the spice rosemary, I think of the spaghetti Ann made. I still like to eat spaghetti, but I pass on the rosemary.

Music at Ann's Wedding

Ann married Tom shortly before Kathy and I were to marry. I wanted to do something special for the reception, so I asked my dad if he would play the piano as I sang "True Love." He agreed to this. I knew Dad was a good pianist, as he was in a band in the twenties when he was dating Mom, and I had heard him pound the ivories on our piano at home. Dad and I practiced several times before the wedding. When the big day came, we thought we were ready. There was an adequate amount of alcoholic beverages served at the reception, and the crowd's conversation was loud. Dad and I wanted to make sure we didn't miss any of the fun, including the drinks, but we also wanted to be in a position to do a good job.

As the time approached to perform the song, Dad and I went on the stage. We were rather concerned because nobody would quiet down so we could perform. After several attempts, we finally had the attention of the crowd. Dad gave me the right pitch and played the right notes throughout the performance. I, on the other hand, started out on the wrong note and consistently kept on it throughout the whole song. My words were near perfect. When we were done, everyone clapped and lied by telling me that I had done a great job. They didn't lie to my dad because he really had done a great job of accompaniment. I had tried so hard to minimize my alcohol intake before the song. I guess none of us is perfect.

Michael John Frederick

Mike was the fifth child. He was two years younger than Ann, five years older than Bob, and five years younger than me. Mike, Walt, Ann, and I have inherited the short stature of our mother. Mike has been a very energetic person his entire life. He graduated from Willard High School where he played football. He has an easy way of working with people, particularly my father. For example, I remember coming in after midnight one Saturday night. Dad "got on me" about his rule to be in by midnight. I told him I didn't think it was fair that I needed to be in so early and that I would not have stupid rules like this for my children (and we didn't). A few minutes later, Mike came in, and Dad read him the same riot act. I quietly waited in the next room to see how Mike was going to handle this situation.

Mike said, "You are right, Dad. I was late." He went to bed, end of the conversation. I should have learned by Mike's example, but I didn't.

Mike married Marge Biesiada a few years after college, and they have two girls, Amanda or Mandy and Melissa or Missy. A close relationship existed and still does between the two families and between the girls and me. They have always trusted me, and my ideas are usually complementary to theirs. I was given a nickname by the girls, and at a very early age, I was known as "the greatest." I can usually do no wrong and have the undivided support of both nieces. I have never questioned their thoughts on this matter.

Mike graduated from John Carroll five years after I did and obtained a job with the Cleveland Public School teaching math in the inner city, a very challenging yet rewarding position. Except for a job as an assistant principal, Mike was always a teacher, and he retired as a teacher. I remember going to Cleveland with my family to visit Mike's family on a Friday night. I couldn't help but notice that Mike had bloody knuckles when he came home from work. When I asked him what had happened, he said that some former students had gotten into the school and caused a fight with the present students in his school. He and other teachers stopped the fight and got a little scuffed up in the process.

Mike also worked in his off hours as a handyman, doing almost any job around people's houses. On one such occasion, he was working on a porch railing. He saw a young man run past him with a sawed-off shotgun. He shot at another young man, and both ran away. The police were called. Mike never did hear the outcome of this shooting. Mike often had many unusual stories about his many jobs.

Marge was a teacher in Parma Schools. Their oldest daughter is Missy, and she is married to John Porvaznik. The youngest daughter is Mandy, who is married to Mike Pritts.

The Knife Fight

One evening when I was twelve years old, I was home with Mike. We were playing in the dining room when I got the bright idea that we should have a knife fight like Davy Crockett. Davy Crockett was big at that time, and Fess Parker was the actor who did such a good job playing Davy. I had a long knife that was in a sheath, so I went to my fishing tackle box and found it. I described to Mike how we could have a fight like Davy, and I demonstrated how I would hold the knife in the fight since I was older. In our household, being older meant you knew more and had some privileges. Mike was to grab my arm below my hand, and I would make the knife go in a circular pattern, which would force him to let go of my arm. It sounded good to me since I had made up the plan, and Mike had no objections.

It went well at first because Mike grabbed my hand, and I circled the knife around his hand while my hand made his hand let go of mine, but he said, "Ouch." I looked at Mike's wrist, and I saw I had cut it, and it was bleeding. The first thing I thought was *I hope I have not cut an artery*. The blood was flowing rather slowly. I found a washcloth, wet it, and applied pressure on the wound. In about five minutes, the bleeding had stopped. Mike agreed with me that there was no reason to tell Mom or Dad about this incident. Our promise to not tell our parents lasted our lifetime.

A Jump in the Garage

The cut to Mike's wrist reminded me of a similar wound that I received when I was Mike's age. I was in the loft in our garage on Clark Street. Wood was stored in this area, and I was looking for a piece of wood for a soapbox I was building. I had found a good piece of wood. I decided to jump from the loft to the ground, which was a distance of about eight feet. I made a beautiful jump and landing, but I was near the side of the garage when I left the loft.

As I hit the ground, I felt a sharp pain, and it was not in my leg; it was in my left hand. I looked at the wall and saw an exposed metal light switch plate. It was the plate that was the culprit. My hand had sprung a huge leak, and blood was on my arm, on my clothes, and on the floor; my hand looked like Old Faithful. This was a terrifying experience. I ran into the house holding my saturated wrists and found my mother where she often put in her time, in the kitchen. A cold compress was applied by my mother, and a trip across the street to the neighborhood nurse, Mildred Rothschild, and her appropriate bandage completely stopped the bleeding. I was inactive for the rest of the day—a rare occurrence for me. From that experience, I learned something about not only looking where I leaped but also looking at all sides for objects that might hurt me.

Herman Joseph the Ram

When I worked on the farm, there were many animals. So I took advantage of a stout ram named Herman Joseph and converted him into a bucking ram. Lu warned me that no good would come out of my animal training exercise with the ram that held part of my namesake. I was fifteen years old, and my brother Mike was five years younger. On this particular day, my whole family was on the farm. I thought it was a good day for me to show off Herman Joseph and his great ability to buck under my supervision. Mike had always been a good sport, so I thought that he should have the honor of being the secondary subject of my training.

I convinced Mike to help me take Herman Joseph for a walk in the pasture. I held the ram close to me as did Mike. The entire walk, Herman Joseph was trying to buck us. I took a buck to show I was a man; Mike eventually took one too. We reached the middle of the field, and I let go of Herman Joseph who continued to buck us. At this point, my mind was kind of fuzzy. I decided to leave Mike fend for himself while Herman Joseph showed off the skills I had taught him. This move was not one of my best Christian acts. As I reached the fence, I saw that Mike was out in the middle of the field trying to hold Herman Joseph's head so he didn't get bucked.

Mom was standing by the fence, and she gave me a direct order to "get out there, and save your brother from that ram." As fast as I had left the two of them in the field, I was back out there and saved my brother from any further danger.

A few weeks later, Grandpa Swartz, Fred's grandfather, went into the sheep pen and bent over to pick up something. He was looking away from the ram. The ram immediately saw the target and bucked Grandpa square in the butt. Grandpa went flying in the air and landed on his hands and knees. Lu was right: no good came out of this whole bucking incident for either Herman Joseph or me. I lost my pet ram to the meat market the next morning.

Snakes

Mike and I again were out on my sister's farm, and we decided to walk to the hickory tree woods. This happened to be the same woods where their sheep were grazing. We noticed that the sheep had done an excellent job of cleaning the woods. As Mike and I were walking, we noticed a small dark substance that looked like the pellets we would light around the Fourth of July, and "a substance that resembled a snake" would fizz out off them.

Mike said, "Are these snakes?"

I said, "I think they are." I knew they weren't, but I thought I'd have some fun with him. Once again, this was not one of my most Christian moves. Mike filled both his pockets and made plans to come back to get more, as he was going to sell them. Mike was so happy that he had made this find, and everywhere he looked, he saw more of what he had identified as "snakes."

We walked back to the farmhouse, and Mike walked into Lu's kitchen as proud as he could be. He told Lu that he had made a great find and was going to be rich. He reached into his pocket and pulled out two handfuls of the pellets. The pellets were in his hands and some also had spilled from his pockets onto the floor.

Lu looked at the pellets and said, "Get that sheep manure out of the house!" That was the end of Mike's great find.

Working with Mike

Now Mike and I are able to work together on various repair projects, but it has not always been that way. Our ability to work together began on a winter afternoon in 1983 as we were preparing to install a new lock in my mother's front door. She had asked us to fix it. We found the tools and another locking system and began to tear out the old lock. I had my way of doing the job, and he had his. The repair could not be done both ways at the same time. We had reached a stalemate, and discussions led to nowhere for about fifteen minutes. Finally, I said, "Mike, we are going to do this your way or my way. Which way will it be?" Mike did not answer and continued to do things his way, so I said, "We will do things your way this time and in the future, and you will always be the boss." Every project we have worked on since that day has worked smoothly as we did it Mike's way, and he has been the boss.

Fishing

Mike had inherited a small fishing boat from our father, and he invited me to go fishing with him on Lake Erie for perch. I learned that going fishing with Mike could also produce the possibility of going to the emergency room. On one occasion, Mike was hooking up the boat and trailer to his ball hitch on the car when his finger got pinched between the trailer hitch and the ball. He permanently lost the feeling in that finger as a result of it being crushed.

The more memorable event was when Mark, Joe II, and I were going out the channel to go fishing, and Mike caught his finger in a hook with three barbs. Now a treble hook that goes in the finger deeply is not easily extracted because there is a barb on the hook, which makes it nearly impossible to pull it out. Mike decided he did not want to spend part of his day in an emergency room. He came to fish, not go to the hospital. We tried to push the hook through the skin so we could then clip off the barb and pull out the hook but no deal. Mike's bottom line remained: he still felt it would be much better to get the hook out of his finger on the boat rather than going to the emergency room. Waiting a few hours in the emergency room and missing a day of fishing was not an option for him.

I had my trusty Swiss army knife and a can of beer as a germ chaser. We poured the beer on the knife blade and saturated the finger. Luckily, Mike had less feeling in this finger than he should have, as this is the finger he had injured on the trailer hitch. After two small incisions, the hook broke free, and we were on our way. Mark and I felt this was the high point of my surgical career. As I thought about this experience later, I should have had Mike finish the rest of the beer, as it would have added at least a small amount of internal germ killer to the operation. Mike's logic about avoiding the emergency room paid off, as we had a good catch that day. The finger healed nicely with no infection.

After-Dinner Drink

Mike and Marge have a favorite restaurant in Cleveland called Mallorca. One evening, Mike, Marge, their daughters, Missy and Mandy; our son, Mark, Kathy and I went to dinner there and had a fabulous meal. After dinner, I wanted to buy a bottle of Portuguese, an almond liqueur called Doirinha, which is bottled and shipped by E. Ferreira Duque, LDA. I was to learn that it was difficult to find this liquor. Mike said he knew a store that sold the drink. We walked a few blocks and found the store closed. Mike said he knew of another store that sold the drink, but it was located a few blocks away in a less desirable neighborhood. Mike and I decided to walk down the eerie alley leading to the shop. After I purchased the bottle, Mike decided to take another route back, which pleased me. As we started down this new route, it was beginning to get dark, and the street felt like it was getting narrower. I looked around, and I began to think that people were looking at us and about to come out of the walls to chase us.

Suddenly I had a flashback of when I was in college and went to Washington, D.C., for the Cherry Blossom Festival. On one of the evenings, my friends wanted to go to the bars in the red-light district. I had some work to do and told them I would meet them later. On the way to the bar, I got lost (an easy feat for me). I continued to walk down the street, and I heard footsteps behind me. I walked faster, and the footsteps came faster. I looked back and could faintly see people coming out of the buildings and running in my direction. I broke into a sprint. I felt like pure terror and was certain that I was going to get mugged and robbed. Something helped me at that point to keep up my running pace. God, a special saint, my twin, or all three helped me because I miraculously came out on the well-lit Main Street known as the red-light district.

I came back to reality and realized that Mike and I had returned to the parking lot where the rest of the group was waiting for us. They asked us what had happened since it took us so long to get the bottle. I told them the first store wasn't open.

Bowling Green State University

In 1996, Mike and Marge had come to our house to visit. Mike and I needed to go to the Ace Hardware located in downtown Bowling Green for a part to finish a project at our house. As we left, Mike asked me to go by a practice field at the university, as he saw a bus from Cleveland. We went by the bus, and Mike asked me to stop. Mike walked over to the field and began talking to a number of participants. He came back and told me they were some of his students. That fact did not surprise me because it seems whenever we go to a public function, such as a Cleveland Indians game, Mike always knows several vendors who are or were students of his. Yes, Mike always seems to know someone anywhere we go. His "people skills" are such that he gives others a feeling of being important, and conversation seems to come easily. Mike inherited this trait from our father who could easily make a conversation with anyone.

Robert James Frederick

Bob was the youngest child in the family, which in the pecking order should have made him last in attention, not so; another overshadowing factor that would play out well for Bob was simply being the baby. As the last child, Bob was to have the benefit of my parents' peak income, which brought with it about anything Bob wanted. He had "first dibs" on a car because Mike was in college. It was very common for Kathy and me to come into Willard and see Bob cruising down the Main Street or Myrtle Avenue in Dad's Chevy Impala, one hand on the steering wheel and the other on the open window. I don't believe he ever saw or acknowledged us in our car. We probably weren't his focus at the time.

My parents' cottage on the Huron River was available for Bob's use, and I believe the sign on the cottage door said Bob's Cottage. Oh, did I mention that there was also a ski boat that went with the cottage? Since it was only Mom and Dad living in the house, and they were gone often, Bob could party about any time he desired. I believe Mom and Dad were a little tired of raising kids, so Bob pretty much had his way. Bob was the tallest in the family. It really didn't take much to beat the rest of us in height, and Bob was a good-looking guy. He was a very good athlete in football, track, and basketball. If you asked him, he was probably good in all sports. Years later at a wedding far from Willard, I was talking to a local banker from Willard. The conversation led to the Frederick family, and this man was Bob's age and played basketball with him. Yes, we concluded that Bob was a good athlete.

If you put all this together, you have a pretty popular guy with many positive resources in a town he knew well and with people he knew well.

Bob had it made, and everyone knew it, especially his brothers and sisters. Bob had a talent of making other people feel good about themselves.

Bob graduated from Willard High School and John Carroll University. My elder brother, Walt, had worked for IBM for years, and Bob always had an interest in IBM, so he got interviewed; obtained a position in Cleveland. He then married Barb Rhodes; and subsequently moved to Boston, Atlanta, Chicago, and Brookfield, Connecticut, all with IBM. Bob works in the area of security, and to me, one of his high-profile experiences was representing IBM in Japan at the 1998 Winter Olympics protecting the scoreboards. Barb is employed in the retail industry. He and Barb had three children, Megan, Matt, and Michael.

My brother Bob is ten years younger than I am. When I was in college, he was in grade school. It was not until he was in his thirties that I began to build a closer relationship with him. Because he was an administrator like me, we probably felt we could trust each other. He is a good decision maker and therefore one of the few people I trust with confidential information. I am fortunate to have not only Bob as a close confidant but the rest of my brother and sisters as well.

Catching Fish

As a boy, Bob enjoyed fishing. One of his favorite spots to go with Dad, Mike, and possibly Ann and me was Willard Conservation League. On one such occasion, the family members were out in their rowboat, and Bob was getting ready to cast his line. Bob had his spot picked out where he was going to cast and was intensely watching that spot so as not to lose it or have one of his siblings steal the spot from him. He placed the pole and line and hook over his head and behind him so that he would have lots of power when he cast the hook and bobber into the opening between the lily pads. Bob was just about to cast the rod and bait over his head when

Dad yelled, "Stop." Bob did stop and turned around to see that his hook was in dad's nostril but had not yet pierced the skin. Dad would have truly been caught if he had not yelled.

The Restroom

Bob was a pretty knowledgeable person about his environment. After all, he had a car to study Willard and the surrounding area, a cottage to study the river, a boat to study the lake, and athletics to study the crowds. I heard that Bob was popular with the girls. You will need to take this statement at face value as I did since I wasn't around.

In his youth every summer, Bob would partake in the Fredericks' two-week vacation to someplace in the United States or Canada. A safe bet on a side or main destination would be something related to religion. Either a shrine, a church, a grotto, a basilica, or a cathedral would be a possible destination. On this particular trip, a restroom stop was needed by the occupants of the car. Once the car stopped, my father usually had a dozen things to do with maps, directions, or money, yet he always wanted the children to be with a parent in the restroom. He was ahead of his time on this.

Since Dad was not ready to go to the restroom, and going to the bathroom with Mom wasn't cool, all the guys waited for Dad. This wait tended to produce extra pressure on the urinary tract, so when Dad was ready to go, all the boys were really ready to go. As we walked into the restroom with Dad, I noticed that the walls were covered with graffiti. Mike also noticed the graffiti but, like me, was more interested in the urinal. As Bob walked in, he began to read the graffiti. At one point, he began to laugh after reading one of the sayings. My dad picked up on the laugh, looked at the funny graffiti, and read the message that had amused Bob. The message referred to male privates. Dad asked Bob if he knew what the graffiti he was looking at meant. Without hesitation, Bob explained the graffiti and several similar graffiti on the walls. I believe Bob asked Dad if he had any questions on the graffiti. Dad never tested Bob's knowledge of the world using the medium of graffiti again.

Beans

One of the big advantages in having Mary Lu live on the farm is that there was always work to be done. This arrangement opened up work for her brothers and sister. When Bob was twelve years old, he was given the opportunity to work on the farm. I was also working on the farm at that time driving a tractor and pulling equipment, which broke down the plowed ground into soil ready to be planted. Once the fields were worked down, the planting would begin.

The first crop to be planted in the spring usually was corn. After the corn was planted, soybeans were next. This is where Bob's work began. Since the soil was ready to plant, Bob's work was to fill the five-gallon pails with soybeans from the dump truck's bed to fill the planter.

There was a definite time span between the filling of the planter and the next time it needed to be filled, so when I made a round with the tractor, I would check on Bob to see that he was doing OK. The day had been going well. The sun was shining, and there were no equipment breakdowns. If a piece of equipment were to break down, it would usually happen at the most inopportune time—planting time.

As I was coming to the end of a round, I saw Bob in the truck. He was waving at me in a strange manner, so I pulled up beside the truck. I asked if he was OK. He told me he had a bean in his ear. I jumped off the tractor and climbed into the truck bed. I looked into his ear, and sure enough, there was a soybean in his ear. The bean was so far in that I could barely see it. I looked in the truck glove compartment and in the tractor toolbox for an instrument to take out the soybean, but I found nothing to give me a remote chance of removing it. I tried to get it out by putting the affected ear down and slightly tapping his head. I was concerned that there was no way to remove the bean easily, as it looked like it would go deeper into the ear each time it was touched. Bob needed more attention and skill than I could give him.

Since I didn't have other transportation, I unhooked the tractor from the disk and drag. At that time, Fred drove up with the planter. I told him I was taking Bob up to the house so he could get the soybean out of his ear.

We went up the road and found Lu in the house. She called Mom, and it was decided he needed to go to the doctor's office. With the issue out of my hands and the three of them on their way to the hospital, I went back to the field. It took me a good twenty minutes to reconnect the tractor to my implements. It is a pretty impossible task for one person to hook up the equipment. The tractor must be backed up perfectly, or it will not hook up. I began to fill the pails and then drive the tractor because without Bob's help, I needed to cover two jobs.

I was concerned that the bean would not come out easily. Word came about ninety minutes later that Bob was fine. There is a tool they have in the emergency room that has a round metal circle on the end of a metal rod that can be maneuvered around the soybean or other offending objects to extract it. After this experience, Bob was careful not to get anymore loose beans in his ear. Bob would admit that this event turned out to be "not such a good way" to get out of work.

The Garden Tractor

My mom and dad would frequently take road trips to visit all their children in whatever location they resided. We were very important to them, and they were important to us. The trips usually started on late Friday afternoon, as the weekend was when everyone had time to spend with relatives. One weekend when Bob was fifteen years old, he and one of his friends also came to our house located on Route 199 just north of Route 582 in Wood County. On this evening, we had invited over our neighbors Don and Marge Trabbic to have a few drinks, eat, talk, or play games.

While we were socializing in the house, Bob and his friend were outside. One of their favorite activities was to drive our MTD riding lawn mower. The mower was peppy, and they could take turns driving on our large yard. It was cold outside, but the spring thaw was imminent. Bob and his friend were busy driving the tractor outside, and we were occupied inside enjoying ourselves.

After about two hours of driving the tractor, Bob and his friend decided to come in the house. When they came inside the back door, they asked for some clean clothes. We gave them the clothes, and they took showers and got dressed. As Mom was putting their dirty clothes into a plastic bag, she commented about the mud on them. I looked at the clothes and decided to go outside and see where they had found mud. It was cold outside, and mud did not seem likely. I looked in the backyard and noticed some mud spots. I opened the garage door to look at the riding lawn mower or small tractor. I was surprised as I got a good look at the tractor. It was covered with mud. With the cold weather, there must have been some warm spots that remained in the lawn. Fortunately, the mud came off the tractor rather easily probably because we ran a hose of warm water from the basement, and we cleaned it. The boys had a good time, and so did we.

The Fourth of July 2007

Bob is a humorous person, and this is an example of his cute side. I had called Bob around seven o'clock the night before they were coming in for the Fourth of July party to get an update on their travel progress from Brookfield. I discovered that they had not left yet and would not be leaving until the next morning due to a complication with one of the boy's ball games going late into the evening. They were to take off the next morning at five or six o'clock.

At six fifty-seven the next morning, we received a phone call. It was Bob checking on Kathy and me. According to Bob, their oldest child, Megan, wanted to know if we sleep in now that we are retired. I tried to figure if this was a Megan question or Bob putting up his daughter to asking questions that took the blame off him for waking us up early. While I had been up till after midnight writing and watering our garden, I answered her question indirectly by saying, "Yes, we are not asleep."

I hung up, and Kathy asked me who had just called. I said, "My brother Bob." I figured in about an hour it was time to call Bob and thank him for the wakeup call. I connected with him as he was going across the Hudson River in New York. I informed Bob that we get up for *Good Morning America* at seven o'clock, and they had awakened us three minutes ahead of our schedule. I could hear laughing in the background, as Bob must be on speaker. Bob and his family did make it for the Fourth of July party, and it turned out that a little late was much better than not at all. I never did find out who was behind our early morning wakeup call.

Chapter 6

Grade School Days and Before

I was born in a small town named Willard (originally named Chicago Junction), on October 4, 1944, at 11:30 p.m. in Willard Municipal Hospital. I weighed eight pounds and ten ounces. According to my parents, my eyes were a beautiful blue, and my hair, eyebrows, and eyelashes were light or blond. I resembled both my parents and looked like my elder brother, Walt. Thirty people were my first visitors in the hospital and at home. I received twenty cards and twenty-two gifts from relatives, neighbors, and friends. The gifts were flowers, money, clothing, a ring, and a baby book.

At birth, I experienced my first life-threatening disease. With many frightening experiences for my mother and father, including extreme and prolonged coughing and a ruptured navel or belly button, whooping cough

The Frederick family in 1944

was the accepted diagnosis. This disease almost took my life, but we beat it. I lived my early life at 519 Clark Street. This picture of the family was taken in the winter of 1944. Front row, left to right, is Mary Lu and Walter; last row is Dad, Walter, and Mom, holding baby Joe.

I was baptized at St. Francis Xavier Catholic Church on October 22, 1944, by Fr. J. B. Fralick. Christmas was not far behind, and I received thirteen presents for my first Christmas. There were toys, stuffed dogs, baby food, and a spoon from my mother's brother Uncle Karl, who was on the front line in the war in Europe.

I had a special supper for my first birthday. My growth was normal in that I sat alone at four months, scooted at seven months, climbed at nine months, took my first steps at eleven months, and walked at one year. My first haircut was at age one by my father, and my mother was the trimmer of my curls. My father cut my hair and all my brothers' hair until we were around sixteen years old. At one and a half, I put together small sentences and said my prayers. At two, I plainly parroted most words my parents said, and I made large, long sentences. Today I still make large, long sentences, but I am not the simple speaker I was at two.

My first friends were my sister Mary Lu and my brother Walt. There were two neighbors I frequently played with, Butch Rothschild and a young girl who lived across the street. I carried a book most of the time, and I loved to hammer nails into a wooden block.

The cutoff date to attend first grade was in September. Since I was born on October 4, 1944, I slipped in under the rule. I was to find that being one of the youngest students had few, if any, advantages socially, intellectually, or physically. I was to find that being the youngest had many disadvantages in my youth and some of my later years. It also meant that I was able to get into the world of work a year earlier.

I attended Willard Elementary School. I was the third child of Walter and Marion Frederick. My elder sister, Mary Lu, and my elder brother,

Walter Jr., did what elder siblings do best: guide me. Willard was settled largely because of the Baltimore and Ohio Railroad known as the B&O. Additional industries developed over the years. My father worked at one of the major industries, Pioneer Rubber Company. The company made balloons, surgical gloves, industrial gloves, and household gloves. Other industries were Midwest Industries Div. MTD Products Inc., where snowblowers and lawn mowers were made, and R. R. Donnelley Company, which printed and bound books.

I can remember many events in my early life. At that time, I loved one neighbor's dogs, another's rabbits, and a third's pigeons. My other interests at this young age were flowers, football, stories about animals, and Jesus. I have always liked cold drinks—the colder, the better—and I was especially fond of drinking from the garden hose, as the water from there was usually very cold. This photo was taken in the side yard of our home when I was very young. The happenings in a person's life that are remembered are most likely the more influential in terms of guiding one's life. We have looked at the early times, and now we will look at the grade school and junior high school years.

I love water!

Willard Public Schools

Kindergarten was not a choice for me, as there was no kindergarten when I started school. As we have discussed, since my birthday was October 4, 1944, my parents had the choice of holding me back until I was six years old or beginning school while I was five years old. My parents agreed that I would start school early. Yes, in years to come, I was to discover that I was always the youngest, almost always the shortest, and socially not as mature as my classmates. In retrospect, I feel we should have waited a year before I started grade school.

I started my education in a relatively new elementary school, and when I started Willard Junior High School, I walked to it behind the elementary school. I remember studying hard in all my school experiences. While in elementary school, I can vividly remember certain events.

When the school nurse came into the class, every student would greet her by her name, "Hello, Ms. Sherman." She would check any wounds, possible infections, or rashes and treat those she was qualified to treat. My classroom teacher in my fourth grade class was single and pretty, and I really liked her. I often wondered if she knew how I felt.

I wasn't too far into my education when a teacher picked up on my lack of skills in recognizing red and green colors. I had testing performed on me to see if I could recognize red and green colors embedded in multicolored numbers. I tried hard to find those colors, as I strived for perfection in most activities I attempted. If I could not see red and green colors, how would that affect others' perception of me? I was not a happy camper being color blind.

One of my jobs in elementary school was to clean the erasers. I liked this job because it got me out of a few minutes of class, and it was something I liked to do—work. There was a large vacuum cleaner with a round suction head and several holes in it. I would put the eraser on the cleaner, and it would pull out the chalk. Well, it would pull out most of the chalk.

It seemed all we did was take spelling tests. Ten words every few days comprised the test. I rarely missed words, and my grades showed that I knew them. An area in which my grades were not so good was penmanship. Things got so bad in this subject I was registering Is for my grade. This meant my penmanship was so poor I was off the charts or got worse than an F. My grade was an I for incomplete. Never had I heard of another student earning the grade of I. It was what it was, and no matter how hard I tried, I could not noticeably improve my penmanship. I have not yet worked out how I will legibly sign copies of this book.

I remember in sixth grade I became attracted to a young girl in the fifth grade. At the time, she was the prettiest girl I had known. She was taller than me—who wasn't? We passed notes in between classes and were developing a nice relationship. I never did understand the part of the relationship where almost exclusively all communications were handled through notes. I can't remember having a conversation with the young lady until years later. I guess some actions just can't be explained from our youth.

Memories of the Frederick Household

Schlotterer Reunion

One of the biggest family events of the year was the Schlotterer reunion, which was with my mother's side of the family. Originally, the reunion was held at a farm where Uncle Lee, Aunt Eda, and family lived in rural Plymouth. In recent years, the reunion has been held at a park in Ashland, Ohio. The day was filled with games, food, and cold drinks for all. One of the most popular games was bingo. For anyone who knew their numbers and the letters BINGO, it was the game. The value of the prize was not as important as winning.

I was always searching for the coldest drink at the reunion. I was on the search one afternoon when I was close to four years old. I was to find the dream of my choice when I discovered several large blocks of ice waiting for me to eat. I knew I had "died and gone to heaven," as this substance was cold, and I loved cold items in my mouth. I must admit that with anything worthwhile, there is usually a challenge. The challenge in this case was to get a good bite into the ice because the block was big, wet, and slippery. Yes, it is still true that anything cold, especially ice, has always been the most welcome and most desirable consumable to me.

As I inched closer to this wet block, it became apparent that I was observing one of the largest pieces of ice I had ever seen in my life. It became more apparent that there was no reason that I could not bite off a section of this beautiful piece of ice. As I got down on my knees and began to sink my teeth into the ice, I heard a clicking sound. This photo shows me trying to eat a block of ice. I was much too occupied with the ice to be concerned about having my picture taken. I enjoyed a piece of the ice, and it was not until a week later that my mother showed me this picture.

I love ice!

At one time, I knew all my first cousins. At my grandmother's passing, there were eighty-five grandchildren, 165 great-grandchildren, and thirty-seven great-great-grandchildren. One of my goals at reunions now is to figure which children are in which family. Everyone's name is a bit beyond me.

The Baltimore and Ohio Railroad

Trains from the Baltimore and Ohio Railroad were an ever-present part of my life. St. Francis Xavier Roman Catholic Church was on the east side of town. This meant that crossing railroad tracks was a constant challenge, as one never knew when trains were going to be dividing the city. The first set of tracks from downtown had no quick alternate route if a train was on the tracks. There was an underpass available if the train was on the second set of tracks blocking the street. Another reminder, besides the sound or sight of the train, was the whistle; this reminder of a coming train was heard both day and night. The whistle was a sound that one heard but didn't really notice. A less frequent but somewhat present reminder of the railroad in those days was the hobos. A hobo was usually a man who lived on or near the train, traveled on the train, and many times slept on the train. There were hobo camps, I am told, where hobos would talk, eat, and sleep when they were not on the train.

As I have already mentioned, several of my relatives worked on the railroad. My grandfather Charles Frederick was an engineer. My mother's father, Karl Schlotterer, was responsible for watering the cars, and both grandfathers worked on the Baltimore and Ohio Railroad, known as the B&O. In fact, as I was frequently reminded, Willard, was named after Daniel Willard, onetime president of the B&O. The B&O was in later years to merge and become the Chesapeake and Ohio Railroad or the Chessie System.

When I was five years old, I remember going to the railroad station late one evening to see my mother off to Pinconning, Michigan, to attend her sister's and her children's funeral. Her sister Rose, on August 19, 1950, was on her way to see her new home that her husband, Kurt, was building for the family. Rose and her three children, Judith, John, and Jean, ages three years, two years, and one month, were all killed in a head-on collision caused by an impaired man driving on the wrong side of the road. This tragic accident was a memory that I will never forget.

I can still see and hear the large steam engines of the B&O. The engines dwarfed my small body as we waited for my mother and her sisters, brothers, and parents to board the train for Michigan. It seemed she was leaving forever as she was engulfed in the large passenger cars. As the train departed, large clouds of smoke left the smokestack and filled the air surrounding the loading platform. As power was built in the boiler, the clouds of smoke grew larger as steam was routed through the piston, which was to drive the large metal poles attached to the wheels of the train going to Michigan.

The loud whistle sounded a whoooo-whoooo-whooo noise, indicating it was clearly time for the train to depart. While exhibition trains of this steam train era are still around now, the trains are not seen on regular routes. They have been replaced with diesel-powered engines. Another reminder of the smoke-filled air from these large steam engines was when the soot from the coal-burning fuel would fill the air and homes located near the railroads at the time of the steam engines. This soot is not missed by the housekeepers and families who have survived this era.

Fishing

If I were to tell you what the favorite hobbies were in the family, they would all likely involve water. One popular hobby was fishing. My father owned some type of boat most of his life. If there were a few minutes of spare time, we would go fishing. Fishing was quality time with my father. My mother didn't fish. When the rest of the family would go fishing, Mom would catch up on her work around the house. My mother was a consistently fast worker. Other than the fun of catching fish, another benefit that came from fishing was being able to eat the fish or give them away so somebody or some animal (cat) would have a good meal.

Before my father had a car, we would go to the fishing hole by riding our bicycles. Since I was too small to pedal the bicycle, I would ride with my elder brother, sister, or dad. It was always a little difficult to steer a bicycle if one's feet couldn't reach the pedals.

It really didn't matter what type of fish we caught as long as it was a fish. Bullhead, bluegill, bass, or once in a while a crappie were the fish we would catch. We always had to bring the fish home to show Mom. Mom pretended to like fish, but we could tell she really didn't. On one occasion, we took a picture with Walt on the left, then Mary Lu, me, and Dad. You can see the bicycle in the background. We did catch a fish, and we were proud of it.

One of many fishing outings

Hunting worms for fishing and learning at the same time

My father, brothers, sisters, and I deemed fishing as a favorite pastime. My fixation with fish and fishing started before grade school. This hobby started when I was first able to use a fishing pole. The water was a great place for us to be, and anything associated with water, such as fish, turtles, frogs, snakes, or swimming, was pure fun. The snakes were fun if they were not near us.

I found at a very young age that learning was essential to my existence. The process involved prior mind-sets and came by way of many potential helpers. One of the prior mind-sets would be to "be open to learning." It is OK to not know something. It is good to not appear to be a "know-it-all." So now I was ready to learn. I found that there were many people ready to teach me, if I was "open." While the people who helped me learn were present, I found that many times I was not aware I was learning from my parents, my neighbors, my siblings, and my friends. In school, our teachers were always instructing us, and we knew this in our formal learning environment.

Some learning came from others who many times were teaching us, although we probably didn't realize it. Another form of learning was independent learning or self-teaching. While some of the learning was fun, when we learned by trial and error, it was not as pleasant to "learn from our mistakes." Let's apply our knowledge of learning to the task at hunting worms.

A prerequisite to fishing was hunting worms, and "being open" to learning the process had the built-in motivator of being able to fish. I realized that I didn't "know it all," as I was constantly losing worms. I learned how to hunt worms in our yard and our neighbor's yard. My father and neighbor helped me to be a better worm hunter. The preparation was quite easy. My teachers explained to me that if there had been recent rain, we did not have to water the lawn. If there hadn't been rain, we needed to water. In those days, it seemed there was never a shortage of water.

I was making the mistake of shining the light directly on the worms, and they would quickly go into their holes. The next step I learned from my neighbor and Dad was to have a reliable flashlight. A light that was too bright would scare the worms before we could catch them, and a light that was too dim would not allow us to see them. It was important that the night crawlers or worms had enough darkness so they would be far enough from their holes so we could catch them with our bare hands.

When a night crawler was spotted by the flashlight, I was taught by my dad that it was important to shine the center beam to the side of the night crawler so that the worm would not be frightened by the bright center light. It was also important to limit the movement of our feet so the worm wouldn't be scared inside its hole. While catching the worm, it was best to pin down the worm with one hand so that the other hand could grab it on the side nearest the hole. Once secured in my hand, slowly pulling the worm out of its hole was important. My friend taught me that there was the right pressure to apply to the worm in pulling it out of the hole. If the worm was pulled too fast and/or hard, the worm could break, and a portion of the worm would be lost. I taught myself how much pressure could be placed on the worm to avoid the broken-worm syndrome.

Sometimes two worms would be attached to each other, and that could be a great catch. My brother Walt taught me that grabbing the worm in my hand instead of pinning down the worm is a bit risky because the worm can be lost in the grass or in the moving hand as I pulled it up. My dad showed me that finding worms in the garden or in other bare spots is an easier picking because you can see the worm part that is out of the wormhole, the soil is easier to pull out the worm from, and there is no slippery grass present. By far, the easiest place to catch worms was on wet sidewalks or driveways. This usually happened after a very heavy rain. The worms crawl on to the pavement and are usually completely out of their holes. It is what is known as easy picking because you can do just that.

Twigs can look like worms, and you can think you have a worm until you feel how hard it is. A fear that I had when hunting worms was that the worm would actually be a small snake. I never picked up nor was bit by a small snake thinking it was a worm. In future years, I would give this knowledge to my younger brothers and sister. Throughout the book, the idea behind the title *People + Me* is present. Here is an example of wonderful people influencing my life by giving knowledge to me. I am then able to give to others. We were now ready to go fishing with our worms, fishing gear, and our bicycles.

Where to Fish

There were several ponds or lakes where my father took us children to fish. There was the old reservoir located west of town near the J Tower and the railroad. The J Tower (named because the building was built in the shape of the letter J) has since been torn down, but it served as a building where railroad personnel could convey a message to the train by placing the message in the middle of a string and then attaching it to a V-shaped piece of metal on a metal pole. As the train went by, the person in the train would grab the message and the string. There was one good place to fish—next to the bridge by the road. The old reservoir has now been drained and is not in operation. In its day, it was a good bass and bullhead fishing hole.

As a young boy, I would ride my bicycle the two and a half miles to the old reservoir. I had to learn how to take bullheads off the hook without getting speared by their sharp, bony protrusions in the sides of their head and on top of their back. Each time I would catch a few bullheads, I would clean them and store them in the freezer until there were enough of them for my mother to fry for a meal.

The second place to fish was the new reservoir also located two miles west of town past the Willard City Park. There were several fishing spots by the road and parking lot, as well as spots by the road that circled around to the back part of the reservoir. I can remember my father taking the car on to the back road and nearly becoming stuck because of high water that covered the road.

The new reservoir was also the location of the hump. The hump or hill was where train cars started from the top of the hill and were separated according to their destination so that they could be hooked with other cars to be pulled by the appropriate engine. I can remember what a treat it was for my parents to take us children to the hump or top of the hill and watch the cars released one, two, three, or more cars at a time. There were many bass, bluegills, bullheads, and frogs at the new reservoir. While worms were the preferred bait, artificial plugs and even maggots were also successful.

Many years later, there was a very new reservoir built, which is located north of town. I have not to my knowledge ever fished in this reservoir.

Maggots

I remember one Saturday night when my father, Mike, Ann, and I were fishing at the new reservoir. There was another fisherman close to us, and he was catching fish right and left. My dad could never refuse the chance to talk to another person, so he wandered over to this unknown fisherman and asked what he was using for bait. About fifteen minutes later, my dad brought back a lure box filled with maggots. The fisherman told my dad that the maggots had to be stored in the refrigerator. I had a very uncomfortable feeling about maggots being in our refrigerator and knew that my uneasiness was not half as bad as the feeling I would have if my mother knew about these small worms in her refrigerator. My father decided that it was safe to put the maggots in the good refrigerator overnight without telling my mother.

This was a very bad move because fifteen minutes after Dad put those maggots in the refrigerator, my mother discovered them. She asked, "Who put maggots in my refrigerator, and why?" Everything was quiet until my father said he had put the maggots in the refrigerator, and they would only be there until tomorrow morning. He also informed my mother that he had double sealed the container, and they couldn't get out. My mother reluctantly bought my dad's argument, but she did say to him, "If one maggot gets out of the container, you will have to clean the entire refrigerator."

I thought to myself, *My dad really did handle that situation better than I would have.* The following morning, as was our custom, the kids and Dad went to the 5:45 a.m. Mass and then retrieved the maggots from the refrigerator. Thank heavens, not one maggot was loose. We found the maggots were good bait but hard to keep on the hook.

Back to Where to Fish

The most commonly used fishing hole that the family used in my teenage years was the Willard Conservation League. This manmade lake was constructed in 1940 by horses and draglines. In fact, my wife's grandfather, Ted Long, and her father, Albert, used the family team of mules to help make the huge basin that became the lake.

My father and one of his coworkers and friend had crafted a small rowboat, which had three seats in it. The boat was perfect for the conservation league, and it was stored near and to the left of the clubhouse. We caught many fish at the conservation league. Among the fish caught were bass, small to very large bluegills, and a few catfish.

Ann and Mike liked to fish, but initially, it was important for my father and me to bait their hooks. It was a proven fact that if I was baiting another person's hook, a fish would often bite on my hook at the exact same moment, and I would rarely catch the fish. Those crafty bluegills could be hard to catch and good at cleaning our hook. My dad and I were to bait the hooks until my younger siblings could put the worms on their hooks themselves.

There were a number of turtles among the lily pads, and we were very good at catching them. Dad would allow us to catch turtles even when we should be fishing. I was one of the better catchers. Dad built a special area in the backyard that held the turtles, and the older of the younger children fed and changed the water in their water bowl. Every once in a while, we tried to catch frogs at the conservation league. They were hard to catch, and when one was trying to catch turtles or frogs, it was necessary that no noise, such as a kick on the side of the boat, was made, for it would startle the frog or turtle, and they would swim away. The Willard Conservation League was also a favorite place for the Boy Scouts to have a camp out.

Fish for the Neighbor's Cats

Mary and her husband, Henry Voight, lived two houses from us on Clark Street. Henry was a retired railroader and was large in size. Henry was usually sitting in a room downstairs reading, and rarely did I speak to him or he to me. Mary was known to be one of the nicest soft-spoken people in the world. Also, she was one of the smallest and oldest people I have known. She wouldn't hurt a thing.

Mary was fond of her many cats. She always welcomed food for the cats. We often gave Mary any fish that we had caught, especially if they were too small to clean. Sometimes we would take our table scraps to Mary. We always knew that she would have some candy around her house, and we were always being rewarded with a piece or two of candy. Yes, this meant that when the fish or scraps were given to Mary, all the Frederick children would also go.

Many years later, I received word from my family that a Willard woman had been proclaimed dead. On the way to the funeral home, one of the attendants had noticed a sign of life, such as a bead of sweat coming down this lady's forehead. Upon further investigation, it was noted that the lady had not died, and she was taken back to the medical facilities. However, she did die three days later. The poor lady who went through this dying process was Mary, our neighbor.

St. Francis Xavier Parish

This seems the most appropriate time to talk about my religious belief starting with my first parish, St. Francis Xavier in Willard. Many of the activities I experienced in my life were connected with the church. The guiding principles of my life come from my religion. Religion has been a major part of my life and still is an important and daily part of it. My parents believed in God and expressed their beliefs through the Roman Catholic faith. Without religion as a part of my life, I would have great difficulty in understanding why I exist. For those who are familiar with the Roman Catholic religion, this should bring back many memories. If you are not familiar, this can offer a perspective on a life that I find gives me a reason to live, love, and look forward to a life of eternal salvation.

A Brief History of the Catholic Church

The Frederick family's lives revolved then and now around the Catholic Church. Much of the information in this section came from an interesting publication on the history of my first church. The original compilation was in 1950 by Fr. J. B. Fralick, and the most recent updating was accomplished by parishioner Larry J. Foran. *The History of Saint Francis Xavier Catholic Church*[23] was provided by Jackie Eckstein, secretary of St. Francis Xavier Parish. The publication provided me with information I had not been able to access previously. For example, in 1879, the St. Francis Xavier Catholic Church "mission" was located initially on the east side of Willard on Keefer Street. In 1897, a new church structured as a reproduction of St. Peter's in Rome was built on Washington Street to serve thirty-eight families, and the original "mission" church was moved behind the new church and was called Xavier Hall. This hall served as a social and educational center.

The last building to be acquired on the east side of town was Charles Clark's home in 1941, and it was renovated for the Tiffin Franciscan nuns to live in. They instructed religion, conducted vacation Bible school, and assisted in the works of the church. The Franciscans remained until 1949–1950. Father Fralick was the pastor when I was born in 1944, and he left in 1951 after serving more than sixteen years. I can remember the play in Xavier Hall, behind the St. Francis Church, when Father Fralick was leaving Willard. At his farewell celebration, there were several songs and skits. My uncle Dick Schlotterer was in a skit with me. Dick was St. Joseph, and at six years old, I was the young child Jesus. We were both dressed in white robes, and I held a globe as I was seated on the shoulder of my uncle. The song had words something like this: "The bells are ringing from Willard to Crestline." I never forgot both the melody and the words as Father Fralick, a truly unforgettable person, was leaving Willard and going to Crestline, Ohio.

It was soon after Father Fralick left that I made my First Communion. The First Communion is a very big celebration in the Catholic religion. It was at that time that I received the body of Christ in the form of bread or a wafer. My godfather was Gene Mink from Cleveland, a family friend, and my godmother was Aunt Peggy, my mother's sister. Since they were sponsors at my First Communion, they were to hold a special lifelong relationship with me. Not pictured was my second godmother, Aunt Anna Pauline. She lived many states away,

My aunt Peggy, Gene, and me on my First Communion day

so somehow her involvement as a godmother was not known until I was doing this research.

The next priest to come to Willard was Father Frederick Mehling. We became very close as he hired me as a part-time maintenance worker. My job was to mow the lawn at the church and the St. Joseph Cemetery located by the Willard Swimming Pool. Every now and then, Father Mehling and I would get involved in a cleanup job, such as pulling out weeds by one of the buildings owned by the church.

I remember one time we had pulled out the weeds, and we were mowing down the stubble. The mower ran out of gas, and Father asked me to get some "bug juice" for the mower. That word has stuck with me, and whenever I need gasoline, I look for "bug juice." I respected him, and I think he also respected me. He would give me a job to accomplish and allowed me the freedom to accomplish the task. If I couldn't finish the task, I would ask for his guidance. Learning to ask for assistance was a valuable lesson in life.

A few years later, I was completely on my own when I mowed the St. Joseph Cemetery. I would run while mowing the lawn and complete it in just a few hours. The faster the cemetery was mowed, the more time I had for other activities. The trimming would take me a short amount of time, and I was always proud of the amount of work I completed in a short time in the hot sun. It was nice not having a competent boss looking over my shoulder. The cemetery was always a special place for me, as my twin was buried there.

I do not remember how much I was paid, but it wasn't a high wage. The important part was I had been paid, even if it was a low rate; my efforts qualified as work. In the future, I was to teach a course in college titled Employment of the Handicapped, and I knew work from the bottom up.

Years later as I reviewed the work I did for the church and especially the mowing of the cemetery, I knew that I was accomplishing a lot of work.

I would ask myself, *Why would I work so hard?* Once again, the principle of doing better and being better was present. The main motivating factor for me to accomplish so much had a logical way of going back to my twin and the ideals of hard work that my parents had instilled in all their children. I have no other plausible explanation for my actions.

In 1958, Father Carmen Nardecchia arrived in Willard. In March of 1962, a new church was opened located near Willard High School. In 1965, Father Nardecchia passed away with a heart attack. He was a very charismatic person who could have given many more years of service. He was almost a professional baseball player, but he had decided to be a priest. Shortly after Father Nardecchia's death, Fr. Donald Klaus became the pastor. I was to graduate from John Carroll University and lost touch with St. Francis Xavier. I will never lose touch with the memories of my church as you will see now.

Special Devotions, Ceremonies, and Practices

Lent, Holy Week, and Easter

The Catholic Church is noted for its ceremonies. Lent provides us with a good starting point. The beginning of Lent is the reception of ashes on Ash Wednesday, commemorative of the fact that we all will die someday and will return to dust. When receiving ashes, which are in the form of a cross on the forehead, the following words may be said: "From dust you came, and to dust you shall return."

In my youth, the Stations of the Cross were said during the weeks of Lent. The Stations of the Cross are fourteen incidents that happened to Christ during Passion Week from His condemnation to His death to His placement in the tomb. According to my early catechism lessons, Adam and Eve had eaten the forbidden fruit and disobeyed God. Jesus's death was essential so that people who had sinned could have eternal salvation. The Catholic Church believes that all people are born with original sin as a result of Adam and Eve's actions. At the beginning of each of the fourteen Stations of the Cross, we are reminded of Christ's death and redemption.

Another part of Lent is Palm Sunday. This is the day that Christ rode triumphantly into Jerusalem on a donkey/colt and paraded down the streets as people laid palm branches on the path He was taking. This happened the week before Holy Week. Palms are still used in the Catholic Church on Palm Sunday, and a procession takes place. One week, Jesus is the center of a parade; the next week, He is crucified.

Let us now reflect more on Holy Week. I can remember the solemnity of Holy Thursday when I was a boy. I would go first to the service of the washing of the feet. The Mass that took place was basically the celebration of Jesus Christ's body and blood being turned into bread and wine. Next was the stripping of the altar and other ceremonies. The last part of the Holy Thursday ceremony was taking the body of Christ in the form of bread to a special place in the church for the adoration of the Holy Eucharist.

As a young boy, I remember my father taking me to church on Holy Thursday at an assigned time to pray for about an hour. This was one time of the year that I could stay up late by going with my father to pray. The time we would go to church varied from eleven o'clock in the evening to two o'clock in the morning. If I was asleep when my father was ready to go to the church that night, my father would wake me. My father, mother, brothers, and sisters would all go to the church. I can remember that the time would sometimes go slow, so getting through the sixty minutes could be hard. The hands on my watch seemed to never move. When we left the church, another parishioner would come to do their time of prayer. After the hour was up, we would go home and quickly go to sleep.

On Good Friday, Jesus was nailed to the cross and died for our sins. On this day, part of the service was the adoration of the cross. This would consist of the cross being transported to the altar and the congregation kissing the cross to show reverence to Jesus. This was one of the most solemn parts of the Holy Week to me.

Holy Saturday customs were related to several parts of Christianity. In the morning, there was blessing of the food. Bread, hardboiled eggs, butter, meats, and even horse radish were all blessed by the priest in the church. The blessed food often would be our lunch on that Holy Saturday.

Holy Saturday Vigil was a special celebration of the Mass. While Mass happens daily, Holy Saturday Vigil was always special. Mass was a time for the community to come together to worship. At evening services, lighting the new fire and lighting the Easter candle was the first part of the service. If rain came upon the ceremony, lighting the flame was much harder.

At the Saturday night vigil, catechumens are baptized and candidates are confirmed and receive their First Communion. At the Mass, the proclamation of the Word of God is celebrated through the readings, including the Gospel. The homily or refection on the Scripture was always important. Yes, the Mass included the celebration of the Holy Communion that was first experienced at the Last Supper when Christ took bread and wine and changed it into his body and blood. This celebration of the Holy Communion is a high point of the Catholic faith. Jesus broke bread, which commemorates his death for our sins. He rose from the dead on Easter Sunday so we may be raised into heaven to enjoy eternal salvation. Jesus is truly present in the Word and in the Sacraments.

The experience of the risen Christ is that Jesus has died so we can live with Him, the Father, the Holy Spirit, and all the good people for all times. Years later, I read a commentary on Easter that very simply placed the risen Lord in perspective. Fr. Roger V. Karban wrote a weekly commentary on the Sunday reading. On the second Sunday of Easter, he related his remarks around the risen Christ. His words were as follows: "If we have yet to experience the risen Jesus in our lives, perhaps it's because we're not carrying on his ministry."[24] This quote meant to me that the proper actions help the proper experiences to happen in the proper manner.

Benediction

When I was young, there was a celebration called Benediction. It usually was on Sunday afternoon, and the Fredericks usually attended this ceremony. The beginning of this service consisted of the recitation of prayers. A while later, there was a ceremony involving incense. This involved the making of smoke using a lighted piece of charcoal in a decorative metal vessel with a top held on by chains. The incense was placed on the lighted charcoal while the top of the vessel was open. When the smoke climbed into the air, the priest would close the top and swing the vessel so that smoke went into the air to pay homage to God.

The Host, a white round wafer, which when consecrated is the body of Christ, was displayed in the center of a monstrance, which looks like gold rays of sun coming from the middle where the Host is located. The monstrance was raised in the air, and the people would bow their heads and make the sign of the cross to pay homage to Jesus. The sign of the cross starts with folded hands and then is made by taking the right hand's extended fingers to the center of the forehead while you say, "In the name of the Father"; then the fingers going to the middle of the bottom of the chest cavity while you say, "And of the Son"; and then taking the fingers and touching the left shoulder and then the right shoulder while you say, "and of the Holy Spirit." The hands then go to the middle front and form a set of folded hands to complete the sign of the cross. This tradition is not lost today but is less frequent.

Crowning of Mary

One of the most well-attended ceremonies at St. Francis Xavier was the Crowning of Mary, mother of Jesus, held in May. The crowning ceremony started at or in the church and proceeded to the backyard of the Spring Street property. At that site, there was a massive display of flowers, as the spring flowers were in bloom and members of the parish also brought flowers. All people, especially women, wore their finest for the crowning. In the middle of the flower display was a huge statue of Mary.

As the procession left the church, several songs were sung to Mary, and a line was formed from the youngest to the oldest children. The students walked two by two to the crowning area. As everyone arrived, they went to a predetermined spot, and the parents surrounded the students and the May altar. One of the older girls was chosen to crown Mary, and she would do so at the appropriate time by placing a crown of flowers on Mary's head. The ceremony was very solemn, and the students did not speak unless they were singing.

In the rare case that someone did misbehave, one of the nuns was there to keep order. This activity was one of the most beautiful and most enjoyable church-related ceremonies. A song titled "Bring Flowers of the Fairest" with the words starting the chorus "Oh, Mary, we crown thee with blossoms today! Queen of the Angels, Queen of the May" was a Catholic hymn, which has no copyright.

Christmas

It would not be right to talk about special celebrations in the Catholic Church without talking about Christmas. As I grew older and had a better understanding of Christmas, the celebration of Christmas was of more importance to me. The birth of Christ is the central theme of Christmas, but the presents really were the icing on the cake. Everyone seemed to be in an extra-positive mood during Christmas. The anticipation of hearing about a baby who was God on earth given by the Father to save mankind from their sins was hard for me to understand. Thus, the idea that God made man was always a mystery. But giving gifts to each other as the Magi had to the baby Jesus made sense to me.

Another mystery of Christ was that Jesus would be with us the rest of our lives. Even though Jesus would die on Good Friday, He rose and is present when we need His help and support. Yes, He is with us always, especially if we ask for His help. The depth and meaning of these mysteries is still with me today and continues to offer me new meaning as I work to better understand them.

Saints

Saints are one of the most misunderstood aspects of the Catholic Church and probably for good reason. The first point that must be made is that people believe, worship, and pray to God as the Supreme Being in charge of all worlds. The Catholics believe that God is three persons in one: the Father, the Son or Jesus Christ, and the Holy Spirit. Thus, people can pray to God or any of the three persons of God.

The Saints are people who at one time were human beings on earth. Each of these Saints had particular qualities that were very desirable. For example, Mary, the mother of Christ, is the patron Saint of mothers. My understanding is that people intercede through Saints because they were particularly good examples or models. Saints intercede with God or go to God with these prayers that have been offered to them to represent one's personal needs. Another practice associated with Saints is the wearing of medals to pay homage to the Saint as a model in hopes that they would also represent one's needs well to God.

While certain saints are ones with a capital *S* or "Saints," others are less well-known and less recognized by the Catholic Church and have a small *s* in their designations. The big *S*aints are more significantly recognized in the eyes of the Catholic Church through a process called canonization. The church has a celebration for all saints on November 1. This celebration recognizes both well-known Saints and those lesser known. A big *S*aint would be St. Mary, the mother of Jesus. A small *s* saint could be anyone who did good on earth but is not recognized as a canonized Saint.

Abstaining and Fasting

There are other practices within the Catholic Church. We will talk about a few of the well-known. Abstaining is usually not eating meat and meat-associated items. Fasting is presently only done a few days a year. Ash Wednesday, and Good Friday, are some of those days. I have heard the story that in order to boost the fishing market years ago, abstinence was created, and fish were eaten instead of meat.

Fasting is eating one big meal and two smaller meals. The reason for fasting is that the person is doing penance or suffering for their sins.

St. Blaise

The blessing of throats on St. Blaise Day on February 3 commemorates this Saint's strength in terms of curing diseases or disorders of the throat. On this day, two crossed candles are placed on the throat of parishioners, and a prayer is recited by the priest to hopefully free persons of disease in that area of the body.

Rules in Church

As an aside, throughout my grade school years, there were always rules to be followed by the children while in church. The first was that there should be no talking. If one whispered, that was just about as bad as talking. It was very easy to look at one's siblings or friends and crack a smile, which led to a muted or loud laugh. This laugh could become cause for parents to look sternly at their children, and if that didn't work, the child was placed next to the parent. A terrible action that could be taken was removal by the parent of their child from the pew to the back of the church. A more severe action would be to go outside the church with one's parents and receive a punishment. This last experience was close to death itself.

Kneeling up straight was a rule that the nuns enforced, and my parents did likewise. Kneeling straight could be interpreted as being a form of being a "soldier of Christ." When I was younger, I always wanted to sit by the aisle, but I never did. Little did I know that the reason my mother was at one end and my father at the other end of the pew was to keep us children in line. I learned about where parents sit in church when we had our own two sons.

The Housekeeper

It was the practice at this time for the priest to have a person, usually a woman, to help him accomplish many tasks. The duties of this person were to make meals for the priest, clean the house, and keep the altar up in the church. I was not sure who did the laundry and some other duties in the home.

The housekeeper also worked with the altar boys in seeing that everything was ready for Mass and that all was in order. Special supplies were required for special occasions, such as the lighting of the charcoal so that the incense would produce smoke when placed on the hot coals. The housekeeper I knew was old, very friendly, and a very soft-spoken woman who was a devout Catholic. This housekeeper was at St. Francis Xavier during most of the years when I was an altar boy. As I look back on this common arrangement when I was a young boy, I heard little about Father being in the same house as the housekeeper. I can imagine that today, the rumors would be flying about housekeepers and priests living in the same house. This practice was, to my knowledge, discontinued years ago.

First Car

I must have been in the second or third grade when my father drove home an early 1950s black Dodge car. It was a big car, so the five kids, our parents, and the sixth child on its way should be able to fit in the car. Before owning the car, we walked everywhere. We didn't have any other way to go places, so we walked. We walked to church, to see friends and relatives, and to shop. Grocery shopping wasn't too difficult, as the nearest store was two blocks away, and we had a child's wagon to carry the groceries.

My dad seemed to like the car the most because it was eleven blocks from home to work. I can remember everyone in the family jumping in the car and going for a ride through town. Mary Lu was very excited about the car because she was old enough to drive. Walt was close behind Lu in age. It was a great addition to our family. Can you imagine not having a car to take you where you wish to go? Now that we have a car, how was our religious activity affected?

Sunday Afternoon Rides

After my parents bought their first car, Sunday afternoon became the time for our family to be together and to visit. This is our first early 1950s Dodge. From left to right, we have Mike, Walt, Ann, Mary Lu, and me. We did not just ride around. We would do one of two things: we would either visit relatives or friends or we would visit shrines and churches. Since my mother had fifteen other siblings and all but two were alive, there were plenty of options in terms of visiting.

Five kids and our new Dodge

My mother's brother George was one of several relatives we visited. Visiting Uncle George and Aunt Rose Mary was fun for me, my sister Ann, and my brother Mike, as there were cousins the same ages as ours. Playmates at this home were Leo, Rose Ann, and George Junior. This convenient arrangement of cousins was good while it lasted. As we were approaching our teen years, my uncle George obtained a position with Fanny Farmer Candies in Norwalk. It never was quite the same after they moved.

My father had one brother, Charles, and visiting him was a possibility when he was not on the road driving truck. Let's not forget our periodic visits to our grandparents. Going to visit Grandma and Grandpa Schlotterer was like an ongoing happening, as my mother was very close to her parents. My father's parents were not seen as often, but we would periodically take time to visit the Frederick grandparents. My grandfather was not used to having children around the house, and there were not many toys there. So we were creative. One of our favorite activities at my Frederick grandparents was playing with the mail slot in the front porch. Ann, Mike, and I would find some form of paper to act as mail, and then one of us would stuff the paper into the little covered slot outside, which connected with the receiving opening on the inside of the porch. One of us would then take the mail out of the opening and deliver it, and we would do it all over again. For some reason, this game would occupy our time for hours and was great fun for the three of us.

Another possibility of visiting friends was going to Len and Ann Playko's house on Park Street, which was about three blocks away from our house. Len also worked at Pioneer as plant 3 manager. I think my dad was involved in helping bring Len Sr. and his valuable job skills to Pioneer. Once again, Mike and I had someone to play with as Lenny was my age, and Rich was Mike's age. Johanna was my elder brother Walt's age. When Johanna was home, Ann would have another female to relate to when we visited. It seemed there was always something to eat whenever we visited anyone.

While visiting family and friends was one option on Sunday afternoon drives, the most frequent destination was to visit shrines associated with the Catholic Church. My favorite shrine was the Sorrowful Mother Shrine located in the rural Bellevue and staffed by the Precious Blood priests. The shrine paid homage to the Blessed Virgin Mary and her great faith and dedication to Jesus throughout her life, and this faith and dedication was especially noteworthy when Jesus died on the cross. When I think of being a parent of the son of God and seeing him condemned for crimes He did not commit and ultimately to die for the sins of all mankind, this had to be a bitter experience. The Sorrowful Mother Shrine is located in the country down a long path or road. There are outdoor stations of the cross and a church. A grotto of Our Lady of Fatima is also one of the high points on the grounds. Today there is a large outdoor shrine used for summer weekend Masses.

An activity that Mike, Ann, and I looked forward to was running in the woods and when we were leaving the premises running out the long pathway leading out of the shrine. Another "gone by the wayside" attraction located next to the original church was a hand water pump. We would get a drink of cold, tasty water and then another until we were full. A new religious article shop that sells a large array of statues, medals, books, and other religious articles has since been built there and operates on a daily basis.

Our Lady of Consolation Shrine, located in Carey was another frequently visited shrine. Our Lady of Consolation is home to the Conventual Franciscan Friars. There is a beautiful basilica and an outdoor shrine to Our Lady. This national shrine is visited by people from all over the United States and other countries. The upstairs of the basilica has colorful leaded windows and a middle altar made entirely of marble. To the left and right of the main altar are other altars. The altar to the right is dedicated to Our Lady of Consolation. There are several sections in which candles can be lit and prayers said for special intentions.

The lower level is a place where people can partake in the sacrament of Reconciliation by confessing their sins to the priest, receive absolution, and do their penance. There is another large altar in the basement and a section displaying the many cures of physical and or emotional illnesses by Our Lady. The area is covered with braces, crutches, canes, a portable bed, and many handwritten documents attesting to having been cured by Our Lady. The miracles that have taken place as a result of Our Lady of Consolation are staggering. I have spent significant amounts of time reading the documentation of these miracles, and I am awestruck at the number of and diversity of present and past miracles. If you are able to take the time and read some of the accounts of the many miracles that have taken place there, it would be an experience you would never regret.

The outdoor shrine is located down the street and to the left of the church as one exits the basilica. Frequently there have been pilgrimages to the shrine, which include walking down the street to the shrine while praying. Upon reaching the shrine, a service was usually conducted by the priests. The Stations of the Cross can be prayed by walking or riding around the path. The stations are very large in size. When visiting, we would usually take a picnic lunch and eat in the shelter house. When my father was the president of an organization for families in the Toledo Diocese, he wrote a prayer, which was recited by the persons on the family pilgrimage.

Another church we visited was Rosary Cathedral in Toledo. This structure is very large and is probably the largest religious structure we had seen until we visited St. Joseph Oratory in Montreal and Saint-Anne-de-Beaupre also in Quebec.

Special Events at St. Francis Xavier Parish

Knights of Columbus

There were many special events connected with St. Francis Xavier Parish. I remember that our social lives largely revolved around the church. The Knights of Columbus (K of C) is an organization that is committed to serving the Catholic Church. Its original four core principles are charity, unity, fraternity, and patriotism. A life insurance program is available to all members as are several other worthwhile programs that emphasize these four core principles of the Knights' programs. Some modern day examples of their programs are supporting the right to life movement, supporting families in need, programs for youth, awards for Family of the Year, sponsoring seminarians, and other needy projects.

Members are eligible to become knights in various degrees. My father was a Fourth Degree Knight and as such was one of the honor guards at civic and religious functions dressing in a colorful regalia of tuxedo, plumed chapeau (hat), cape, sword, and white gloves. My father encouraged all his sons to be knights and several attained the role of a Third Degree. My favorite part of my dad's outfit was his sword. Practicing "touche" on a suspended ping-pong ball was a great activity, which improved our extended eye–hand coordination. However, this is not a K of C–related activity, just kids having fun.

Some of the Knights' family-related events in the Willard Council were parties, which consisted of potlucks, dancing, and conversing about the happenings in our lives. The K of C Hall was formerly located over a grocery store in downtown Willard. The food at the potlucks was always excellent. There was one entrance open to the public that assisted the parents in keeping tabs on their children. It seemed in those days most children listened and obeyed their parents.

The floor was huge and allowed the opportunity for the children to slide on the freshly salted or dusted floor in preparation for dancing. Once the dancing started, the children found other activities because the adults loved their dancing, and they occupied the dance floor. Dancing allowed the parents the chance to give an educational lesson. Few, if any, of the children were allowed to pass up the opportunity to learn dancing from their parents, usually the mother.

I can remember my mother giving me the opportunity at each dance to be her partner by coming up to me and saying, "Joey, it is time to dance." I would usually say, "Mom, I don't feel like it." She would without losing a beat say nothing and grab my hand, and I was out in the middle of the dance floor. My mother would hold me tightly partly because that was the way they danced and probably partly so I didn't try to get away. I can remember looking around the dance floor and seeing most of my friends, boys and girls, dancing with their mothers. It was a very successful conspiracy, for each mother at the appropriate time was dancing with her children.

As I look back, those were some of the most memorable dances of my life. It forced me to learn how to be in front of other people, and I also did learn how to dance. At the time, I did not enjoy these lessons, but in later years, I should have thanked my mother for teaching me. When I was old enough and interested enough to dance, I was a pretty good dancer. I didn't try to get away from the girls then, as I had asked the girls to be my dance partner. Thanks, Mom!

St. Francis Parish Festival

Another special activity was the St. Francis Xavier Parish Festival. The major purpose of the festival was to raise money for the church. It started with the first fundraiser being kicked off several weeks before the festival, and that was the selling of raffle tickets to win either cash or other prizes. Committees had been formed for bingo, the beer wagon, games for kids, the food, and other fun activities. Not only were the various supplies needed, such as the booths and prizes, but workers must also be scheduled to cover the length of the festival from late afternoon to late evening. A short time before the festival, the bingo playing area was erected out of wood as were the other game and food areas.

The night before the festival was a big night of anticipation for the kids of the parish. Dreams of the games to be played and the prizes that could be won were more than the mind could bear. When the big day came, church was on the schedule for the morning, and after lunch, there was the long wait until everyone would leave for supper and the games. There were always two certain happenings when we reached the festival: everyone needed to eat supper with the family, and we always discovered that there was never enough money available to play all the games.

Confirmation

First Communion was the sacrament before Confirmation. Holy Communion is receiving the body and blood of Christ while Confirmation is receiving the Holy Spirit. There is much preparation for the sacrament of Confirmation, as the bishop at that time, George J. Rehring, would come to the parish and would ask questions of the persons to be confirmed in the public setting of the church. The bishop would also give a tap on the cheek to the persons being confirmed as part of the ceremony. The bishop was not usually seen much in our parish, other than for Confirmation, and since more than one age group was receiving Confirmation, the bishop came only every few years. My parents told me that the bishop was a busy person and had many parishes to visit.

On the day of the big event, May 9, 1954, all the boys dressed in a white shirt, a bow tie, and dress pants. Girls dressed in a skirt and a white blouse. As the boys prepared for this sacrament weeks ahead, there was a continuous practice of the tap to the face that the bishop would deliver. I can remember when the time came for the questions to be answered by the persons seeking Confirmation, I was really uptight. The whole church was filled, and there would be only one chance for me to get the question right in front of the congregation. There were several questions in my head. If I gave a wrong answer, would I be confirmed? Did I get a second chance? Much to my surprise, I found the questioning very smooth and very fair. If someone didn't have the whole answer to the question, the bishop would help the person answer the question. The next part of the ceremony of great concern was being tapped by the bishop as one was given their

Confirmation name. My name was Leonard, the same as my sponsor. It turned out that all our concerns about the tap from the bishop were for no reason at all. The tap came after we were confirmed, and it was very light.

The part of the celebration most positively anticipated was the party. The party was composed of food, drink, and gifts. On this occasion, my father was my friend Lenny's sponsor, and Lenny's dad was my sponsor. Lenny's mother was the sponsor for another girl in my class. A three-way party was given at Lenny's for all three of the youth receiving Confirmation. It was a grand party, and I knew that Lenny's parents always threw a great party as did my parents.

St. Dominic Savio Club

Dominic Savio was a young Italian boy who led an exemplary Christian life. A club was formed in America, and one was specifically formed for boys who were around junior high age going into high school. Several of the boys at St. Francis joined the club. One of the sisters was the moderator, and officers were elected to guide the direction of the club.

One of the basic purposes of the organization was to imitate the Christian life of St. Dominic Savio. There was a listing of various prayers to be offered and activities that could be done and checked off each day. The list included attending Mass, saying the rosary and other prayers, and activities that could be accomplished on a daily basis. These activities were very influential in my life because they taught me that I could do many activates each day if I set my mind to it, and I would know how well I was doing by the number of checks I had made beside each item. I tried completing 100 percent of the items and was pleased with how many items I accomplished. A great deal of energy was needed for daily Mass because one would need to get up very early, ride one's bike to church, complete the

Mass, return home, eat breakfast, and be at school on time. Organizational skills and much energy were required for these tasks.

It wasn't until many years later as I was looking closer at my twin's influence and trying to pinpoint when in my life I was trying to do more that it hit me. The prayers, the Mass, and the other spiritual activities were all documented on paper. I thought I was doing the same number of activities as all the other boys. I believed this until, by accident, one day I saw the documentation sheets of others. I immediately noticed that I had far more checks than were on anyone else's sheet. I had so many checks that I didn't want anyone to see my sheets because I was sure that they wouldn't believe I had done all of these activities. I felt trapped because I didn't want anyone to see the documentation that to me was now looking suspicious. I wasn't close to being within a normal range of activities done and documented. Yes, I was doing better and being better; the only explanation that I now have was I was doing at least some of it for my twin. There were driving forces every day to accomplish those activities, and two of them were God and my twin. So way back in grade school, I was fulfilling a need that I had to do better and be better, or it must be a result of my strict family upbringing.

One of the big activities that the St. Dominic Savio Club undertook for the year was the Easter egg hunt for St. Francis Xavier Parish. This activity required that prizes for each age group, several dozen eggs, and dyes be purchased. The eggs needed to be hard boiled, colored, and hidden. When the big day came, it needed to be decided if the weather would allow the egg hunt to take place outdoors. If so, the eggs were to be hidden outdoors and the prizes awarded. I remember one year being more interested in hunting the eggs than in hiding them, so I decided to be in the egg hunt. I should have stayed away from the hunting of the eggs because it wasn't nearly as much fun hunting eggs that year as it would have been helping the Easter Bunny hide them.

Some members of the club lived on a farm near Willard. It was at their farm where we held a picnic and had other adventures. After lots of food, we decided we would ride their horse. I am neutral about horses, neither greatly liking them nor greatly disliking them.

Everyone was taking their time, and it became my turn to ride. I had apprehensions about riding, as I usually had a hard time getting my feet in the stirrups since I was short, and the stirrups usually did hang low. I got on the horse and the stirrups were adjusted. They were still too long for me. When they had adjusted them up to the highest point possible, my feet were still not supporting my legs and body. The horse had traveled very slowly with all the other riders, so I thought that I didn't need to worry about my feet fitting tight in the stirrups. After all, it was only around the house that I would be riding.

The rather large brown horse began to slowly go around the house. As the horse was making its second turn, it acted like a fly had bit him because he was instantly in a full run. I held on to the reins and tried to pull them back to stop the horse. It did not work. I pulled my legs as tight as possible around the horse and tried to get some support from the loose-fitting stirrups. Once again, it was not much of help. I was literally bobbing on the horse, and the world was one big dizzy spell, as I could see nothing but a blur.

I felt the end of the world was near, as I had no confidence that I would be able to complete the ride on the horse; I was sure that I was going to fall off the horse and, at best, die. The horse began to run faster around the third and final turn. By this time, all my friends were standing watching me nearly fall off the horse. As I came to the end of the ride, the horse miraculously slowed down and stopped. I was happy the horse had stopped but very surprised. I vowed that it would be several years before I again ride a horse, and it was.

The *Catholic Chronicle*

The newspaper for the entire Diocese of Toledo was named the *Catholic Chronicle*. In this paper, activities were reported from the several parishes in Northwest Ohio. Each year, there was a drive to renew the subscriptions of all the persons receiving the paper and to find new subscribers.

Whenever it was announced in catechism class that it was time for the annual *Catholic Chronicle* drive, I was first in line for my seller's packet. In those days, there were not many jobs available for me to make money, so this was a big chance for me to earn some cash. I learned something about competition from these drives. I do not remember talking about nor encouraging my classmates to be involved with the drive. When I either called on the phone or rang a potential customer's door bell, I wanted to be the first in line to get the sale. Losing a sale to another Catholic boy or girl was not doing my wallet any good. The least amount of competition allowed me the greatest chance for success. Encouraging others to sell the *Catholic Chronicle* hurt my chances of winning or being successful.

Selling was not a task without its challenges. The initial contact with either someone I knew or someone I didn't know always produced a few butterflies in my stomach. When someone was wavering about buying, one had to think fast on his feet. The time needed to make a sale was time borrowed from having fun.

After my first year in the contest, I had a number of clients who gave me a good base on which to build my future sales. In the two years, I had sold the most subscriptions in the category Parishes Without Catholic Schools, group B. I sold eighty subscriptions in 1955 and seventy-seven in 1956. The next three closest competitors in 1955 sold thirty-four, thirty-one, and twenty-two. My next closest competitors in 1956 sold forty-one, thirty-seven, and thirty-five respectively. I always enjoyed being a young winner and having my picture taken free for the newspaper.

Catechism Class

My Early Religious Instructions

When I was in grade school and high school in Willard, it was the expected practice that all the Catholic students attended catechism classes. Since we attended Willard public schools, there was no religious instruction during school time, and the only method of instruction would have been after school or during the weekend. If the sisters or nuns were available, they would give the instructions; if not, trained laypeople, usually parents, would teach. For as long as I can remember, the nuns who gave the instruction were from the Order of Christ the King. I remember that there were three nuns who lived and taught in the church facilities. Each order of nuns had a special habit or their own distinctive dress, and Christ the King Nuns had a gray dress with a crucifix necklace and round dark-colored hats. Their hair was done up in a bun and hidden beneath the hat.

The instructions came largely from a book called *Baltimore Catechism*. This book contains the teachings of the Catholic Church. I can remember that my Protestant friends were knowledgeable about the Bible. I rarely was encouraged to read the Bible with others nor on my own. The *Baltimore Catechism* was my "Bible." I remember the structure of catechism was in a question-and-answer (Q & A) format. For example, one of the first questions was "Q. Who made us?" The answer was "A. God made me." Another question was "Q. Why did God make us?" The answer was "A. God made us to show forth His goodness and to share with us His everlasting happiness in heaven."[25]

This was the formal start of my understanding of God. I had been exposed to God for years by my parents, siblings, my mother's relatives, and our friends up to this point. The fact that God had made me showed that I had a special relationship with this being. At church, I would pray to the Holy Trinity, which is God the Father, God the Son, and God the Holy Ghost, later changed to the Holy Spirit. Part of this relationship with God is that since He made me, I am an instrument of God. I am to do God's will for eternity. I have a direct link and a responsibility to please God more than anything.

If God made me, I wanted to please Him, and I could do that by being a good boy and obeying His rules. Since I had learned that God was responsible for making me, I thought He must think a lot of me. He must love me. I certainly believed in Him or had faith in Him. Likewise, I trusted God. I could not bring myself to seriously think about deserting God for several reasons. The first reason is that I really had no better option. The second was that I could not explain to my father and mother why I would want to leave God. Also, it never seriously entered my mind to desert the Being who had given me life and who was always with me and watching over me. This was a great relationship, and I was very comfortable with the importance of God in my life. This is to be the thread that held my life together.

Pagan Babies

While attending religious instructions, the topic of missions and pagan babies was discussed. Each year, there was a mission time, and there was an emphasis on saving money so that babies in underdeveloped parts of the world could be fed, clothed, and offered the chance to become Christians, in our case Catholics. There was always a film from an association called Pontifical Association of the Holy Childhood. At the beginning and ending of the film, a catchy theme song of the Holy Childhood would play. The attractive part of sponsoring a pagan baby for a very small amount of money was that the sponsor also would have the privilege of naming the baby.

In later years, I began to have questions about this practice. One was how long would the name stay with the baby? If someone did not donate funds on a continuous basis, would the baby retain its original name, and what would happen to the individual in terms of food and clothing? Regardless of my questions, babies were clothed and fed for some periods, and that was the positive outcome.

I always wondered, and so did my wife who can still remember the names of her pagan babies, if it is possible to meet those persons we sponsored in the early 1950s. An investigation of my archives showed that while I may have sponsored several babies, the only one that I could find documented was Bernard Michael. This was a combination of my middle name, Bernard, and my brother's first name, Michael. Yes, I still have many questions now that I am not sure I had when I was younger.

Attending Religious Education Classes

Attendance at religious instructions was very important in the lives of the Frederick children. I remember going to religious classes once a week during the school year. I have already relayed the experience I had with my shoe being caught in the railroad tracks and my brother Walt saving my life. I also have fond memories of going to catechism or religious instructions with one of my classmates.

When we had catechism, one of my friends would usually invite me to go to a relative's house before class. We would hurry to their house so we wouldn't be late for class. The first trip we made, his relative asked us if we had time for milk and donuts, chocolate-covered donuts. I about fainted. That was like asking, "Would you like the greatest snack in the world?" We sat at the kitchen table and had at least one or, I believe, two donuts before going to class.

We would usually talk to his relatives about many subjects. I learned a lot about giving from my friend's relatives. I wish I had thanked them more times than I did for inviting me and giving us all the snacks as I went to catechism during my junior high years. These experiences also reminded me how fortunate I was in my childhood to know and experience people who were so considerate of me.

Knowing People with Special Needs

Little did I know that my experiences with special-needs persons in my younger years would give me confidence when I began my career working in the area of developmental disabilities. The basic lesson learned here is that people with special needs are people like you and me, and they, like you and me, use their skills in adjusting to the world. The more I was around and communicated with persons with special needs, the more I would not see our differences but our similarities.

Restrooms

Willard Catholic students in the lower grades usually had their instruction in the large building in Spring Street in which the sisters or nuns lived. The living quarters for the sisters were on the second floor, and classrooms were on the main floor. During one of those classes, I needed to go to the restroom for a sit-down experience. I asked Sister, "Could I go to the restroom?" and she said yes. I don't know what I would have done if she had said no.

The restroom was a unisex restroom and was located in the basement and accessed from outside the building. In order to use the restroom, there was a door that needed to be lifted before one could arrive at the door to the restroom by a set of steps. As I looked into the restroom area, for some reason, I made sure that there was nothing in the toilet bowl that could harm me. I was shocked to see that there was a large bat in the bowl. Without thinking, I flushed the toilet before I could see if it was dead or alive.

I waited a few minutes before I did my business, and as I did, I was hoping that I would not have another problem such as a clogged toilet from the flushed bat. Everything went OK for the rest of this experience. Because of this experience with the restroom, I have learned a very valuable lesson. That lesson is to look before using all spaces. It was good I had looked on this occasion but wanted my goal of looking to be a planned experience in the future.

---

[23] Fr. J.B. Fralick, *The History of Saint Francis Xavier Catholic Church*, Willard, Ohio, 1950's, updated by Larry Foran in 1975, 1-12.

[24] Rev. Roger V. Karban, "Second Sunday of Easter: Acts 5:12-16, Revelation 1:9-11,12-13,17-19, John 20:19-31," Commentary on the Sunday Readings, *The Messenger*, the Catholic newspaper for the Diocese of Belleville, (April 11, 2010), 3.

[25] Right Rev. Msgr. William R. Kelly, L.L.D. and others, *Living for Triumph VII*, (New York and others: Benzinger Brothers, Inc., 1949), 8.

Chapter 7

Other Memories of My Grade School Years

The grade school memories were too numerous for one chapter. These memories deserve the attention of this separate chapter.

Ann and Mike

In my preschool and early school days, my sister Ann and brother Mike were my constant companions. Since both of them were only a few years younger than me, we were to form inseparable bonds of friendship, which lasted years into the future. Many of our activities centered on playing ball and board games and of course riding our tricycles, which would in a few years be replaced by our two-wheelers.

Sister Ann enjoying a ride with me

My prized three-wheeler was very large and had a platform on the back for my sister or brother to ride. In this picture, it is Ann enjoying a ride.

Water Puddles

An inexpensive activity occurred when a big rain fell, and it pounded on the street in front of our neighbor's house. What made it more inviting was that the rain pooled next to the curb section where the street and the alley met. It made a large puddle in the alley in which we could play. Since the puddle didn't last long, quick action on our part was important.

While we had one or two small wooden boats to float in the puddle, it did not take us long to realize that we had many boats at our disposal. This is the way the project proceeded. Mike, Ann, and I looked through our father's scrap wood. Anything that vaguely resembled a boat was extracted from the woodpile. The next step was to decide which boards were going to be sailboats and which were going to be barges or speedboats. The sailboats were given a nail in the middle of their decks. The other boats floated as they had been cut by Dad. What a good time we had racing and floating the boats in the street pond.

Children and water are not easily parted. I vaguely remember slipping on the curb and having one of my shoes buried in the puddle. If I continued playing, my shoe would eventually dry, and my mother would never know about the wet shoe. It worked.

The next day, we went back to play in the pond and were disappointed to see that much of the water was gone, and the loose dirt from the street was now becoming mud. Our total expense for the boating extravaganza was nothing. After all, Dad had already bought the nails, and all they were doing was sitting on the shelf.

My Pet Frog

Some people have dogs or cats; others have birds, snakes, or chameleons as pets. Early in grade school, I had a pet frog. I do not remember where I found this frog, but it was mine, and I took very good care of him. Each day, I would put the frog into a bowl of water and allow it to swim and get its skin wet. I also would catch flies for it. If I couldn't find flies, I would use some of the food my dad had for his tropical fish, as it looked like dead flies. My frog's name was very original; it was Frog. One of the favorite activities that Frog and I had was our daily walk. I would follow Frog, and if he didn't move, I would nudge him, and he usually would go forward.

On this particular day, I had taken Frog out of his box and put him down on the sidewalk. I had urged him to go forward, and since that did not work, I nudged Frog. Frog started forward, and I started forward. I began going a little too fast for Frog, so I slowed down. At the same time I was slowing down, Frog had stopped. I tried to stop myself, but it was too late. I stepped on Frog. Frog was motionless, and I was crushed.

I cried as I took him home and prepared him for his burial in a matchbox. I buried Frog before lunch. That afternoon, I began to doubt if Frog had actually died. I dug up Frog and found out the inevitable. Frog had truly died. The final burial took place, and I vowed to be more careful when playing with my pets. This was my first experience with death, and I wished it were my last.

Davy Crockett

In my early grade school years, there was a big fad for boys my age and maybe a few girls. It had to do with a man born on a mountaintop in Tennessee. Davy Crockett was big! There were coonskin caps, toy flintstone rifles, and Davy Crockett leather clothing.

The prize I could afford was a yellow Davy Crockett shirt with a picture of Davy and, I believe, a bear or "bar" on the front. I could have worn that shirt every day of my life at the time, and in fact, I almost did.

I loved that shirt as much as anyone could. Since my mother insisted on washing it each time I wore it, I was restricted from wearing it all the time. One day, I wore the shirt to school. It was a big deal to possess this shirt, as there were not too many boys my age able to buy a Davy Crockett shirt.

As I sat down at my desk, I placed my pencil on the desk. I liked to cover the pencil with my shirt and make a tent. I realized that the pencil lead was facing up. I quickly took the shirt off the pencil and noticed that I had already put a hole in the T-shirt. I was sick about the hole.

My only Davy Crockett shirt was now going to be displayed with a hole in it. I had my shirt washed that evening, and I was able to wear it to school the next day. Since I could see the hole in the front of the shirt, others also may have noticed. I decided that this was still my favorite shirt. I wore that shirt to school for many days after that, and the shirt was threadbare when I finally retired it to the rag box. I would still love to have a yellow Davy Crockett shirt—without the hole.

The Unforgettable Chase

One Sunday morning when I was about six years old, it was looking like a beautiful day. It was summer, and we had gone to the eight-o-clock Mass at our church, St. Francis Xavier Parish. We were going home to eat breakfast, but Dad decided that we would take the long way home. The long way meant we were to head to the north of town and into the country. As we left church to turn north, we passed a few houses. As we headed out of town, there were houses on the right side of the street. I saw some people sitting on their front porches and others just walking around their yards.

As I looked at one of the homes, I noticed a person running in front of a house with another man chasing him. I couldn't see the first person well, but I did see the other man dressed in a sleeveless undershirt, chasing him around the house. As we passed the front of the house, I looked a little closer at the man doing the chasing. I saw a very long butcher knife in his hand. The knife had to be twelve inches long. I looked to see what the man was going to do to the first runner, but the car passed the house, and the men had disappeared around the corner of the house and were out of sight.

Most of that day, I wondered what had happened to the person being chased by the man with the knife. I hoped that there had not been a stabbing. I never found out anything more about that event, but I never forgot the sight of the man chasing a person with a twelve-inch butcher knife.

The Hobo in Hiding

When I was seven years old, my bedroom was located next to the roof of the garage on the right side of the house with a door from my bedroom that connected to the garage roof. My bedroom was located in the back of the house, and there was a window overlooking the backyard next to the television antenna tower. The idea that someone could have access to my bedroom from the television tower or to the garage roof from the antenna constantly played in my mind. I frequently thought that a burglar could have access to my bedroom by using the tower, or he could get to the garage roof and then my door.

On several occasions, I thought I could hear someone on the garage roof coming toward my door next to the roof. On those occasions, I would sometimes wait it out, but no burglar entered my room. Other times I would go to one of my parents with the story that someone was trying to get into my room. My parents, being the concerned people they were, would check the roof and the tower and tell me it was safe in my room; no burglars were present. Was anyone ever on the garage roof trying to break into my bedroom? I know I heard some strange noises on the garage roof, but I did not know what they were.

Just about the time I began to think nobody was on my garage roof, a very strange incident occurred. I would sit often by my window, located next to the tower, and look out to see if anything "funny" was going on in the neighborhood. I had a great view. A spotlight below my window pretty well lit up the backyard.

One evening, I was looking out my window making sure no one was in the backyard, and no one was climbing the TV antenna. It was summer, and I had my window open. As I looked at the alley behind my house, I could see a police car slowly going down the alley and shining his spotlight in the neighbors' backyards. I had never seen a police car going that slow down the alley before.

I could easily see the police car because of our spotlight and my neighbor's spotlight on their shed next to the alley. As the police car again passed down the alley, I could see him shining his spotlight on the sheds. Then I saw someone come around to the now unlit side of the shed after the patrol car went past it. This action placed the trespasser on the dark side of the shed out of the policeman's spotlight until the officer's next trip down the alley. The mysterious person continued to move out of the light into the dark side of the shed.

The trespasser continued to hide from the police each time they passed down the alley. While I never heard whether the police caught him, I had my fears rekindled that the person by the shed might try to come up our tower to elude the police. I had thoughts of him coming up the antenna into my bedroom from the roof to hide from the police. It never did happen that way, but my fears were alive for most of my childhood.

The Willard Roundhouse and the Subways

As one left town on North Main Street, there was on the right side of the street a large open piece of land owned by the Baltimore and Ohio Railroad. This space was commonly used by youngsters to play baseball and other games. As you proceeded further to the north, you could see a large building. The building was very well-known because of its shape; it was called the roundhouse. For years, the structure housed the repair of trains.

The roundhouse was designed with stations around the outside of the building in which the machinists would repair the trains. The trains reached the various workstations by coming into the middle of the building on train tracks. When an engine was on the large turntable located in the middle of the roundhouse, it would rotate until it reached the spot where it was to be repaired. When the tracks from the turntable matched the tracks at the workstation, the engine would go to the designated repair area. When the repairs were completed, the roundtable would again line up with the workstation, and the engine would access the turntable and go to an area in which the engine could reach the main line.

My brother-in-law Fred Eldred was a machinist and worked in the roundhouse until it was demolished, and another area was designated to repair engines. In earlier years, I had the opportunity to see the roundhouse when I delivered lunch to Fred at work.

Continuing our trip north, there was a downward ramp, and at the end of that ramp was a double-car underpass. The first underpass goes under the first set of railroad tracks. After the double underpass, there is a single-car underpass, which allows traffic from both directions but not at the same time.

The single underpass from town leads to a hill that takes one back to ground level. Before going into the second underpass, it is important when going in either direction to check for oncoming vehicles by swerving to the left and putting the car in a position to see oncoming cars while keeping enough distance from the tunnel so an ongoing vehicle would not hit you. If nobody is coming, one can go up or down the hill. The right-of-way was reserved to the car going up the hill should there be two vehicles arriving at the tunnel at the same time. A real treat while traveling in the tunnel was to ask Dad to beep his horn. The beeping horn would echo and could be heard for a long distance. While we enjoyed the beeping of the car horn, the people who lived nearby probably did not.

The Votive Candle

My next lesson was to be as important as any lesson I learned when I was young. It started with wax. I loved to play with wax. One exposure to wax was in the form of candy. At this time, the candy manufacturers produced wax bottles, which looked like miniature pop bottles filled with sweet syrup. After sucking the syrup out of the wax bottle, it was always customary for me to chew the wax bottle in hopes of extracting a few more drops of the scarce liquid. Another manner in which I could fulfill my love for wax and sweets was the (imitation) wax teeth, black mustache, or red lips.

My love of wax continued one day when I found a few matches and one of my mother's small votive candles. Votive candles were used by Catholics as a sign of paying tribute to God or Saints who had lived their lives in a manner pleasing to God. Therefore, lighting a candle and praying to God or to intercede through a saint was a way to get to God. Interceding through a Saint means to me to put a Saint or Saints in an intersection between God and us. We have Saints intercede because of their desirable qualities. If one wanted to be a better mother, Mary, as a good mother, may help us to more effectively pray to God.

On this particular day, I was lighting a votive candle. I found it in a cupboard, so I reasoned that I could obtain some wax to chew if I light it. Since I burned papers in our backyard, I had access to the matches.

I proceeded to light the votive candle, blow out the match, and blow out the candle when some wax had liquefied. Then I would scoop out the wax with my finger and put the wax in my mouth to chew it. I realized very early that it took several matches to get enough liquid wax. I was getting low on matches. I looked at the clothes hamper and the lid looked like some type of stone. I lit the match and then the candle; I laid down the lit match on the clothes hamper top so I could reuse it. I scooped out the wax and put it in my mouth to chew.

I reached for the burning match to again light the candle. The match was still lit but so was the plastic top of the clothes hamper. I was terrified; the house was on fire, and I had caused it. I immediately took a big towel and hit the flames time and time again. The fire was still blazing bigger now than ever. I then took a cup, filled it with water, and threw it on the fire. I don't know how, but I do know that the house fire was contained on the top of the clothes hamper.

When I reported the fire to my parents, they saw that I was afraid, and I had learned my lesson. My gift of ruining the top of the hamper and almost burning down the house required a reassessment of my actions.

My father removed the rest of that marble-looking plastic top and painted the top a soft color.

This experience was certainly one very close call, which taught me respect for fire.

Night Games

While my father had a very good job, he also had six children and his wife to feed, clothe, spend time with, and provide for other essential needs.

Walt and Mary Lu were a bit older than Ann, Mike, and me. Bob was either not born yet or too young to play these games. So Ann, Mike, and I were the ones who played games with each other or the neighbors our age. To amuse ourselves, we would play games that required little or no money because money was scarce. Two such games played in the summer were kick the can and hide-and-seek. Both games were usually played in the dark.

The two games were well-known to many people and pretty similar in terms of rules. Usually, one person would be "it" or was responsible to catch all the "hider" players before they kicked the can or touched the safe zone. If the "hider" was caught, they would become "it."

Kick the can required the "hiders" to be in a place out of sight of the person who was "it." My brother Mike, sister Ann, and I would rotate the two roles. The "hider" had to kick the can before he/she was caught by the "it" person in order to be safe. Rules varied as to what discovered or caught meant for the "it" person. For example, if I was the "it" person, I would try to catch the "hider," Ann or Mike, by saying the words, "I see Ann," or "I see Mike." I might be required to touch Ann or Mike before they kicked the can. Touching was much harder than seeing and saying their name.

Having clear rules can help avoid disagreements. An acceptable yet unpopular practice against the "it" person was to have Ann and Mike rush the can at the same time. Another practice for Ann or Mike was to hide close to the can so that when I finished counting to 100, Ann and Mike would kick the can just as I uncovered my eyes. Do you think I ever practiced this technique? You bet I did. The only expense in kick the can was a discarded can.

Hide-and-seek on the other hand had a space called the safe zone. A safe zone was a designated place, usually a tree. If safe, the reward would be to continue as a "hider" in the next game. Conflict would arise if I, the "it," and Ann and Mike, the "hiders," arrived at the tree at the same time. If I caught the "hiders" by words or by touch, I would win the game.

An acceptable yet unpopular practice against the "it" person was to have several "hiders" rush the tree at the same time. Another practice in hide-and-seek as in kick the can would be for "hiders" to hide close to "it" and the safe zone so that as the "it" person finished their counting, they would rush to the safe spot. It is hard to catch many people at one time.

There is no expense in hide-and-seek as using trees or other safe spots is free. The 1950s were a fun, exciting, and inexpensive time in my life. At this time, we were learning some valuable lessons about life. One was that we all knew we could lose, especially if we didn't play by the rules.

Buckeye Trees

On Clark Street, there were two large buckeye trees near my house. All summer, the neighbor kids would watch the growth of the buckeyes. When the buckeyes were ripe, the neighbor kids, and especially the Frederick kids, would take either long poles, footballs, other balls, or all three over to Mary and Henry Voight's yard and harvest the buckeyes. When the buckeyes were out of reach, one person, usually me or my brother Mike, would climb into the tree and shake the limbs. Buckeyes were a free treasure to us.

There was one big caution about being in the buckeye tree. If one shook the branch too hard, the branch could break. Fast action was required on the part of the climber if a branch broke. The cleanup job at times was more than challenging, but the owners never said one word to us about harvesting the buckeyes probably because we cleaned up our mess. We were to find that cleaning up our messes was important in many aspects of our lives, especially if we cleaned them up before being told to do so.

Because of the owners' assumed approval, there were many years of anticipating and harvesting the buckeyes. There were many uses for them. One is storing them in a glass jar and observing the treasure. A more common usage was to drill holes and string them so that necklaces could be made. I had my own tool chest and used my drill and my dad's bits to make the holes. Today we could make money selling the necklaces to the Buckeye fans of Ohio State.

Winter Means Sledding

Anytime we could go outside was a good day. When snow came, we waited until there was enough outside for the two runners on our sled to be able to slide down the hills in the neighborhood. When we were very young, the backyard of our home was a good place to enjoy sledding. While the hill was not steep, and the backyard was not long, it would provide us with a big enough thrill. If the snow was not deep, and the temperature was cold, we would pour water on the hill and have an icy slide.

As we grew older, my brother Mike and sister Ann, as well as our neighbor Butch Rothschild, became more daring on the street hill in front of our houses, as the longer, wider, and steeper hill provided us with more adventure. Cars were constantly using our hill as a street, and we competed with them in using it as our sledding hill. While our parents did not like us sledding on the street, they had given us strict instructions that the moment we saw a vehicle, we should steer our sled to the side, pick up our sled, and exit the street. This technique worked, and there never was an accident between our sled and the cars using the street.

It was on one such outing where I was waiting for a car to leave our sledding hill that I wondered what it would feel like to touch the metal on my freezing sled with my tongue. When I did one of my experiments—and this was an experiment—it was not always a simple task for me but one that needed to be carried out so there was no doubt about the outcome. Carrying through any task is important because I may never have the chance to do it again. On this evening, I stuck out my tongue and placed it on the metal of my sled. Much to my surprise, the tongue was completely glued to the metal of the front top of my sled. I couldn't talk. I had very little movement in the front middle section of my tongue. I thought of running water over my tongue and the sled. However, I couldn't move very far as it hurt my tongue. Finally, I reasoned that my tongue was frozen to the metal, so if I pulled it off the metal, it would be frozen a little, but there wouldn't be much harm to me when I removed it.

I was wrong and had made a foolish mistake. When I pulled my tongue off the metal, I felt a sharp pain, and I looked down to see a large portion of my tongue stuck to the sled. I put my hand in my mouth to feel my tongue. When my finger came out, it was covered with blood. I was afraid I had permanently injured my tongue. Would I be able to taste food with many of my taste buds gone? I hurried home and ran copious amounts of cold water over my tongue until it began to stop bleeding. A complete stoppage of blood was not immediate. Eventually before I went to bed, the blood had stopped enough to make me feel like I was not going to bleed to death. The urge to put my tongue on a cold surface, such as metal, has completely left my thoughts now.

The Temple Theater

The Temple Theater was in downtown Willard. This was the indoor theater that housed the only public motion picture show in town. As my brother Mike and sister Ann and I approached the theater, the first eye-catcher on the theater walls was the posters of present and future motion pictures. They were usually bright colors, and the characters and the background scenes were very noticeable in the design. After opening the large doors, there was a walkway down the corridor, which was covered with plush carpet. The ticket booth was embedded in the left wall, a little more than half the distance of the corridor. The ticket seller would take the money for the show through a small half-circle cutout on the glass. The opening was located high enough for adults yet low enough for most children. After paying for the movie, the next attraction was the candy, popcorn, and "pop shop." Sometimes we had a little money for JujuFruits candy, a bag of popcorn, and a drink. Usually it was our money that we had earned, so we would make careful purchases. My parents would at times pay our way into the movie but not always. Money management was an educational opportunity for each child.

As we entered the theater, we had the choice of sitting downstairs or in the balcony. It only took me, an eleven-year-old, one time seeing the lovers in the back row of the balcony for me to decide I preferred the downstairs. There were many good pictures. A few examples of the flicks were westerns with cowboys and Indians, animated pictures, comedies, and always the world news and previews.

The most interesting, exciting, and memorable show I remember seeing was *Ben-Hur*. The part I remember most vividly was the chariot race between *Ben-Hur* (Charlton Heston) and his archrival. During this chariot race, each of the charioteers would try to knock the other person out of the race. The scene in the chariot race that stuck with me was when one of the charioteers, I believe the archrival, worked himself next to *Ben-Hur's* chariot. Then the spoke cutters mounted on the middle of the wheel would touch the wheel on *Ben-Hur's* chariot and begin to cut the wooden spokes off the wheel. *Ben-Hur* saw the cutter and moved his chariot away from it and saved his wheels. *Ben-Hur* did beat his archrival. I can still picture myself in the dark theater watching the chariot race and biting my fingernails.

Another majestic building downtown was the Willard City Hall. On the first floor was the police station and jail. Also located on the first floor were city offices. The second floor was located up a wide cement stairway. A large mural of George Washington crossing the Delaware River was located at the top of the first set of steps. The library and other city offices were on the second floor.

There was a basement that no grade school student wished to visit as it was cold, dark, and spooky. The only reason to visit the basement was it housed the public restroom in the downtown area.

First Television Shows

At about the same time, my parents purchased a car and a black-and-white television. In the early days of television, I remember placing a see-through piece of clear plastic on the television screen so that at the appropriate time in the show, I could draw lines on the plastic and solve a mystery being presented on television. Color televisions came along much later.

Super Circus Band

A vivid TV memory was viewing the *Super Circus Band* on Sunday night. The show had many different circus performers, but I remember the most famous of all the performers was Mary Hartline, the head majorette of the band. The ringmaster, Claude Kirchner, introduced Mary. Mary had long blond hair and was the "leader of the band." The band was composed of many brass instruments and made music with the best of them. In fact, Mary was featured in the theme song of the show and took special recognition as she went to the stand to lead the band.

I have always had a special liking for blond hair probably because I am a blond. I really liked Mary's beautiful blond hair.

Other Cowboys

The other classification of TV shows that "tripped my trigger" were the many and varied cowboy and other action shows. There were Roy Rogers; his wife, Dale Evans; Trigger, Roy's golden palomino horse; and Pat Brady. Roy's friend Pat drove a jeep named Nellybelle, although a motor vehicle seemed out of place in a western setting. Like Roy Rogers, Gene Autry, the singing cowboy, also captured the bad and helped the good. Another cowboy, Sky King, flew a plane named Songbird to uphold justice. His niece's name was Penny.

The Lone Ranger

One cowboy and his sidekick who in my mind stood above all the others was the Lone Ranger and his friend Tonto. The Lone Ranger's white horse was Silver, and his trademark was a silver bullet. While the Lone Ranger wore a black mask and light clothes to protect his identity, Tonto did not. He rode his faithful horse Scout and referred to the Lone Ranger as *kemosabe*. I believe this means "my faithful friend."

There were many crimes committed by the bad guys who were always caught by the Lone Ranger. At the beginning of each show, the Lone Ranger would ride up a hill with featured large rocks. After he reached the top of the hill, he would have his horse stand on its two hind legs. The Lone Ranger then would ride down the hill and say "HiYo, Silver! Away!"

While there were guns involved in cowboy movies, rarely was there any blood shown on the screen and certainly not any victims bleeding.

Standards were conservative, and violence shown on television was much less than shown today.

Lassie

Another set of adventuresome TV shows were those in which animals were the defenders of law and order. Two shows come to mind. The first show was *Lassie*. Lassie was a beautiful full-grown collie which was able to sense the villain with a sniff of her nose. Lassie could do about anything to catch villains, such as fetching needed materials to solve the crime. She was also the perfect pet.

Rin Tin Tin

The other show I dearly loved was *Rin Tin Tin*. Rin Tin Tin was a German Shepherd whose master was an orphan boy named Rusty. Rusty was a survivor of an Indian raid in which both of his parents were killed. When the cavalry came upon the massacre, they found and adopted Rusty and Rin Tin Tin.

The most moving of all the episodes I saw on *Rin Tin Tin* was entitled the "White Buffalo." As I can best remember, a white man killed one of the Indian chiefs. Rusty and Rin Tin Tin tracked and found the culprit. As the villain was making a break from Rusty, a buffalo stampede started, and they killed the villain.

The buffaloes then headed toward Rusty. The white buffalo came out of nowhere like a miracle of miracles and changed the direction of the stampede.

Several years after that show, I was in a gift shop and found a small figurine of the white buffalo. The buffalo occupies a position of honor on my computer desk. As I look at the figurine, I can hear the theme song "The White, White, Buffalo, Buffalo."

It is important to note that my parents maintained a balance between television time and other times such as outdoor play. If my mother felt we were watching too much TV, she would tell us to go outside and play as it would "blow the stink off us."

Other Interesting Happenings

Halloween

In 1953 when I was nine, I was allowed to go trick-or-treating within a three-block distance from my home. I started out by myself, but within a few houses, I recognized two classmates and started walking with them. I usually dressed as a bum since I could be warm and get away without wearing a mask. Masks were not a favorite of mine because I couldn't see where I was walking, and masks had a piece of thin white elastic on them that would always cut into the skin between my ear and my head. We were having a good time that evening and had filled the better part of a large bag of candy.

As we were moving up the next street, Park Street, and were getting close to my friend Lenny's house, which was a block from the high school, little did we know that we were entering a trap. We saw some big kids coming down the street dressed in pirate outfits. As the pirates passed us, they grabbed the candy of my two friends walking on both sides of me. My friends screamed at the pirates, but the pirates took off running and disappeared into the solid flow of masked trick-or-treaters. We regrouped in the front yard of one of the homes and talked about what we should do. We couldn't come up with a plan. I looked down the street and a miracle happened. A Willard police car was slowly coming up the street. Normally the Willard police car was not the automobile that I wanted to be near to, but this time was different.

I ran out into the street and waved my hands over my head in front of the police car. The car slowed down and then stopped. I approached the moving vehicle and told them about the pirates taking the candy. There were two policemen in the car, and they told me to get my friends into the backseat, and we would look for the pirates. I yelled to my fellow beggars, and they came running to the car. At this time, there was a large group of onlookers gathering on the curb looking at the car.

I hurried the two friends who had lost their candy toward the car and told them that they needed to get going so we didn't bring any attention to the police car and scare off the pirates. As the car moved forward, I was in awe. I had never ever seen the inside of a police car let alone rode in one on official business. All the while we were in the car, we hear people talking on the radio. The officer wrote down our names and told us that if we saw the pirates, we should tell them in a normal tone of voice. They explained that yelling might tip off the pirates, and then we would not get a chance to get the candy back.

We drove up and down the adjacent streets and then went back to the scene of the crime. We were about to give up when sure enough across the street from where the candy had been stolen, we saw the pirates. Almost in a whisper, we said, "There they are." The police drove past the pirates, and then one of them walked back and stopped the culprits. He brought the pirates to the edge of the street where the car was now parked, and he told them not to move, as his partner was watching them.

The policeman went around the car and opened the door, and when we were out of the car, he asked my two friends if the two bags of candy in his hands were the bags that had been stolen. My friends said it was, and the officer told us we were free to leave and to go to the opposite side of the road from where the pirates were standing.

The boys thanked the officers for retrieving the candy, and the officer reminded us to keep a tight hold of the bags. The officer went to the other side of the street and dealt with the pirates. We took off but looked back to see what was happening to the pirates. The officer was standing next to them talking. We figured that we better get going, as we didn't want any more action with the law or the pirates. We never found out what happened to them, and to be truthful, we didn't much care. We all felt good about getting the stolen candy back.

Marbles

Marbles was a very popular game when I was in grade school. I had a mixture of marbles in my old sock, and in the middle of that sock was my prized steelie. A steelie is a larger-than-normal marble that was made out of steel. The steelie was actually a ball bearing out of a wheel, and the large ones came from railroad car wheels. I never had a really big steelie, but I did have one almost an inch in diameter.

During recess or before school, we would play marbles. I remember two games of marbles: one was tag, and the other was circle marbles. I was pretty good at both games. The game of tag usually was played with two players, but there could be more. One person would roll their steelie a distance, and the other would try to hit it. If the player hit the steelie, he would be given a marble by the player who was hit. The players would take turns until they would call the game. The teacher would usually call an end to recess and thus the end of the game.

The other popular marble game required a circle to be drawn on the ground, usually a foot or larger in diameter. Each player would put in the same amount of marbles, maybe three to five from each player. From a specified distance of, say, one to two feet from the outside of the circle, each player would on a rotating basis try to hit a marble out of the circle.

It was important that the shooter didn't get closer to the circle than the rule. If he did, he would be known as a huncher. A huncher's shot did not count. A good player might be able to hit out one or two marbles with their steelie in one shot. The steelie had to land outside the circle in order to claim the marble(s) he had hit out of the circle. I remember over five people playing, which sweetened the pot to at least fifteen marbles in the circle. What a pot!

One Sunday afternoon, I was walking around the neighborhood. I saw a neighbor boy walking around his house. I said hi to him, and he returned the greeting. Somehow we started talking about marbles, and he told me that he had a collection of blue marbles. I was all ears and eyes; I had never seen more than one or two blue marbles at a time. He offered to show me the marbles, and I was really impressed with them. They were the most beautiful marbles I had heard of, let alone seen.

Somehow we decided to play a game of marbles. I ran home and was back, it seemed, before I left. As we began to play, I was having great luck and probably some skill. I won a great deal of his collection of marbles. I went home and was not feeling real good about winning so many marbles. I talked to one of my brothers and decided that I should take back some of the marbles. I felt better about taking some back, but it still didn't feel right winning as many as I did.

A Baby Is Born

My baby brother Bob was born in December of 1953. I didn't remember much about Ann's or Mike's births, but I do remember Bob's. He was usually referred to as Bobby in his earlier years. At this time, I was nine years old. This was an age in which sex was being talked about by fellow students with various levels of knowledge. My level of knowledge was at the lowest level or practically nothing. When I explained to some of my friends that I had a baby brother, I was at the level of understanding that the stork had brought my baby brother.

Some of my friends were at a higher level of understanding than me; this gave them a chance to share their in-depth knowledge about how my brother came to be a baby and how he came into this world. I was confused and upset about all the facts they were giving me on sex and birth. I really didn't want them to make fun of me due to my lack of knowledge, so I decided to listen and pretty much bite my tongue.

As time went on, I learned that my friends knew what they were talking about and that the whole issue of where babies came from was a beautiful mystery that we all learn someday. I was glad I had bit my tongue.

Coin Collecting

At a very early age, when I was about ten years old, I first became interested in coin collecting. It happened when I was in a toy store in Sandusky, and I saw foldout coin books for sale. These books had holes for the coins for all the dates, mint markings, and the number of coins minted from the first coin to the present. I believe the cost of the book was around 35¢. I wanted that book, but I had little money and was tight with the money I had. I hated to see my money spent on something that wasn't making money for me. I decided that rather than starting my collection with the Washington quarters or the Standing Liberty 50¢ pieces, I chose the Lincoln penny book. I figured I would fill that book and then go back for the Buffalo nickel and Jefferson nickel books.

I began to check my mother's and father's change. I graduated to going to the bank and asking for rolls of pennies. I had limited funds, and penny rolls at 50¢ were within my range.

As I began to do more odd jobs, mostly mowing lawns, I had more money to put into collecting coins, mainly by checking rolls of coins.

Sometimes my father worked late at the Pioneer Rubber Company, and there was a petty-cash box there with some coins. I would periodically check the coins in the box. I was finding pennies that I needed everywhere. I graduated into nickels and dimes. Several years later, I got into quarters and I collected a few 50¢ pieces and silver dollars.

In my earlier days, some of the pennies I had collected were Indian Head pennies. It was at this time that I had a chance to own what I considered the best penny in the world. The Flying Eagle penny was a penny that really turned me on. Larry Ayers, a friend of mine for several years, had this penny. I really didn't think he would be interested in trading it, but he indicated he would be interested in a trade. I thought I would never obtain this penny. I wanted that penny more than any other penny in the world. We struck a deal, and I walked away with my prized penny. I obtained other coins, some through coin magazines and others by trading but most often by working the rolls of coins.

It was in a roll of nickels that I was to make one of the biggest finds of my life; that would be the discovery of two near-perfect 1913 Buffalo nickels. The 1913 Buffalo nickel was the first year of mint, and the coins were in uncirculated condition. When I saw these two coins, I couldn't believe it. I scooped them up and put them in a safe hiding place.

It was not until several years later in 1969 when Kathy and I were leaving Mansfield to come to live near Bowling Green, that I parted with one of my prized Buffalo nickels. Benny, a friend of ours in Mansfield, had been very generous to Kathy and me on a number of occasions, and since Benny was a coin collector, we knew he would appreciate this gift. Benny was beside himself and wouldn't take the nickel at first. We explained that we really wanted him to have this gift to remember us. Benny finally relented, and the Buffalo nickel became part of his collection.

Cedar Point

My father was the treasurer/comptroller for the Pioneer Rubber Company. The company made balloons, Bluette gloves, household gloves, surgical gloves, industrial gloves, and other specialty gloves, such as veterinarian gloves.

When I was in grade school, each employee, their family, and others were given the opportunity to go to Cedar Point at the expense of the company. Cedar Point is, and has been for years, an amusement park located near Sandusky.

Included in the packet each family received was a free pass into the park and a picnic lunch with more food than an army could consume.

As soon as summer started, I would begin counting the days before the picnic. Since the picnic was in August, I had to count lots of days. I would save my money for the arcade because I loved to play Skee-Ball. Skee-Ball involved rolling a ball that was a little smaller than a softball up a piece of carpet about ten feet long. At the end of the flat carpet, it continues into a hump that the ball would hit and, if thrown hard enough, would jump into the air and hopefully go into one of the small rings around a bull's-eye. The bull's-eye was worth the most points, and each ring out was worth fewer points than the rings closer to the bull's-eye. I would receive coupons for the points I had successfully rolled. The coupons were then traded in for prizes, such as fuzzy animals and other trinkets. I was a sucker for trinkets, so this was a natural way for me to spend my money. Besides, I was a good Skee-Ball player.

I also saved money for the miniature scoop shovels. The shovel would be activated as soon as I placed the money into the machine. Inside the glass case was the crane with an open scoop. I could move to about any spot in the enclosure where the prizes and loose-covered candy were located. I would find the controls, put in my money, and manipulate the open scoop over the prize I desired. I would then lower the open-faced shovel over the prize. Rarely did I receive the prize I desired. I usually did receive some sugar-coated peanuts.

The day of the trip to the Pioneer picnic never came soon enough for me. I usually slept little the night before the picnic and rides. We would travel toward Cedar Point a little over thirty miles away from our home. The last few miles of the trip would be spent on the Cedar Point Causeway. This road ran next to the water of Lake Erie. On one side was the water, and on the other side were beautiful cottages. One of my fantasies was to live in one of those cottages—it still is.

Upon arriving at Cedar Point, my father paid for the parking. We would all be instructed by my mother where the car was if we were lost, and we were further instructed to check back to the car periodically to see if anyone was lost. At least we had a plan if we couldn't find anyone in the family. Having a member of the family lost at Cedar Point was a periodic occurrence, and this plan did produce a lost child into a successfully found child. My parents always had a plan. The biggest part of their plan included a prayer.

Walking down the midway was like a child walking down the Main Street in heaven. There were games in which balls were thrown, water was shot into tubes while horses raced each other according to the amount of water sprayed into the tube, darts were thrown at balloons, and rings were tossed onto pegs. Prizes were won if you were skilled and/or lucky at the games. One big drawback was the expense of the games. As I continued to walk down the street, I came to the fun house. I always went through it because it was fun and scary, and my pass covered the entrance fee. At one point, I would be tiptoeing through a dark corridor and see light at the end. At that moment, puffs of air would hit my ankles and scare me. I would run to another section of the house. I will always remember the mirrors that made me look tall, short, and overweight. It truly was a fun house.

Next on the agenda were the rides. Roller coasters have always been a big deal at the Cedar Point. When I was very small, there was a section called the kiddies' rides. In the kiddies' section there includes a small roller coaster that made only one short trip around the loops, but as a kid, I thought it was a long ride and lots of fun. There were, of course, several rides in which I would travel around and around in circles and have little control over the ride. In the early days, Mike and I would ride the boat.

Mike and I at Cedar Point

A few years later, there was a new ride in a round metal container that allowed two or three youngsters to sit facing each other. The ride I remember was the one that spun around as fast as I could turn the wheel in the center of the cylinder where I was sitting. I had just eaten a number of chocolate-coated peanuts from the crane game. Instead of prizes, I had won peanuts. I was with two friends who took control of the wheel and made the ride spin in circles as fast as they could. I grabbed on the speed wheel, and the three of us spun and spun. We laughed as the world spun by us. I was to pay a big price for my fun. As I exited the ride, I "lost my cookies." While getting sick ruined the rest of my day, the good part was that the incident happened near the end of the day. It was years before I could eat those chocolate-coated peanuts again, and that was the last time I was on that type of ride.

Dr. Dentist

One of the most dreaded experiences I can think of was going to the dentist. In more recent times, there have been many advancements in dentistry but not in the 1950s. When I was in the fourth grade, I took a trip to a neighboring city in which dentistry was in a very crude state of existence. For example, in the dentist's examination room, all the various utensils were in plain sight. My anxiety level was at an all-time high from what I thought was about to happen. If an examination was to take place, all the picks would be open for my inspection. If a tooth extraction were to take place, the pliers would be visible. The basin in which waste was to be discarded after the patient spit into it was in operation instead of a suction tube with a hook that cleanly and with little effort extracted the waste.

On my first visit to the dentist, the teeth were examined, and I would wait anxiously to see if I had any cavities. On one visit, I learned that I had three cavities. This pretty much ruined that day and all the days leading up to my next appointment to drill the tooth and hopefully fill the hole with metal.

I clearly remember going to a neighboring town with my mother to have the three teeth drilled and filled. This was the first time that I had that experience. I didn't know what to expect other than knowing that I was going to be drilled. As I walked into the office, my mother checked in with the receptionist. I was hoping the receptionist would say, "The dentist is ill, and we need to reschedule the appointment." In fact, I prayed that the dentist was sick. We waited for a few minutes, and I was asked to come into the office. At that point, I was walking and not even knowing I was walking because I was terrified of the drill.

The dentist came into the room. Up until that point, I had not seen the dreadful drill, but the dentist walked over to the drill and began to run the drill to see if it was running properly and inspected the various drill bits about to be used. Finally, the fateful moment came, and he asked me to open my mouth. He began to drill without any numbing chemical, such as novocaine. I immediately smelled something burning coming from my mouth. I knew that it was going to get worse. It didn't take long for the dentist to penetrate the enamel on the tooth, and it seemed he hit every nerve there. Not surprisingly, he continued to hit several more nerves. The hitting of nerves, the smell of something burning, and smoke from the drill went on for what seemed like hours.

Finally, I decided I had enough pain, and I would need to come back again to be finished. I don't remember if or when the tooth was filled. All I remember was that I was in pain, and I wanted out of that office. I went shopping with my mother that day, and the pain from that nerve inside my tooth was excruciating. My mother told me, "If the pain is that bad, I will take you back to the dentist." Those words were enough for me to understand that going back to the dentist was much more painful than the pain I had then, so I didn't say another word. Somehow the procedure on my tooth must have been treated by someone because I do not have any pain with that tooth today.

I did learn a lesson from this experience. That lesson is to know that pain is usually going to be present, so one would do best to accept the pain that cannot be ignored and plan to minimize pain whenever possible.

Another First Communion

It has been established that First Communions were a big celebration in Catholic families. As I was very close to my younger sister Ann, her First Communion was also very important to me. Family portraits

Early family portrait

of the children properly dressed were another must for this day. In this picture, I appear first sitting on the family couch and then come Bobby, Ann, and Mike. In the second row are Mary Lu and Walter. It is easy to pick out the First Communicant as she is wearing the white dress and the head piece.

Vacations and Visits to Sites Close to Home

Sainte-Anne-de-Beaupré

When I was ten years old, my family made its first trip to a Catholic shrine in Quebec. Within the next few years, two more trips were made. The name of the shrine was Sainte-Anne-de-Beaupré. The trip was long, and it seemed that we would never make it to Quebec in our Mercury station wagon. There were my mother and father and six children. Bob was a baby, around six months old, and every night, we looked for a motel with a washing machine. The first thing my mother did was wash Bobby's diapers. I don't know if there were no dryers or they were just too expensive, but each day, cars would see our station wagon going down the road with white flags (diapers drying) waving out of the window. Disposable diapers would have been a good alternative, but they were unheard of at that time.

Our travels were slow because periodic restroom breaks were a must. We didn't always stop for lunch, and fast-food restaurants were in their infancy. Sandwiches, vegetables, and fruit with a drink on the road were lunch. If we didn't eat breakfast in a restaurant, milk and cereal in the motel room also helped save money. Supper was a big splurge, as this was a big meal and was very expensive. I never was able to figure out how my family was able to take a two-week vacation for all those years with six kids and two parents. My mother was an excellent manager of money.

Sainte-Anne-de-Beaupré was a particularly overwhelming shrine. The main building was a huge structure with two huge steeples. The steeples were not finished when we were there. It was like they were built, and then the upper part of the steeple was cut off. Inside, there were many stations to pray and ask the saints to intercede for us with God. I can remember going to a station of prayer for St. Anne. My major concern was a case of poison ivy was not healing and was rapidly spreading. I prayed to St. Anne and asked for a cure. It was either a cure or my parents would shortly be finding a medical doctor to treat my affliction. To my surprise, the poison ivy stopped spreading almost immediately and within a few days was gone. I was impressed and very happy.

Across the shrine is a building that has several steps. The object is to climb the steps on your knees and to say the rosary at the same time. To a child, it seemed like a long trip up, but it did feel good to make it to the top.

The country roads around St. Anne offered many exciting experiences. There were numerous craft shops. The one I remember most was a woodworking shop. Inside this shop, there was about any imaginable form. My father and mother were taken with a beautiful nativity scene of the Holy Family, the shepherds, sheep, the cow and donkey, the three kings and camels, the stable, and the angels. Years later when my mother went to the rest home, one of my brothers was fortunate enough to obtain this family heirloom.

The next stop we were to make was at an outdoor bakery. The baker was just finishing a large round loaf of bread as we pulled up to the roadside bakery. My parents purchased the bread and butter, found a vacant table and chairs, and treated the children old enough to eat solid food to the best bread we were to ever have in our life.

A side trip was to the Plains of Abraham Battlefield, where the English under James Wolfe defeated the French under the Marquis de Montcalm.

This grassy area offered the children a chance to run on some beautiful and open spaces next to the St. Lawrence River.

Years later, my wife and I were able to make this trip with my brother Walt and his wife, Judy. This trip brought back many memories and created many new ones about these holy and historic places.

Piano Lessons

I must have been ten years old when my mother informed me I was to take piano lessons. The lady I was to take the lessons from was my neighbor lady. She lived less than two blocks from our house. I didn't know a lot about her other than she had a daughter who was much older than me and a son a few years older, who later in life was to become my chiropractor. He was to be my chiropractor in Ashland when I lived in Mansfield. I don't know why my neighbor took me on as a student. I rarely practiced and would much rather be outside playing. If I must play piano, I would have been happy to walk into the room with a piano and just have the skills to play, with no practice needed. I took lessons for many years and learned two songs, "Marines Hymn" and "William Tell Overture" (*Lone Ranger* theme song).

Meanwhile my mother had found another piano instructor who was a nun. My family was very Catholic, so a nun would be about the best instructor one could find. This instructor was in Bismark, Ohio. Bismark is a rural community ten miles outside of Willard. The nun I had for piano lessons was also a grade school teacher. I wasn't sure I would be helping this nun's reputation as a piano teacher. We started our lessons, and I did about as well as I could. My five years' experience prior to these lessons and these next few years' experience did not qualify me as a great student by any standards.

On one occasion, a man came into the room during my lesson. I could tell he was a priest. He was the pastor of St. Sebastian Church and was responsible for the school we were in, as well as the parish of St. Sebastian. As the priest began to talk, I could tell that he was a very thrifty person. He talked about putting the temperature in the building down very low. He also talked about coffee soup. Evidently, one can take coffee and make a soup with it. It is inexpensive and tastes pretty good according to the priest.

I never followed either practice that Father John Keller imparted to me. I was impressed with the man's knowledge and sincerity. I also did not believe that playing the piano was my calling, and the lessons came to a halt shortly thereafter.

You will be hearing about St. Sebastian Church in the future because one of the young girls who was attending school where I had taken my piano lessons was to become my wife. This experience helped me understand my future wife and her experiences at the St. Sebastian or Bismark School.

Ohio State Fair

It was the end of August in 1955. In my youth, one of the most sought-after events in the summer was going to fairs, and the big one was the Ohio State Fair. Yes, I was to have the opportunity to go to the Ohio State Fair in Columbus.

I don't remember where I obtained the tickets for the fair; it must have been from my school. I was to attend two big outings in one month, the Pioneer Rubber Company picnic and the Ohio State Fair. I was very excited about the fair. I was so excited I could not sleep the night before, as my mind was occupied about the events of the next day when I was to go to Columbus.

The ride to Columbus was much too long. All I could think about was the carnival rides, the drinks, and a cow made out of butter. I knew that I was going to have some experiences that I would never forget.

As we arrived at the fair, I saw cars and pickups parked for miles in the parking lots. There were people walking everywhere, most going to and a few coming from the fair. We parked the car, and I approached the entry gate and handed the attendant my ticket.

I walked through the gate, and I immediately saw the midway. There were ball-throwing games to be played and places to eat and drink. The amusement center had a very large ferris wheel and other rides. I was skeptical of riding, as they looked like they could easily make me sick again.

I had to have a cinnamon-flavored candy apple. The candy covering was bright, red, and hard. It was difficult to bite through it. I finally found a weak spot in the candy covering and proceeded to eat the apple. It was good, but it didn't last very long.

It was time to look for the cow made of butter. I asked a few people for directions until I found someone's guidance I trusted. I traveled down the path leading to the cow and noticed many people around a display. As I pushed my way into the crowd, I saw a calf but no famous cow. It was the correct size of a calf, and it was kept refrigerated so that the butter did not get soft or melt in the summer heat. Seeing the calf made of butter turned out to be the most memorable event of the day. I couldn't imagine how they could make a calf that big. Thanks to the calf, my day had been memorable and a lot of fun. I still think there was a cow made of butter somewhere at the fair.

Conger's Grove

My father had gone through the steps and attained the Fourth Degree in the Knights of Columbus. The purpose of this organization was to strengthen the faith of the men who were knights; to have a life insurance program so that if something happened to the knight, there would be some income for the widow; and to provide activities for the entire family of the members.

From the time I was old enough to remember, my father was a member of the Knights of Columbus. I also remember that whenever a new child was born into our family, my parents would purchase a K of C life insurance policy in their name.

Periodically there were social events such as dances, potlucks, and other events that the Knights would schedule for their families. The most memorable event of the year was the potluck and corn roast at Conger's Grove near Willard. At this event, there was an unlimited supply of ice-cold drinks in a big metal container filled with ice. The other popular part of this menu was the boiled sweet corn. While the sweet corn always tasted great, it was even better at Camp Conger because it was boiled over the open fire in a large metal pot.

While there were many games to play for children of all ages, many of the boys wished to explore the river and the fields on the property. Depending on the rainfall of the summer, the river might or might not have rapidly flowing water. A game of skip the flat stones on the water was always fun. However, I thought the most fun was to explore the fields of the surrounding property. I remember an occasion where five of us went out to see the wildlife.

On the first exploration, we were crossing a fence to access the next field. We immediately came upon a large dark-colored snake, which startled all of us. We lost it in the heavy grass, which covered the field. We wanted to identify the snake and see if it was poisonous. We armed ourselves with big sticks and began beating this huge field to find the black snake. We searched the area where we thought the snake might be with no success. We were just about to give up on our hunt when we got a break.

At this time, one of the younger boys yelled out "snake." In a flash, the entire group of hunters was at the site of the most recent snake sighting. After a few more minutes of hunting, the snake was spotted, and before identification could take place, the snake succumbed to the club of one of my friends. The snake was long and large in diameter. Everyone agreed this big snake could have bit us. At that time, I decided that we would place the near lifeless snake over the fence because it would be easier to spot the snake on the fence on our trip home. We were somewhat sure of the name of the snake, and we thought one of our fathers might know for sure if it was a blue racer.

The rest of the hike was to prove as adventuresome as the first part. We began to climb a strange, rather high, and long trail, which was unfamiliar to all in the group. As we started up the hill, we noticed in the distance a small old shack. The closer we came to the shack, the better we could see that the building was about to fall down.

In front of the building and to the right, there were a couple of white tombstones. As we approached these stones, we noted that there was an inscribed image and some dates on one of them. I got on my hands and knees and was able to make out a date. While I do not remember the date on the stone, I do remember the image in the middle of the top section of the tombstone. It was the image of a woman's neck, head, and shoulders, and around the woman's throat was a hand. The hand looked like it was strangling the woman. I have often wondered if I could find this spot and see if my memory was correct. I have my doubts.

It was getting late, so we headed back. On the way back, we stopped to pick up the black snake. The snake still twitched its body, so we left it and decided to come back later. As we went back to camp, we told our parents about the snake and the tombstone. It was time to eat, and there was no time to do any further checking on either.

After supper and games, it was time to pack up. But before ending our outing, the boys decided to get a flashlight and check on the snake. It was still hanging on the fence, but now it was lifeless. The old saying about snakes must be true. Snakes never die until sundown.

The Blue Hole

One of the most memorable natural wonders that existed near Willard was the Blue Hole in Castalia, Ohio. The story about the original discovery of the Blue Hole was very simple. Some pioneers in a wagon and a team of horses were going through Castalia. The team of horses went into the Blue Hole and dragged the wagon, the pioneers, and all their possessions into it, never to be seen again.

As a young boy, I can remember going by the Trout River, which led to the Blue Hole, and seeing many large trout feeding on whatever the tourists would give them. I remember dreaming of catching one of those large trout.

I would continue walking until I came to this large pond with fencing wrapped around the perimeter of the water so no one would fall in. As I gazed down into the hole, I would try to see if I could see the remains of the wagon. It was very clear, and it must be blue because that was its name. I would strain my eyes to see, but I never did see anything on the bottom, and that would go well with the Blue Hole story that it was bottomless.

I would think that someday I would be a diver and try to find the bottom. Those thoughts never became serious because each time I would picture myself near the bottom of the hole, I would be sucked down into a huge hole that existed in the bottom of the Blue Hole.

Another story I heard is that the Blue Hole is drained into by the underground river that flows under and around a nearby town named Bellevue. My childhood fantasies that were fed by visiting the Blue Hole are now gone. An adult fantasy is also gone because the property containing the Blue Hole was sold and now is closed to the public, and the depth is probably greater than I wish to dive.

Tricks of Youth

Whoopee Cushion

When I was young, I was always on the lookout for any type of gadget that I could scare, trick, or catch someone off guard with. There were many such gadgets in variety stores (5¢ and 10¢ stores) or, sometimes, grocery stores. The items were reasonably priced, but they were not always easy to find or to buy without our parents' knowledge or permission.

One of the most well-known gadgets was the whoopee cushion. The cushion looked like a large balloon and made out of heavy rubber with a flat flap, which one could use to inflate the cushion. The flat flap kept the air in the balloon-like round structure. When sat on, it would produce a sound like the passing of human gas. The cushion was to be secretly put on someone's chair so that they sat on it without knowing it was there.

Placing the cushion on the chair without the person knowing it was there required a great deal of good timing. As the person was sitting down, they must be looking forward, thus not behind, to not see the cushion. Laughter would fill the room when the loud noise came out of the cushion sounding like passing gas. It could be embarrassing to the person sitting down for at least the first time. The cushion could last for a long time unless abnormally large amounts of pressure were placed on it.

While catching my brothers and sisters on the whoopee cushion was fun, catching our parents on it at mealtime was the best. When my father came into the dining room to sit down for supper, one of the brothers or sisters would distract his attention so he was standing in front of his chair ready to sit down but not sitting down until the cushion was in place.

As my father sat down, this loud, embarrassing noise would echo in the dining room, and my father would look around at all us kids laughing so hard we were crying. Pulling off a successful whoopee cushion trick was one of the most rewarding experiences to us. Mom was caught less often than Dad, as she was usually serving supper.

Handheld Shocker

The next two tricks, the handheld shocker and the Chinese finger lock, involved the hands. The first was a small round metal device held in place with a stiff wire near the palm of the hand. The windup device had a small trigger that when pushed by a handshake would buzz or "shock" the hand. People tend to automatically extend their hand, so having someone shake your hand is common. While the gadget made a small noise, it was possible to use it on several people in one room before being detected. A notice that something unusual was happening was often given by the receiver of the "shock" by a yell. While the trick was harmless, it was attention getting. The device can be placed on a chair, and when sat on, the shocker would be triggered. This device proved to be fun with my younger brother and sister.

Chinese Finger Lock

The Chinese finger lock is a round braided cylinder made of heavy paper. It is around five inches long and easily slips on any finger of either hand. Slipping on a finger from each hand and pulling it apart usually caused the fingers to lock. Most people do solve the gadget by pushing in both fingers and loosening the gadget. Continually pulling on the fingers tightens the finger lock. The finger will be released if the fingers on both hands are pushing in. I can remember allowing my friends the challenge of using the finger lock. I also remember my friends getting very frustrated because they were unable to get out of this device.

Alum Gum

Gum holds another option in the world of trickery. Alum was a type of gum that when chewed would cause one's mouth to pucker. It looks just like regular gum. I would place a piece of alum gum in a regular gum wrapper and position it so that it was the next piece to be taken out of the pack. The unsuspecting person would pull the alum gum out of the pack.

Another way of getting someone to take the alum gum is to take the piece of alum gum out of the packet and offer a piece of gum to someone. As the gum is placed into their mouth, it is usually not easily detected. After a few chews, the mouth becomes so puckered that it is impossible to chew. At this point, the trap has been sprung. I can remember offering this gum to my friends and almost losing them as friends.

The Spring Trap Gum

Another gum trick was having a pack of gum and a flat piece of fake gum with the kind of a spring that resembles the common mousetrap. After setting the spring, it was slid into the package of real gum. When offering a piece of gum to someone, the booby-trapped gum is placed further out than the real gum. As the other person takes the fake gum, you can watch the gum trap snap on the thumb. It is important to have a weak spring on the trap so that nobody is hurt.

A Noise Maker

To make a simple noise maker, cut a medium-size rubber band, and string it through the two holes in a large button. Next, tie the rubber band on to both sides of a small slingshot made out of a paper clip. Turn the button until it is tight, and place the assembly in an envelope. When a person opens the envelope, the button rotates very fast, scaring the person with its noise. This is harmless and sure to get a laugh.

Cigarette Loads

This last trick I periodically pulled on my father. He would leave his cigarette pack lying around, and I would insert what looked like a small piece of wood that contained a small explosive in one of his cigarettes. The trick to successfully insert the load into the cigarette was to push it in far enough so that when my father lit it, it wouldn't immediately explode. The explosion was timed to go off when he was taking a big drag a bit later. As my father took the crucial drag and the end of the cigarette would explode, it was an extremely funny event for everyone but my dad. I usually told my brothers and sister when it was going to happen. Lucky for me, my father had a sense of humor, and lucky for my dad, the loads were only powerful enough to slightly blow apart the cigarette. It was a given that the explosion provided a good scare for my father.

Physical Activities

Wiffle Ball

One of the most common and enjoyable toys in the Frederick household was Wiffle ball. My younger brother Mike and I would play this game in the alley between our house and our neighbors for hours. Since the alley was used by bicyclers and walkers, we needed to have a "heads-up" so we were not hit by a bike or other moving vehicles.

A Wiffle ball is made of plastic with holes on the outside, and it is open in the middle. When the ball was thrown, it would travel at a slow pace because the holes would cut down the speed of the ball. Wiffle ball was played like baseball, but its slow speed would make it hard for someone to get hurt if hit by the ball. The bat was usually plastic but could be a wooden bat. The Wiffle ball was easier to field because of its slowness. A variance of Wiffle ball was stickball. This game was played like Wiffle and softball, but a broomstick or similar wood stick was used as a bat, and the ball was usually made out of masking tape rolled tightly into a ball.

Often I would play one on one with my brother Mike, and other times, we would have two or three players on each team. My cousins Leo and George Schlotterer were frequent players as was my sister Ann. During those days, winning was a big deal, which is not much different than today. I can remember getting physical with my brother Mike if he missed a fly ball or grounder. As I think back, I probably missed a few plays myself, so I should have gotten on myself.

The alley where we played Wiffle ball connects to the property of our neighbor. From the second floor of our house, we could see much of what was going on in the backyard of our neighbors across the alley. I can remember one Saturday morning we were looking out our second-story window and saw the neighbor boy climbing the apple tree to pick and eat apples. We would softly say his name and tell him to "get out of the apples."

Our neighbor boy would then yell out, "Who is this? What do you want?" My brothers, sister, and I thought this was funny as we continued our little game.

Our neighbor boy never did find out who was telling him to "get out of the apple tree."

Snowing

When the winter season arrived in Willard, there was one place that you could often find me—the back room of our house. I was there to watch how fast the snow was falling in my hometown. I was always looking for a snowstorm that would be capable of canceling school. Whenever the first flakes of snow began to fall, I knew it, and if it were night, the big spotlight in the backyard was my key to a day off school. My sister Ann was only three years behind me, so we would take turns watching the snowfall. If the snowfall became especially heavy, we would both look out the back window with an aura of excitement and hope.

The heavy snow would prompt us to begin planning what we would do on our day off school.

That evening, we might take a walk in the new snow where the world seemed to be silent except for the falling snowflakes.

If school was called off, it was usually because of a huge snowstorm. Some superintendents would cancel if the weather was "iffy," and one would hardly ever cancel. The "hardly ever cancel superintendent" was not on my people list of "I like him best." I had no idea at this time that later I would be in the position of superintendent and would make the decision of calling off school.

If school was called off, I would attempt to sleep late. These plans usually were not to come to fruition, as my mother would want the sidewalk and driveway shoveled. Early in the morning, the world seemed to be very active with everyone shoveling out their driveway and sidewalks. The city trucks were always plowing the streets.

Many times my friends and I would try shoveling sidewalks to earn some money. There was a private service that had a huge roller brush on the front of the tractor, and the driver would clean all of the main sidewalks. This left only the sidewalks to the house and the driveways, and few people were interested in paying for the rest of the shoveling, as they were already paying for the clearing of their main sidewalk.

If no work was available in the snow-shoveling business, we would usually end up sledding. While the day off school may not always be very exciting, we felt that it was better than a day in school.

Boxing

Another activity I participated in was boxing. Jeff Hartzel was my sparring partner, who lived nearby and had set up a boxing ring in a back room of his house. The ring consisted of an old mattress, boxing gloves, and the room. It had the essentials. Jeff was a little bigger than I was and really liked to box. I was learning from Jeff the hard way. The fight usually had both Jeff and me throwing and taking a few punches.

The best part of my match was the first few seconds. After that, I would get tired of throwing punches and would go into a defensive mode of protecting my body with my gloves and arms.

If the fight had been scored, Jeff would have won the matches. I did learn one important fact from those boxing matches. I was not a fighter, so maybe I would be a better lover of people.

Unforgettable Friendships

Butch Rothschild

There is one friend from my youth with whom I would do about anything and one of my few early friends with whom I have maintained an ongoing friendship. That person is Butch Rothschild. Butch's name came from his father's name; Butch's father was known as "Big Butch."

Butch lived across the street from me, and it would only take a hop, skip, and jump to get to his house.

Butch was a few years older than me, but that didn't seem to matter in our relationship. I would fish with Butch, ride bikes with Butch, skate with Butch, and always know he was there to hang out with me.

If there was nothing to do, we would find something to do. Sometimes our activities got the approval of our parents, and others were our secret.

A bike ride was always one good option. For a time, there was another neighborhood pal named Denny. While Denny lived in Willard, the three of us had a bicycle club called the CSBS. The initials stood for Clark Street Bicycle Club. The meetings were short, but the riding activities we planned were much longer and more fun.

I remember one afternoon in the summer when nothing was happening in the neighborhood, so we decided to write down the license numbers of cars to see how many cars and states we could register. We had copied down several license numbers, but the writing and organization was sloppy. The poor penmanship may have been because of the fact that I had been the one writing down the information.

Butch found a new yellow legal pad in his house and copied all the car license numbers and the states on it. Butch's handwriting was very legible, and the end product was worthy of winning a contest. We didn't do anything with the list of license numbers, but we could tell you how many cars from what states passed on Tiffin Street. We were proud of our research project. Cars were to be an important part of our lives in our high school days.

Those carefree summers before high school were some of the best days of my life. Butch and I were inseparable, and this childhood bond was so great that I have no doubt it will last a lifetime. Butch has never left my life.

In our adult years, Butch and his wife Phyllis were good friends of Kathy and mine. Phyllis is a talented seamstress, painter, quilter, woodworker, hairdresser, and anything else she wanted to be. What fortunate people we are to have such good friends!

Lenny Playko

Another close friend of mine was Lenny. Lenny's father worked with my father; they were both Fourth Degree Knights in the Knights of Columbus. Both families were Catholic, and both fathers were knowledgeable Boy Scout leaders.

As a result of these relationships, our parents would have social events with the families. Lenny's parents, Ann and Len, were gracious hosts. When we visited Lenny's home, one could count on the good china and excellent food. Visiting friends' homes was common practice in my youth probably because there were fewer restaurants and other entertainment establishments. Home entertainment would have been less expensive than going out to those commercial establishments.

Lenny was a great outdoor person. Sometimes I wondered if he slept outside his house in a sleeping bag, as he was that comfortable with the outdoors. Over the years, he had studied animals, birds, and almost anything related to the outdoors, especially the woods. When we played nature games in Boy Scouts, Lenny was the one to have on your team.

Lenny always had a dog, usually a beagle. His most famous beagle was the smallest one I had ever seen. This beagle was so small that he could penetrate a rabbit's hole, flush out the rabbit, and then come back out of the hole and chase the rabbit.

Lenny and I, like my other friends, had a relationship built on trust and friendship. Lenny was a friend in grade school, high school, and college.

Coincidentally, Lenny married a girl from Norwalk, named Ann, the same name as his mother. Unfortunately, I lost meaningful contact with Lenny after college until I contacted him on this book.

Neighbors

Neighbors have been an important part of my life and probably yours. My parents' viewpoint on neighbors could be taken from Matthew 25:31–46: A relationship with a neighbor in need will be a measure of judgment our last day.[26]

The role of a neighbor changed for me as I grew older. As children, they were playmates; as adults, they are confidants and friends. We will deal with some of my neighbors I grew up with on 519 Clark Street before my high school days.

Each of the other parts of my life will have their own set of neighbors.

As I think of these neighbors, I cannot help but think that my twin would have loved to be present physically rather than in a spiritual sense because my neighbors were fun, thoughtful, and the most wonderful friends. A common thread I have felt with my neighbors has been their recognition of my positive and high energy.

The Bench

When I was in the first grade, I was cutting through the neighbor's yard located two lots from my house.

Beside the neighbor's garage was a concrete bench about four feet in length. I decided to walk on the bench, which was over a foot high. As I walked on the bench, I discovered it was wobbly, and it fell over, breaking the seat into two pieces.

I couldn't decide what to do, so I did nothing. The bench was eventually thrown away. In fact, I remember watching the bench being carried away. I thought it might be repaired, but it wasn't.

Over the years, I have reflected on what I should have done after I accidentally broke the bench. I wish I would have told the neighbor lady that I had broken it accidentally and taken the consequences of my action. She was an old lady then and of course is not alive today.

Since that event, I have worked to admit my part in any misdeeds whether accidental or otherwise because that is the right thing to do, and guilt is minimized.

The Sour Cherry Tree

Each summer, we had the privilege of picking cherries. Usually we would pick the yellow Queen Anne cherries at Grandfather and Grandmother Frederick's house in Willard. There also was a sweet red cherry tree, but Grandfather Frederick reserved those cherries for himself.

The other tree available was a sour cherry tree at Chet and Madeline Kostoff's house next door. I asked Madeline if I could pick some cherries, and she said, "Sure, but be careful." I set up the ladder and began to pick. I began to note that the bigger cherries were beyond my reach. I positioned the ladder so that I could put my feet in the crotch of the limb and then began to climb up the tree to pick the larger cherries.

Everything was going great. I had filled two containers and had only one more to go. I proceeded to go higher up the limb when I realized the tree looked like it was starting to rot. I continued picking over my head when I had a strange sensation; the sky was moving. Not only was the sky moving but the tree limb I was standing on was moving too, and I was moving with it. I was over ten feet in the air, and the ground was beginning to move up very fast. I couldn't jump, as my feet were entwined in the limbs of the tree. I couldn't grab anything but the branch I was on, as it separated itself from the rest of the tree. I decided to calmly ride out the fall, and much to my surprise, the limb went slowly to the ground and allowed me to step off it as if the smooth landing was made to order. God was with me on this easy descent.

I went into the house and told Madeline what had happened, and she said the tree was getting old and that I should pick the cherries off the downed limb and then cut off the limb as best as I could. I felt pretty good about this experience since I didn't get a scratch on my body, the neighbor lady was not upset with the results of my picking, and no cherries were lost.

A Bearded Man with a Drinking Problem

One summer evening around ten o'clock (and that was late for me to be up), I was in the kitchen with my parents playing a board game. We had a number of games we could play, such as checkers, chess, dominoes, a dice game, or one of several card games such as old maid. We played them all and had lots of fun in the process.

Games were important then, and little did I know that nineteen years from that date, I would be coauthoring a book on games and their use in various body movements.

As my parents were encouraging the children to go to bed, we heard a knock on the back door. My dad descended to the landing and opened the back door. My mother went over to the top of the steps to see who was there, and she began to talk to my dad and this man. I did not know this man well.

As I began to slowly go down the steps, my mother told me to go to the kitchen and play with my brothers and sister. As I was playing with my siblings, I heard the loud voice of the visitor.

I decided to see what was going on in my house and if my help was needed. I knew my parents did a fabulous job of teaching all the children to help other people when we saw help was needed, so I was confident everything was going OK. My younger siblings told me not to go to the door, and as usual, I did what I thought was best. I don't remember Walt and Mary Lu being at home or in the kitchen at that time.

I arrived at the steps to the basement, and I saw a man with a beard and a straight razor hanging out of his pocket. I could tell the man had been drinking. I could see that my dad and mom knew the man. I also knew that it wasn't unusual for people to come to our house to see my parents when they needed help. I was not sure how my parents knew this man. My father knew people from the Pioneer Rubber Company and my mother from the various downtown shops. After over an hour, my parents convinced the man that it was late, and he needed to go home and get some sleep.

As the man left, he said he would be back at noon the next day to see us.

My parents talked about the incident after the man left, and it was decided that the family would leave the house before noon the next day and go to the Willard Municipal Swimming Pool. My father did not want my mother and the children at home alone with this man.

I went to bed but did not sleep as well as I would have liked because the visit by this bearded man had scared me. I wondered if the man would come back that night or maybe the next day before noon.

The next morning, we were all up early.

Dad had gone to work and by nine o'clock, I had packed my towel, swimsuit, and anything I would need for that afternoon at the pool. I was ready to leave at nine o'clock that morning for anywhere because I did not want to be near that bearded man. As the time got close to eleven o'clock, I began to ask my mother when we would be leaving the house. She would tell me, "Soon." At eleven thirty, I was very uneasy about being at the house and started to look out the window overlooking the alley that I thought the bearded man would be using to come to the house. That was the direction I saw him leave last night. It was eleven forty-five, and noon was fast approaching. I told my mother I was going to the car. If everybody else wanted to be in the house when he came, that was their problem.

Finally at eleven fifty, we were all in the car and ready to leave the house for the Willard Municipal Pool.

Incidentally, this would be the very same pool that I would be managing eleven years from this date.

As we pulled out the driveway, I looked to see if the bearded man was near our house. I saw nobody.

My mother decided to go around the block and check if anyone was going down the alley to our house. I can still see us slowly going past the alley that led to our house, and I can still see the man headed toward our property. We didn't have a minute to spare in leaving our house because I saw the bearded man approaching our back door. I felt sorry for the man, but I also knew we needed to protect ourselves.

I had a great day swimming at the pool for two reasons: One, I didn't have to face that visitor. The second reason was that we didn't have a lot of money to spend on recreation, and as a result, we enjoyed the pool the few times we did go. Our home recreation was fun and pretty inexpensive; however, the pool was great fun.

As I reflect on this incident, I saw much positive energy coming to my house that evening. The ability of my parents to keep calm was noteworthy while facing an inebriated man with a razor protruding out of his pocket. This was one of the most fearful incidents of my youth. I often think that I must have received much support that evening from my parents, my God, and maybe even from my twin.

Bicycling

The first story about bicycles happened in the front yard of my house and two neighboring houses on Clark Street. I was about to ride my bike without my training wheels. I was getting close to being able to ride a bicycle, probably five years old, when my dad went with me to the front yard.

He somehow knew that I was ready to ride the bike alone and had me get on my bike after removing the training wheels. He waited till I was well positioned on the bike, and he slowly pushed me across the neighbor's yard. I began to pedal the bike and felt I was doing very well, thank you. It was then that I noticed my bike had taken a turn toward the neighbor's shrubs. I tried to turn the wheel away from the bushes, but it didn't work. I drove directly into the prickly mess, and I fell on my side with my bicycle on top of me.

The next story involves Charles Edward "Butch" Rothschild, my closest neighbor and best friend. Butch was followed in popularity at this time by Denny, another neighbor. Both of these neighbors had the distinct privilege, as did I, of being members of the previously mentioned CSBC or the Clark Street Bicycle Club. This elite club had the unique features of low dues, 5¢ for life, and meetings in which everyone got their say. The usual topic of discussion at the meeting was where we would be going on our next bicycle trip. Money was usually not a big topic of discussion as the 15¢ in the treasury was never used and never discussed.

This memorable experience happened when I was in fourth grade and was on one of the CSBC outings. I remember the other riders dared me to ride sideways down the huge hill at the old park entrance. There used to be a set of stairs that angled down to the bottom of the hill, and the path led to a bridge over a creek, a few hills, and another bridge until we were at the Willard Municipal Pool. At this time, it was pretty hard to go down the hill because the steps were gone, and all that was left was an open spot where the old steps used to be at this old entrance.

I seemed to look for recognition. I blamed this fact on my short stature. I told both of the other bikers that I would go down the hill on my red Schwinn bicycle, and I would live through the experience. After some words of encouragement from my two friends, I was going down the hill. I lined up the angle of the bike so I wouldn't roll over on the way down. As I listened to the cheers of my friends, I made my first mistake and started down the hill at a very fast rate of speed. My second mistake was that I increased the angle of my descent. This sent me into a roll down the hill. I held on to my bike and rolled down the hill sideways over and over. At the bottom of the hill, the bicycle was facing straight up in the air on top of me. Somehow the handlebars had twisted themselves into my shirt, and I could barely move.

Coming down the hill, I could hear Butch and Denny running and saying, "Is he alive?" Well, I wasn't about to move with all this attention coming. The bike was taken off my body, and eventually I got up without a scratch. I know someone was watching over me again, and it certainly was God and could have been my twin. By the way, I continued as president of the CSBC.

The last story on biking happened when I was going into junior high school. I was riding down the street on my bike with my pedals even and my legs and body straight. This made me look tall on the bike. As I looked ahead, I saw a couple of young ladies about my age. I was just getting into the boy-girl thing, so I took a long look to see who was walking down the street and to "size them up."

Since the girls were walking the same direction as I was, I had to look hard to find out anything about them. At this moment, I felt my bicycle abruptly stop, and I went flying forward. I would not have had any injuries, but my bike (like all bikes) had a piece of metal between the handlebars that attached the handlebars to the front tire connection. I caught my "privates" directly into this piece of steel and felt an excruciating pain between my legs.

I got up after the accident and was going to scream out in pain when I realized the girls had now switched their gaze on me. I gave a fake smile, got on my bike, and gritted my teeth as I continued *not* to yell out in pain.

I was very concerned after this experience because I was pretty sure that I had somehow compromised my ability to father a child. I found out years later that I had no permanent injury.

Chicken at the Farm

The Niedermeier farm was located about five miles north of Willard. While I generally knew the entire family, I specifically knew many of the children. Mr. and Mrs. Niedermeier ran the farm. Along with their farming activities, they raised scratch chickens. A scratch chicken is a chicken that has free reign to the barnyard as opposed to being caged. Their food is obtained by scratching the soil and finding the feed that had been scattered in the barnyard.

Periodically my family would go to the farm and ask the Niedermeiers to catch a chicken. After the chicken lost its head, it would be dipped in hot water so the feathers could be removed, and it could be butchered. One of the neatest parts of this process was how the chickens were caught. I had spent a great deal of time trying to just get close to the chickens before they would run away. The Niedermeiers, like other scratch chicken farmers, had a five-foot hook that they would run along the ground until it would catch the leg of a chicken. When they had caught a chicken's leg, the chicken would make a loud squawking noise. I would always stand back when the chicken was caught, as I

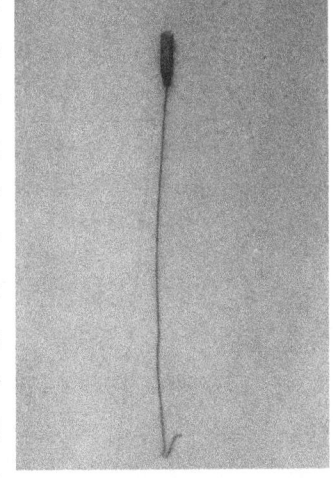

Hook used to catch chickens

was concerned that I might get pecked. To my knowledge, I never did get pecked while harvesting chickens.

Once we had paid for the chicken, we would be on our way home to enjoy a fresh chicken dinner. Food is always better when it is fresh from the farm.

Hornets' Nest and a Cocoon

Sixth grade was about the time that I was very lucky in finding various dwellings used by insects. To the best of my memory, this was the grade I put up for display a hornets' nest I had found in the winter. Luckily, the nest was an inactive nest, or the change of cold to hot temperature could have produced a classroom of active stinging hornets. An active hornets' nest would have made me unpopular with the teacher and my classmates.

I found a cocoon a day or two before the Thanksgiving vacation, so I took it to school; it was a hit. It was very cold outside prior to Thanksgiving, and the cocoon was warmed up with those old-fashioned iron water heaters, which stood next to the wall in the school. It turned out that this warm, moist air and the warm temperature of the classroom was just what the cocoon needed. This warm temperature was exactly the kind of spring-like weather that warmed the cocoon and triggered it into thinking it was spring. When the class left on Wednesday for a two-day vacation, we did not know what, when, or if any type of insect would be coming out of the cocoon.

On the Monday after the holiday when we came into the room, we saw miniature insects on our desks, the bulletin boards, the walls, the ceilings, and any other exposed surface. We needed a good set of eyes and even used magnifying glasses to identify the insects as none other than the praying mantis.

Our joy was short lived as the insects began to die due to a lack of nutrients. We were both happy and sad. At least we knew what a praying mantis cocoon looked like for future reference. I have seen several praying mantis cocoons since that experience, and never again have I disturbed the cocoon's ability to hatch naturally.

The Chase

When I was in junior high, I was allowed to go to the Willard High School football games. Sometimes I would go with friends, and sometimes I would meet friends at the game.

On this particular occasion, I decided late in the evening to go to the game. As I walked outside the front door, I saw that it was dark but that the moon was bright enough to allow me to have some vision. I closed the front door, walked down the steps, and proceeded to cross the alley.

As soon as I had crossed the alley, I could faintly hear the band playing at the football game. The football field was over three blocks away from my house. Within a fraction of a second, I heard the sound of stones flying as someone was running down the alley in my direction. I looked and saw within a few feet away from me a bearded person. I immediately began to run as fast as my legs would take me toward the football field.

It would have been foolish for me to go back to my house because I would have met the person chasing me. Besides, I didn't have a key, and if I did, it would have taken me too long to open the door before the man would have caught me.

I ran a half block and still heard the man running behind me. I was well into the next block, and I wasn't sure if the man was close. I ran all the way to the football field before I stopped running.

There was nobody behind me when I stopped, and to this day, I can only guess what he wanted to do to me. I felt there was nothing good my pursuer wanted from me that evening. I can't help but think how lucky I was not to be caught by him.

I am convinced that I received a great surge of energy that evening from somewhere to be able to run as fast as I did. When I first saw the man, he was within an arm's reach from me. I could see and can still see his face. As I reflect on this incident, I would have no trouble attributing help from God and my twin, as the speed and endurance needed for this run was extraordinary. I am still amazed that I was within the grasp of this man and escaped by running three blocks without stopping. I have read about people being kidnapped and killed, and I am lucky I am still alive and unharmed.

Snakes, Snakes Everywhere

In Willard, there were some new houses being built several blocks from my home.

One day, I was riding my bike and noticed some other kids standing around a big pot in a field. I pulled up to the pot and noticed that there were several garter snakes in the bottom of the container. I asked the boys where the garter snakes had been found. One of the three boys told me that they had caught them in the field where we were standing. I looked around carefully making sure that no snakes were near me. I was almost late for supper, so I asked if I could catch some garter snakes tomorrow, and they said, "Sure."

The next day was a beautiful summer day, and I decided that I was going to catch some snakes. I was somewhat afraid of snakes, so I figured this was a good time to cure that fear.

I got an early start that morning and was at the snake field in about five minutes. I came alone that day partly because I didn't want to have someone see that I was afraid of snakes. As I began walking through the field, a small garter snake took off in the grass. I ran up to the snake, stepped on it lightly, and picked the snake up with my hand. I took the snake over to the pot since I didn't have any place to hold the snake. I knew my mother would have wanted no part of a snake! I found other small garter snakes and was feeling good that I was overcoming my fear of snakes.

As I walked along, I found a large garter snake, a bigger snake than any others I had seen that day. I followed the garter snake and stepped on the snake with my foot. As I reached down for it, I noticed that the snake had opened its mouth and was about to strike or bite me. I drew back my hand and just stood there looking at it. I decided to let the snake go, as I really didn't feel like getting bit. This was the first time I had hunted snakes barehanded, and that was also the last.

My Relatives

My relatives have always been a very important part of my life. When I was very young, I remember the parties and get-togethers on my mother's side of the family, the Schlotterers. There were originally sixteen children, and now there were fourteen alive. At that time, most brothers and sisters were married, and several had children older, of the same age, or younger than me. At this time, all but a few of the original Schlotterer families lived in Willard. Since my father had only one brother, who was frequently on the road, there were not many get-togethers with his side of the family. Additional relatives and families were added with the marriage of my eldest sister. These are some of my memories about relatives in my early years.

The Towel and the Underwear

My aunt Esther from New York City was one of my favorite aunts on Grandmother Schlotterer's side of the family. It seemed as if each year my aunt Esther and my uncle George, who lived together and were brother and sister, would come to visit relatives in Ohio, and my family was one that they always tried to visit.

On one occasion, my aunt Esther was talking to my mother in the front room of our house, also known as the parlor or living room. I had been downstairs in the basement taking a shower, so I would be clean and almost ready to visit with my aunt and my family.

While I was downstairs, I decided to make and carry out a very strategic plan. Since I had to go through the front room to get to my bedroom and my clean clothes, I was very uneasy about going past my aunt with only the towel covering my body. I knew my aunt Esther could be somewhat of a cutup, and I didn't put it past her to pull off the towel as I passed everyone in the front room. In fact, I was so sure that someone would try to pull off my towel that I felt I must have a secondary plan if this towel-pulling thing materialized. I brought a pair of underwear with me to the shower.

I walked up from the basement after I had showered, walked through the kitchen, and began to pass by my mom and Aunt Esther. Sure enough, I couldn't go through the parlor room unless I walked directly past Aunt Esther. She was sitting in the front of a stuffed chair with a big smile on her face. Did I mention that Aunt Ester is a mischievous woman who dearly loved a good laugh?

That was the trap in which I thought I could be caught. As I said hello to everyone in the room, I saw my aunt's hand move and saw her smile, and her voice began to chuckle as she grabbed my towel and pulled off my protective cover. Well, the laugh was on Aunt Esther because all she saw was my underwear that I had decided to wear up to my bedroom. I can still hear her say, "He has his underwear on." I began to laugh, and everyone laughed as I proved that a five-year-old boy could outfox an elder woman.

Parties

It seemed that with so many brothers and sisters of my mother and so many other offspring, there were constant weddings, birthdays, graduations, and holidays when everyone got together and celebrated. These were the times that I looked forward to and enjoyed myself when I was a young boy. There was always a potluck, something to drink, cards, and balls to be played with someone.

The biggest of all parties were the reunions. These were always held in the summer and usually at a farm or one of the relatives' homes because in those days, there was little money to be spent on building rentals.

On this particular year and day, we were having the reunion at our house. We had a large enough backyard for a party, and we could play ball in the alley beside our home. That is exactly what some of the older generation was doing, playing ball in the alley beside our house.

I remember that someone was trying to take a picture of one of my female relatives. I was standing close to her, and I turned her so she would be more photogenic. What I didn't see was that she was about to hit the ball as I turned her toward the camera. She continued her follow-through with the bat as I turned her, and the bat hit me in the head instead of the ball.

I immediately developed a knot on my head, which was to be with me for the rest of my life. I developed a new respect for a baseball bat, and from that respect, I learned to stay outside the batter's box unless I am batting. When I see the knot on my forehead, I now am reminded of that reunion day and the fun we had at our house.

My Cousin from Chicago

David Bapst would travel from the Chicago to Willard, and for many summers, he spent time with Grandma and Grandpa Schlotterer and his uncles, aunts, and cousins, which included me. David's mother was one of the senior daughters in the Schlotterer family and a sister to my mother. Each time he visited, David would bring information on what was happening in the big city. My brothers and sisters also enjoyed David as can be seen in this picture. On our front porch, we see in the front row from left to right my brother Bob, sister Ann, and me. In the second row from the left, we see David Bapst and my brother Mike.

David had a very good memory, an infectious laugh, and a sense of humor. In our many exploits in Willard every summer, David would recite a poem, which was very funny. One year, I asked David to teach me the poem, and he did. The poem went like this:

David Bapst visits the Fredericks

>Ladies and gentlemen,
>hobos and tramps,
>cross-eyed mosquitoes,
>and bull-legged ants,
>I'm here to address you,
>not to undress you;
>I am here to tell you of a subject I know nothing about.

Christopher Cucumber sailed down the Missis-sloppy River with
The Declaration of Indigestion in one hand
and The Star-Speckled Banana in the other.

There shall be a meeting in the men's hall for women only.
There shall be no fee;
pay at the door,
pull up a chair, and sit on the floor.

Since the initial memorization of this poem, I have used it several times at parties and other occasions where a little creativity with words was appreciated. I found that there are variations of this well-known poem, but I could find no person or source possessing the copyright.

David and I grew up; we both married, he to Kathie and I to Kathy. Our time together was scarce, as we rarely saw each other than at family gatherings, such as our yearly Schlotterer reunion.

Even this time together was to end on Monday, November 19, 2007. On this day, I received an e-mail about David. David had had a heart attack and wasn't expected to live. I learned later that day that David did pass on. I thought constantly about him the rest of that day. Within a few hours of receiving this e-mail, I completed this section on David as a memorial to my friend and first cousin.

Pizza with My Aunt Theresa and Uncle Tom

Relatives continue to be a big part of my life. We had fun visiting relatives, and that usually meant having some type of edible treats in addition to playing with my cousin's toys.

My uncle Tom and aunt Theresa lived in Bellevue, during their early years after their marriage. Bellevue is in the northwest part of Ohio. My uncle Tom worked for the telephone company. I believe he was a lineman early in his career and was an instructor once he moved to Mansfield, from Bellevue. My aunt Theresa "kept things together" at home, ultimately caring for their twelve children.

It was on one of those summer trips where I was in grade school that my aunt decided to have pizza for lunch. At that time, my family wasn't "into" pizza. I was a particular eater, so I wasn't sure of melted cheese and all that tomato sauce on dough. The day I was first served pizza, I took a big bite out of my first piece of *hot* pizza. While the taste was good, it stuck to the roof of my mouth, and then the cheese slid off the pizza and stuck to my face and my clothes. The pizza was hot, and it almost burned my mouth and my face. It also stained my pants.

Despite the fact that it had heated up the roof of my mouth and my face, I grew to like pizza, and it opened my eating habits to Italian food. This was not the last time that I was not careful and felt the ill effects of hot pizza.

Frederick versus Schlotterer Team Sports

My cousins George and Leo were the Schlotterer team, and my brother Mike and I were the Frederick team.

While these teams played several sports, the biggest rivalry was football played in the neighbor's backyard behind George and Leo's house on Dale Avenue. Two members on one team against two members on the other necessitated a limit on play options. Since there were no substitutions, continuous energy on the part of all players was required. While the running game was used for short gains, the pass play and frequently the long pass or the "Hail Mary play" was very important.

A team composed of brothers added a hazard for the younger brothers; they must face the big brother if they missed an easy play. Leo and Mike, being the younger brothers, probably have some valid tales on how their elder brother could have treated them more fairly.

Those junior high years and before, while George and Leo lived in Willard and before their move to Norwalk, provided memories and a closeness among the four brothers/cousins that has been present and treasured to this day.

Rabbit Hunting

Rabbit hunting was one of the outdoor activities I thoroughly enjoyed. My first experience with rabbit hunting came when I was in junior high school. I was working on the farm at that time, and my first rabbit-hunting experience was with my brother-in-law Fred and his grandfather Fred Swartz. Grandpa Swartz was the father of Fred's mother. Grandpa lived with Rose and Russel, Fred's parents, across the road from Fred.

As we entered the field, I felt as if someone had just stocked the brushy hunting area. I never saw before nor after that day so many rabbits in one field. After the first shot, there were rabbits everywhere we looked.

I had never shot a rabbit, so I really didn't know what I was doing. I did have the chance to shoot a rabbit that was sitting. I hit the rabbit in the middle of the body and ruined the chance for us to eat it. Grandpa Swartz told me that when shooting a sitting rabbit, aim high so only a few pellets hit him.

Everyone else had at least one rabbit to take home. I lost the chance to bag a rabbit, but I learned how to shoot a sitting rabbit, an opportunity which I don't remember experiencing again.

The Community

Trinkets from Cereal Boxes and the Gum Ball Machines at Rager Store

Every family had a store where it faithfully shopped for food and other needs. Our neighborhood store was Rager Store. This store was located on Tiffin Street about a block away from our house on Clark Street.

There were several other small grocery stores located throughout the city, and each of these stores served a geographic area of its own. It was nice not to have to get in a car to purchase groceries.

The supermarkets soon became the death notice to the neighborhood grocery stores.

I never had much money nor did any of my friends, but any money I did have went straight to the 1¢ gum ball machine at the neighborhood store owned by George and Erma Rager. The gum ball machine was, of course, filled with gum balls and small trinkets. On very rare occasions, you might receive both a trinket and a gumball as a prize. These trinkets were usually made of plastic. They could be a small cowboy hat, a small silver horseshoe with a horse's head or four-leaf clovers in the middle, or a small record the size of a quarter. Each of these trinkets usually had a small hoop so it could be attached to a piece of string to make a necklace or to attach to a material. One of my favorite prizes was a miniature set of cards. My absolute best prize was a miniature lighter, which would actually light.

In later years, my mother made me a "trinket tree" on a large pine cone. Where have all those gum ball machines gone with all those neat prizes for just one penny?

The other source of trinkets and prizes was the cereal box and the many mail-in coupons contained in the box. For me, buying cereal was usually based on one criterion: the type of free giveaway in the cereal box or the mail-in coupon generally requiring money. I preferred the trinket in the box to the mail-in prize, as the enclosed prize was easier to obtain.

It was usually easy to convince my mom what cereal I wanted. It was called diversion and worked like this. I would go to the cereal section as soon as I hit the store. I would choose the cereal I wanted based on the trinket contained or the coupon attached. I would then slip the cereal into the shopping cart under other groceries. The checkout counter was not the place to go back and look for a more nutritious cereal. Usually, I would wait until my mother's attention was on something other than my cereal box and then I would hand the box to the cashier. It was a "fun" game, and I rarely lost.

The big stumbling block in sending in coupons and money for the (almost) free prize was that the cereal box was to be emptied before sending for the prizes. I tried once to send in the box top and/or coupon before finishing the cereal. My mother spotted the full box of cereal with no coupon and the cuts into the bag that held the cereal. This was a dead giveaway something was wrong. My mother had a completely different take on eating cereal, and I learned to eat the cereal before mutilating the cereal box and its contents.

I guess it could have been a different story as I reviewed the facts. One of my siblings could have taken the mutilated box from the shelf without a side coupon or no top, and the cereal could have fallen out of the side or top of the box and hit the floor, with cereal flying in several directions. My alert mother would have had many more questions about my cereal prize management had that happened.

Which brother or sister would have most likely innocently pulled out the damaged box of cereal on that fateful day? Well, I can't say for sure, but my brother Mike would have been a likely prospect, as I was a champion of getting him into trouble.

Obtaining the prizes from within the cereal box was an easy matter. Simply opening the outside cereal box and then opening the inside wax wrapping would allow my small hand to explore the bottom of the cereal for the prize.

For the mail-in prizes, it would be much harder to obtain the prizes because the U.S. Mail is in charge of the time line and setting the rate of postage. I can remember that I would wait from the time of mailing in the necessary materials until I would receive the prizes around five to six weeks later. The mailman was a very important person to the Frederick family. One of the longest waits I had was for the twelve rings from a cereal company. I still have most of the rings, which included a dice on one enclosed ring, a game of tic-tac-toe on another ring, a rotating piece of metal on a base that produced a high-pitch whistle, a referee-type whistle on a ring, and eight other rings. How great it was to get something in the mail! I always enjoyed choosing my cereal by the toy inside or available through the mail.

Later in life, I was to learn that at middle age, I would be choosing my cereal by the fiber it contained, not the toy inside the box.

My Dentist

I had more than one dentist when I was young. I have written about one earlier, and now I would like to write about a dentist I didn't mind seeing. This dentist had been my family dentist for years. He practiced in an office near downtown Willard and was familiar with all the Frederick children and parents. My sister Mary Lu worked for him. That is why I most recently saw my childhood dentist and his wife at Mary Lu's funeral.

When I was younger, I visited Dr. Charles Piller to have my teeth examined. He was a positive person and a competent dentist. He always was careful with his instruments, procedures, and medications. He constantly was concerned about my pain level when he was drilling my teeth and watched very closely the amount of novocaine he administered to me. He gave not too much nor too little.

I remember one day after he worked on me, I hung around for a few minutes. I believe he was working on a set of dentures, and either the dentures or something else seemed to occupy his mind. I sensed that we needed to talk, and we did. I don't remember the exact conversation, but I know we had a pleasant conversation. I felt good about it and then went home.

A few days later, my mother had an appointment with him, and he mentioned to her that I had brightened his day with our little talk. As a young boy not yet in high school, I was very pleased and uplifted by his comments. This incident was a seed in helping me to decide that I should look into the area of the social sciences as my lifework.

By the way, he remembered me thirty-five years later at my sister's funeral. Our last face-to-face contact had been 1968. I don't believe he knew that my mother had told me the compliment he gave me and the influence his comment made on my life.

When I moved to Mansfield, I was lucky to know two other wonderful dental professionals. You shall read about them when you read about Kathy and our first year of marriage.

The Gypsy Funeral

Periodically the Gypsy caravan would come through Willard. When talking about the Gypsies passing through town, I had an uncertain feeling since I knew little about Gypsies other than what I had heard from my friends; they also had limited information.

When I asked my mom and dad if the Gypsies would steal from me, they would tell me we must always know where our money is and not allow anyone to have a chance to get our billfold or other possessions.

I can still remember the uncertainty in Willard as the funeral and burial of the queen was discussed. I was in the third grade when the shocking news came to me; the queen of the Gypsies had died, and the funeral was to be in Willard. My parents informed me that the queen was to be laid out at the Secor Funeral Home.

I asked if my parents were going to see the queen, as they seemed to go to visit about anyone who died. My parents informed me and all my other brothers and sisters that the queen of the Gypsies was Catholic, and we as a family were going to visit her at the funeral home and pay our respects.

I was really concerned about going to the funeral home because the rumors were flying high about Gypsies stealing money and whatever else "shifters" would do. I couldn't think or talk about anything else. I had talked to some of my friends and asked them if they were going to the funeral home to see the queen, and hardly anyone was going.

The big day came at last, and I was still concerned that I was going to have someone picking my pockets at the funeral home. This made little sense as I reflect on it because I had no money. My parents loaded everyone in the car and gave us specific instructions on being nice to the Gypsies and keeping our hands to ourselves.

As I walked into the funeral home, my worst fear was confirmed. There were so many people in the home that everywhere I turned, there were chairs and people sitting on them. The aisle between them was less than two feet wide. As I began to walk down the aisle, it seemed every person was looking at me, and when I went by someone, their hands seemed to be touching me.

I clutched my mother's hand so tightly that I must have cut off any blood flow going through her hand. As I looked around, I saw that the body was only one room away from the entrance, but it seemed like it took me several minutes to get to the casket. When I looked into the casket, it was the first time I had ever seen such a sight; it was different than I had expected.

The casket was filled with jewelry and money, especially coins. The queen looked very old and was wearing lots of brightly colored silk clothing. There were many colorful silk scarves around and in the casket. I don't remember well, but one of the Gypsies must have said something to my parents about coming. Since my mom and dad will talk to anyone about anything, I was hoping they didn't put me on the spot because I simply could not talk.

Instantly I felt good about coming and seeing the casket. I felt like God was in that room helping me get through this experience. I still had to get out of the room with my shirt on. I can't remember if I closed my eyes to go through the aisle or just closed them halfway so I wouldn't see the Gypsies sitting along the aisle. In either case, I walked out and felt great relief about making it through that challenging situation. I often wondered if my parents wanted us kids to see the queen as a good Christian gesture or as a good educational experience or both. That will be another one of those questions not answered on this earth, as neither of my parents is alive to answer my inquiry.

The Muck Fire

My parents were very familiar with Celeryville and the black earth that comprised that region. Celeryville is located a short distance south of Willard. The black land was called muckland, and it is soft coal. Since there were many labor-intensive crops on the farms near Celeryville, much of the work was done by migrant workers.

For years, my mother had gone to the muckland and helped people with food, clothing, and their practice of the Catholic faith.

Mysteriously, around 1952 one day the land in the muck caught fire. There were stories about how the fire started, such as someone throwing a live cigarette butt out the window of a car or someone else intentionally starting the fire.

The reality was that the muck was on fire, and because of the very heavy smoke, it was impossible to travel through certain parts of that area. The fire caused many problems for the farmers and for the migrant workers who lived in the muck. The smoke was thick, and the air became hard to breathe. After an extended period, the fire went out.

In 1968, Kathy and I were traveling through the muckland, and there, to our surprise, in the middle of one of the field was smoke coming out of the ground. The muckland still must have been on fire.

Scouting from Generation to Generation

An Overview

Scouting has been a big part of the Fredericks' leisure time. My father had been a Boy Scout leader mainly so his sons could be involved in the Boy Scout activities. My mother was a Brownie and a Girl Scout as well as a Cub and Boy Scout leader for the same reason.

I was one of the six children to become involved in Cub and Boy Scouts having gone through the ranks up to and including Eagle Scout. I was the first Eagle Scout in eighteen years in Willard.

My youngest sister, Ann, was a Brownie and a Girl Scout. She traveled to several places with the scouts, including Washington, D.C. These Girl Scouts were an attraction to me, so I always tried to get close to where the Girl Scout activities were.

My youngest brother, Mike, was also an Eagle Scout.

Here are many scouting-related activities that I will share from my youth. Also, there will be activities that I will share about adult Boy Scout days.

Camp Firelands

Camp Firelands was the camp all Firelands Boy Scouts would attend. Since I was in scouting for many years, there were a number of scoutmasters and assistant scoutmasters who gave their time so that boys could have this fantastic growth experience.

Don Albright was one of our scoutmasters. He was a lieutenant in the Army. He knew a great deal about the outdoors and about the ins and outs of marching or drills. These exercises included lining up, facing off, facing different directions, and marching. In high school band and in ROTC in college, I had a head start in marching and drills because of Mr. Albright's training.

Len Playko; Walter Frederick, my dad; and John Leitz were some of the assistant scoutmasters that I can remember. All of these men knew scouting and devoted many hours to the weekly meetings, advancement, training, and the many campouts.

Another scoutmaster, Lance Young, was in construction work. His big truck was very useful when we would canvass the town of Willard for scrap metal that was converted into money for the troop treasury.

The next scoutmaster was Bill Schlotterer, who was a Navy veteran and also my uncle. In addition to knowing scouting, he was a good fundraiser. His spaghetti suppers seemed to draw the entire town into the Knights of Columbus Hall located downtown near the Willard Times. The spaghetti was great, and the money we made was even greater.

The Skunks

Boy Scout Camp lasted almost a week, starting Sunday afternoon and ending Saturday morning after checkout. We usually had at least two leaders to keep the troop in line.

One of the unique features about Camp Firelands was that there were an abnormally large number of skunks in the area. If there was any food in the Adirondack sleeping cabins, we made sure it was stored high in animal-proof bags.

The cabin looked like the one in this picture in which Mr. John Leitz, a leader, is entering while I was having my picture taken. The other leader was my father.

Even if food was stored reasonably high, it seemed the skunks would find a way to get to the food and wake the inhabitants with all the noise they created.

Me at Camp Firelands

One evening, we had popped TV Time popcorn on the open fire. This was quite a task to accomplish as TV Time popcorn needs a consistent fire so it does not burn the popcorn or the carton. This evening, the fire burned the popcorn and the container that held it. In other words, popcorn covered the ground.

We tried to pick up the loose and burned popcorn and threw it in the fire because if we didn't successfully accomplish this task, we would have skunks in camp all night. Lenny Playko had gone to his cabin and heard paper rustling near the stone fireplace located in the back of the room. His roommate entered the cabin, and they both stood in the dark trying to identify the paper-crunching sound. The roommate turned on his flashlight and discovered the intruder was a huge fat skunk eating his saltine crackers. The light was blinding the skunk, so Lenny told his roommate to keep the light on the skunk as he was going to pick it up by the tail.

This move was to be expected because earlier that day Lenny, master of nature, informed the other campers that he had read that if you pick up a skunk by the tail, the skunk can no longer spray. Since Lenny was a man of the woods, we had triple dared him to try that feat. As Lenny got in position to grab the skunk, it began to raise his tail to spray. Like clockwork, as the skunk raised its tail, Lenny grabbed the tail and pulled it up. The skunk was not able to spray, as it couldn't push on anything with its hind legs.

Much to his fellow scouts' surprise, Lenny was correct—picking up the skunk by the tail prevented the skunk from spraying its smelly scent. He showed everyone in camp that his earlier prediction had been proven.

One of the scouts (it could have been me) encouraged Lenny to visit the next campsite with the skunk and instruct them on the art of rendering skunks' spray temporarily inactive.

As Lenny started on his instructional campaign, several smaller skunks had caught the scent of popcorn, and they were all over the campsite. Unfortunately, seeing the skunks wasn't the worst part of the experience because all the yelling and activation of flashlights was exciting a few of them.

One by one, the scouts began following Lenny's lead of picking up a skunk by the tail and discarding it in the brush surrounding the campsite. This allowed the bewildered skunk to run off into the woods and leave our campsite. A few younger skunks did spray, so the campsite had an offensive aroma of fresh skunk scent around its perimeter.

As I walked by my cabin, I spotted a less-than-full-grown skunk and slowly grabbed the tail. Unfortunately, the skunk was getting ready to spray, and I was directly in the line of fire. I quickly lifted him by the tail and walked over to the edge of the campsite.

Someone flashed a beam of flashlight on my skunk. As they did, I saw a visible faint mist near the skunk's behind. I decided to release the skunk and place myself out of any more danger. By this time, most of the skunks were gone, and the only remnant of these animals was the offensive smell.

Meanwhile Lenny was approaching the next campsite and yelling "hello" to them so he wasn't treated like an intruder. It didn't work. The sight of the skunk coming into camp was not seen as desirable.

The scouts did not want the skunk in their campsite, and they didn't want Lenny there either. They yelled and threw objects at Lenny and the skunk. Lenny had had enough of this treatment. He released the skunk and took off for his campsite. A quick look told him the skunk he had released was going toward, not away, from the neighboring campsite. The yelling and throwing of objects continued, and Lenny smelled skunk as he left.

Word had it next morning that the campers next to us had to move to another location. Hopefully, the neighboring campers learned that one does not throw objects and shout in the presence of a big fat skunk.

As it turned out, stories of our successful encounter with the skunks had spread to all the troops in the camp. As our troop took its place by the flagpole to go in for breakfast, the constant buzzing and the looks directed to our troop 207 occupied exclusively the idle time before the raising of the flag. I can't remember seeing the scouts who harassed Lenny and his skunk during breakfast. I heard that the camp eventually found a way of reducing the skunk population.

Merit Badge Classes

After breakfast, we all went to our merit badge activity areas and worked on such badges as nature, reptiles, and swimming, to name a few.

My luck wasn't much better at swimming than it had been at camp the night before. As we entered the pool, we were greeted by cold water as the night air prevented the water from holding the heat of the day before. After learning the side stroke, the back stroke, the breast stroke, and the crawl, the lifeguards allowed us to have a free swim. During those days, there were diving boards, and I enjoyed the springboard.

As I came up from my board dive, I began to swim to the side of the pool and grab on to the side ladder. As I reached the side ladder while underwater, someone released my grip on the ladder and proceeded to sit on me. It seemed like more than one body keeping me underwater. At the time, I did not have this thought, but as I reflected on this incident, the thought came to me that my twin must have gone into high gear because I received two forms of energy. The first form of energy was the ability to hold my breath longer than I had ever held it in my life, and the second one was to push off the swimmer(s) holding me under.

I really thought that I was going to die. I weakly exited the pool and made my way to the edge of the pool to regain my breath and energy.

I made a promise to myself that I would never again allow myself to be in a position where other swimmers could cause me to face that kind of danger.

---

[26] Hickey, op. cit., 57.

Part III

Approaching Adulthood

Chapter 8

Willard High School

Oh, Willard High Forever

There were 109 students in the graduating class of 1962. I knew and enjoyed interacting with many of these fellow students. There were also many students in other class years both younger and older who provided me with many memorable experiences.

I entered Willard High School in September of 1958 and enrolled in a college preparatory curriculum.

My father was adamant about me attending college, more specifically John Carroll University. These four years were to be my advanced preparation for life through this private Jesuit university in Cleveland.

Since I had an elder sister, Mary Lu, and an elder brother, Walter Jr. or Sonny, who had gone through Willard Schools, it was a foregone conclusion that I would also graduate from Willard High School. Both of my parents were also Willard High School graduates.

The Willard High School structure was an old brick building when I attended and is still the same high school as of 2013. Plans are now underway for new buildings.

In high school, I was to find that my classes were either easy or almost impossibly difficult. While I had to study for all classes, I either was good at a class and worked to learn it or had to work very hard to get through certain subjects and barely "skid" through them.

I was not good at most sciences except for biology, and most math courses were tough except for algebra. My foreign language class, Latin, started out easy for me but became progressively harder. Problems of Democracy or Government and typing were special loves of mine.

I enjoyed choir and band probably because I could converse with the girls and my male friends who sat close to me (as long as I wasn't caught). Another positive was rarely was there any homework in band and choir.

There were many good teachers and some exceptional teachers at Willard High School.

Memories of Willard High School Classes

Yes, I was enrolled in the college preparatory classes and took subjects that focused on acquiring the skills needed to succeed in college.

Some classes affected both my intellectual growth as well as my daily life. English, physical education, biology, and Problems of Democracy were classes that affected both areas.

Classes in how to use one's social skills to interact with others would have been useful for me in my daily life adjustment. Since I was planning on a major in college related to the humanities, high school was in many ways not useful to me. Courses such as psychology and sociology would have been very useful.

The graduate college curriculum where I was to be involved with individuals having developmental disabilities would be very strongly based on instruction that involved everyday living skills. I suffered through the sciences constantly wondering how I would consistently use this knowledge.

It was the space age, and sciences were big. Somehow persons who were interested in humanities were not the priority.

Physics

One of the many science courses I found a challenge was physics. I understood some of the basic principles, such as levers, but others went over my head.

I remember one class in which the teacher was conducting an experiment with two twelve-inch-diameter wheels mounted side by side and periodically containing pieces of metal. Also mounted next to the metal on the wheels were metal brushes. As the wheels turned in the opposite direction, the wire brushes hit the metal on the wheels, producing electrical currents. The goal of the experiment was to have the wheels produce so much electricity that a pop sound would be made. As one student turned the wheels, the rest of the class earnestly waited to hear the pop.

About five minutes into the experiment, one of the students in the back of the class decided to end the experiment. The student put his finger into his closed mouth and with a quick push of the finger out of the mouth made a large pop. Some of the students knew where the sound originated, but I am not sure whether the teacher or the rest of the class knew.

Chemistry

If one were to rate the classes I had liked, chemistry would have been at the bottom of the list. Although Mr. Zulauf tried to make the subject come alive, I was never able to get it.

One of the conclusions I have drawn about chemistry classes is that the actions that students took outside the regular experiments proved to be more interesting to me than the regular lessons. For example, the water hookups and the gas hookups were both located over the water troughs at the experimental areas. Each of these hookups was physically the same. One was located higher than the other so students could differentiate between the two functions. If a student hooked up the Bunsen burner to the gas outlet and lit it, it would burn. If the gas was turned up too high, it would burn high and draw the attention of other students and the teacher. If the Bunsen burner was hooked up to the water, a water spout would develop. If the water was turned up too high, a large spout would shower everyone nearby.

At times highly flammable materials would be used for experiments. When these flammable chemicals were discarded in the water trough, it was very possible that someone lighting their Bunsen burner would throw a lit match into the trough. Flames could erupt from the point of the flammable discard until the end of the water run. The further away the end of the trough the flammable liquid was discarded, the longer the flame in the trough. The concentration and the flammability of the fluid determined how high the flame would erupt. Any flame was a high point of interest. I would guess that in today's world, many of these setups would be changed to ensure greater safety.

Unusual circumstances seem to foster unusual responses. Chemistry class could be a lecture and/or an experiment.

On this day, class was done in a lab, and the students were busy working on their experiment. Someone noticed an unusual object in the sky, a blimp, and the attention of all was drawn to this. A blimp was a rather unusual sight in Willard. The windows in the chemistry lab were located higher than normal. Several of the male students jumped up on the radiators or chairs next to the wall to obtain a better view of the blimp.

All eyes were on the blimp except for one, a male classmate. That one classmate took a match and put it into the shoe of another student standing on the register and lit it. As the match burned closer to the shoe, a hot foot was experienced by the student on the register. There was a commotion and a bit of a physical altercation, but the incident quickly became a memory.

I was aware that chemistry and a few other science courses were extremely difficult for me. I remember no matter how hard I studied, when I took the test, I still did not do well.

This opened up the option of studying with a friend, Beth Lewis, before the test. The tests were still very hard, and passing them was nearly impossible for me regardless of the help I received.

Teachers at Willard High School Who Had a Lasting Effect on My Life

My Biology Teacher

I will never forget my biology class and the many useful teachings from my biology teacher, Mr. Ronald Sbrissa. From the first A grade I received on my first biology test, I just knew that this class and this teacher was for me. The lesson was about the many aspects of living beings.

My teacher also taught useful matters about humans, and it was called hygiene. One of the many facts he taught was that after a shower or bath, it was wise to use two towels when drying so that one's body was completely clean and dry. Especially important was drying between one's toes to prevent athlete's foot. I rarely had athlete's foot as an adult.

Later in life, my wife had a different take on the two towels probably because she does the laundry.

Years later on November 16, 2005, I came upon my teacher's address from a former childhood neighbor, Carole Winemiller Reed.

I wrote to my teacher and expressed my thanks to him for the individual attention he gave me. I had been taught that thanking people for sharing their gifts was a worthwhile response (hence the basis for this book).

I filled him in on the course of my life and thanked him for being an inspirational influence in my life. I also thanked him for relating to me in such a respectful manner. He was a teacher who treated me as a man before I became eighteen years old.

His handwritten response came about a month later. He mentioned that he was surprised to receive my letter, and he thanked me for the compliments I had given him. After relating information about his wife and children, he filled me in on his professional career.

After reading his letter, I knew I had done the right thing by writing to him. Life has shown me that unsaid or unwritten words usually have little value, especially if they are complimentary.

The Owl in the Classroom

I remember one winter day when Butch Rothschild, Dick Ellis, Rich Buss, and I were trapping and found a baby owl in one of our muskrat traps. The owl was unhurt, and we decided to place it in a bag and take it to class, as it would be a good lesson in biology.

As we walked into Mr. Sbrissa's classroom proud as a peacock, we slowly opened the bag to show the teacher and the class our owl; it looked like a horned owl. Well, the surprise was on us because the owl wanted out of the bag and immediately flew toward the ceiling of the room landing on the light fixture. Word got around that there was an owl in the biology room, and many students walked by to see this baby owl. Toward the end of the school day, a high window was opened, and the owl regained its freedom.

My Typing Teacher

I eagerly signed up to take personal typing. Before taking the class, I was able to type with only a few of my fingers in what was called the "hunt-and-peck" method of typing. There were many reasons for my excitement about learning the skill of typing. One was that I will always possess the attributes of "extremely poor penmanship."

When I was in grade school, one teacher creatively gave me the final grade of incomplete. It was nowhere on the list of recognized grades that could be awarded a student. It wasn't considered a pass or wasn't a fail.

People always had a problem reading my writing as did I. Some doctors' writings in those days resembled my penmanship or I theirs. With my doctoral degree, I now feel I have an excuse for my poor writing skills. Yes, typing would give me a chance of improving my communication with others. A second reason that I was looking forward to typing class was I needed to type in my later high school years and my future years in college.

My typing teacher, Mr. David Hirschy, was a likable person, yet he was able to make sure that his class was under control. I will never forget the rapid rate of learning to type with both hands and with all of my fingers.

From the beginning of the class, I found that I had one secret skill that was about to emerge before the entire class. That skill was the ability to break typewriters. At first, I thought that it was a coincidence that my typewriters would break. For example, where the spring was attached to the shift lever, breaking the spring rendered the typewriter useless. On those many occasions when I would break a typewriter, my teacher would calmly ask me to move to another typewriter. I cannot remember how many typewriters I broke, but the number fourteen sticks in my head. About anything that moved on a typewriter was subject to my damaging fingers. As I remember, the shift carriage was one of my favorite targets, but various keys and shift keys also were acceptable ones. I became convinced there was a little bad luck and some skill involved in breaking typewriters.

I was to master all the keys on the typewriter except for the number keys. We ran out of class periods, and I didn't have sufficient time to practice learning these keys.

In graduate school at Bowling Green State University (BGSU), I would see my former typing teacher; he was taking classes there. I don't know if I ever told him how much I had learned and appreciated his typing class. He must have known because he always would smile and exchange small talks with me when he would pass me in the halls at BGSU. That always made me feel good that my former teacher would take time to greet me.

My Gym Teacher

My gym teacher, Mr. Herbert Hart, was the type of person who would take time from his busy schedule and listen to others' concerns. He was also the head basketball coach, and his successful teams won several Northwestern Ohio League championships.

I can remember when I was on break from college, Bob Schodorf, a good friend of mine who was attending Bowling Green State University, and I visited our gym teacher to discuss old and new times. It was enjoyable and helped us all bring back many good memories.

My Track Coach

I enjoyed my track coach at Willard High School. He was a coach who always worked with his athletes, especially if they tried hard and put a lot of effort into the sport.

My position on the track team was that of a mile runner. Although I was not the best miler, after trying hard at many positions, I ended up running the mile. My true goal was to be a pole-vaulter, but despite the fact that I practiced vaulting away from and at the track, I was to learn that I couldn't do everything I wanted to do. This was a tough lesson to accept.

I can remember the beginning of track season when the coaches were trying to find which position was the best for each athlete, and I was running the 220-yard run with several others. I was closer to the back than the front of the pack. As I was running by the coaches, I overheard a discussion about keeping me on the team. The consensus was to keep me on the team because I tried hard to succeed. The coaches did not know I had heard that comment, but the comment stuck with me, and I was inspired to take whatever energy I could muster from within, from without, from God, and from my twin and to give whatever I was doing just a bit more effort.

A second lesson for me in this experience was how influential comments can be in a person's life. Influences can be encouraging or discouraging; in either case, they can be real.

Problems of Democracy Teacher

My Problems of Democracy instructor, Mr. Robert Moomaw, was an excellent teacher who always presented the material in such a manner that I felt students would be able to understand. I worked in local, county, and state government for over forty years. He must have influenced my life.

Fate brought me and that teacher together at Bowling Green State University. He had earned his PhD and was a professor at BGSU. I was a doctoral student there. Although I did not have him as an instructor in college, he was a constant motivator in college, and I would see him often in the department of education.

In all those graduate years, he was an extremely inspiring person, and when I would see him at the university, he would always introduce me as one of his best high school students. Never once did I argue the fact.

He was a teacher in the education department, and I was a student in the department of educational administration and supervision. His time on earth was cut short, and I miss his kind smile and exemplary communication skills.

Willard Government Day

Mr. Moomaw was a very talented person. His course was designed to help students learn about forms of government.

The end-of-the-year project was to run the city of Willard. It was up to each person to choose the job they wished to assume on the big day. There were positions for city council, city manager, director of maintenance, fire chief, police chief, finance director, and all positions in the city of Willard table of organization. There was a job for each person. After each person chose a job, if they were the only one who wished to have that job, that was their position. If more than one student wanted a job, the teacher would talk with the involved students and find a job for each of them.

Announcements were made about the class of 1962 running the city in the local paper, the *Willard Times*. I chose and was given the position of mayor of Willard because it sounded good to me.

We prepared for the event, and on the assigned Saturday, everyone assumed their positions. I had a new suit with a vest since I thought I could at least dress the part. The day of the event, I was at the city hall early. The activity I remember most about the day was signing papers, one being a proclamation announcing that the students of Willard High School were to run the city that day. I remember my picture was taken as I signed the proclamation, and the 1962 high school annual, the *Chief*, displayed the photograph.

Students learned much from participating in the activities of the day. I learned I enjoyed administration so much that this experience was a driving force in my becoming an administrator. I do not know if this practice of students running the city of Willard is still taking place each year, but this hands-on form of learning was to be one of several stimulating and enlightening activities. In fact, years later, I was to be the appointed mayor of New Rochester.

My Latin Teacher

My Latin teacher, Mrs. Naomi Wiebe, and her husband, Peter, spent much of their careers at Willard High School. Languages were always a very hard subject for me to master. Mrs. Wiebe was a very understanding and fair teacher. My first-year course in Latin was much easier than the second year. She was constantly challenging her students into working for a life filled with success.

Extracurricular Activities

I had the good fortune to be involved in many activities both school related and non–school related. I was in band for four years, track for three years and choir for two. Studying consumed a good portion of my life, and I worked on the farm for two years while attending school.

I was very involved with my church, St. Francis Xavier Catholic Church, Boy Scouts, and my family. I would like to share some of my memories that were connected to these activities.

In fulfilling the title of this book, *People + Me*, I wish to honor as many seniors and other classmates as possible for supporting me and for their contributions to the class of 1962 and to our alma mater, Willard High School.

Band

The band was both a marching band and a concert band. The marching band played at the football games and the Memorial Day Parade. I started playing the baritone and ended up playing the tuba in the band. I always enjoyed playing the tuba because it was one of the largest instruments.

The band director was easygoing unless students began to forget about the music and began talking inappropriately. At this point, he would bring people back to the fold. Hard work on the music for concerts and the music for marching during football season was the menu.

Band was structured and required constant new learning. Performing in front of large crowds was a risk, and success was a group and, at times, an individual accomplishment.

Three Baritones

I had the pleasure of playing the baritone with two other classmates. The other baritone players were Sally Rapp and Bobbi Richards; both were majorettes in the marching band. Sally was a sophomore as I was, and Bobbie was a junior.

In 1960, the band director asked the three of us if we were interested in being involved in the band competition as an ensemble. We were interested, so the practicing commenced.

We practiced and practiced and practiced for the big day. The amount of time the band director gave us for practice was amazing.

When the big day came and we were to compete, I was uptight and thought the others may have been the same. As we entered the room where we were to play, we tried to relax. While the competition was not perfect, we did OK. We didn't get the first prize, but we did get the third.

I didn't feel this was too bad for the first year, and it was a good experience to perform in front of a judge in a stressful situation.

In years to come, I was to find that performances in front of judges or other people in stressful situations were a common experience.

Memorial Day Parade

In Willard, the Memorial Day Parade was the biggest annual parade. The purpose of Memorial Day was to honor veterans both living or deceased and particularly those who had fought in the wars. The parade was held on May 30 but was changed in 1971 to the last Monday in May to allow for a three-day weekend.

The band participants in the parade would meet at the Willard Elementary School wearing our wool-like band uniforms, not suitable to march in weather that was usually very hot. There was always a big crowd along the parade route. The route from the school went directly downtown and across the main railroad tracks under the railroad tunnel to Spring Street. It was an unusual experience to hear the music, especially the drums, as we went through the railroad tunnel.

Grandpa and Grandma Schlotterer lived at 119 Spring Street, and their front yard was always filled with family and friends to view the parade and watch their friends and family in it. I would look out of the corner of my eye to see the people at that address pointing at me as I passed them.

Spring Street led us directly to the Willard Cemetery where one of the hills in Willard was to be climbed. This hill was the true test of endurance not only because it was at the end of the parade route and most people were tired but also because it was steep, and—don't forget—it was usually hot!

The parade started with the police car and the color guard. The color guard was composed of Willard men and women, active or veteran, who had served in any branch of the military. Sometimes there were a few and sometimes many. The number depended on how many past and present men or women were available and willing to walk the distance. At times there was more than one row of servicemen. I think people were very proud to see the many local servicemen and servicewomen.

I remember when my brother Walt, a Marine veteran, was in the parade. On at least one occasion, Walt was in his dress blues, with his Expert Pistol and Expert Rifleman medals on his chest, and was in charge of the color guard. Walt's Uncle George Schlotterer, the parade marshal, was proud and excited that his nephew was in charge of the color guard. I also was very proud of my brother for his place in the parade and his service to our country.

As the flag went by, people would stand, and many would put their right hands over their hearts. I always knew that was the thing to do, but I often don't see people at public occasions today show their respect for the flag like I feel I must.

There were other participants in the parade who will now be listed in no particular order. The band was in the parade and played music almost constantly. The band director would march beside us making sure that we were in perfect line. The word *perfect* for the members of the band was not always defined in the same manner as the band director. I was one of the tuba players and always felt that people couldn't help but see the tuba. The size of the tuba was to me a compensation for my size. It made me taller as the tuba was tall.

There were always bicycles decorated in red, white, and blue crepe papers with streamers flowing from their handlebars. The clinging sound of cardboard placed on the spindles of the wheels could be heard by the crowd. Most bicycles displayed the American flag. There were large bicycles, small bicycles, and some tricycles. It was always fun to see very small children in the parade, so small that the parents had to help them along by pushing the tricycle or bicycle. There was no argument that this section of the parade was very colorful.

Several organizations marched in the parade. The Boy Scouts and Girl Scouts were two I remember. If my memory serves me right, there were also fire trucks and other city vehicles. I also can remember the many horses of beauty, size, and obedience that graced the parade. The horses were at the end of the parade followed by the cleanup crew armed with shovels and buckets.

After the parade, the crowd entered the cemetery and was greeted by flags placed on the veterans' graves the week before and often flowers placed by the families. There was always a solemn ceremony, which included a speech and the salute of guns. After the firing of guns, the shells were removed from the chamber, and they fell to the ground.

Initially I remember kids picking up the shells as souvenirs. I also remember the military being concerned if each of the shells had fired. If they didn't fire, live ammunition could get into the children's hands. As a result, a new practice was that the shells would be gathered by the servicemen, inspected, and then given to the children.

Observance of Memorial Day also marked the beginning of the summer break, a time filled with sleeping in, fun, and some work. It also marked the opening of the Willard Municipal Pool.

Sports and Fun

My Track Experiences

The sport that I felt I could do best was track. Since stamina was one of my strong qualities, I began to work on distance running. The mile run became my event, and I practiced during the season, after the season, and any time I had a few minutes.

I would also wear weights on my ankles most of the year to build up my leg muscles. The ankle weights would at times get the attention of members of the opposite sex and did not hurt my chances of attracting them.

I wasn't the greatest miler, but I was a competitor. I learned that everyone contributes to the team according to their abilities and shares in the victories and defeats.

There were a few times that things didn't go as planned in track. One of the things I learned right away was that I shouldn't get far behind the competitors because I could get boxed in and lose the race. Boxing in is accomplished when some members of the opposing team position themselves ahead and beside a competitor. When I tried to pass, there was no place to go. If I slowed down, they would slow down. Meanwhile the other opposing runners were gaining time and distance because they were not part of the boxing.

An unusual practice I experienced was running against a person who had been hypnotized. I experienced it only once and had questions about its legality and effectiveness.

After track, we would occasionally have a pickup game of basketball. That was lots of fun until I landed on my ankle and twisted it so bad that I was on crutches for several weeks. I wasn't able to run, and l lost valuable competition time.

There were many occasions before, during, and after track where some unusual happenings occurred. In my freshman year, my friends Dick, Rich, and Butch all went out for track. A mishap we had was when a few of us found the track dressing room too crowded and decided to use an old dressing room under the theater stage. This arrangement worked out fine until we found a mouse running along the baseboard. We eliminated the mouse. We did not eliminate the damp floors, which likely spread the athlete's foot we all contracted. After much medication and a move back to the regular locker room, we began to beat it.

A Fellow Track Teammate Goes Fishing

One of my friends on the track team was an avid fisherman. Bob Kennard knew how, when, and where to catch fish.

On this occasion, my friend had told me that the old reservoir by J Tower was going to be drained and closed. This would be accomplished by draining out all the water in one day. He was excited because he was going be there as they drained the reservoir, and he was going to catch as many of the big fish as possible and transfer them into other ponds. I thought about going with him, and then I decided that it would probably be a mess and not worth the effort.

I didn't go with my friend to catch the big fish as the reservoir was being drained, and I did regret my decision. The report came back to me that there were many large fish, and they were pretty easy to catch. That's what can happen when one misses an opportunity; one can miss out on the fun.

Stulls' News Center

The high school hangout in Willard at this time was easy to remember and easy to find. It was located in the middle of downtown Willard and the owners were Renna and Jeanne Stull. The Stulls knew and loved every kid in town. There was music, food, and drinks. It was a place where everyone was happy. It was an experience I will never forget.

Classmates in High School

As I reflect on my Willard High School friends, it is difficult for me to have anything but affirmative feelings about my classmates. A book rather than two chapters would have been an option for my writing on Willard High School. For the present, short spurts of memory will be documented of high school classmates I have never forgotten. While some are mentioned in this section, others have been or will be mentioned in other sections of the book.

Remembering a Few Classmates

In my years of education in Willard Schools, I was to have the good fortune of knowing many classmates. All of the classmates were not close friends, but many of them at one time or another were involved in my life and as such were an influence on me.

One of the major purposes of this book, *People + Me*, was to tell how other people, in this case classmates, did influence me. Here are a few examples I remember.

There was "Roach," Butch Snook, our fearless class leader displaying his natural "Mr. Popularity" ways and friendly mannerisms. Larry Ayers was a long-term buddy and a fellow Boy Scout and coin collector. John Bailey was a friend who allowed me to use my first-aid skills when he ran his arm through the glass of the door at Willard High School. Jack Richards could lift me up when I was down with his smile and a few words.

Ralph Webb was the accomplished ball dunker and dribbler. Sally Rapp was a special friend who sat next to me in band. Don Elmlinger and Tom Androsac were interesting friends I rode with on the school bus when I worked on the farm. Ruth Shrader was a friend and all-around popular person. Bobbie Moore always had time to talk and had represented our class as prom queen in 1961.

Nancy Cok was a friend always ready for a conversation. Janet Heisler was a congenial friend with great people skills. Tom Gray was an interesting person who could always access his mother's great pizza. Beth Lewis used her knowledge to tutor me in science and math. I cannot forget Bob Bauerle, a friend in high school and one of the most useful and supportive persons in the process of my authorship of this and my next book *God Keeps on Giving*. There were other classmates I never knew well, but I wish I had.

Seniors Receive Outstanding Awards

Several seniors received awards and other recognition for outstanding services. The Harlow Staff Award for athletic accomplishments was presented to Richard Holmes.

The National Merit Scholarship Semifinalist Award and the Paul Hargrove Senior Math Award were earned by Elizabeth Lewis. The Girls' Athletic Association Award went to Susan Sage. Jerry Eitle was presented a trophy for the WHS Best Farmer Award. Ruth Montgomery and Robert Schodorf received citizenship medals. The state homemaker degree pin went to Ruth Montgomery. Congratulations to all these award winners.

Lunchtime Intramurals

I remember the lunch intramurals in which I had the privilege of participating in badminton and ping-pong tournaments. Lunchtime was an extended period giving students a chance to both eat and participate in activities.

In the badminton tournament, Sue Sage was my mixed-doubles partner. We had worked our way up the bracket, and we were in the finals.

Unfortunately, we couldn't have things our way and couldn't come in first. I was sure that we were going to win the tournament. Instead, I learned a lesson on the unpredictability of life and being a gracious loser.

I remember another lesson in the finals of the ping-pong tournament. Denny Reed and I played in the finals, and he beat me. I, of course, wanted to win this tournament, and I didn't. Once again, I tried to be a winner but ended up being—you guessed it—a gracious loser.

My Close Friends in High School

I was fortunate to have many close friends in high school. Each of these friends will be involved in some interesting stories in this chapter and possibly others.

Rich Buss

Rich was a year older than me, was a member of my Boy Scout troop 207, and was a member of St. Francis Xavier Church as a server. He was a reliable friend in that he was fun but not at the expense of his friends. Whatever Butch Rothschild, Dick Ellis, and I were doing, you would usually find Rich.

Rich lived a distance from the rest of our homes. Butch and I lived across the street from each other, and Dick lived about two blocks away from us.

Rich's father was a mailman, his mother was a housewife, and he had two younger brothers.

On one occasion, I remember walking into Rich's house, and immediately Butch, Dick, and I went to the back room. There were other high school classmates present. One of the guys sat down on a barstool. One of the others put a towel around his shoulders and began to cut his hair. It was not long before the haircut was finished. The "barber" did an acceptable job. When the hair was cut, the barber called for the next person. I decided that I had something else to do and left before I was the next.

Dick Ellis

Dick was in my class and lived a few blocks away from me, and I spent a lot of time at his house. I could be at his house in a few minutes if I tried.

Dick had three sisters, one elder and two younger. Dick's mother and father were always willing to take time to talk with me.

Dick always seemed to have a job. When he was in grade school, he delivered papers. Sometimes I would help him when he needed help, and on a few occasions, I remember doing the route. When Dick was in high school, he worked at his uncles' filling station located across the street from the city hall. When I visited Dick at the gas station, I noticed that working in a gas station during the summer can be a little hot; however, working in a filling station during the winter was really hard with the snow and when the temperature dipped into the teens. I remember standing in the gas station while waiting for Dick to get off work and freezing each time the door opened. In those days, the gas attendant filled your car with gas, checked the oil, and also washed your windows.

Dick was a good runner in track, a fellow Boy Scout, and a member of my church. When my friend Butch graduated from high school and went into the Army, much of the time I used to spend with Butch was now spent with Dick.

Bob Schodorf

Bob was in my class and another of my good friends.

Bob had an elder and a younger sister as well as a younger brother. Bob's household was an uplifting place to be since cracking a smile or laughing was not unusual.

Bob's dad had been in the dairy business and the insurance business. I can still see Bob's dad delivering milk to our front door. I remember Bob's mother as the church organist at St. Francis Xavier Church. She always wore a smile and was a pleasant person to be around.

Bob also was a runner in track, and we spent many hours on the track together. Bob ran the 880-yard run, which has since been renamed.

Lenny Playko

Lenny was a year behind me in school. Our families were close, and we went to the same church.

Both of our fathers worked for the Pioneer Rubber Company and were Boy Scout leaders. We both enjoyed Boy Scouts, and while I spent a great deal of time in the outdoors, Lenny spent even more time there than me and taught me a great deal about nature (more about Lenny later).

John Gibson

John was in my class, and our fathers worked together at the rubber company. John's father was the president of the company.

John and I scuba dived for years in high school and had many experiences diving in various locations.

In years to come, Kathy and I would arrange enjoyable dinner engagements with John and his wife, Mary Jane.

Scuba Diving

Diving Indoors

My friend and classmate John Gibson convinced me that scuba diving is a great sport. I loved the water and decided to initially pursue winter scuba diving in the pool at Sandusky High School and then at Margaretta High School. John and I both loved the water and while in high school joined the Erie Island Diving Club.

My brother Walter was in the Marines part of this time, so he dived when he was able.

I had a Voit single tank and regulator, as I liked the color of the tank, and it was reasonably priced.

The experienced divers were good at giving instructions to new members. Instructions on clearing the mask, scuba safety equipment, and diving depth on descent and ascent were given. Additional necessary scuba knowledge was imparted in the sessions.

Playing underwater hockey was by far the most enjoyable part of indoor scuba diving. Few people I have talked to are able to immediately comprehend underwater hockey.

This is how the sport is played. The first piece of equipment needed is a hockey puck filled with lead. A weighted hockey goal is the next item. The last one is the hockey stick, preferably lead weighted. The game starts with a face-off similar to real hockey. As soon as the puck hits the pool floor, players begin to take the puck toward the other team's goal. The concentration for the hockey player is the puck and the people who are closing in on his/her progress.

There was no rule on turning off the air valve to the tank of another diver. This would mean that if another team member had control of the puck, one way to stop their progress to the goal was to shut off their air valve. Shutting off the air was a relatively easy move as the person with the puck cannot see who is behind him, as the mask does not offer the opportunity to look behind. Once the air is off, it is impossible to go much further with the puck. As one tries to turn on the air, control of the puck and the stick becomes difficult, as breathing is the most important task at hand. It is not easy to try to turn on your air especially if you do it with the same hand that you are using to hold the stick. Remember, you are out of air, and you are trying to turn on your air valve.

I do remember making one goal; it seems that goals were infrequent, and I believe it occurred as someone closed my regulator. Having one's regulator (and consequentially the air in the tank) shut off was good practice in learning how to act if the regulator is not functioning.

The Ride Home

It was at one of these indoor diving practices that my brother Walt became interested in diving. When he was home on leave from the Marine Corps while stationed at Parris Island, South Carolina, he participated in the indoor dives at Margaretta High School.

Walt was always "first class," and he purchased an Aqua Lung tank and regulator in which the air hoses came around both sides of the head to feed him air.

One evening after the dive, we started on our way home to Willard. Our route would take us through North Monroeville, Ohio. We were about three miles from North Monroeville while Walt cruised along in his white 1959 Chevy convertible. His cruise was not to last long because an Ohio highway patrolman was, unbeknown to Walt, following him.

Walt, John, and I were having a good time joking around and talking about areas of common interest. Our laughing stopped as we realized that the "gumball" was on, and we were the only car in sight. I was mentally calculating the amount of money that the fine would be as Walt left the car and went back to the Ohio highway patrol car. Yes, the rule today is the driver waits for the officer to come to the car.

Walt was gone for only a short period when he returned to the car. Walt took off, and John and I asked him how much the fine was. Walt said, "I am not going to pay a fine." I gave the patrolman my Marine identification, and we talked a little about the service before he said, "Have a nice evening."

John and I were pretty impressed with Walt's ability to avoid a ticket. Getting out of a ticket was a new experience for both John and me, and I bet both of us were not to forget how Walt successfully managed that feat.

Open-Water Diving

The next part of diving was open-water diving. I remember one Lake Erie dive when John and I were in high school. We had gone to Catawba Island with his mother and father for a weekend at their cottage and a day of scuba diving. Lake Erie was in those days a very polluted lake. John's father transported us out to the diving spot in their pleasure boat. Lake Erie is a shallow lake, and it took us a while to find a deep spot. The deep spot at Lake Erie would not be that deep in comparison to the other great lakes, so we were talking about thirty feet.

We checked all our equipment in the boat and in the water and proceeded to buddy dive into the lake. As John and I began to descend to the bottom of the lake, we noticed the pollution in terms of algae and other particles around us that looked like dirt. As we approached possibly twenty feet, we went through a thermal climate. A thermal climate happens when the water is warm at, say, eighteen feet, and then at twenty feet, it is very cold.

We reached the bottom of the lake only to find that in order to see what was on the bottom, one needed to place the face mask against the bottom of the lake. I remember seeing a ruler on the bottom and felt fortunate that I was able to find anything at all. There were no visible fish; it was cold, and John and I decided to go to the surface. This experience helped motivate me to take up scuba diving forty years later when Lake Erie was clean enough to dive.

Farm Pond

A snorkeling experience I had during the summer was at a farm pond near Willard. Snorkeling is diving without a tank. I wish I knew where that pond was, but I do not. It was a swimming party with some friends. As I snorkeled in the pond, I was surprised that the pond was loaded with many fish, and I could see from one end of the pond to the other. The pond was as clear as any swimming pool. There were bass in the middle of the pond as well as near the shore. I likewise saw several schools of bluegills. Both of these species of fish were nice in size, and I wished I had an underground fishing pole to catch enough fish for a meal. That was truly a dream dive.

Ice Diving

Ice diving was an experience I would have enjoyed. It was a Sunday morning in the middle of the winter. The day started out with my brother volunteering to drive me to Lake Erie where our club would be diving under the ice. During the winter months, once the ice was frozen, it was not unusual to drive cars onto the ice and safely survive the experience. During my senior year in high school, the ice was very thick and did allow cars to navigate safely on the ice.

My brother Walt and his friends had some necessary stops to make before we arrived at the diving spot. As we approached the site, we noticed that there were ropes going into a hole large enough for a diver to enter the ice. As we looked closer, we saw that a person had come out of the water and had the rope attached to him. He had on a diving suit (to keep him warm), tank, mask, and gloves. It was only a few minutes later that all the equipment and all the divers left the hole. I knew that I had missed my chance.

As I thought about diving under the ice later that night, the possibility hit me: *What would I do if I were under the ice with only one way out of the water and the rope became untied from my body?* Maybe my brother and his friends did me a favor by *not* making sure I was on time and able to dive that Sunday afternoon.

Butch Rothschild

The friend who was also my neighbor was Butch Rothschild or "Little Butch." Not only was he my very close friend growing up but he also was to be my friend for life. We shared many experiences. His 1953 Chevy was our "wheels" in and out of town. The Rothschild boat provided many fishing trips and water ski expeditions. The large garage located behind his house off the alley provided tools and supplies to experiment with wood and metal. A look at a few of these experiences is next on the agenda.

"Laying Rubber"

Butch's black 1953 Chevy was a well-known car in Willard because it was constantly on the road, and the driver possessed great skills at "laying rubber." This means squealing the tires so rubber was placed on the pavement.

Butch's car was also well-known because it had a standard transmission, which meant the gears of the transmission were shifted manually. Standard shift transmission is the opposite of automatic shift transmission, which does all the shifting of the gears automatically in the forward position.

Successfully "laying rubber" required a standard transmission. Butch's technique of "laying rubber" rested first on his ability to put the transmission of the car into the reverse gear. Running the car in a fast reverse motion while keeping the car on the road was the second step. Knowing when to put the car in first gear as the car sped backward was crucial. This step required putting the shift stick into second gear and then first gear with the clutch disengaged. At that time, the clutch was engaged. This put the transmission into first gear to move the car into forward motion while the car had been moving fast in reverse.

"Laying rubber" was successfully achieved if the tires were running forward and the car was going backward so that rubber came off the tires onto the pavement. Butch was a master and, to my knowledge, never lost a transmission in this process. The success of "laying rubber" rested on the amount and length of rubber left lying on the road as the tires struggled to have the car go forward when it was in fact going in a reverse motion.

One of the most satisfying aspects of being involved in the "laying of rubber" was returning to the scene of the previous evening and measuring the length of the rubber marks while observing the darkness of the tracks. The unexplainable part of this activity was that I never remember Butch buying any new tires.

The Broken Window

Butch and I were with a few friends on a weekend night by the bowling alley near downtown Willard when we saw two cars pull to the curb, and some large males from the first car approached the second car and began talking to the occupants. We stopped to see what was going on.

The talk escalated as we sat looking from our car behind the second car. Out of nowhere, one of the tallest men took his bare fist and hit the side window of the second car. Glass went flying, and so did we. I never did find out what the altercation was about, as we were more concerned about getting out of there before our windows or something else was broken.

Water Skiing

Water skiing was an activity that I had grown to love. Butch was a few years older than I was, and he had taught me how to ski. One of the hardest skills of skiing is coming out of the water. The trick is to come out of the water as fast as one can without losing one's balance. If one stays in the water too long, a large volume of water will push against the skier's body and will make it impossible to hold the tow rope, let alone to go up on the skis.

When Butch and I were already pretty good skiers, a new towline was added to the boat so two skiers could ski at once. The length of the ski ropes was different so that it was impossible for the two skiers to collide. Skiing double was exciting, as there were not many skiers who had mastered this feat. Double skiing provided a chance for skiers to master a new trick. It was possible for the skiers to jump over or cross over the other skier's rope and switch positions with them. I was constantly cautious when jumping to another rope because having the rope wrap and entangle my body was a possibility.

I felt the most dangerous part of basic skiing was not jumping over waves or to the other ski line but circling the outside of the boat when the boat made a sharp turn. The speed of the skier was so fast that if the skier fell off his skis, he would be thrust into the water at a very high and dangerous speed. I never went down while the boat was turning, nor was I interested in the results.

Another dangerous part of water skiing was ramps. In Ohio, the use of ramps must have been prohibited, as we never saw one. We still could always dream about this adventure.

Another challenging part of skiing was to ski with more than two people behind a boat. This task was attempted late one summer by Butch, me, and another skier behind Big Butch's boat. Unfortunately, the waters were too rough to ski, and we did not attempt this feat again after one attempt. Skiing is an exciting sport but must be approached with caution and respect.

The Raccoon

During the winter months, Butch and I and sometimes Dick and Rich trapped wildlife for their furs. We had a spot close to Daniel's Corner where trapping was good. We were successful at trapping some muskrat and once in a while a raccoon. We would rise a few hours before school started so we had time to check our traps in the dark.

On one occasion, the night had not been very cold, and the streams were still running where we trapped. We had one spot on our route where two drain tiles came in from opposite directions, and water would run between the two large tiles. We had a few number 2 traps set, and as we checked them, we couldn't find one of them. We turned around and looked behind us. There was the trap and a small portion of a leg leading under the grass and dirt that had grown out and over the sidewall of the ditch. Butch shined his flashlight on the leg and cautiously touched the leg in the trap with his hatchet. A loud animal scream was heard. We sensed it was a raccoon, probably a male or boar looking for a female. It was mating season, and it made sense that the raccoon would be very aggressive. The animal wasn't coming out, and we couldn't see it. Time was of the essence since we needed to be leaving for home so we could dress for school.

Butch said he would put his hunting coat over his hand, have his hatchet in the other hand, and pull out the raccoon so that he or we could subdue the animal. There were no objections to this plan, and we needed to make our move or lose the pelt, which was worth a few bucks.

Butch pulled hard on the foot of the raccoon, and the animal came out roaring, madder than anything I have ever seen. It was trying to get at Butch, and Butch was defending himself by swinging the hatchet at the raccoon. After a few minutes, Butch got the best of the raccoon. It was a fight none of us will forget nor would ever want to be a part of again.

The Lost Watch

On another occasion, we were near the spot where we had previously trapped the raccoon. This time, we were trapping muskrat, and we were checking the many traps we had set in the creek. Butch was resetting the traps and found his watch was touching the water. He asked me to carry the watch so he wouldn't damage it. I put the watch on my wrist but noticed shortly afterward that the watch had vanished from my arm. I had lost it.

We were all unhappy about losing the watch. I told everyone that I would be especially careful that evening when we ran the traps to try to find it. That afternoon, I walked the entire trail but was especially careful around the creek because that is where we took time to stop and inspect the traps.

Shortly after reaching the spot where Butch had given me the watch, I looked in the middle of the creek. To my amazement as well as everybody else's, I reached down into the water where I saw something shiny and pulled up Butch's watch. To me, that was a miracle, and another miracle was the watch still kept perfect time.

Enjoying My Free Time in Boy Scouts

Scouts Fly to Kelleys Island

During the summer of 1960 when I was a junior at Willard High School, I traveled with my fellow post 207 Explorer Scouts to Kelleys Island from Willard Airport. In the picture from left to right, we have pilots Art Heck and Russ Harter, myself, Scoutmaster Bill Schlotterer, and scouts Jim Leitz, Barry Seaholts, and Randy Robinson.[27] Free air transportation was provided by the airport. Rich Buss and Dick Ellis met us on the island.

Flight to Kelleys Island

This was the first flying experience for most of the scouts. While on Kelleys Island, we fished, swam, hiked, and slept in tents. In the evening, large schools of white bass would swim by our campsite. A silvery minnow proved to be the best lure. The fishing was hot and heavy as the school passed by us.

The most memorable experience, not necessarily enjoyable, about the trip was that we unknowingly slept in the middle of a colony of chiggers. Chiggers are small insects that burrow into the skin and cause the skin to swell up into a mound, which will also irritate the skin and cause it to itch. While clear nail polish applied to the source of entry may kill the chiggers by suffocation, it takes a few days to kill them, and one will still have the insects in the skin. Chiggers like warm places like the crevices in the body and any place in which the light of day will not hit it. Yes, this unfortunately included the very private areas. And yes, we endured many uncomfortable experiences with the chiggers for days to come. Other than the chiggers, we had a great time!

Counselor at Firelands Scout Camp

After my junior year at Willard High School, I had the urge to be a member of the staff at the Camp Firelands scout camp near Wakeman, Ohio. I had gone to this camp as a Boy Scout.

My mother took me to the camp as I didn't own a car, and I don't think I would have been able to have a car as a camp counselor. On the way to the camp, we spotted a large snapping turtle on the road. I asked my mom to stop, and she reluctantly did. I thought that this would be an interesting animal to take to summer camp, and I looked for something to contain the turtle until we got to the camp. I discovered that the only container I had was my official Boy Scout backpack. I "encouraged" the turtle to enter the pack with sticks. The turtle was of good size at over twelve inches in diameter. We began to finish our journey to the campgrounds as the turtle tried to free itself from the pack. When we arrived at the camp, I took the turtle over to the nature building where it was later used in their displays.

The first week was the time when we selected the skill area that we wanted to work in at the camp. I looked into several areas, and the dining hall chief had his eyes out for good workers. I was hired for the dining hall before I had a chance to try another area. Working in the kitchen wasn't that bad, as there were a few hours during the morning and afternoon when I had some free time, and I had access to the food.

I had one secret tool I could use if the food was not to my liking: sugar bread sandwiches. Since there was always bread, butter, and sugar on the dining table, I was always sure there would be something I like to eat. I could spread some butter on the bread and sprinkle some sugar on top of the butter and enjoy a meal that was second to none. I lived on sugar bread sandwiches during the better part of my early scout years at Camp Firelands.

I checked on my turtle from time to time at the nature center and found on one occasion that someone had let the turtle out of the pen, and it had escaped.

My final big event at the camp one evening was heavyweight boxing; Ingemar Johansson was fighting for the heavyweight boxing championship. As the starting bell was heard over the radio, I cut a piece of wood out of a necktie holder I was making. The knife I was using was a carving knife that had a blade like a surgeon's scalpel. That knife slipped off the wood and went straight into my right leg, laying open a rather large section of the skin.

I was off to the hospital for stitches, and I, as well as the senior counselor, missed the entire fight except for the opening bell. The doctor also missed part of the fight, but he didn't seem to be interested in it; he was interested in sewing up my leg.

Shortly thereafter, I left the scout camp, as I was needed at the farm. After a few weeks of farming, I knew that it was more challenging than scout camp and felt I had made the right decision to go to the farm.

Philmont Scout Ranch in 1959

In the northern part of New Mexico, there is a very large scout ranch located in the Rocky Mountains called Philmont. The ranch was given to the Boy Scouts of America by Waite Phillips Company owned by Mr. and Mrs. Phillips. While there is a more mountainous region in the ranch, there is also a less mountainous area. Either of the terrains will open up a world of nature and beauty. In 1959, my father was taking a weeklong training session at Philmont to advance his volunteer efforts with the Boy Scouts of America.

The four youngest children traveled with Mom and Dad to New Mexico and reached Taos, New Mexico, the night before my father's training and my hiking tour in Philmont. On that night, we had eaten at a Mexican restaurant. My father had eaten pig hocks, and everyone else had traditional Mexican food. At about three o'clock in the morning, I heard my mother asking my father if he was OK. Since we were all sleeping in adjoining rooms, I went over to my parents' room and asked Mom what had happened. She was in the restroom with my father, and she said, "Something is wrong with Dad because he just fainted and is not very responsive to me." I helped move my father to the bedroom, and he began to feel better. I asked him if he needed to go to the hospital, and he said he was fine. I asked if his heart, hands, or arms felt numb or different. "No" was the answer to all my questions.

The following day, we arrived at Philmont, and I parted ways with my parents as they went to the training area for adults and their families who were not on the trails. I met a number of scouts who were from all over the United States. At less than five feet at the time, I was the shortest as well as the youngest scout on this trip. Our leader was a teacher during the school year. Leading hiking expeditions was a summer job for him.

We were to hike in the northern region, which was also the more mountainous region of Philmont. Due to the mountainous terrain, we were to use mules to carry some of our supplies when we were on the trails. We began our hike, and I quickly understood why we had the mules. The mountains were not very forgiving to any hiker.

At the end of the first day, I took off my hiking boots and felt an uncomfortable pain in my left foot. I couldn't imagine anything being wrong as I had broken in my new hiking boots for many weeks before this adventure. I pulled off my sock and saw a blister on the back of my right foot about the size of a half dollar. This blister hurt and was threatening to send me back to the base camp and end my experience at Philmont on the first day. I went to our leader and showed him my blister. He said that blisters were not uncommon in this rough terrain, and he would be happy to fix it. He cut off the loose skin and poured Merthiolate (thimerosal) on the blister. Initially, I went through the sky from the pain, but after the initial shock, the blister gave me little pain, and I had no trouble walking on it the rest of the trip.

The mules were great on the trail, but every morning at the break of dawn, they were up heeing, hawing, and making sure everyone was up and ready. The country was beautiful and the hiking very challenging. Whenever I was having a rough time hiking, I would grab on to the straps holding the supplies on the mule and allow the mule to give me a little break as we climbed the mountains.

It would not be unusual for us to eat breakfast, hike most of the morning, have a quick lunch, hike in the afternoon, and stop for our evening meal. The evening meal was prepared by the scouts except for the final night. On the final night, our leader cooked in the Dutch ovens the best pizza I had ever had.

While bears were on the grounds, our group never saw them. Mule deer, which are deer with very long ears, were abundant at Philmont.

A pleasant trip back to Ohio provided the family with the most enjoyable experience. We all knew that Dad needed to visit the doctor when he returned to Willard. Our doctor felt that the ham hocks may have been the culprit in Dad's fainting episode.

Philmont Scout Ranch, 1961

My second trip to Philmont Scout Ranch was before the beginning of my senior year. Two of my friends, Larry Ayers and John Gibson, also went on the trip. The trip was organized by the Firelands council, and scouts from this district were able to participate in the two-week expedition.

We left from Sandusky, for Philmont in the middle of the summer for two weeks. We traveled via Greyhound Lines all the way to New Mexico. The seats in the bus were not very comfortable, even though they did have a button to push so the back of the seat could move back and down. One of the buttons controlling the movement of the back of the seat was stuck, so one of the Scouts held in the button and moved the seat back and forth manually. This proved to be a bad move as the back of the seat would now not hold in any position so no one could comfortably sit in the seat for the rest of the trip.

When we reached Philmont, I expected we would have mules to carry our supplies as on my previous trip. I found mules were not used in hiking in the southern part of Philmont. The terrain was not as challenging. That was a disappointment to me because carrying all our supplies was now a necessity. We were told to be on the lookout for poisonous snakes while on the trail. On both trips, I never heard or saw a poisonous snake.

Several leaders from the Firelands district also were on the trails with the Scouts. At one point, one of the men was complaining about pains in his chest. He decided that it was not worth it to become sick on the trails, and he went back to the base camp and waited for us to finish the hike.

One evening, we were very close to a stream with rainbow trout. I had learned how to tie or make flies back at the base camp. I also knew from my previous visit that I could find a stick for a fishing pole, but I would need some eyelets to screw into the pole to hold the fishing line and a fishing reel and line used for fly fishing. I had all the necessary items for a fishing pole, so I hooked up the rod and reel, and I hiked up the mountains to find the trout stream.

I began to fish using the method I had learned at base camp of not letting the fish see me by fishing behind a hill a short distance from the stream. While it was difficult not seeing the stream, I had seen the success of this methodology. My efforts paid off, as I caught three rainbow trout of nice size.

I traveled back to camp, cleaned the trout, and put some twigs across the top of my mess kit frying pan to keep the fish from touching the pan. The fish were slowly cooked over the fire, and they were the best fish I have ever eaten in my life.

After our stay at Philmont, we were on the Greyhound bus on our way back to Sandusky. What a privilege to have two chances to hike the hills and mountains of Philmont.

An Eagle Scout

I had always been told that being an Eagle Scout is the highest honor a Boy Scout can attain. I had been working on advancing in rank in the Boy Scouts for years, but I was stuck on my first-class badge. I could not pass the challenge of the signaling requirement.

I went to my father and told him what a challenge this requirement was for me and several other boys. As usual, my father addressed the situation in a positive manner and said that he would work with some other fathers, and the signaling requirement would be accomplished.

My father was no stranger to the scouting program, as he had been involved in Girl, Cub, and Boy Scouts for many years. I thought if anyone could make this happen, it was my father.

Within a few days, my father and other men in St. Francis Xavier Church met and decided to help with advancement. It took at least three talented and experienced adult leaders to make it happen. John Leitz, Len Playko, and my dad worked hard to find a way so that the signaling requirement could be passed by any scout willing to take the time and effort.

They came up with a plan of methodologically approaching signaling, and all the scouts in troop 207 passed. It wasn't easy, but it demonstrated to me that with the right people and hard work, a task usually can be accomplished.

I always admired my dad and the other leaders for how they addressed issues and how Dad and other people worked together to solve a challenge.

I used this participatory management approach with people in addressing my future administrative positions.

While other scouts advanced in rank while working on the Eagle Scout requirements, I was the only troop member to attain this goal at this time.

When I was in need of passing twenty-one merit badges, many of those being required, I went to knowledgeable people in these areas to ask for their help as counselors. To my amazement, all those people, who were very busy themselves, volunteered to be counselors and worked with me to earn those merit badges.

For example, my doctor's daughter, Roberta Kauffman, helped me attain the swimming and lifesaving merit badges. My gym teacher, Herb Hart, who was also the head varsity basketball coach at Willard High School, was the counselor for me on the personal fitness merit badge. My father worked with me on the citizenship merit badges. I learned a big lesson from this experience, and it was that I will never know what people are willing to do for me unless I ask them. People were more than happy to be a part of my life and to make that award a reality.

My Eagle Scout board of review was conducted in Norwalk, at the old Huron County Health Department building by a respected Boy Scout leader. I remember being very concerned about passing the board of review because failure would affect me and many other people. In particular, my father would be affected, as he had done so much to make sure many Boy Scouts could advance in rank.

I have always felt indebted to all of the adult leaders and persons who had helped me with the merit badges, especially all the past scoutmasters. It is said that repaying one's Boy Scout leaders for their time is done by volunteering time to Boy Scouts in your future. I was very relieved to find out that I did pass the board of review and a court of awards was scheduled in 1961, my senior year at Willard High School. It had been eighteen years since anyone had received the Eagle Scout Award in Willard.

There were many people present at the Eagle Scouts awarding ceremony. The ceremony was held at Madonna Hall, located behind the St. Francis Church. I was very surprised to see a packed house. It was a humbling experience to realize so many people would take an evening of their time to honor my accomplishments. I can still picture all my merit badge counselors, family, neighbors, and community members being present for the ceremony.

I was equally surprised to see a large picture of me and a long article on my reception of the award on the front page of the next edition of the *Willard Times*.

It was not until after the ceremony that I started to realize how important this Eagle Scout thing was. Dealing with this recognition in a humble manner was an important item on my agenda.

That award was a great example of the individuals in this book, *People + Me*. The Eagle Scout Award I received was not exclusively my award; it was for everyone who had helped me attain the award, including my fellow Boy Scouts.

At the time, it was relayed to me that becoming an Eagle Scout carried with it the responsibility of being a positive role model for other boys and the community. Also, I was told that being an Eagle Scout is something that will always be with me, and I will be known for this accomplishment the rest of my life.

I did always list that I was an Eagle Scout on my resumes. I usually received the positions for which I applied for whatever reasons. It was one of my accomplishments that I was to be very proud of for the rest of my life.

I would like to think that I was a good model, not a perfect one, for others who came in contact with me.

I am sure everyone involved, including God and probably my twin, shared in the congratulations I received in achieving this rank.

Memorable Events in High School

Fox Hunting

Fox hunting has a definite relationship to rabbit hunting. If there are too many foxes, there will be too few rabbits to hunt. Fox dearly love to prey on rabbits.

Rabbit hunting was not allowed on Sunday even when the rabbit season was in full force. What was allowed on Sunday was fox hunting, which was organized by some of the local farmers.

I probably learned more about fox hunting from my friend Lenny than anyone. Like me, Lenny was an avid hunter. The hunt was done in a certain way so that the chances of harming other hunters while bagging a fox would be eliminated.

The hunt would commence with all hunters meeting at a designated spot.

Next, the pickup trucks would take everyone to their appointed position. A line of stationary shooters would be placed at one end of the block. At the other three sides of the block would be drivers. The drivers opposite the stationary line would move directly toward the stationary line yelling and making noise so that any fox that was in the block would run toward the stationary line. To prevent the fox from running out of the sides of the block, additional stationary drivers would be placed on both sides, and they would join in the main moving line where the two meet.

Hunters would be placed on all lines. When a fox was sighted, the person seeing the fox first would yell out, "Fox!" This would tell the rest of the hunters, usually thirty to forty hunters, where the fox was located. Hunters close to the fox would try to shoot it if they could, or if they were too far away for a good shot and if it looked like the fox was going to get through the line, the hunter would turn the fox into the line by shooting at it.

On one occasion, I was one of the side stationary drivers waiting for the pushing line to come by me. On this particular day, we were shy on hunters, so everyone needed to cover more ground. This meant that there were larger openings in the line for the fox to leave the block. I saw a fox going between me and the next hunter, and it looked like it knew how to get out of this mess.

When the fox got close, but not close enough to bag, I shot a few volleys of buckshot. The fox turned toward the stationary line, and it was bagged a short time later. After all the hunters had cleared the block, a new block was hunted.

A block was a section of land with roads usually on four sides of it. A block could be several hundred acres of land. Landowners were asked ahead of time if the hunters could go on their land. Each hunter had a hunting license and could shoot fox on Sunday.

At the end of the hunting year, a big party was thrown by the hunters. The hides of the fox were sold, and refreshments and food were provided with these funds.

A big feature of the fox hunting party was the pigeon shoot. Members of the fox hunt would go to area barns at night and catch pigeons to be used in the shoot. Farmers were very happy to have someone take away the pigeons, as their main contribution to the farmer was defecating on his beams, his equipment, his floor, his vehicles, and even his house. The pigeons one by one were thrown into the air, and as they were thrown up, they would try to fly away. Any unlucky pigeon was cleaned, and the meat was prepared for the evening meal.

Almost a Fox

One winter day when I was working on the farm, I had some free time and decided to go rabbit hunting.

I dressed warmly and put on a plastic raincoat, as it was drizzling. I thought I would hunt in the woods behind Fred and Mary Lu's house. While it was a long walk through the fields to reach the woods, I thought it was worth the trouble. Some brush had been cleared in those woods, so there were piles of brush. That was fine with me because rabbits stay in a protected area, such as the brush piles. I had gone to three or four brush piles and was headed to the next one when everything in the woods went quiet.

I looked around carefully and saw nothing. I looked closer and saw something moving on the other side of the brush pile. I was standing close to a fox unaware of my presence. I felt like I was paralyzed; I wasn't able to shoot the fox.

Just as I thought I wouldn't be able to move, my fingers and arm loosened up, and I slowly raised the gun to my shoulder. I released the safety, had the fox in my sight, and pulled the trigger. I heard a click but no shot. The fox looked directly at me and quickly ran in the other direction.

The shell I had put into the gun was old and had malfunctioned. The primer that ignites the powder in the shell did not function. I had to wait a few seconds before I took out the old shell to make sure the shell didn't have a delayed reaction and blew up in my face. I placed a new shell in the chamber. By the time I was able to put another shell in the chamber, the fox was gone.

This was probably the only time in my life I had a good chance to shoot a fox, and the shell misfired.

Such is life; we win some, and we lose some. I just lost one.

At least I do have a good hunting story.

The Race

One afternoon after catechism, we decided to have a car race. My adversary, Bob Schodorf, was a fellow classmate.

We went east of Willard to a less traveled road. My friend got the jump on me as the race started. We were racing along at a good pace with his car being a little ahead of my parents' 1956 Ford Fairlane. As I began to gain on my friend's car, I noticed that the passengers in the other car were waving their hands about something as we passed them.

I looked ahead and saw two hills, one on each side of the road that blocked the view of traffic both ways on the railroad. It was too late to stop, so I crossed the railroad tracks.

As I looked through my rearview mirror, I saw a small utility cart cross the road on the tracks behind me. Then I knew why the passengers in the other car had been waving their hands at us. Everyone in my car was lucky to be alive. I learned that I should be more attentive to other people's actions.

I don't remember doing much car racing after that close call.

Horses Are Other People's Best Friends

After band practice, it was a common practice for girls and guys to socialize.

On one fall evening during my junior year in high school, I had access to my brother's white 1959 Chevy Impala convertible. One of my friends called this car a "chick magnet." I asked a group of lovely young ladies if they wanted to cruise the Main Street in my brother's convertible. I had no trouble filling the car on this beautiful warm fall night.

We buzzed Myrtle Avenue a few times, and then I thought it would be a nice evening to show the girls how really great it was to have the wind fly through your hair in the country. We went out to Tiffin Street, a main street in town, and drove past the Pioneer Rubber Company where my dad worked and past the Pullman Lanes and Club, a bowling alley and nightclub. None of us was old enough to go into the club, so we proceeded to the next corner, which is known as Vance's Corner.

As we went up the hill to turn right, I noticed that there was a bright light in the ditch on the left and a man and a horse. It became clear as we pulled closer that there had been an accident, and the horse had been hit in its side. The farmer was trying to replace the intestines of the horse back into its body. Evidently, a car hit the horse and left a large gaping hole in its side. Some of the intestines had fallen out.

That sight caused everyone in the car to question our ability to remain well. The farmer had the situation well under control, and it was time to take the ladies home. I felt a little better having all the girls with me instead of one because the sight of the horse would not have produced a good setting for any type of romance that evening.

An Embarrassing Date

My brother Walt and I double dated only a few times in our lives. We decided to have a boating date on Lake Erie.

We both asked beautiful young dark haired ladies from neighboring towns to double date. We picked up our dates and proceeded to my dad's boat docked near Lake Erie at Bay Bridge. The day looked promising, and I was happy that the weather was sunny.

Dad had a sixteen-foot fiberglass boat powered by a sixty horsepower Mercury outboard engine. On more than one occasion, the motor just wouldn't start. Expecting a similar hard start, I held my breath as I hand primed the motor. Walt turned over the motor, and with his good luck and mechanical abilities, the motor started. I was not surprised, but happy, that it started promptly.

We headed out to the lake enjoying a beautiful summer day as we headed for the Marblehead Lighthouse.

As we came close to the lighthouse, we knew that we were getting close to our destination, Johnson's Island. This plot of land was a prison for Confederate soldiers during the Civil War. At this time, the island was a little more than the site of many old Confederate tombstones.

We quickly anchored off the shore of the small island so the boat wouldn't be destroyed on the rocky shore. The wind was picking up, and the sun had disappeared. All of us had our bathing suits on, but the girls decided to stay on the boat as Walt and I swam to shore. After a quick survey of the desolate island and a brief look at some of the tombstones, we decided to get back to the boat, as it was beginning to rain, and the wind and waves were escalating.

After boarding the boat, Walt and I attached the top canopy so that we were protected from the rain and wind. We had a small window in the canopy located in front of the water well and the motor. I opened the window and reached into the well for the hand pump on the fuel line to prime the motor with gasoline.

As I was pumping the line, I saw the rain coming down faster than cats and dogs, and I observed that the anchor wasn't holding. We were headed with the waves into the rocky shore. I grabbed the anchor and began to pull it in as I yelled to my brother to start the motor. At this time, I was standing outside the canopy in the space created by the open window in the boat cover. I pulled the anchor out of the water and saw that the boat was dangerously close to the shore. I told Walt, "Get us out of here."

As Walt began to inch forward in the water, he was looking for large rocks. Walt did well avoiding rocks until we were about halfway from the rocks to the open lake. A huge wind came up with a large wave appearing out of nowhere. As the boat went into the swell after the high point of the wave, the prop hit a rock. Luckily, the hit was not enough to make the prop inoperable. We left the island, and then we were in the lake.

Walt decided to stay as close to the shore as he could to avoid the waves of the lake. Lake Erie is the shallowest of all the great lakes. Depths are normally in the twenty or thirty feet-range. Due to the shallowness of Lake Erie, the water produces large waves. These waves are very high and dangerous, and they were pushing our boat around like a bobber. The day of boating had turned into an extremely serious and dangerous experience.

Walt and I had been on the lake when there were storms. Having dates on the boat made it more serious, and we saw this concern in the eyes of our dates. We assured the girls that we had experience with these types of storms, and we felt we were able to safely get all of us back to the dock.

After the assurances to the girls, in the middle of the storm, I developed a case of seasickness, and I could feel in my body that I was about to lose my breakfast on the occupants of the boat as well as the interior of the boat. I was beginning to panic, as I was becoming even sicker.

In desperation, I quickly made my way to the back of the boat, the only place on board that allowed me some freedom from the inside of the boat. I raised my body through the now open back window and stood up straight seeing the waves and the lightning and hearing the thunder. As I held on to the motor and the steering mechanism of the boat located in the water well, I hung my head over the back of the boat and "lost my cookies."

The wind and waves were so noisy that I was sure nobody in the boat had a clue that I was ill. I pulled myself completely out of the covered part of the boat into the water well onto my knees and zipped down the window so that nobody could see me.

After vomiting, I was having a bladder attack. With great effort, I relieved my bladder despite the wind and rain. I was lucky to hold myself in the well by holding on to the motor. By this time, I was completely drenched. I had to get inside the main part of the boat, or I was sure to be thrown into the water.

I began feeling better for several reasons. I zipped open the left side of the back window on the canopy and carefully moved myself to the safety of the inside of the boat. I had taken a nice natural shower in the rain.

My brother asked what I was doing, and I said, "Fixing something."

As I was sitting down in the boat, my brother noticed that in the activities surrounding the relieving of my bladder, I had not followed through on one matter, zipping up my bathing suit.

There had been just a few chances for the occupants of the boat to see that my zipper was down. I will never know if either of the girls noticed.

As we were about halfway back to the boat dock, the sun came out, and we all decided that the water was now our friend. A few dives into the lake were refreshing and reassuring to all that it had indeed been a stimulating experience for the most part. At least we had all come out of the storm with no major injuries.

My brother and I did not make double dating a high priority after this experience; maybe each of us thought the other was bad luck.

---

27   Times Photo, "Explorers Become Air Minded for Fast Trip to Lake Camp Site," *The Willard Times*, date unknown in summer of 1960.

Chapter 9

My High School Neighbors, Community Activities, Family, and Work

During high school, much of my time was spent with neighbors, community, family, and work. A large portion of the day during my teenage years was spent outside my home. That is usually the way I feel that most people's teenage years were spent.

"Big Butch" and Mildred

Our Good Neighbors

Mildred, Big Butch, Butch, and Debbie were close neighbors to the Frederick family. Mildred was a nurse who frequently administered medical assistance to everyone in need and did so in her kitchen. If we had a cut or sore throat, she would administer first aid. If it needed more attention, she would say, "I think you had better go to the doctor or the hospital." Mildred had worked in the local hospital for years and knew medicine. She was an inquisitive person and formed her ideas on many subjects from the facts she acquired. She also was a very compassionate person and like a second mother to me.

Her husband was a person of many skills. He was a carpenter, plumber, electrician, mason, and painter, and he could do just about everything you expected a tradesman to do. He was a very direct person, and thus, you always knew where you stood with him.

Big Butch and Mildred had a large homemade wooden boat that they constantly used during the summer and autumn to fish, ski, and cruise. I waited every weekend to be invited by Big Butch and Mildred to go fishing with them in Lake Erie. Fishing has always been one of my favorite pastimes.

Rescuing Three Fishermen

It was on one such an occasion in the autumn of 1961 when I was in my senior year at Willard High School that I was asked if I wanted to go perch fishing. Perch is a small fish with vertical stripes on either silver or yellow bodies. Yellow perch are usually larger than silver perch, and they seem to be available more in the fall than any other time of the year, especially using silver minnows as bait. In those days, it wasn't uncommon to catch 100 to 200 perch or more in one outing. Perch are said to be the best-eating fish in Lake Erie or other bodies of water.

On this day, Big Butch, Mildred, Debbie, and I had been fishing for several hours. The ice chest was full of perch when Mildred said, "I have been watching that boat over there"—she pointed to a boat—"and something is not right." Big Butch had the best vantage point to see the boat in question since he would always fish by the steering wheel, and he was facing the front of the boat where the mysterious boat was located.

Butch said, "Bring in your lines." All lines and the anchor were pulled in, and we started to go toward the boat in question. It was a rather brisk fall day. The water was getting cold, as summer was over, and the colder weather was arriving. As we approached the boat, we could see that there were three men in it, which was almost completely underwater. The boat could take on maybe one more inch of water before it sank. Big Butch and Mildred told me that since Big Butch had recently had an operation, I would have to do all the heavy work. One look at the three men convinced me they were afraid but a little more relieved since we showed up. There were no other boats near them.

The first thing I did was to secure a rope from our boat to their boat. As I did it, I could see that they had caught a fishing net in their boat's propeller, and it had begun to pull the boat into the water. I asked who wanted to come aboard first. The man driving the boat said he was very weak and had just had an operation and needed to get out of the cold water. With the help of Mildred and Debbie, I carefully pulled the first person onboard. We then helped the second and third persons to board. We asked them where they were from and how long they has been in the water. They said they were from Crystal Rock, a small community a few miles from our present location. They had been in the water long enough to be very cold. Lake Erie is not the warmest body of water in the late autumn.

I retied the small boat to our much larger boat, and as we pulled the boat, much of the water was drained out of it. We helped each of the fishermen out of our boat to shore and tied their boat to the dock. Several people onshore were helping the men too.

There was a large article about the rescue in a local paper. Until her dying day, Mildred was very upset with a public official in Willard because he would not recommend me for a national award from the Boy Scouts of America.

I didn't think I did that much and was much happier to see my son Joe II receive a National Medal of Merit from the Boy Scouts of America years later for saving a young boy's life at Middle Bass Island while we were on vacation.

In August of 2009, the story about the rescue of the three men from Crystal Rock was run in a review section of two local papers. I was informed of this fact by relatives Jim Ruffing of Berlin Heights, Ohio, and George Schlotterer of Centerville, Ohio. Strangely enough, neither of the cousins had been aware of the incident, and both were checking to make sure that I was the right Joe Frederick in the article.

St. Francis Xavier Church

The Catholic Church was extremely important in my life, and its influence has been, is, and will always be strong as long as I live.

Easter Weekend 1961

Easter week is important for members of the Roman Catholic Church. Our parish was St. Francis Xavier, and we were at Easter services and a Mass longer than usual. High Masses and the several blessings and other rituals are well-known to Catholics.

Altar boys (yes, I was one) occupied a unique position in the church. We were physically closer to the priest at the altar than any other members of the congregation, as we prayed, stood, and knelt near the altar.

Altar boys, if properly positioned, would have the best view of the congregation since they were frequently on a raised platform. To an outsider, altar boys assisting the priest must have looked saintly. Behind the scenes, altar boys were not always perfect, nor did they claim to be. There are stories where altar boys strayed from the straight and narrow and could be considered an embarrassment. Such is the next story.

It was the Saturday night Mass before Easter Sunday that provided the reason for my attendance at church. Five boys and I had been chosen to be the altar boys for this special occasion. As four altar boys and I were putting on our black garments called cassocks, the remark was made that Lenny Playko was late. The conversation rapidly degenerated into playing a trick on Lenny.

His fate was quickly set. The growing accusation was that he was late for serving once again, and there were only a few minutes left before services would start. The plot thickened as it was decided that we would take Lenny's cassock, a black long robe that looked like a graduation gown, and put it over his head and body as he entered the sacristy to get his attention about being on time. We felt that this act would definitely scare him into having a more compliant behavior. The other purpose of this prank was to show Lenny that others were capable of playing tricks on him.

We had to move fast because Lenny was coming in or may have already come in the church. Services were starting soon, and we had little time to execute this plan. We were all snickering as we passed from our dressing room on the other side of the church to behind the altar and into the sacristy where the priest dressed. We were all experienced altar boys and knew well most of the nooks and crannies in this room. A few doors were locked, and we did not know what was in the locked doors. We picked out the best position to nab Lenny. We had turned the light off, and we all assumed our assigned positions. Some were to cover Lenny with his cassock while others were to grab his feet so the cassock could be perfectly secured on his body. One person was to turn on the light after Lenny was completely subdued. It was a great plan; it could not fail, and every altar boy present was extremely proud of this surefire "teach Lenny a lesson" approach.

We had just gotten in place and turned the light off when the outer door opened and shut. We heard a hand placed on the entrance door to the sacristy. We heard the hand turn the doorknob. My heart was beating louder that a bass drum, and I felt the perspiration on my forehead. As a person entered the dark room, the cassock was masterfully placed over his head while the rest of the altar boys secured his feet and body. We heard the victim yell, "Here, here!" Everyone froze as they realized that this was not Lenny's voice. It was the voice of an old man. Lenny was not under the cassock. We turned on the lights to experience one of the worst nightmares of our lives. We had "jumped" Father John, our parish priest.

At that exact moment, Lenny walked in the door and asked, "What is going on here?"

God could not have vanished from the room any faster than the four other altar boys and I did.

Our priest never mentioned the attack. We felt it best to follow his lead.

The sad truth about this story is that Lenny's payback must wait for another day. Lenny had somehow turned the tables on the involved servers, and in my mind, I wasn't very confident that we could ever "get Lenny."

Happenings as a Server

Being a server was a "before the congregation" and a "behind the scenes" position. Since servers are in front of their parents, relatives, friends, and the congregation for many of their duties, there is a good deal of pressure to do it right. When lighting the candles, it was possible that one of them could just go out a short time after it was lit. A final check after all the candles were lit was necessary. The consequence of seeing an unlit candle upon entering the altar area at the start of the service would be embarrassing for the responsible server. Muted laughter from the servers' side of the altar before the service began signaled that something was going on "behind the scenes."

The older churches had a communion rail that divided the congregation from the altar area. In the St. Francis Xavier Church on Spring Street there was a long cloth that hung on the inside of the communion rail and was held by metal clips. When it was communion time, two servers, one on the right and one on the left, would go to the communion rail and place the cloth from the inside dangling position to a position in which the cloth was laid on and over the communion rail to the congregation side of the rail. The challenge made by several servers was to flip the communion cloth and have the entire cloth go over the altar rail. It would take an accomplished server to get it right the first time. Flipping too hard could cause the cloth to pull loose from the metal clips holding the cloth to the rail. If one were to flip the cloth not hard enough, only a portion of the cloth would flip to the communion rail, forcing the server to walk down the line and flip up the rest of the cloth. It was usually elder servers, ones with practice, who could successfully flip the cloth with one movement of the hand and arm.

Another area of expertise for a server was being able to light the candles on the altar. The first step to successful lighting was to make sure the wick in the candle lighter was long enough and properly bent. A straight candle wick on the candle lighter was sure trouble. It wouldn't allow the lighter to ignite the candle, as the angle was not right. There was a round metal ring found on the top of the candle, which contained the melted wax. In lighting the wick with the candle lighter, it was important to have the wick out a little over an inch and bent down so it would light the candle surrounded by the metal ring.

If one had the wick in the candle lighter out, say, two inches while lighting the candle, it could very likely flame up and light the entire section of the wick. This occurrence is very embarrassing because the server could be forced to pull the wick back into the wick holder, which would extinguish the fire on the wick. The server would then need to go back to the servers' quarters for a new flame if no candles were lit on the altar.

The lightning of the candles could be rather complicated and trying because, at times, the wick on the candles can break. A broken wick requires removing the large candle and holder from the altar. This was a rare and difficult task to accomplish, especially with the congregation watching your every move.

Work

I had several summer jobs from painting my parents' house to working on my brother-in-law's farm. Most of these jobs were physical in nature and were usually outside, many times in the hot sun.

In two winters, my sophomore and senior years, I worked before and after school milking the cows on the farm.

This is a closer look at the jobs before my freshman year through my high school years.

My Motivation to Work

Before we look at the jobs during this time frame, it is important to address what motivates me to work. While this analysis could apply to all phases of my life, I have chosen to address it now. There are many possible reasons I am motivated to work. Money is a big motivator, as it can be a satisfier, and it provides a sense of accomplishment.

There are other possible reasons I am motivated to work. We have analyzed the fact that although I did not always consciously remember thinking that my twin was a force at the time of my actions, as I think back to these challenging jobs, my commitment to do better and be better may have been a factor. On the other hand, it may also have been the examples of my hard-working parents that I was modeling.

Another motivator in my life is God, as He controls the entrance to heaven. I believe in the mystery that there are three persons in one God: there is the Father, the Son, and the Holy Spirit. I usually pray to God the Father. There is logic in linking God to everything in my life, as I believe He created the world and all that happens in the world. God gave me life and skills to work. I believe I must use, not misuse, my work skills. I owe it to myself, the world, and God to positively use them.

As I grow older, I understand and appreciate more the world God has given us and the fact that He is always with me helping me in my work. I keep in contact with God by praying. One component of prayer is asking God to help me in my work and thanking God for everything He has given me.

While I do not pray as often as I would desire, I continue to improve in this area. I owe it to God to do His will and work. I believe one manner that God calls on me is to read the teachings of the Bible. Meditating on and following the Bible is essential to my life in preparation for the next world after death. Developing my relationship with God in this world is an ongoing process necessary for the greatest of all motivators, being with God in the next life.

Sealing the Fence

One summer, my father informed me that he had purchased supplies for me to seal the fence that surrounded our backyard. As I looked at the fence, I was overwhelmed at the amount of fencing that needed my attention. The time that I would need to complete this job seemed to be endless.

As I began the project on the first day, I noticed that the sealant was very thick. I completed the first section, and it took the whole gallon. I was done in the middle of the morning because I had run out of sealant.

When Dad came home that evening, he quickly decided that we needed to dilute the sealant. He purchased enough supplies to finish the whole fence. As I proceeded brushing on the sealant, I noticed that the weeds were getting in my way. I had to add the job of pulling out the weeds and brushing around the flowers. I finished the fence in less than two weeks and was glad to get out of the sun and away from the sticky sealant. I received whatever energy was needed to complete the project, and the project went as smoothly as could be expected.

Painting the House

Our house was a two-story white wooden home. It was very large and even had a dormer on the third story. Dad must have liked the job I had done on the fence because he asked me to paint the house. This project unlike the fence project required painting on several levels. In order to paint the higher portion of the house, ladders were used at times, and a scaffold structure secured to the house was used to paint the higher sections.

Since the higher levels of the house were to be painted first, I had to learn how to avoid dripping paint on the concrete below and on the ledges, which were covered by shingles.

One wrong step on the boards while painting the second floor could mean that I would fall on grass at the best and at the worst concrete. I was lucky enough not to fall on either surface mainly due to the fact that I learned how to move slowly and cautiously on the boards. Safety was a constant learning factor and one that would help me in many jobs in the future.

Painting windows proved to be another challenge as some of the caulking was deteriorated and needed to be replaced and then primed before the final coat. Completing this job at a fast pace was not a likely prospect. Trying to paint the dormer on top of the house was another challenging job, as it was very high, the windows all needed to be caulked, and the ladder barely reached the dormer.

It took several weeks to paint the house, and in the end, everybody in the family was happy with the result. No member of the family was happier than I was to finally experience the completion of this massive accomplishment.

The Farm

The First Day on the Farm

I remember the first day on the farm as if it were yesterday. My brother-in-law Fred Eldred had told my parents that he was in need of a farmhand on his parents' farm and wanted to know if I was interested. I had the summer off and wasn't particularly busy around the house. I was flattered that someone would want me to work for them. It was agreed that I would work on the farm.

On my first day of work, Mom gave me a five-mile ride out to the farm. We stopped about a mile from the Section Line Road on Boughton Road or what is now Old Military Road. I was to help clear the woods located next to the creek that went through Fred's parents' property. Their names were Rose and Russel Eldred.

I walked into the field and was ready to work. Russel told me that I could load up the small trees that had been cut down. He told me to be careful, as the trees have thorns. I began to load the small trees on the wagon and thought that this isn't too hard of a job. As I was feeling pretty confident in my ability to work, I felt a pain in my foot. The pain was extreme, and I yelled for help. Rosie came over the fastest and asked what happened. I said, "I must have stepped on something." She looked at the bottom of my tennis shoes and said, "You sure did step on something. I can see the broken end of a thorn from one of the trees." Since we had nothing to use to pull out the thorn, I loosened my shoelace and began to pull my foot out of my shoe. The thorn was in the front of the shoe and was holding my lodged foot in the shoe. After more pain, my foot finally came out of the shoe. Looking into the shoe, I could see a two-inch thorn sticking up in the bottom of my shoe.

We cleaned out the wound and patched it up, and I was back to work. I have been more than careful when working around thorn trees after this incident. I didn't run into any problems clearing the rest of the woods. I also bought some work shoes, as my tennis shoes couldn't protect me from the thorns. My choice of shoes became more important then and now.

Driving the Tractor

Learning to drive the tractor was pretty easy for me. I had the ability to make the steering wheel do what I wished. There were several tractors used for various jobs on the farm.

There was an old Silver King, which had one tire in the front of the tractor and of course two tires in the rear or beside the driver. The Silver King was by far the fastest tractor on the farm. It was used for working up the ground and pulling wagons on the road. The only fear I had while driving the Silver King was that when it was newer, the metal piece that held the front tire on the tractor broke and was repaired. I always had a fear when I put the tractor in high gear that the tire would break off again, and as the front end was jammed into the road, the end result would be that I would be catapulted over the tractor and into the road ahead. Thank God that fear was never fulfilled.

The next tractor I remember driving was the Allis-Chalmers. This tractor was used for plowing and working ground. It was one of the more powerful tractors and was very reliable.

There was a second Allis-Chalmers called a WD45. This tractor had the same qualities as the regular Allis-Chalmers plus a hand clutch. This unusual accessory when pushed forward stopped the motion of the tractor and when pulled back placed the gear into active drive. Sometimes the clutch would easily work, and at other times it would lunge forward. The advantage of the hand clutch was that if you wished to stop the tractor without pushing in the clutch, you just have to merely push the hand clutch forward, and the tractor would stop. No foot clutch or foot brake is necessary if the hand clutch is used. The hand clutch is especially useful when one is bailing because it can be pushed in to go over a ditch, and one can creep over the ditch rather than jerk the tractor and the baler over the ditch. A hand clutch allows the tractor to stop while the PTO (power take-off) and the baler keeps on running.

The hand clutch was also nifty in hitching the tractor to various pieces of equipment. Some pieces were very forgiving when it came to hitching up to them, such as the hay wagon's tongue that could be moved a few feet so the tongue of the hay wagon and the hitch on the tractor could match up perfectly. The task of hooking up large stationary equipment was much more difficult. Larger pieces of equipment had little variance when being hooked up; their position was stable.

The cultipacker, a round piece of equipment that breaks up clods, weighed several hundred pounds. The tractor hitch and the tongue on the cultipacker needed to meet exactly. The hand clutch allowed me to move the tractor easier than the foot clutch in hitching up to the cultipacker. Even with the hand clutch, it could be very difficult to hook up a piece of equipment by myself in the middle of a hot field. For example, backing up to a piece of heavy equipment by myself meant I had to guess where the tongue would be when I picked it up to attach it to the tractor. Any unusual movement such as getting on or off the tractor could cause me to go into a heavy sweat, so it was always the goal to move slowly and not often when working in hot, humid weather.

The last tractor, which was also my favorite, was the Ford tractor. The Ford tractor was a tractor that sat lowest to the ground, was peppy, and could plow or plant. The Ford tractor was used to run equipment such as a rotor hoe (a round disk with spikes), to break up hard ground after a rain, or to pull or push wagons loaded with straw, hay, or grain. A nice feature of the Ford tractor was that it was easy to stop. If I would be coming down the road and wished to stop, all I needed to do is shut down the hand accelerator and push hard on the brake.

On one occasion, I found that stopping required a certain amount of timing. I was coming down the road leading to the farmhouse for lunch when I had slowed down the hand speed control, and I slammed on the brake. The tractor stopped, but it was about a foot too late after the tires lost their footing on the stones. I had traveled through Fred's garage door breaking it in two. This was to be seen as a bad move on my part.

A Day on the Farm

To appreciate the flavor of working on the farm, a look at an average day would provide a good overview of farming.

Our day would start at around 6:00 a.m. with milking cows. Before we could milk, we needed to bring the cows in from the pasture to the barn and to ready the milking equipment. Initially, milking was done by hand, so the udders, buckets, strainer, and milk cans need to be cleaned and sterilized. After milking and placing the milk in a cooling area, all the equipment again was sterilized, and the cows were returned to the pasture.

After a breakfast of a drink, eggs, meat, potatoes, and toast, we would go out to the fields to drive the tractor, to ready the ground to be fit for planting, or to do whatever else needed to be done.

Later in the summer, other activities were rotor hoeing beans or possibly bailing straw or hay.

Usually there was one water break in the middle of the morning. The water break was one of the highlights of the day after working for two to three hours. When I saw the car or a truck coming down the road, I knew that I was going to have a cool drink of water and a bottle of pop. That drink was like a message from heaven saying you have worked hard and well that morning.

At noon, it was time for lunch. Once again, meat, potatoes, vegetables, drinks, and dessert were the order of the day. Since Rosie was the cook, or sometimes my sister Mary Lu, I knew that I was having some of the best food possible.

In the afternoon, there was more work on the tractor and another cool drink. I would finish the work in the field, milk the cows, and eat supper at six.

While breakfast and lunch was taken with Rose and Russel Eldred, my brother-in-law Fred's parents, supper was usually with my sister Mary Lu and Fred. Similar to the two previous meals, a full dinner of meat and potatoes and all the side dishes was presented.

After supper, I would work if needed, especially during planting season. If there was time, Fred would join me for an evening of shooting varmints, such as rats and birds.

There is no doubt in my mind that my basic knowledge of work came largely from my farm days.

Unloading Barley

Barley is a grain that looks like oats, only it has a longer beard. One hot summer day in one of the first days I worked on the farm, I was informed we were going to unload barley into the granary in the barn. I didn't think much about this process until I climbed into the bed of the truck to shovel out the barley. As I planted my feet on the grain, they immediately sank out of sight. I had an abundance of grain in my boots, which made it uncomfortable to walk. Immediately I discovered the itching caused by the beard of the barley touching the skin on my lower legs and ankles. Itching and shoveling are compatible because the more one shovels, the more grain is disturbed and the more itching takes place. Unloading grain in the hot sun was becoming more unbearable by the minute. The longer I worked, the hotter I became and the more barley pricked my skin causing more itching. I was never so glad to see a job done as I was that day with barley.

The neighbor, Charlie and Fred's father, Russel were also unloading the barley. A little background information on Charlie was that he was known to be a practical joker from the word go. If there was some way he could do something to get a laugh, he was first in line. Charlie's wife was Amelia. Rose and Russel and Charlie and Amelia were close friends as well as neighbors, and they would do things together, like go to the lake.

Let's go back to the barley story. We were done unloading barley, and giving the new kid a hard time had been very successful.

With the job complete, it was time to eat lunch. Big meals provide the extra nutrition needed by farmers. As Charlie, Russel, and I walked into the back door of Rose and Russel's home, Russel said, "Let's tap the barrel of new wine."

Charlie agreed, and I followed them downstairs. Russel drew two glasses of wine from the barrel. Charlie and Russel each had a glass, and they asked me if I would like a little.

I was so thirsty I could spit cotton. I said, "Sure, I would like some wine." I sampled a glass of wine that Charlie had drawn for me. It was excellent. I drank a little bit more, and it went down so smoothly that I drank the whole glass.

I didn't think anything about drinking the glass of wine as I went upstairs to the kitchen and began to fry and smell the sausage. As I cooked, I noticed that I wasn't feeling so well. My head was spinning, and when I walked across the kitchen, I didn't end up in the desired spot. The more I tried to fry sausage, the harder the task proved to be. I tried eating some sausage and soon found myself on the couch.

The room began to swirl around, and I couldn't remember having this type of experience before. It didn't take too long before my stomach began to churn. I became sick to my stomach and lost the little lunch I had eaten.

As I lay on the couch all afternoon, I realized I had never been sick this way before, and this was not something I wished to repeat.

When the time came to milk the cows, I was happy to be feeling better and be out of the house doing something constructive.

Since that day, I have always tried to be cautious about drinking too much wine or other alcoholic beverage. I watch closely so drinks don't sneak up on me. My first experience with homemade wine was not good.

Later in life, I would begin making homemade wine myself.

Manure Loader

I had just finished the ninth grade and was working on the farm loading the manure spreader. The manure spreader is usually loaded with a pitchfork. The substance to be loaded was the cow manure that had been collected outside the milking section of the barn. Cows do not always defecate in the fields, but when nature calls, they relieve themselves in the milking stalls.

While I had loaded manure in the past, this was the first time I was to spread the manure, so I wanted to get it right. I had the spreader loaded as high as I could pile it. I asked Rose and Russel how to set the controls so that the spreader would distribute the manure on the field as fertilizer. I was shown which control to move so that the spreader would be engaged.

When I reached the field, I set the control so the manure spreader would be engaged, and I moved down the field to spread the manure. Nothing much was happening, but I did hear the chain click. I moved a few more feet and heard a snap.

I stopped the tractor and inspected the manure spreader. After a few minutes of inspection, I saw that the chain was lying on the ground and had broken.

I drove back to the farm and explained what had happened. They explained that there were two levers I was to set because setting the one lever, as I had done, would move the manure along the bottom, but the other lever was for the spreaders to distribute the manure. I never did figure out why I didn't know about the other lever.

I asked how we were going to fix the spreader. The answer was simple: I needed to empty the spreader by hand so that the chain in the bottom of the spreader would be exposed, and the chain could be repaired. I had just lost several hours of work, but I had learned how to set both levers and run the manure spreader. I became a first-class manure spreader, just a little too late!

Chickens

One of my jobs on the farm was to butcher the chickens on Saturday morning. I had seen the process of butchering chickens when I was a young boy at the Niedermeier farm, which was about five miles from the Eldred farm where I was presently working. Rosie, Fred's mother, was there to butcher with me because we would prepare more than one chicken at a time. If we were going to the trouble of butchering, it didn't make much difference if there were one or three chickens. One of the most time-consuming tasks in butchering is to prepare enough hot water to be able to accomplish the plucking of the feathers.

Since I was now doing the butchering instead of watching, a few more facts need to be explained. When we were to catch free-range chickens, it would take more than one person to corral the chickens into the fenced area so we could catch the chickens by the legs and tie them up until we had all them.

Next, we would go to the butcher block and use either an ax or a knife to cut off the head. It was very important after the head was gone to hold the feet and the wings of the chicken until they had no life left.

I remember one time the chicken's wings came loose from my hands, and the chicken took off, wildly flapping its wings and bumping into anything in the barnyard. It acted like a chicken with its head cut off!

When the chicken had no life left, it was dipped into hot water for a short time, making it easier to pull out the feathers. If the chicken was left in the water too long, the skin would begin to peel. Once all the feathers were off, the small hairs on the now dry body were singed by using a rolled-up newspaper, lighting it, and rolling the chicken over the flame.

After a washing, it was time to extract the various organs of the chicken by cutting into the cavity. A thorough rinsing of the chicken would allow the option of cutting the bird into its various parts.

Homegrown free-range chickens are more delicious than any caged chicken. It is hard to beat homegrown chicken for a Sunday dinner!

Another Chicken-Related Story

One of my favorite delicacies is meringue. Meringue is made from the whites of eggs by whipping them with a mixer and putting air into the meringue. It is like making thousands of white bubbles. Then sugar is added. Some people like baked meringue on pies, such as lemon meringue pie; I like it raw.

One afternoon in the summer when it was a slow day, I decided that I was going to make meringue. All I needed was eggs, sugar, a beater, and a bowl. I began to look for the eggs first, as the rest of the ingredients were in the kitchen.

I found a dozen eggs by the corncrib behind Mary Lu's house. I picked up an egg to see if it was good. Eggs can spoil and be rotten. As I cracked the egg, it sounded dead. I opened the egg, and there was a chicken embryo.

I never tried making meringue on my own *after this experience*. I was practically sick thinking of killing the chick, and if that didn't do it, placing the embryo into a bowl to make meringue would have done me in.

Experiences while Milking Cows

I was exposed to milking cows very early in my farming career. This was the first duty each day because milking started sometime around six o'clock in the morning and lasted around two hours.

In the afternoon, milking started around four thirty and went for another two hours.

In the morning, particularly in the winter, the cows stayed in the barn all night, so cleaning the manure that had accumulated and spreading fresh straw on the floor would have been the task before milking.

In the summer, the cows had usually been in the pasture all day, so we would take the tractor down the road to the pasture and bring them to the barn so they could be milked. In my early years of farming, hand-milking cows was the only manner in which we milked.

When I was starting to wean myself from the farm in my last years of high school, milking was done by machine, and this didn't seem like much work at all.

There were twelve cows and a bull in the herd. The breed of cows was a mixture, meaning they were about any breed you could think of individually and collectively. You were to find out early in the game that the size of the teats varies from cow to cow. I remember one cow, which was mostly Holstein, had the thinnest teats of all the cows, being the size of a medium finger. Usually when one milked, you would wrap the thumb and the pointer finger around the top of the teat, close off the milk in the teat, and squeeze it from the top to the bottom to ensure the milk reached the pail. This particular cow's small teat made it impossible to place the thumb and pointer finger around the teat, so one would need to strip the teat. Stripping was accomplished by placing the thumb and the pointer finger on each side of the teat, not completely around the teat, and then pulling down the thumb and finger so that the milk would be forced down into the pail. I could see the foam formed on top of the milk because of the pressure from the incoming milk.

Another of the cows, named Whitey, had teats that were very large. They were so large that one could barely place one's hand around the teat. Milking Whitey would take longer and because of the large teat would be very taxing on the hand and arm muscles.

I remember milking Whitey one evening. It is important to note that Whitey always gave more than a full bucket of milk. When I had filled the pail, Whitey picked up her right back hoof to kick at a fly. I don't know if she got the fly, but I do know she set her foot down in the middle of the pail. This action contaminated the milk and the pail and gave me the job of trying to figure out a method of removing the leg from the contaminated milk and pail.

The cats were more than pleased to see milk on the barn floor, and I was not pleased to see the mess and the loss of milk and my time.

There were two sides of the barn for milking. Rosie and Russel were the other two milkers. Sometimes Fred's sister, Carol, was the other milker. Carol was a few years older than me. Most of the cows were milked on the left side of the barn, and two or three were milked on the right side.

On the left side, there were wood divider stalls that held the cows in place. One stood two or three feet away from the cow when she was being released from the wood stalls so they were not stepped on or hit by the cow.

On the right side, there were chains to hold the cows in the stall. In order to place the chain around the cow's neck, it was necessary to stand next to the cow.

On a cold winter evening in November of 1959, I was standing next to the cow I had just milked when she moved her front right foot toward me as I was trying to remove the chain from her neck. The cow placed her foot in the middle of my foot. Yes, this was very uncomfortable. The strange thing about a cow is that one can hit them, push them, or yell at them, but they do not acknowledge your existence and consequently do not move. I must have waited for the cow to move its foot for over ten minutes. I felt I was very lucky at the end of the ten minutes to have no broken bones.

The next night while I was milking the same cow that had previously stepped on my foot, I was to have another unusual experience. I was on the right side of the barn milking the cow that liked to stand on my foot. I heard noises in the rafters over my head. I looked up only to see the tin that formed the floor of the granary. The granary was the storage container for oats, an ingredient used in the chopped feed eaten by cows when they are being milked.

A little while later, I noticed that some kernels of oats were falling into my lap as I was milking the cow. It was now pretty dark in the barn, so I decided to pick up the bucket, empty it, and find a flashlight. I then proceeded to finish milking the cow that liked to stand on my foot.

It wasn't five minutes before I again heard something in the rafters overhead. I shined my light at the ceiling and saw a mouse crawling between the wood slats of the rafters and under the tin from the granary. I found a frog spear and set out to eliminate the pesky mouse traveling over my head.

The Art of Shooting Rats

Living with my sister Mary Lu and my brother-in-law Fred on the farm provided me with freedom of movement, excitement, and many varied experiences. Since there was not much peer socializing available, hunting was the best way to spend my time. Hunting around the barnyard was a favorite pastime, as I could shoot birds, mice, and rats. All three of these animals were considered pests, and the Willard High School Future Farmers of America (FFA) received points for turning in mice and rat tails, as well as sparrow heads. Sparrows were usually in the trees during the day and under the overhang of the barn roof at night. There were usually not many mice available until we cleaned out the granary. Rats, on the other hand, were plentiful and required great patience to hunt.

Hunting rats would usually be centered in the main barn. My favorite spot to find rats was by the chopped-feed box or in the granary. I would sit and wait for them to come out when it was dark. Hearing rats move in the dark around me was unnerving at first. Later it was something I got used to, as they never hurt me. The chopped-feed box held the ground feed of various grains, which is used to feed the cows before and during milking. When hunting rats, I found it essential to turn off all the lights and wait until I heard the rats crawling close to me and away from their hole. Patience is required.

When the proper time comes when one thinks the rats are in the open, the barn light or the flashlight would be turned on. I had rigged up a long string to the barn light so I could pull it on from many vantage points in the barn. Again, patience is required. Pulling the light switch from a distance frees up both hands, allows one to be back far enough to see the area being hunted, and minimizes the amount of movement to turn on the light.

On a good evening, it was not unusual to have several rats scatter when the light was turned on. If you see none or a few rats, you didn't give enough time to allow the rats to come into the open.

It is important to note that rats travel between bales of hay and straw and can be seen and shot if found by the beam of a flashlight. On this particular night, Fred and I went directly to the granary at the back of the barn. As we walked into the granary, rats were seen everywhere. It looked like a convention was in progress. We made as many good shots as we could, and then we entered the largest part of the granary, the back bin. The gun used to hunt rats is usually a .22 caliber rifle or a pistol using .22 bird shot or a cartridge that contains several small shots that scatter when it is fired.

As we both walked into the back of the granary, we noticed a large dark-colored rat crouched down in the corner, and the rat gave the appearance that it was about to attack. I pulled up my rifle as Fred cocked his .22 pistol, and he pointed the barrel directly at the large rat. The rat was cornered, and as the saying goes, a rat will attack if it is cornered. As I cocked my loaded .22 rifle with a bird shot cartridge in the barrel, the rat lunged directly at Fred who was standing next to me. Without thinking, Fred quickly aimed his pistol and pulled the trigger as the rat lunged toward him. Fred's shot hit the rat in midair. He was the last person that rat jumped on.

The Practice of Neutering Young Pigs

The neutering or castration of pigs is an unusual task. I found out what it was all about when Russel Eldred informed me that the pigs must be castrated when they are the right size. Being a male gave me some personal identification and sympathy with the pig's position in this process. My position didn't matter because we were already set up and ready to go. There was a scalpel or knife, there was plenty of antiseptic, and there were two people, one to hold and the other to do the deed. I held the pig after catching it so Russel could do the first few by applying antiseptic to the scrotum, doing a small vertical cut on the outside bag or scrotum, and then squeezing out and cutting out the testicle. We were finally coming to the noisy part where we cut what looked like veins going to the testicles and then applied antiseptic. The cutting of the veins to the testicles caused the pigs to squeal for a long time.

It was my turn, and I thought I was ready to go. Russel held the pig, and I applied the antiseptic and made a small cut in the scrotum. I squeezed out the testicles and then cut the large and small cords around them. The reapplication of antiseptic was the last part of the operation used to ward off infection. Russel told me that the testicles were good to eat (I heard of Rocky Mountain oysters years later), but I still don't have the desire to investigate this fine cuisine.

The Bus Ride

When I was in high school, I was needed on the farm to milk cows in the morning and in the evening. The work hours were as expected, early in the morning and late in the evening. Latin never was an easy subject for me and for that reason required a great deal of effort. My work hours on the farm left me with less time to spend on this subject.

Living in the country required me to ride a school bus. I was to discover a pleasant surprise on the first day my elder sister took me to the bus stop. There were two young country girls on the bus. I was not shy, so I walked toward the girls and sat next to a couple of cuties. They were sitting together as friends. Their names were Kathy Long and Pat Elmlinger.

Each day, we talked about many subjects on the bus. I remember one of the subjects was food, specifically their potato chips. Potato chips were a commodity that had a special appeal to both of them, and as a result, they had devised a technique to stretch their chips. Instead of eating the whole chips, they would smash them so there were more pieces of chips to eat; it seemed there were more chips to share. I imagine they may have been into sharing their lunch with each other, but I was never certain.

Kathy Long was to be in my mind forever; I just didn't know it at the time.

The Tiring Snowstorm

I had attended a basketball game at Willard High School on a Friday night in January. When the game was over and I walked out of the gymnasium, I was to be picked up by my brother-in-law Fred Eldred. When the game was over and as I began to push on the door of the gymnasium, I noticed that a snowstorm was in progress. About four to five inches of snow had already fallen, and cars were slipping on the road and in the parking lot.

I saw Fred and Lu and walked over to the car and opened the door. As I settled in the backseat, Fred said, "We are due to get quite a bit more snow. Do you feel like pushing the car if we get stuck?"

I said, "Sure." I was to find out that my answer was going to be one I would regret later that night.

As we began leaving the parking lot, larger snowflakes began to fall. We headed out of town toward the farm and found slippery roads everywhere we traveled. The snow continued to fall very hard. Fred was able to maneuver the car ten miles to his road with only a few pushouts. We did not get stuck often since the road had been traveled by other vehicles and was somewhat packed down and passable. There was now between seven and nine inches of snow on the ground.

Fred turned to the road where they lived and said, "We are going to have to do quite a bit of pushing to get to the house." The house is located over a mile down what is now called the Old Military Road. Fred gave it the gas, and we started down the road to the first low and snowy spot.

The tires began to spin, and I said, "Let me try to push." I put on my gloves and already had on my boots and snow clothes, so I was ready to go. I started to push, and Fred gave it the gas. That was how it was for the next two hours! After Fred got going past the first low spot, he proceeded toward the top of the hill, which leads to the bridge.

Now the snow was deeper than ten inches, and the car's tires were spinning as Fred "gave it the juice" as he began to approach the big hill. I was out again to push the car to the hill. As we reached and looked down the hill that led to the bridge, we could see that the road turned to the right immediately after the end of the bridge. If we were going down the hill and started going into a spin, we could end up with the car going sideways into the bridge and crashing.

I started pushing the car down the hill, as the snow has drifted, and Fred could not get it through the deep snow on his own. The harder I pushed, the slower the car would seem to move. We were about halfway down the seventy-five-yard hill when the car began to go a little faster. The car was not going fast enough, nor did it have enough power to go down the hill without me pushing. I continued to have both hands under the back bumper and pushed as hard as I could. Every time I would stop pushing, the car would not move. We were now a little beyond halfway, and I decided I was going to have to push all the way down the rest of the hill. I pushed, and Fred gave the car the throttle. We began to pick up steam about thirty feet from the bridge, and at the same time, the car began to slide sideways. I knew that the car could not go through the bridge sideways. Fred also must have noticed that because he began to steer the car in such a manner that the car began to straighten itself. As we reached the bridge, Fred gave the car some gas, and it straightened out enough so that it did not hit the sides of the bridge. I fell down at the beginning of the bridge and just lay on the ground watching the car go through it.

On the other side of the bridge, Fred continued to accelerate for a short distance until the snow was too deep for him to go forward. I picked myself up and went up to Fred's window. I asked him what he thought we should do now, and he said, "I will drive, and you will push." That response did not surprise me, and I began to ask God for some energy, as I was completely exhausted, and we had only covered about one-third of the distance from the main road till we would reach home. I began to push, and Fred gave it the gas. As we went forward, we settled for a gain of twenty or thirty feet at a time, and each time we stopped, I was becoming more tired than before.

We went on until we finally reached Fred's house. He told me to go into the house with Mary Lu and take a shower. I had never been so tired in my life, and I had never physically endured such a trying experience. I knew that there was no option but for us to reach the house once we had started down the Old Military Road. Fred could not have turned around, and we could not have slept in the car all night because it was too cold, and we would have run out of gas.

From that point in my life, I knew that I could never have pushed Fred and Lu's car down the road if it had not been for the energy that I had received from someone other than myself. I took my shower, and I went to bed. Getting up to milk the cows the next day was hard, but it was much easier to get up and milk than to go through the ordeal that I had experienced the previous evening.

The Issue of Pay

Several years after working on the farm, I found that my pay could have been either a gun or a Cushman motor scooter. My parents were afraid of the dangers of a scooter, so I had received a gun. I have tried to figure out without success which would have been the better item for me.

My Breaks on the Farm

At lunchtime or after supper, I would take a break if possible. Since work came before pleasure, and there was always plenty of work, breaks were not a daily occurrence, especially during the very busy part of the summer. When the work slowed down, or it was raining, I enjoyed fishing or shooting birds. Shooting birds was a common occurrence forty-five years ago because there were pest birds, such as blackbirds and sparrows.

Fishing was also a common sport. I have always loved to fish. There were two spots that were available near the farm to fish. The first was a small creek located off the next road from the farm. The fish I would catch and eat here were called chubs. Chubs are a small fish, and they have a somewhat large middle section (or were chubby) and are about six inches long. Chubs were not prized for their gourmet taste, but they are easy to catch, and there is usually a large school available.

The other fishing spot was a pond located close to the farm. The pond was within walking distance. The two major fish in the pond were bluegill and largemouth bass. A stray catfish would be another possibility. Bluegills are a colorful fish with yellow, orange, and blue tones. They are about six inches long and are round and flat in appearance. They are known as panfish and as a great fighting fish. Largemouth bass are usually several pounds in weight. They are long, rather bulky in appearance, and light in color with a black streak on their side from head to tail.

One afternoon, I was not working because there had been a heavy rain the previous night, and water had saturated all the fields. I had an old metal fly-fishing rod that my father had given to me. It was ten feet long with a very thin pole. Fly fishing is an art. It is accomplished by slowly moving the line forward and backward and then forward allowing the line that is in one of your hands to extend out several feet. The line is pulled back to the fisherman by retracting it in a short distance at a time. The line is not wound around the reel, as it will soon be cast out into the pond again.

On this day, I was fishing with a wet fly. Wet flies sink below the waterline, and dry flies float on the water. As I was about to pull the fly out of the water and recast it, I felt a tug on the line. This can have several causes. It could hopefully be a fish, a piece of wood, or the bottom of the pond. I began to pull hard on the line, but there was little give. Within a few seconds, the line began to move back and forth in front of me about thirty feet into the pond just like a bass. As the fish moved closer to shore, I could see that it was an enormous largemouth bass, probably the largest bass I have ever seen at that time in the wild.

As I tried hard to bring in the fish, I found it was moving either from side to side or further from me. After a long fight, the fish began to tire. I walked backward, so I slowly began to bring it to shore. Finally, the bass was within five feet from shore. Since I didn't have a net, I began to slowly drag the fish to the shore and to the grass behind the shoreline. I had a large pail with me, so I filled it with water and placed the fish into the five-gallon bucket. When I reached the house, I asked where I could keep the fish alive. We had fifty-five-gallon wood barrels in which we stored the milk until the milk truck arrived. This five-pound largemouth bass was according to my records the largest bass taken from this pond. The fish was so large that it did not fit well into the fifty-five-gallon wood barrel. We had the fish for supper, and I was very proud of my catch.

The Hornets

One afternoon, I was mowing the grass around the pond with the mower behind the tractor. It was going well until I noticed that hornets were attacking me. I stopped the tractor and ran to the house. The hornets were still biting me. Mary Lu and Fred took off my T-shirt as I ran into the kitchen. There was still one live hornet in my shirt.

Next time, I decided to jump into the pond and take off my shirt when I hit a hornet's nest.

The Farm

I was to finish my career on the farm the year before I entered John Carroll University. The farm had been good to me by providing me with many problem-solving, physical, and emotional skills. For example, when a tractor runs over a rock, and the rock becomes lodged in the drag or another piece of equipment, or the hookup on the equipment doesn't line up with the hole on the rear of the tractor, and there is no one around in that hot sun to help but me, I needed to solve the problem. When a heavy piece of equipment needs to be picked up, or the front wheels of the tractor are bouncing everywhere but where I want them to be on the plowed ground, I needed my physical skills. Another challenge was when I had been on the tractor for ten hours, and I was ready to stop for the day but couldn't.

Also, it was challenging when I became tired of being without my friends, but I needed to retire early and be up early the next morning. I had to use various skills to see myself through these circumstances.

I have never learned so much in my life about so many areas as I did on the farm. I still miss the farm and like to go back to visit. I found that regardless of one's physical stature and size, the farm is always a challenge. It provided me with many good problem-solving skills and memories.

My Senior Year and Beyond

My High School Girlfriend

Senior year was my time to experience a relationship with one of the attractive freshman girls. I don't remember how it began, but I started my visits to a place called Pioneer Hill, which was located near the company where my father worked. As I began to visit Dianne Brubaker's house, I wondered about the frequency I was visiting. In my mind, I was thinking, *How long will it be before Ruth and Les, Dianne's parents, tell me that I am visiting their daughter too often?* The fourth member of the family was Dianne's younger sister, Vickie. I wasn't concerned about her acceptance of me because our relationship appeared to be good. Luck was to be on my side because not a word was ever expressed about the number or length of my visits, even though those remarks would have been in order.

My senior year, and I think Dianne's freshman year, passed quickly. Dating was lots of fun with many good experiences. Thoughts of college began to occupy my mind, and I wondered where this relationship with Dianne would go.

The previous year, I had had an experience with a horse accident on Vance's Corner, and I hoped that my unpleasant horse experiences were a thing of the past. I was now getting ready for college, and little did I know that I was to have another experience with a horse. Dianne had always wanted a horse, and she finally had one. She invited me out to see it. I was never fond of horses but decided to make the trip to see Dianne and to make her happy.

I pulled into her driveway and noticed that she was with a few other friends across the road in a field with the new horse. I walked over to them. My knowledge of horses was limited, yet I wanted to be socially appropriate, so I complimented Dianne's horse.

She invited me to ride the horse. This was not the direction I wished to go. I was a little leery about riding the horse because of my previous negative experiences. I didn't want to hurt her feelings or look like a nerd in front of her many friends, so I said, "Sure, I would love to ride your horse."

I mounted the horse and began to ride it at a slow pace. The horse had other ideas. Dianne's horse must have sensed my insecurity because it immediately took off running. I felt like I was repeating an experience from grade school when a horse disregarded my commands and decided to take off with me clinging to its back. In this experience with Dianne's horse, when I pulled back the reins, the horse showed me who was the boss and decided to go faster. At this point, I became more than concerned, as the horse's direction was beginning to edge toward the main road. I glanced toward the road and could see that a car was coming down the road setting up a direct collision with us. I held on for dear life and desperately tried to come up with a plan to save the horse, me, and the people in the car.

When the horse jumped over the ditch and was on the road, I was not sure if either the horse or I was going to live through the next few minutes. I lost track of the car as I pulled back on the reins, and the horse's feet slid on the pavement. We both fell on our sides in the middle of the road. Unfortunately, my leg was under the horse when it went down. The more important part of the experience was that I could not feel or see the car hitting the horse or me. The car had missed us. I never knew why that car didn't hit the horse or me.

Both the horse and I were able to stand up, and it appeared we were not seriously injured. As Dianne and her friends looked over the horse and could find no injuries, I thought that things were looking up. Meanwhile I felt my leg burning and looked down to see a scraped left lower leg with surface bleeding. I felt lucky that the horse appeared not to be hurt, but I decided that I needed to go home and treat my wounds. It would be forty years before I rode another horse.

It was getting close to the time I was to leave for college. Something told me that my time at home and my relationship with Dianne also were coming to an end. My next four years were to have many failed female relationships, attributed mostly to my commitment to my books.

Another unpredictable event was about to happen that would convince me my bad luck was not yet over that summer.

A Major Mistake to End My High School Years and Start College

My brother had bought a twenty-year-old car, a purple Plymouth. I had used it to make one of my last visits to Dianne's before going to college. As I was coming home on Tiffin Avenue, I looked up at the Myrtle Avenue stoplight and saw it was changing from green to caution. I didn't think I had time to stop, so I pushed the gear shift into second gear and went through the intersection on a caution light. The light was yellow when I entered the intersection!

It was my luck that a Willard policeman was sitting to my right in his cruiser as I went through the light. He activated his flashing lights, which triggered me to pull over. He told me I had run the red light. I respectfully told him the light was yellow when I entered the intersection. He didn't believe me and issued a ticket.

I was seventeen years old and within a month of starting college. I began college and received a summons to appear before the probate judge in Norwalk. I came home from college and went with my parents to appear before the judge. The patrolman also was present, and he gave graphic details on how the incident happened. I wasn't prepared for all that information. I just knew the light was yellow. The judge believed the patrolman, and I lost my license for a few months.

I learned a lot from this experience. First, I learned that I needed to do my homework. While it takes time to prepare, I will not have to try to remember the facts at the last minute. The information will be on paper in front of me, and my memory will be open for other issues. Second, being ready to speak for myself is another factor related to having the homework completed. These two principles proved to be essential to me in many facets of my life, even though they were not helpful to me in this circumstance. The third fact I learned was that I never knew when I was to run into someone in the future. Judge Don Young was to become a federal district court judge, the same judge who would hear a lawsuit filed against me professionally several years later.

A Speeding-Related Incident

One of the only Supreme Court cases that originated near my hometown involved the Police Department of the City of Monroeville. Reviewing my ticket in Willard helped me remember this incident in Monroeville. I cannot say the incident happened exactly in this manner, but it did take place. At this time, I heard this story more than once. This incident happened around the time I graduated from college.

As I remember, many trucks traveled through Monroeville on Route 20. As the trucks passed a curve going west near downtown Monroeville, the speed limit suddenly changed. The police were Johnny-on-the-spot and ticketed drivers in their speed trap.

It seems one truck driver was very upset about what he saw as an unfair treatment by the police. The word *speed trap* was used as the manner in which the Monroeville Police were raising the revenue of the city of Monroeville. The Supreme Court did rule against the local court. Every time I drive through Monroeville, I slow down, think of this story, and look very hard to see if there are any "officers of the law" present. While I didn't win my stoplight case, a truck driver did better than I did.

Unforgettable People Known Before My College Years

Dr. William "Bill" Kauffman

These are memories I had as a young boy, as a high school student, as a college student, and with what my family considered the "greatest medical doctor in the world." I will present in this section the memories my family had of Dr. William Kauffman, Doc for short. At various times in our growing-up years, all six children and the two parents in the Frederick family were in need of medical help. It seemed the four young Frederick boys who were constantly exploring the world were in need of a little more attention than some of the other members of the family.

The children in the Frederick family didn't know that Doc had a first name. It was always Dr. Kauffman or Doc, the frequently smiling man, who was good natured, not so thin, and often seen making house calls. He never seemed to sleep, as he came to our house all hours of the day and during the night.

Dr. Kauffman rarely asked anyone to leave the room at home or in the office when he would treat a family member. It was as if he wanted to teach everyone everything he knew about medicine because it was good for their health. He, to my knowledge, was never negative with anyone. When Dr. Kauffman was around, there was an aura of trust and hope. He was so respectful and respected by everyone that all our actions with each other were very giving and understanding.

Our family members loved about everything this man did. A few of the boys modeled their penmanship, so they say, after Dr. Kauffman. It was not known if this modeling was on purpose or was used as an excuse for their hard-to-read writing. In all fairness, my penmanship was by far the most illegible and Dr. Kauffman–like.

My eldest sister, Mary Lu, would quote my mother saying she couldn't afford to have Doc go on vacation. When one child was sick, that usually meant more than one would be sick. If Mom took three children to Dr. Kauffman, he would only charge for one visit. It did so happen that three of the family got sick with high fevers and sore throats while Doc was vacationing with his family.

Mom made an appointment with another doctor, and when it came time to pay, the other doctor charged for three separate appointments.

Dr. Kauffman had a good laugh when Mom told him this story. The next year when Dr. Kauffman went on vacation, my mother told us that we were going to have to stay well until Dr. Kauffman came back to town.

My eldest brother Walt tells the story about the delivery of his second son, Peter, in April 11, 1968. Judy, his wife, was to be released on Easter Sunday, but Dr. Kauffman was not scheduled to be in town to release her. Judy told the nurse that she would prefer Dr. Kauffman releasing her. Dr. Kauffman postponed his trip to Columbus to visit his daughter when he heard his patient had requested his services.

My most frequent memory of Dr. Kauffman was his visits to see my mother because of her persistent migraines. Mom's migraine made it nearly impossible for her to travel to the office, so Doc would come to our house. When Doc was coming to the house, one of us kids was posted by the door to open it as soon as Doc's foot hit the front steps. It was a known fact that Doc had many calls to make, so every second was important in helping him to see her as quickly as possible.

When Doc arrived, we could be sure that his big black bag would arrive with him. The black bag contained the supplies and equipment of an entire medical office. Doc would always set down the black bag and say, "Marion, how are you feeling?"

Mom would always say as she clutched her rosary, "Not so good, Doc."

After finishing his questions with Mom, we all wondered why Doc would ask those questions because he would say on many occasions, "I thought so." Then Doc would open that big black bag, and all the kids would look with amazement at what was in it. The bag had two top compartments, which flipped open, one to the left and one to the right. The base was the largest section and supported all the large pieces of equipment, such as the stethoscope.

At this point, Doc would usually bring out the hypodermic needle and load it up with liquid from a small bottle with a rubber top and metal cap. The sight of this needle was enough to send all the kids out of the room, but out of respect for our sick mother, we would grit our teeth and wait for the shot to be completed. If we kids were being treated, they would always hope for Doc to take out a small white envelope and place some pills in it rather than placing a needle in our arm.

Mom would usually feel better later in the day. Her recovery was good for two reasons. One, she would have less pain, and two, she would be well enough to complete her work around the house rather than having us kids do it all.

Dr. Kauffman was part of the staff at Willard Hospital and therefore practiced medicine at the hospital. My father's contribution to the hospital was serving as a member of the board of directors. He used his skills as an accountant and as a problem solver. I always felt that Dad helped make it easier for the doctors and nurses to practice medicine since it was the board who saw to it that the necessary buildings and resources were available.

Ann, my youngest sister, is a storyteller, so she has three short stories to relate about Doc. The first occasion was a house call from Doc because of her tonsillitis. Doc came to our house on 519 Clark Street to see Ann. Quickly, Doc judged that she needed a shot. Doc tried to give Ann a shot, but her body was so tight the needle bounced off the skin. A light touch to another section of her body was a distraction and caught her off guard. This gave Doc the challenge of making the needle enter the skin.

A few years later, Ann was older and sick. Doc judged over the phone that instead of going to the emergency room, she should go to his house for treatment. Since it was very early in the morning, Dr. Kauffman was in his pajamas. Being in his pajamas didn't bother him, as he simply administered his medicine.

A third event happened on June 6, 1971, when Tommy, their oldest son, was born. Ann had the flu, and during delivery, Doc lost Ann for a short period. Doc revived her, and she is still alive today.

Mike and Bob, the youngest brothers, worked at the same city park system in Willard where I had worked. One of the drawbacks of working in various sections of the park was the poison ivy along the creek. As Mike and Bob were clearing the weeds along the creek, they also unknowingly cleared out some poison ivy and developed a wicked case of it. It didn't take long before they realized what had happened, as their bodies began to itch. The solution was a trip to Dr. Kauffman and a shot to knock out the itch.

Bob had always been known as the Frederick most likely to hate any shot in the arm. This day was no exception. Mike took the shot first, and

Doc kidded Bob that he was next. After Doc gave the shot, the needle somehow became dislodged from the syringe, and the needle remained sticking in Bob's arm. Mike immediately noticed the needle sticking out of Bob's arm and began to laugh. Mike started to point to the needle as Doc developed a smile on his face and pulled out the needle. Mike will attest to the fact that to this day, this was one of the best laughs he has ever had at the expense of his younger brother Bob.

Dr. Kauffman's family was very well-known in Willard. His wife, Bettie Kerr Kauffman, was very active in community organizations. Their eldest daughter, Roberta, was my merit badge counselor for swimming and lifesaving. These two merit badges were two of the hardest required badges for the Eagle Scout Award. Chuck, his only son, was older than I was and played tuba when I played baritone in the Willard High School band. A younger daughter completed the Kauffman family. I have always thought of the great sacrifices that the Kauffman family made by gracefully supporting Doc in the many hours of service he gave to the community.

Roy Doster

When I was in high school, it seemed everyone knew Roy Doster. Roy was of African American decent, was proud of it, and spent his life trying to foster positive relations between all people regardless of race.

As I remember, Roy worked on the B&O Railroad and did odd jobs on his off time. I remember as far back in my childhood as possible that when spring came, Roy was at our house hand washing all the walls. Roy would start early in the morning, and if you walked through the room where he was working, he would strike up a conversation with you while working. Talking would not slow down his work nor affect its quality. During our conversations, he would mix laughter with his talk and work. How could one not grow to love such a magnetic person?

In Willard, most persons of African American decent lived on the east side of town at this time. That factor had no bearing on Roy's ability to work for racial and community change. Roy was very active in the community and always strived to see that the various races were having positive communication as they worked together on community activities.

I remember well my junior year in high school when I was in an honors study hall. This meant that I had a study hall without a teacher. Another student in the class had gone to the restroom. He did not come back for the longest time. When he came back, it was apparent he had been in a fight. It seems an African American student who had moved into Willard from the South and my friend from the honors study hall had an altercation in the restroom.

I was afraid that some type of major racial confrontation was going to happen in Willard like the ones in the South I had seen on television. It was scary. I would bet big money that the quick solution to this incident and more positive steps to better race integration were influenced by Roy. A little sidenote on this incident was the honors study hall disappeared immediately.

Roy's wife also was committed to getting along with all people, and once a year, they would open their house to a summer party. It seemed the whole town, regardless of race, social class, or wealth, would attend Roy and Martha's party. My parents always enjoyed going to this party, as they were friends with the Dosters. My father and mother enjoyed working in the area of civil rights. I was always amazed at the food and drinks that were served at the Doster party.

I can never forget Roy, as he was, and is, a good man trying to do positive things for other people. When my sister Mary Lu passed away in early 2007, I knew Roy would make an appearance at Secor's Funeral Home and with his smiling face and positive comments would make things a bit more bearable.

I saw Roy Doster after his ninetieth birthday. Roy was still working by cleaning the medical center every Friday and Saturday. He always said, "When God calls me home, I'll be working." He is a man after my own heart.

A Summary

The fond memories in this section of my high school days and the previous sections remind me that there are precious memories that many people have of their surroundings and people they had known as they grew up. Memories comprise the majority of our knowledge, which allows us to relate to where we came from, where we are, and where we are going. I was very lucky to have had the many experiences I had as the product of a small town and the goodwill of so many wonderful people.

Part IV

On My Own

Chapter 10

My First Years at John Carroll University

Introduction

My years at John Carroll University (JCU) were to be a great adventure and full of challenges and lessons that I will never forget. It was my first long period away from home, and I was to spice up my life associating with many talented, intelligent, giving classmates, instructors, and others. The chapters on the four years at John Carroll are a presentation consistent with the other chapters. My classes, extracurricular activities, dorm life, summer employment, and summer activities will be the focus.

Why John Carroll?

My father had decided that my attendance at John Carroll University, an all-men Jesuit school in Cleveland was to happen many years before it transpired. My father's business friend Justin "Bud" Noetzel, a certified public accountant with the company of Peat, Marwick, and Mitchell (now KPMG), had graduated and lived a few blocks from the school. Bud's brother Arthur was the dean of the prestigious business school.

When I first visited the school, I was overwhelmed by its beautiful campus, old stone buildings, and staff. The wealth in University Heights and the neighboring community of Shaker Heights is impressive. After all, I was a simple small town, country boy and to see a lawn that one could sleep on was beyond me.

Starting College

In the beginning of my freshman year, my parents drove me to John Carroll. The first site we saw was the highest point of JCU, Grasselli Tower. As we came closer to the campus, we saw the Grasselli Library. It hadn't completely sunk in yet that the library was to be my home away from home. It was there I would be spending a significant part of my life for the next four years.

As we unloaded my possessions, I could see that my parents were very happy that the big day had come. I was very unsettled because I didn't know what my future would be. I did know that the school I was attending was academically respected and very expensive. At the time, it was one of the most expensive schools in Ohio. To be truthful, I never understood how my father and mother could afford sending five of six children to Catholic private colleges with three of us graduating. My two younger brothers Mike and Bob were five and ten years respectively behind me as graduates of John Carroll.

As we approached my dorm, Pacelli Hall, I could see that there were still beautiful flowers and landscaping. The grounds were green and had to require the services of several groundskeepers. As I walked into my dorm, I felt like a lost puppy. Here I was in Cleveland and knew no one except for my dad's friend Bud. I was to soon meet his family. Fortunately for me, Bud had a very attractive, cultured, and intelligent daughter named Mary Beth. I met her, her mother Frances, and the rest of the family on my first day. A thought went through my head that my relationship with my high school sweetheart was dying, if not dead, so here was a chance to meet someone new. When my father and Bud shook hands, I could see that it was a very respectful and trusting relationship.

After tours of the campus, it was time for my parents to leave me to my new life. Before my parents left, we took a few pictures of Mom, Dad, my sister Ann, Mary Beth, me, and in the front row my brother Mike.

My family leaving and Mary Beth and me staying behind

Everyone knew that this was the start of my new life and their lives without me being a fulltime resident of 519 Clark Street.

As orientation and classes started, there was some spare time, so I tried to spend some of it with Mary Beth. I took Mary Beth to one of the first mixers at John Carroll. I wore my freshman "duffer" or small hat and a tie with the school colors. These two pieces of clothing were to be worn during the first few weeks of school by all freshman students. As Mary Beth and I were leaving the mixer, an upperclassman began to harass me. This too was part of the orientation process. Mary Beth told him in no uncertain terms to leave me alone. Despite the fact that Mary Beth was a girl of smaller stature, the upperclassman did just that!

It was the same evening that Mary Beth, a student at Regina High School, a local Catholic girls high school, was chairperson for one of their dances. She wanted me to go with her, but for some weak reason, I wanted to go to the dance at John Carroll.

As I reflect back on that decision, I wish I would have attended Mary Beth's dance. I do know that while one cannot reverse decisions in life, I did learn a lesson about taking other people's feelings into consideration. I bet I missed a better time at her high school dance than I had at JCU. I now know an apology to Mary Beth, a true friend and a joy to be around, was in order.

I was happy to have some free time in the first week because I was about to adopt my study rule of one night out a week. This rule was to last four years during the school's academic year.

Another experience I was to have in my first few weeks of college was to learn how to drive in Cleveland and what it was like to eat at a fancy restaurant. Mary Beth had suggested that we go to downtown Cleveland to eat. Classes were not in full swing, and I wanted my college education to be full in every way possible. Mary Beth asked her father for the use of the family car and asked me to drive. I had driven tractors and my parents' cars, and I had been pretty successful (but not perfect) back in Willard. I found out that I was not in Willard anymore; I was in Cleveland. There were more cars and more traffic lanes, and everything seemed to move faster. As we approached the downtown area, driving became more challenging in the rain. Mary Beth said our exit was approaching, so I began to switch lanes. The lane switch was a good and bad move. In my blind spot, there was a car with a horn, and he used it to keep me from changing lanes and hitting his car.

We moved on to the downtown area and came upon a triangular-shaped building in the middle of the street. Mary Beth said, "There it is!" I saw a restaurant named something like either the Black Angus or the Black Bull. I pulled into a parking lot. Another new experience unfolded with the use of valet parking. I did not know what the procedure was with valet parking, so I cautiously gave the attendant the keys to the car. Meanwhile Mary Beth began walking into the restaurant like it was something she did every day.

We were seated in the middle of this beautiful restaurant. By the middle I mean there was the same number of tables surrounding us in all directions. I felt like I was on display. Mary Beth began to point out to me various local political figures and socialites from Cleveland. She was having the time of her life, and I was going along for the ride. This restaurant was definitely a hot spot. I began to look at the menu to see if I had enough money to pay the restaurant bill, tip, and now the valet parking. I remember ordering chicken while Mary Beth ordered steak. When the chicken was served, I looked around to see how others might be eating their dinners. I realized that fingers were out, and knife and fork was the rule. I managed to eat the meal, but I continued to feel like every person present was watching my every move.

It was a delightful meal, and Mary Beth was most interesting despite all the attention I felt. On the return trip, I tried not to switch lanes unless it was absolutely necessary. If it was necessary, I took several precautions to see that there was definitely no car next to me. We made it to Mary Beth's house after what appeared to be a mutually pleasant experience. I had learned much from her about the big city that evening and was on my way to learning much about the many happenings at JCU.

Thanks, Mary Beth!

Settling In

John Carroll was the biggest single transformation experience in my life. This was a culture shock filled with challenging paths, and my safety ropes would be my fellow students, my teachers, and my family. Quickly, I found that the learning process required much time and energy. My past study experiences were not comparable to those of some other students, as they were able to have more free time than I did. I continued to judge that going out one night a week was all I could afford, as studying was necessary the other six nights. My friends not only seemed to have more free time, and less study time, but also got better grades on their tests. For me, to successfully keep up with other students, I needed to do better and be better by working harder, longer, and faster. These traits related directly to the commitment I had made to my lost twin.

College life was a challenging adventure leading to the successful start of an interesting and rewarding adult life. In making each day a better day, the challenge to me was to work harder so that I felt good about my accomplishments and tried to enjoy each day and each experience. Studying was a process, and tests led to the end of each course. Professors were in the giving situation, and my giving was to return to the professors what I had received from them.

Every class was like an internship, offered and monitored by the professor. Each class had elements of learning that were essential, sometimes uncomfortable but vital, to the process of acquiring new knowledge.

I knew that my goal of graduating from John Carroll was the most motivating aspect of my life and a direction that would ultimately provide much personal satisfaction. The specific motivation was not yet marriage, and it wasn't money. The path was a lonely one because I had to be the one who made the grades. In meeting the daily challenges of college, one of my major guiding forces came from my father. He taught me that looking back was not always a helpful practice. His words of wisdom emphasized looking forward so I knew where I was going. The past was the past, and the present quickly led to the future. I use this simple guideline constantly in my quest to help me go forward.

Freshman Year

As I began my studies at John Carroll, I noted that I was respected by the teachers as a man. I was to find that the Jesuits were not only concerned about me as a man but were equally, if not more, concerned about me being a man for other people. While this was not a foreign concept to me, it was a welcome reinforcement of the ideals my parents had always instilled in my siblings and me.

Classes

At the beginning of each course, I reviewed the information relative to the course and the professors. While there were many different areas of study related to my major and minor, there were also required courses. This practice gave me a chance to understand how the course fit into my academic goals. When entering college, I had the belief that I wished to have as happy a life as I could. This motto had a different meaning in college, and after I had finished college, I saw much work and little play in the last four academic years.

No God

During orientation, I met many other young men. One of the students I met told me as a matter of fact that he didn't believe in God. At first, I thought he was putting me on, but it didn't take long to see that he was serious.

This was the first time in my life that I had a serious conversation with someone who didn't believe in God. That is not to say that I hadn't met someone that didn't believe in God, just that the subject hadn't been discussed in detail.

I asked that patient gentleman several questions about his beliefs concerning the life hereafter, prayer, support of God, and religion in general. I realized his belief was so strong that I did not think it would ever change. As I remember, he advocated several points such as there is no Supreme Being, no life hereafter, no value in church services, and no prayers needed. These were pretty cut-and-dried beliefs of his. In future years, I was to come across many people who did not believe in God, and I was to study several philosophers who challenged the belief in God.

I had been taught that if I believed in God, I would have a chance to attain eternal salvation. I was not sure what a person's chances for heaven would be if they didn't believe in God. My religious beliefs have always been, are now, and I think always will be essential to my life. While I do not believe in judging other people's religious beliefs, I have always been interested in learning others' thoughts on religion. I must admit that talking about not believing in God is an uncomfortable experience for me.

First Semester, Freshman Year

In my first semester at John Carroll, I registered for seven classes or seventeen semester hours. As I began the semester and was struggling to find enough study time, I talked to a few upperclassmen about my number of hours. The advice of the upperclassmen was that I should have taken fewer hours and courses during the first semester. While I appreciated their advice, I was not going to drop a course; I saw this as quitting, and I did not wish to be a quitter. I studied harder and played less while taking this number of hours.

As I reflect back on my classes, if personal computers had been in use, I would have saved many hours. I remember using erasable typing paper. Thus, the ability to store data in memory and to make changes in the memory rather than making new draft copies would have saved so much time. I was born a few years too soon.

I did enjoy several of my classes; one of my favorites was moral guidance. I enjoyed this subject because the material was extremely relevant to modern-day living and helped me form a more solid basis in my approach to morals in my life. Speech communication class was to help me in developing and giving speeches. I did not have the opportunity to take speech in high school, so this course was a new experience. I remember one talk on smoking that I gave in this course. During the presentation, I blew up a balloon, which symbolized a human lung. I lit a cigarette with a pin embedded in the cigarette. I was making the point that cigarettes could harm your lungs. I explained that it would be like a cigarette blowing up a balloon. As I popped the balloon, I jumped and so did the class. Dr. Austin J. Freely was impressed with my presentation, especially my visual aids. I was not familiar with debating, and because of my instructor's expertise in this area at John Carroll and other universities, I learned the rudiments of this subject. I rather enjoyed this experience.

Military science and world history were required courses that did not have a great effect on me. Every male student at John Carroll was required to take military science for the first two years of his academic career. This was due to the fact that John Carroll is a land-grant college, and the Army carries out the required training for these two years.

One of my first experiences with military science was learning how to shine shoes—excuse me, how to spit shine shoes. I was given a new pair of shoes, and the leather on the outside of these shoes was not shiny; in fact, the leather was so dull it appeared it could never be shiny. After trying for several hours to shine my shoes with no success, I decided to do that which I always do when I do not know the answer to a problem, ask someone. I was to have inspection the next day, and I did ask someone how to shine my shoes fast. One of my friends offered the best solution: buy a can of instant spray shine and apply it to your shoes, and your shoes will be spit shine perfect. The spray worked, and I was saved hours of work shining my shoes. I had heard that using this spray to shine shoes was not looked on favorably by the instructors. I never got caught, and my friend who gave me the idea faded into the background.

Composition rhetoric courses are about writing. Each student had several compositions or papers to write for the course. The grading of these papers has always been a question in my mind because I didn't understand the criteria.

My sister Mary Lu was an excellent writer, and she helped by tutoring me. I improved my writing skills in this course, and they were to be improved more when I wrote my dissertation for my PhD.

On the other hand, French was one of the courses that tested my ability to graduate from John Carroll. I was actually spending more time studying French than on all my other subjects combined. This was called frustration, and I had to take three more semesters excluding the present one.

As I remember, the instructor was from somewhere in the Mideast. The most interesting and enjoyable part of the class were the stories about his past. One of his stories, as I remember it, put him in the position of driving a vehicle and coming in direct contact with a camel.

Latin had been my language of choice in high school, and enrolling in French in my freshman year was one of the biggest mistakes I made at Carroll. Spanish must have been easier to master and much more usable in society. After French, I learned to stay away from language courses.

My language requirement for my PhD was the computer language.

Snowstorm in the First Semester and the Bus Home

It was in 1962 when a snowstorm hit on December 7. Classes were canceled, and our Christmas vacation began early, as our exams were postponed until January. That was not good because our Christmas vacation was cut short so we could take our exams in January. The exams that were usually two hours long were now compacted into sixty minutes. The snowstorm turned out to be a big inconvenience.

I usually went home via the Greyhound bus. I would take a rapid transit bus to the Cleveland Union Terminal or the Terminal Tower. Due to my class schedule, I usually had about ten to fifteen minutes to get from Terminal Tower to the bus station. This was one of my first lessons in finding out that money talks. Unlike the conventional manner of paying, I would give the driver his fare plus a tip upon entering the taxi and tell him, "The Greyhound Station, and make it fast." I never missed a bus, but on occasion, I was seen running after the bus as it was backing out of the terminal.

The inside of the station was a bit of a sideshow. If you are ever looking for jewelry, there was usually a man with a trench coat walking around the terminal selling some. I will never forget the time this man came up to me and said, "Need a watch?" As he said that, he pulled up both the sleeves on his coat and showed his shirtsleeves. There on his arms were several watches. After he showed the watches on his arm, he opened both sides of his trench coat and displayed more watches. His stock approached the average display case in a jewelry store. I would guess his watches were stolen.

Another first for me was the shoeshine stand. On a few occasions, I reached the Greyhound Station early, and I liked to treat myself to a shine. I learned very fast that dark socks should be worn instead of white socks. Dark socks did not show any of the black polish that may have missed the shoe.

Traveling home on the Greyhound bus also was a big inconvenience when there was snow on the side windows. While it was safe as a mode of travel, being able to see out the windows, especially the side windows, was impossible. I usually was able to see out of the front windows if I was in one of the seats in the first few rows. Of course, the seats in these rows were always taken. I never did like sitting in close proximity to another person, as it was very cramped, so the back of the bus was my spot. When two seats were open, two seats were used.

My limited other transportation option was to take the train to Sandusky. While I could catch the train in Sandusky, catching the train from Cleveland to Sandusky was not an option. The train was a definite improvement over the bus, as one can walk around, and there is usually plenty of room on the coaches. I never did run into a man selling watches at the train station.

Second Semester, Freshman Year

I was to continue more of my same frustration with French class in my second semester; I would study hard but not receive very good grades. Once again, I figured I was spending half my study time on French and learning very little.

I continued my composition class and found that I had learned a lot from the previous semester. Writing was difficult for me for two reasons. I had not had as much helpful individual guidance in this area, and writing anything in long hand was difficult for me and the professors, difficult for me because I possessed terrible penmanship and difficult for the professors because they could not read my handwriting. It probably took the instructor twice the time to read my test material.

Statistics and sociology were enjoyable classes, and I did well in them. I enjoyed statistics, as it allowed me the opportunity to work with probabilities in my daily life. My studies in sociology allowed me to better understand the organization of society and how it functions.

World history, Christian origin, and military science were required courses again.

Extracurricular

I always felt that extracurricular activities are important, as they help round out one's interests and abilities. Books alone do not make a well-rounded student. I had the pleasure of being involved with several extracurricular activities at John Carroll, which I will share. The areas of concentration that I will cover are the band, French club, glee club, and sodality. There were many other sports of interest such as football and basketball.

Band

The tuba was the instrument I played in the marching and concert band in college for three years. I was five feet two inches tall when I started college, so I needed to exert more than the ordinary energy to play the tuba or take up another smaller instrument. The band, like the glee club, performed two concerts on campus.

A trip to the Mardi Gras was planned by the band for 1963. A large mixer called the Collegiate Caper Mixer was held under the capable leadership of our band president. All the band members were involved in helping to make the event successful.

One of my duties was to obtain balloons as a donated entity. I contacted Jack H. Gibson, the president of the Pioneer Rubber Company, for an appointment to request a donation of several hundred balloons. As I entered his office, I was a bit intimidated by the aura of power that arose from this office. His desk was large as was his chair, several awards were on the wall, and he projected a sense of authority. He gave us the balloons despite the fact that it probably wasn't a profitable advertising venture.

Since my father was the comptroller/vice president of finance, and I was a friend of the president's son, John, he was probably being nice to me by giving us the balloons. Regardless of the reason, I had accomplished my goal and had several boxes of balloons. I did get the balloons, and that's what counted. I learned a valuable lesson from this experience. Sometimes it is better to get the job done than to accomplish it in the manner you wished.

The big night came, and all the balloons had been blown up and were placed on the catwalk above the gym floor for the big dance. The appointed time came, and my crew pushed the balloons over the sides of the catwalk. It was a beautiful sight to see the hundreds of balloons fall on the crowd. It was a great feeling to know the mixer had been a financial success.

Unfortunately, our good luck ran out, as the plane we had procured to take us to the Mardi Gras did not meet the safety standards of the university. All the work did not produce a trip to the festival, but we did gain some great experiences in fund-raising.

The band also provided spirited music for the basketball games and other events.

The sixty-member band performed two concerts that year under the direction of Jack T. Hearns, the conductor. The concerts that academic year were with the glee club at home. Instead of traveling to New Orleans, we participated in the Cherry Blossom Festival in Washington, D.C. The trip to the parade is a trip I will never forget. While the parade went well, my evening was something quite different.

My friends wanted to meet at a bar in the red-light district earlier than it was convenient for me. I was ready to leave the hotel shortly after dark and began to follow the directions I had been given. I was following the map to what I thought was the right street. Shortly after I turned to the street, I began to hear footsteps behind me. As I looked around, I discovered I had gone down a side street instead of a main street. I looked over my shoulders to see how far I was from the Main Street and also to look for the person making the footsteps. By the dim light, I began to see people coming out of the walls. It hit me like a ton of bricks; I am being followed, and they probably are going to rob me. I walked faster only to realize that the footsteps were beginning to close in on me. I couldn't go back, and my instincts told me to flee this dangerous situation—now! I began to sprint faster than I have ever run in my life. I prayed and looked for a main street. My hopes were beginning to wane when a well-lit street with people on it appeared.

When I felt safe, I looked back and realized that I had taken the wrong street. I knew I was a very fortunate to walk and run with God through this situation in which several people, not my friends, may have robbed, beaten, or even killed me. As I think back on this event, I wonder who else was there with God helping me run and pointing me in the direction of a safe street; it could have been my twin. No doubt I had just experienced one of the most dangerous events in my life, and I was very lucky to be safe.

Then I went into one of the bars to find my friends. I discovered that they were not there. I traveled to several bars with the same result. Finally, as soon as I sat down, I was asked if I wanted a drink. I said, "Not yet." I had not given the correct answer. I was quickly informed that unless I purchased one of their expensive drinks, I would need to leave. I had to have a drink or two to keep my table. I left and used the well-lit streets to arrive at my hotel. When I ran into my friends, they asked where I had been. I told them the story and knew they were happy that they had not been with me that evening.

French Club

I had thought it wise to join the French club for no other reason than to improve my grade. The French club of over twenty persons was very active in furthering the French language and advocated a better understanding of the French culture. Films and lectures were the main media for providing this better understanding. Studying the French culture was much more interesting to me than learning how to speak French.

One interesting happening for me in the French club was when I was introduced to a French cigarette and had the opportunity to smoke it as part of the French club meeting agenda. The oval cigarettes looked like a cigarette, but they tasted like cigar. This was a onetime experience with French cigarettes.

Glee Club

The glee club fraternity is known as Beta Tau Sigma or "Brotherhood Through Song." The glee club, like the band, practiced several days each week. The success of the band and glee club could be directly attributed to Jack Hearns, the conductor, as he worked tirelessly to see that he was fair to every member. He was a good listener and a patient person.

One of the big draws for the glee club was the members went on tour each year to sing with girls' choirs. I sang tenor all four years at John Carroll. There were ninety members in the glee club. The past year, two concerts with Siena Heights College and Alverno College took place. In the second semester, the Midwestern Concert Tour took the club to St. Mary's College at South Bend, Indiana; Alverno College in Milwaukee, Wisconsin; and Rosary College in River Forest, Illinois.

Alverno College Glee Club then traveled to Carroll for the pop concert in Kulas Auditorium. The auditorium was decorated as a sidewalk café for a weekend of melody. While in Chicago at Rosary College, I had the good fortune of meeting a young lady named Christina. We were to write back and forth for a few years while I was at John Carroll.

Sodality

The sodality at John Carroll was named the Sodality of the Annunciation. The purpose of this organization was to provide training for the Catholic Action Apostolate. This goal was accomplished through ongoing meetings, a leadership retreat, and days of Reconciliation to name a few.

Mixers or dances after the basketball games were the major fundraising events.

Helping in the spiritual growth of each member was of primary importance. I grew spiritually with my involvement in this organization. Growth in my relationship with God was of primary importance to me then and remains so today. A staff member guided the progress of the sodality and spent many hours with the group, as well as with individuals. This staff member was rarely without a smile. Members of the sodality were run-of-the-mill students who happened to faithfully follow their religious convictions and practices. I learned that the reason I was on earth was very simple: I was to have a relationship with God and all his creations.

At this time, I tried hard to understand my relationship with God and how my life would grow with God. I was to find in years to come that understanding God was to be a lifelong venture. I believe in the mystery that there are three persons in one God: the Father, the Son, and the Holy Spirit. Thus, God can be one of the three or just God in general that I am addressing. Usually it is God in general that I am referring to. There is logic in finding God in everything in my life, as He created the world and all that happens in it. God gave me life and skills to do many things. I must use, not misuse, my skills and abilities. I owe it to myself, the world, and God to positively use my skills. As I grew older, I tried to understand and better appreciate the world God has given me and the fact that He is always with me.

I try to keep in contact with God by praying. One aspect of prayer is asking God for help in my life and thanking God for everything He has given me. While I do not pray as often as I would desire, I continued to explore meaningful prayer. I owe it to God to do His will, and I believe God called on all His people to follow His son's example, which is given in the Bible.

Meditating on Jesus's life was a form of prayer that I favored, but finding a set time varied as my schedule changed. I would like to meditate on Jesus's life more. I find Jesus's life as a man more concrete, and thus, the lessons are easier to relate to. Developing my relationship with God is an ongoing process. Thinking about God should be an everyday activity and more consistent in my life than it is now. It requires constant attention and can be hard to understand, but I do believe in Him.

Other Organizations at John Carroll

There are approximately thirty other organizations at John Carroll whose purposes ranged from service to John Carroll, being dedicated to a particular subject area or coming together because of its point of origin. These organizations are essential to the goals of this school. While time and space do not permit discussion of each of these organizations, this should not lessen their importance or positive contribution to JCU.

Sports

Football and basketball were big at JCU. During my freshman year, I saw the Blue Streaks football team win the PAC (Presidents' Athletic Conference) championship with a 7–0 record. The "Wolfpack" set four NCAA records in defense and twelve PAC records. The "Roadrunners" always scored enough points for the win.

That year, the basketball team finished with an overall record of twelve wins and five losses and a 9–3 PAC record. The team was close to winning the PAC but "no cigar." The reserve team won the "Little PAC Co-Champs" with a 5–3 record. I knew two players from our class who were on this team, John Minaudo and Jim Scanlan.

Entertainment

Entertainment helped to develop a well-rounded Carroll man. The fifth anniversary of the University Series included Hal Holbrook, Odetta and Leon Bibb, and the San Pietro Chamber Orchestra of Naples. Fr. Herman S. Hughes, SJ, has guided the University Series to be one of Cleveland's leading cultural attractions.

Dorm Life and Pranks

As I started classes at JCU, I was overwhelmed! At best, JCU was going to be a difficult and challenging experience. As a result of uncertainty in my abilities, I prayed to God to help me graduate from this excellent, but difficult, university. I was not sure where I was going, but I knew I needed help. I knew that I would need to use my education in a Christian manner, but I was not able to produce any specifics. I also knew that I had an obligation to use wisely the many skills that other people had shared with me. Yes, it was a time of uncertainty and few answers. I saw no way that I could be effective in this world without an education.

The other adventuresome part of college was that with the fast pace of studies, dorm life, and social life, there were many incidents that happened that produced some serious and lighter parts of college life. This time in one's life is the time to experience what comes one's way, have fun, and take some risks along the way.

A Visit to Youngstown

In my freshman year, my next-door neighbor in Pacelli Hall John Mulcahy received a phone call that his father had a heart attack and had passed. Many of us from the dorm decided to go to Youngstown, Ohio, for the funeral. When we arrived, we took a tour around the town. We noticed a large man standing beside a Cadillac. The man had the largest cigar I had ever seen in my life. The cigar must have been nine inches long or longer. As I saw the man wave at someone, I asked who this person of distinction was. One of my fellow students from Youngstown said that he was a known mobster. I didn't ask any more questions.

The funeral Mass was a very solemn affair. The homily that the priest gave was one I will never forget. My friend's father was referred to many times in the homily as a "pillar of the church" and was a well-known attorney in Youngstown. As the priest talked about him, I remember that he placed his fist a number of times on the coffin emphasizing to me and the congregation his importance and that he would be missed.

Fleeting thoughts of my own father's mortality and service to the community immediately came to my mind. It would be nineteen years later that my father would pass at the rather young age of seventy-one.

After the funeral and the meal, we decided that it was time to see more of the town. The bar district was first on the list. As we slowly drove through the neon-sign-lit area, I saw a man stagger through two parked cars to the Main Street we were traveling. As the man staggered in front of our car and stopped, the driver of our car slammed on the brakes. As it turned out, the man who obviously had been drinking came over to our car and fell face first onto the hood of our car. After a few minutes, he picked himself up slowly and staggered off in a new direction.

That evening, we stayed and enjoyed the hospitality at another student's home. As I again began to reflect on the day's activities, it was impossible to think of the mortality of my friend's father without thinking of my own parents' mortality. While their deaths were to come years later, it always seemed that they passed on much too soon.

Pranks

Many pranks occurred in the dorm. A wastebasket of water is the first prank. A wastebasket is filled with water around three-fourths full. The wastebasket is leaned against the door, and a knock on the door sets the trap. As the person opens the door, the wastebasket tips, and they receive a wet floor. (It was probably time to clean the floor anyway.)

A brief sleep in the daytime was a frequent happening in college. Staying up late and studying the night before promotes the need for sleep. One day, a friend was sleeping on his back, and his hand was in a position like he's holding shaving cream. A generous portion of shaving cream was sprayed into the palm of his hand. A feather tickling his nose prompted him to hit his face with the handful of shaving cream. Voila! The deed is done.

Friends

During my whole college career, I associated mainly with my various roommates and students from Youngstown and Chicago. A friend from Chicago was about the only other person my height. In the evening, we would all go to supper together. It was a ritual. One person would go to another person's room. Then those two or three would go to another room until everyone was assembled in one area. Finally, we would all go to eat together. At JCU, it was imperative that each man wore a sports jacket and tie for dinner. The condition of the ties and coats was anything but pretty after a few weeks of wear. Yes, the "prettiness" was lost since somehow food and drink had a tendency to jump off one's plate and stick on the tie or sports jacket.

Roommate

I was to have several roommates and others who seemed like roommates. My freshman roommate was from Detroit and had many friends. On occasion, he would go home on weekends to work in a butcher shop to earn extra money. In the butcher shop, he would rapidly cut up the item of the day. As a student, he used his study skills so well that he could accomplish about twice as much as I could.

Fr. Joseph O. Schell, SJ, was the prefect of Pacelli Hall. At times, Father Schell was in need of a carryout from shops on the Warrensville Circle. Running an errand for such a well-respected person was always a pleasure.

Food and Drinks

This topic was one of the top concerns of any JCU student. Our three basic meals were provided under the room and board plan by SAGA foods. I had nurtured a few duodenal ulcers in my high school experiences. When I thought I needed it, I could ask for special food. One of my favorite special meals was broiled steak for supper. If I thought the main course was too greasy, I would ask for the steak. It was usually a little tough coming from the kitchen trying to conceal my steak, as others were being served the greasy entree. Students would constantly ask me, "Hey, where did you get that steak?"

I would reply, "I sometimes need a special diet."

They would respond, "What's your diet for?"

I would respond truthfully, "Ulcers." Since no one wanted to have or admit having ulcers, that would satisfy their brain but not their taste buds.

Had I been born years later, the treatment of ulcers with Maalox, Tums, or similar antacids may not have been the best treatment. Instead, antibiotics to control the bacteria in the stomach would have been a preferred form of treatment and more effective than what I was using. One of my own forms of treatment was my supply of jarred fruit baby food.

In the evening, one of the most common dorm foods was popcorn. The smell of popcorn had the ability to permeate brick walls in less than one quarter of a second. The trick in preserving the morsels for oneself was to lock your entry door and maintain silence while you consumed the popcorn. If there were leftovers after you and your friends inside the locked door had your fill, opening the door would invite many hungry occupants of the building to clean up the scraps. Scraps were usually defined in this incident as kernels that did not pop.

Other types of food also were stored in the dorm. Items such as cookies, preferably homemade, and anything sold in the vending machines were common.

Beverages usually came from the machines located in the lounge. Of course, there were pop machines, but my favorite were milk machines. One can of pop was usually satisfying for a limited amount of time, but two milks were the start of fulfillment for me.

The most sought-after drink was beer. The seeking and consumption of this liquid had to be done outside the walls of the dormitory at the local establishments set up for such an indulgence. Some members of our class were to find out that if one decided to consume the beer in the dorm and was caught by the authorities, living outside of the dorm was the option preferred by the administrators.

Although I would at times drink beer, I believed that the pain and suffering were not worth the few moments of pleasure. Studying with normal stomach pains from ulcers was challenging, but studying after consuming beer was more challenging. I usually had to endure some pain from my ulcers while studying for good grades. I did not feel that the additional pain caused by beer was worth it.

One more memory of my freshman year associated with drinking was at Halloween. Some of the students got the bright idea that instead of trick-or-treating, a good variance would be to go "trick or shot." A few brave souls found a shot glass and launched their newfound idea. Two types of neighbors greeted the JCU entrepreneurs. It was either a laugh and a shot or a scowl perhaps followed by a call to the police. Fortunately, no JCU students were apprehended by the arm of the law in this escapade.

Summer Break

Pioneer Rubber Company

After my freshman year in college, I was a summer employee at the Pioneer Rubber Company in Willard. My major job duty was painting. The summer of 1963 was the most eventful. Pioneer was a company that made balloons and several types of rubber gloves. The Frederick household usually had a good supply of balloons. The gloves made there were surgical gloves, Bluette gloves (a household glove), industrial gloves, and veterinarian gloves. The most interesting of these gloves to me was the approximately three-foot-long veterinary gloves used to examine and conduct other medical procedures on animals such as cows. Another interesting product was bull condoms for a bull farm in Tiffin to catch the semen from the bull to be used in artificial insemination.

I largely, if not entirely, obtained this job since my father was an employee and vice president/controller at Pioneer. The summer jobs were reserved for employees' offspring attending college.

I came to know very early in my employment that the entire workforce was watching the summer employees; I was never sure of the reason. After almost every action we took, it was somehow known by the entire workforce, especially if the action was the least bit shady. I realized I was under the microscope and tried to make myself look good in the eyes of the administration. We will see shortly how unsuccessful I was in this venture. It wasn't hard to know that we were under the microscope, as many of the fulltime workers would stand by the entrance doors to catch any indication of what we might be doing that day.

The Fence

I started a week earlier than other college summer workers at Pioneer since classes at John Carroll had started earlier in the fall and were out earlier in the spring. One of my first jobs was to cut the weeds along the fence surrounding the plant. I began cutting everything close until I ran into a large growth of flowers, which looked like irises to me. I walked back to the shop and asked Ernie, the maintenance director, if I was to cut down the flowers by the fence.

He told me "everything goes" by the fence.

As I cut down the flowers, I thought it was a shame to waste them. On my next break, I took the flowers back to the shop, found a glass jar, and put the flowers and water on the director's desk. I never did find out what he thought of the flowers, and I felt comfortable with my decision to add a little color to the office with a gift that he could either accept or throw away. I did find out, however, that I did not like the poison ivy I caught clearing the weeds.

The first job assigned to the five summer workers by our direct supervisor was to paint the fence surrounding the property. There are two key words in this undertaking: paint and fence. The painting was accomplished by brushes and rollers on a long stick. The rollers were not the typical rollers but looked like cutoff mops. One had to be careful not to roll too fast, as the silver paint would flip onto all the painters.

That is exactly what happened on the second day of work for us college students; the paint that was to go on the fence went on another painter. There was some discussion as to whether I had intentionally flipped silver paint on my good friend Lenny Playko, who was painting opposite me on the fence. Lenny felt there was no discussion on my intent. Lenny thought that one flipping deserved another, and my roller flipper was answered by a silver paint can. When I saw the big blob of silver paint coming toward me,

I lowered my head so as not to have my face covered with paint. It didn't work; the paint hit the top of my head. It was dead center in the middle of my hair, and when I looked up, the silver paint rolled down on my face, including my eyebrows, my eyes, and my lips. In short, my entire face was pretty well silvered.

Well, the action was over, and I definitely got the worst end of the deal. To be perfectly clear about this incident, I do not believe that I splashed more silver paint on Lenny than he did on me. I felt Lenny was due for a payback.

I walked into the maintenance building, which was about two years old, and was greeted by the big boss. Now he was three times my size and had this booming voice that everyone could hear in the shop. In fact, he asked me in his booming voice, "What happened?"

I am not a liar, and I don't like to get my friends in trouble. I told him that an incident had happened and a pail of paint fell on my head. It was the best explanation I could give. I think he eventually heard the whole story, but under the circumstances, I thought I came up with a good reason for having paint on my head. I was expecting to get to the restroom unnoticed and clean up before anyone knew what happened. As I came out of the washroom from cleaning up, I saw Ernie standing at the door.

He told me, "Now that you have yourself cleaned up, get the silver paint off the floor, as two people already have slipped on it." I got the worst end of the deal that day.

The Tanks

On another occasion, the five summer workers were painting two cylindrical tanks that contained a chemical called xylene and were at least ten to fifteen feet tall and fifty to seventy-five feet long. We were instructed to paint the tanks with large paintbrushes. As we finished up a morning of painting, we had a discussion over our lunch. The outcome of the discussion was that we were going to take our mops used on the fence out of mothballs and activate them instead of the paintbrushes. Since that would reduce the amount of time significantly, we decided that we should just do it and surprise the boss with the good news.

That afternoon, two teams approached the two tanks. With one painter on top of the tanks pouring the silver paint down the side of it and one or two persons with mop rollers on the ground distributing the paint, we were in business. It did take a little time to get the method working smoothly, but after the right amount of paint was poured on the tank, and the rollers were able to properly distribute the paint, the new system worked much better than the old system. The tanks looked good so far.

We were not ready for an inspection that afternoon, and I don't think the boss was expecting to give one as he and some other big shots walked through the grounds close to our tank-painting project. All at once, the boss looked over and saw what we were doing and shouted, "You are supposed to paint those tanks with paintbrushes!"

Since we had made a team decision, I informed the boss that we felt it is much faster with the rollers than the paintbrushes. The boss shook his head and headed off to another job.

Break Room

Each morning and each afternoon at a specified time, each worker was given a break of fifteen minutes. The break room was a nice room, and it had a good selection of snacks and drinks. The tables and chairs had a shine on them and were impeccably clean.

Since we were painters, we had to remove any paint on our arms, hands, and clothing before going into the break room. Removing all paint from our bodies and clothes that might come in contact with the tables, chairs, or floor was a very difficult task.

It happened on more than one occasion that a painter would sit down and unintentionally leave a trace of the silver paint. The kitchen would then call down to the maintenance shop and ask for someone to clean up the paint before it touched anyone's good clothes.

There was talk about painters not being able to come to the break room. We were lucky that no one followed through with that proposal.

Plant No. 3

In addition to the main plant, there was a plant in Attica, Ohio, a nearby town, and another plant in Willard called plant number 3. Lenny Playko's father was the plant manager of it. The workforce was largely women. At this plant, the cloth lining inside the gloves was made. The college students were working a job at plant number 3. We came into the building to take a break with the rest of the workers. Lenny's dad worked closely with his employees, so I was not surprised that he took his break with his workers. The break was over when Lenny's dad would crush his coffee cup. It was amazing how everyone was out of the break room a minute after the cup was crushed.

On one particular day, the college students were leaving the inside of the plant. One of them touched a hot handpress used to iron the cloth that lined the glove. He burned his hand very badly and had to be treated. We all learned that when one doesn't know what something is, we should keep our hands off it.

Painting Houses

Be Careful

In the evening during the summer, Lenny and I would paint houses to earn a little extra money. We were already painting together at the Pioneer Rubber Company, so this extended our ability to earn money. One of the houses we painted was owned by my brother-in-law Fred Eldred. If Fred had time, he would paint with us, but most of time, Lenny and I painted together.

Since this house in Willard was a two-story home, we would paint from a ladder to access the second story. On one occasion, I was painting the second story over a first-story structure, which jutted out from the house. This extended structure had a slate roof on it. I was painting over my head on the soffit or the bottom part of the roof. I was reaching over the first-story structure and needed more paint on the brush. As I was lowering my arm to dip my brush into the paint bucket, my elbow hit the corner of the slate roof of the first-story structure.

I felt a terrible pain and looked down at my elbow. A large amount of blood was coming out of my elbow and dripping into the paint, on the side of the house, and on the ground. Lenny took one of the old T-shirts used to clean up, and he wrapped my elbow with it to stop the bleeding. A trip to the local medical expert confirmed a nasty cut. The cut needed to be cleaned and wrapped tight so the elbow couldn't bend. That was the end of painting that evening, and that was the end of my right-hand painting for several days.

A Trip to the Country at Night after the Painting Ordeal

Of all my experiences, this story is the one most requested at campfires and the one that I enjoy recalling. It was a Friday night, and I was at a nightspot called Friendly Corners in Norwalk. I was with my friend Lenny, and we were having a drink and talking. There was not much going on except for a story that Lenny was telling. His story was about Sam, a hermit who lived near Willard.

Lenny's story went something like this. One evening, Lenny was driving down Sam's road, and he decided to drive in his driveway to see if he could see him standing in his Dutch door with his big coon dog standing beside him. Sam usually had a long rifle, which he kept by his side. Sure enough, Lenny pulled in Sam's driveway, and there was Sam, his dog, and his rifle standing in his house's open Dutch door. This was a scary sight, according to Lenny, and as I listened and asked questions, the whole story was intriguing, interesting, and scary.

I said to Lenny, "Let's go see Sam." Lenny agreed to go to his house, but he could not promise me that we would see Sam. He did promise to give it a good shot. Being young and in college made the trip a little easier to try. I was not sure if Lenny was telling the entire truth about Sam, but I wanted to find out. We left Friendly Corners and headed toward Sam's road. As we approached the road, I noticed that it was a very dark evening. There was no light from the moon, the stars, or any pole lights. As we started down the road, I was looking everywhere for Sam or his dog. I was soon drawn into the scary setting of that road because both sides were covered with tall cornstalks coupled with weeds. There was limited vision, and the headlights of the car shone on a path that was dark and small.

A few minutes after turning to Sam's road, the car began to shake. I said, "Lenny, quit playing around with the car."

Lenny said, "I am not making the car shake, and I am not sure what's causing this vibration." Lenny stopped the car, and we walked around it. There in the darkness between the small opening of the cornstalks and weeds, we saw that we had a flat tire. We decided that we needed to change the tire quickly because Sam might see the lights from the car and come to investigate the trespassers.

I pulled out the jack with my good left arm; remember, my right elbow had been hurt. Before we placed the jack under the car, we decided to loosen the nuts on the tire. Lenny tried to loosen the nuts but said they were frozen and would not budge. I told him, "They can't be frozen because we have a flat, and we need to change it." At this point, one person was standing guard with a hammer in hand, and the other was trying to loosen the nuts on the tire. Since Lenny couldn't break the nuts loose, it was my turn. My right elbow was wrapped so that it would not move or bleed and would heal.

I tried loosening the nuts and was only able to stir up a few mosquitoes, which bit both of us on that hot summer evening. Lenny continued to hold the hammer and search the road and the corn with a flashlight hoping *not* to see Sam, his dog, or his rifle. Lenny decided to move the car a few feet. Finally, one nut broke loose followed by all the others. The nuts were loose, but Sam and his dog had to know we were near his house, and we knew we still needed to change the tire. Using the jack, we lifted the car and continued. We took off the flat tire and placed the good tire on the axle.

The mosquitoes continued their biting frenzy while we tightened the nuts, loaded our equipment, and started the car. I looked around one more time for Sam, his dog, and his rifle. Lenny started and drove the car. I really wasn't sure what I would have done if Sam and his dog had walked out of the corn or down the road.

We moved down the road a few feet, and I asked Lenny, "Do you think it is safe to pull into his driveway?" Neither of us was sure, but we were close to the house and had been close when we changed the tire. The headlights were bright enough that we could see the outline of his house. Before I knew what had happened, Lenny had pulled down a small hill into the driveway and was looking in the yard so that he didn't run over anything. I looked up and was in shock. All I could do was to point straight ahead at Sam, his dog, and what looked like a gun. They were standing in the open Dutch doors located at the entrance.

As I was pointing at him, Lenny was still avoiding obstacles in the front yard. He was completely unaware that anyone was standing in the doorway. Finally, Lenny looked up and saw Sam, his dog and the gun, and said, "Holy cow." Lenny quickly put the car in reverse, gave it the gas, and left the front yard much faster than we had entered. We were both in disbelief about the evening and were glad we got off the property safely.

As I look back on this experience, I don't want to leave anyone with the impression that Sam ever hurt anyone; to my knowledge, he did not. I do know that this experience was very scary, and I was looking for adventure at this time in my life. I concluded that our "adventure" to have a quick look at him, his gun, and his dog would have been better done during the day, if at all.

After-Hours Summer Activities

I always had the good fortune of easily meeting young women. Even though it seemed they were not around, I could usually find them. It may have been at church, a visitor to the neighbors, at a store, or at a bar lounge. I knew that I wanted to marry the young lady who would best be a good mate for me and I for her. That was my constant goal.

It was not surprising that I would squeeze more than one date into a day. I had three months during the summer to make up for the nine months of "lean" dating at school. I even successfully arranged three dates in one day. One of the more unusual dates in which I was fortunate enough to participate will be presented along with some information about my height. If I had one thing in my life I would not change, it would have been the active dating in my high school and college years.

My height did limit me in my choice of dates because tall ladies usually did not perceive dating shorter men as desirable. At times, shorter women did not wish to date shorter men. My height had been a factor in my ability to adjust to the world. In grade school, I was usually the shortest boy in the class. Everywhere I looked, my male classmates were taller than me. I felt I was at the bottom of the ladder. Being the smallest carried the distinction of having to deal with less weight, less strength, less ability to see over others, and other factors depending on the situation. Although I was only five feet two inches as I entered college, I was more accepting of my size as a result of a discussion I had with my aunt Mary. I reported this incident in an earlier chapter.

In summary, she said, "It is not the size of your body that is important. It is the kind of person you are." Since this quote came from an extremely successful horticulturist and a lady who always treated me like I was a great person, I believed her. From that day forward, I slowly replaced the feelings of being someone less, because of my height, to a person that I could be very proud of—me. I took off work to be at my aunt Mary's funeral. I wish now that I would have had the opportunity to say a few words to honor her at the service. African violets adorned the outside of her casket. This reminded me that she had an African violet named after her; her legend lives.

The Lady from Work

It was the summer after my freshman year at JCU, and I was at home working at Pioneer Rubber Company. My elder brother, Walt, was always looking out for me when it came to finding single young ladies. One evening, Walt told me that he had spotted a single young lady named Barb that worked at Pioneer Rubber Company. She worked second shift, and my brother had noticed her one evening when he worked late. Somehow he had obtained her name and phone number. Walt told me to give her a call. I told Walt that I didn't know what the girl looked like, had never met her, and had no "lead in" to asking her out. Walt told me that it was very simple how I should approach Barb. I was to call her and tell her that I saw her one evening when I was picking up my brother Walt and thought that I would like to go out with her. If she asked how I got her name and phone number, I would tell her I had asked around and come up with them. I had not had a chance to meet her, as I wasn't usually at Pioneer in the evening hours. She believed everything I had said and agreed to go out with me the following Sunday evening at seven.

On Sunday, I started out for my date with Barb. Since I didn't know what she looked like, I thought whoever comes to the door will be Barb, and if someone who couldn't be Barb (because of age) came to the door, I would just go in, sit down, and wait for her to come into the room. I got to thinking Barb doesn't know what I look like either. I arrived in the neighboring town and could see that I was going to be fifteen minutes early. I killed some time by riding around the town.

As I pulled up to the house, panic feelings developed, and I was horrified by what I saw. There were several cars parked at Barb's house, and people of all ages on the lawn were having what looked like to me a reunion. I started to sweat. There were several young ladies about my age walking around. I didn't know any of them, and any one of them was "fair game" to be Barb.

As I left my car and had no idea what I was going to do, I saw a picnic table with some elder people around it, so I walked over to the table and asked them if they were having a reunion. They said they were, and some small talk developed. I thought I had broken the ice with these people, and I didn't know where I was going from here, but I sure was sweating and causing my shirt to become very damp. I continued to talk and waited to see what was going to develop. I was going to ask where I might find Barb. However, if Barb was standing close to me, I didn't want to tip my hand and allow anyone to know I didn't know her. I continued to sweat and hope for a good solution.

God must have intervened because an attractive young lady walked up to me and said, "Are you ready to go, Joe?" Was I ready to go? I had never been more ready to go anywhere in my life! I was afraid that something else would happen, and I wouldn't successfully get out of the circumstances I was in.

I said, "I am ready," and we left.

I found out how lucky I was that evening to find Barb because my neighbor lady Pat shared with me how she and her identical twin sister, Eileen, would switch dates as a trick on their escorts. That evening would have been a primetime to switch dates on me because I didn't know anyone at the reunion.

Scuba Club

The Willard police decided that having a standby scuba club was needed in the city. The club's members could assist in finding a person's body and locating needed evidence relating to various crimes. A small number of scuba divers was assembled. The ones other than myself that I can remember are the police, John Gibson, my brother Walt, and four or five others. We periodically had practices in the lake at the Willard Conservation Club.

There were a few calls that came in for diving assistance. One was for a boy who had drowned in a small pond near the edge of town. We checked this one out, and it turned out to be a false alarm. The other was a drowning near town. Divers and persons in boats searched for the body and did recover it after searching for many hours. I was out of town when the second incident happened and was unable to participate in the dive. Although the task of diving for a body can be viewed as gruesome, the need for the family and loved ones to know the outcome of the incident is important. It is a job that must be done by someone. I learned that doing a task that might not be appealing may fall on each of our shoulders.

The Pond and the Frogs

After work, the tradition was to stop at the local establishment where a quick cold beer and sausage were waiting for me. Since I didn't have the time to enjoy this tradition at John Carroll, I enjoyed this time by "forgetting about time" and savoring the moment. On occasion, I would buy a round, and someone else would return the favor. Well, "forgetting about time" was to get me in a little trouble. When it was suppertime, my mother only knew one time, and that time was when supper was ready, and anyone who was going to eat needed to be at the table "on time." On a few occasions, I can remember "forgetting about time" and supper.

On those occasions, my mother was thoughtful enough to call me at the tavern and say, "Do you know that it is suppertime?"

My answer was "I am just walking out the door." Well, I wasn't walking out the door when she called, but I surely was after I talked to Mom.

I was within my time line on one particular day, and I was spending my time talking with a friend about frog hunting. Eating frog legs was a favorite of mine, and frog legs were not easy to come by where I lived. My friend knew of a spot where frogs were plentiful, and the pond was very large and shallow. I have been known to be a very prompt person, and if there is something to be done, then I often say, "Let's do it now." If I didn't accomplish the task now, I may never have the chance to do it in the future. My friend liked my philosophy, so we agreed to meet later that evening to try this newfound pond. The location of this pond was then, and is now, a mystery to me. As we arrived at it that night, we found that we could not drive my friend's pickup truck close to the pond. Instead, we parked the truck off to the side of the path so others could go around it.

When we reached the pond, the sound of bullfrogs was everywhere. Hearing the bullfrogs was good because it meant that larger frog legs were likely. As we began to look around, we discovered frogs everywhere. Their eyes would sparkle in the beams of our flashlight, and we found them easy to obtain. Within an hour, we had more frog legs than I ever thought existed. That frog hunt was the most indescribably great frog hunt of my life.

We found the path we had used to come in to the pond area. As we started to walk down the path, we immediately heard dogs barking a short distance ahead of us.

My friend said, "Maybe we didn't have permission to be hunting here." If someone is bringing dogs after us, we probably shouldn't be here. We decided to get off the path as far as possible, so hopefully, the dogs didn't pick up our scent.

As we lay in the weeds several feet from the path, I could hear the dogs trying to sniff out our scent. I stopped breathing, as they were passing directly in front of our location. After they passed us, I began to breathe again. When the dogs were far enough away we ran for our truck. As we found the truck, we also found a vehicle parked in the middle of the road blocking our easy access out of the property.

We cleared out a few dead limbs and were able to drive our pickup around the vehicle. I went back to college a few weeks later and always had several questions, which I would have liked to pose. The first was "Did we have permission to be hunting frogs?" Another was "Was someone training his dogs to coon hunt?" The license number was on the pickup we used; yet to my knowledge, we were never contacted about frog hunting that evening. Why not? Some happenings in our lives will be a mystery, and it looks as if this is one of those in my life.

Sophomore Year

Classes

First Semester, Sophomore Year

I was pleased to note that I was still in college and beginning my second year at Carroll. I no longer was the lowest of all in existence—freshman. I wore no duffer and no tie symbolic of incoming freshmen students. I was still apprehensive about French but had been told that my new teacher could teach the language to anyone. It turned out that this teacher helped me learn French, and I received a B that semester. I actually was learning the language, and my new instructor shall always have my heartfelt thanks for his efforts. This semester was to expose me to a philosophy course, which I enjoyed. I learned a lot and have been able to use the information. The course was logic, and the teacher was Fr. William Bichl, SJ. The A I received in this course was a crowning accomplishment to a course well taught and well learned and to a subject matter I could really apply.

Biology was another course I enjoyed because of the subject matter and the labs. I enjoyed living organisms of any type, and the powerful microscopes allowed the class to clearly see the amoeba, paramecium, and other biological organisms. Military science, English literature, and the New Testament were among the required courses. I learned a great deal about the interpretation of words through my exposure to English literature and the New Testament classes. These courses were not high on my priority or my most enjoyable lists. In military science, I learned the art of lining up in formation and marching, skills I had used in my Boy Scout days.

Second Semester, Sophomore Year

I felt more secure during the second semester of my sophomore year than I had before. I was anxious to start courses in my major area of study, psychology. It appeared to be impressive to the young ladies. This semester was my chance to see if psychology was really a good fit for me. The head of the department of psychology was an approachable person, and he "lit my fire" of learning. Introductory psychology was for me the beginning of a love affair about people's behavior as influenced by the mind, feelings, desires, and other aspects of human behavior. I have never lost my desire and respect to study and apply psychology. Psychology was to help me in my future career, which involved working with people.

Genetics proved to be a challenging course. The instructor made sure that the terms *genotype* and *phenotype* were words the class would never forget, and there was a high probability of these words coming up in our sleep. While the classroom work was not easy, the lab work was very challenging. I had an especially threatening time in the lab. In the first week of class, each student was given a jar with nutrient and live fruit flies. Cotton was used to keep the fruit flies in the jar and allow them to breathe. My first generation was composed of five pairs of fruit flies. Now each of the jars had fruit flies with different characteristics. Some had short wings, different types of eyes, and other unique characteristics. My concern came in the second generation, as I had three offspring. I relayed my concern to the professor, and he helped me understand that I needed to take my fruit flies to bed with me because the offspring was the only way I could explain what had happened with the genetics of my fruit flies.

I was more than careful every time I administered the sleeping gas to the fruit flies to examine them, as I did not wish to kill them by oversedation. I was anxiously waiting to see what, if any, offspring would be in the third generation. I had ninety-seven offspring. I sedated each of the fruit flies, recorded the results, and came up with a theory to explain why I had so many flies with short wings or dark eyes.

My French teacher continued to be the kind of instructor I needed to pass my fourth semester of French. I was always amazed to see that a person can do about anything to be successful at a task that is so difficult. I was done with French after this semester. My roommate, Don Gresko, and I studied and studied and then studied more French. It paid off when we passed the course. I also had completed my military science course this semester since I had fulfilled my two-year requirement. I must say that I was always impressed with the Pershing Rifles when they were on the parade field after practicing hour after hour.

Extracurricular

My sophomore year involvement in organizations was a continuation of my freshman year. I had the pleasure of being involved again with the band, French club, glee club, and sodality. A quick update on these organizations is in order.

Band

The band was to adopt the Greek name of Phi Theta Mu with its emblem being attached to its new burgundy blazers. Fraternities that were based on friendship and not fostering the idea of elitism or "I am better than people who are not in my fraternity" appealed to me. While a number of concerts were given with the glee club, two concerts were presented in Kulas Auditorium on campus. One was with Rosary College of River Forest, Illinois, and another with St. Mary-of-the-Woods College of Terre Haute, Indiana. The big trip was to the St. Patrick's Day Parade in Chicago. True to tradition, the river was dyed green for the day. It was very cold that day, so cold the valves on the brass instruments were freezing. After the parade, a very nice social event was held with food and drinks. At that event, a well-known celebrity from Chicago made his appearance; the man was none other than Mayor John Daley. Mayor Daley had come to visit the JCU band on the most important of all important days, St. Patrick's Day.

When I was in Chicago in my sophomore year, I traveled the loop one evening to visit a lady friend. She and I had a platonic relationship arising from a meeting a year earlier. I was in hopes we could be a bit closer. Using the loop for the first time was an experience to remember. I must have walked a mile on the platform hoping the train would stop at what looked like a stop. I did not know that I needed to stand close to the train's loading platform to have the train pick me up. That was the last time I saw Christina. We continued writing for a while, but the relationship never became a close one.

French Club

Since I was doing so well in French, I decided to allow my membership to go to someone else.

Glee Club

Concerts with Rosary College and St. Mary-of-the-Woods College occurred during my sophomore year. The glee club continued to be known as one of the best.

Sodality

The spiritual life was molded by daily religious exercise and, where possible, helping members of the community. This type of growth was essential in building and maintaining a relationship with God.

Sports

For the second year in a row, the Blue Streaks football team was the PAC (Presidents' Athletic Conference) champions. An exciting year-end game with Washington & Jefferson and a score of 14–6 gave JCU the victory. The basketball season saw the John Carroll team go 12–6, which let the PAC title slip through its fingers.

Entertainment

The University Series outdid itself with some big name performers and many other notables. Louis Armstrong entertained with his jazz music, the Vienna Boys Choir sang to the crowd's delight, the Spanish guitarists, The Romeros played, Cornelia Otis Skinner performed in *The Wives of Henry VIII*, Lotte Lenya was in *Brecht on Brecht*, Shakespeare's *Henry IV, Part I* was presented by the Canadian Players, and The Old Vic Company's *The Hollow Crown* rounded out the entertainment. Stunt night proved positive for the class of 1966 with "The College Bull" between day-hops (commuter students) and dormies hosting a second place.

Dorm Life

A Trip to Downtown Cleveland

My roommate in my sophomore year was from Michigan. On a Saturday in the fall, my mother and sister Ann were in Cleveland with a group of Girl Scouts who were taking in the sights. I wasn't adept at getting around downtown Cleveland yet, so my roomie said he would go with me. Well, he did know his way around town. We found my mother and sister, and we were on our way back to the rapid transit to catch our ride to JCU when a gentleman came up to me and asked me something.

My roomie saw me trying to talk to the man, and as he got close enough to see what was going on, he said, "Let's go now."

I wasn't quite sure why we should leave because I had not found out what the gentleman wanted. I asked him, "Why did you want to leave?"

He looked at me and said without skipping a beat, "Because the man was propositioning you." Yes, my roomie did know his way around town, and I was learning a few lessons myself.

A Cleveland Indians Baseball Game

In my sophomore year, two of my friends, Tom Pruse and Don Gresko, went to a Cleveland Indians baseball game. After the game, they were walking through downtown Cleveland to catch the rapid transit to campus. As they were about halfway to the terminal, they were attacked by a gang. Don got away; Tom didn't.

Don came back to campus thinking Tom also would be there. Don was safe, and Tom was nowhere in sight. The resident staff member called the police. After twenty long minutes, they called back and told us Tom was located at one of the police stations. The staff picked up Tom. It seems

Tom was jumped, and he fought five to seven attackers. Tom had a black eye, a cut and bruised face, and a bloody T-shirt. I was very cautious about going down to the Indians game after this excursion.

A Late Night with the Maintenance Worker

My dorm room was next to a parking lot and had buildings on both sides. During the evening, I saw a maintenance worker with a wheelbarrow and tools walking across the parking lot about eleven. As he was about halfway through the parking lot, we began to do a ghost call through our open window. The ghost call went something like this: "OooooooooOOOOOOOOOOOH." To our surprise, he dropped the wheelbarrow and ran across the parking lot. The next morning, we rose early, and there in the middle of the parking lot sat the wheelbarrow in the same position as it was the previous night. The worker was nowhere in sight.

Onions

I had gone home in the fall for a brief visit with my family. After a night out with my friends, I decided to "hit the hay." At about three o'clock, I heard my elder brother, Walt, take a fire call. Walt had been a fireman for some time, and a call in the middle of the night was not unusual. As Walt was dressing, he came over to me and asked if I would like to go on the call too, as he was to drive a piece of equipment, and he needed someone to drive his car to pick him up after the fire. I had gone with Walt to a few parades and thought that this might be interesting. He told me that a storage building full of onions had caught fire.

I dressed very fast and took Walt to the fire station where he drove what looked like a pumper that delivered water. I followed my brother at a safe distance, and when we arrived at the fire, I parked his car in a spot that was away from it, yet I could still see the blazing fire. Unfortunately, the fire was quite advanced when we arrived, and the smell of onions was in the air. The fire was out in a short period, and the damage was more than I guessed. I followed my brother to the fire station and drove him home. As you might have guessed, I can easily recognize the smell of burned onions anytime.

Hoz Loses His Car and More

In my first few years in Pacelli Hall, one of my friends was John McManus, and his nickname was Hoz. Hoz seemed to have the ability to attract trouble and work out of it. This incident is about a time he traveled home to Youngstown. While at home on a cold winter evening, Hoz decided to cruise through the neon light bar area of town.

As Hoz was waiting at a stoplight in town, a man jumped into the backseat of his unlocked car. He informed Hoz that he had a weapon that would harm him unless he cooperated and drove the car into the country. Hoz did that and was asked to remove some of his clothes. The robber then took off with the car and his possessions. Hoz had some clothes on and was very cold; he began to walk. He looked ahead and saw his abandoned car. He approached the car noticing the keys were still in it, but his clothes were nowhere to be found.

He started the car, and since there were no cell phones at that time, he drove to a pay telephone. As Hoz was talking to the police, he noticed a car pull up to the telephone booth and shine its lights on him. He reported this suspicious action to the police. They told him to stay on the phone, and they were on their way. When the police arrived, they ran a check on the suspicious driver and found he was wanted, so they arrested him. The police asked Hoz to get in their cruiser while they filled out the report.

One of the officers loaned Hoz a police jacket to keep him warm. With their investigation complete, Hoz gave back the police jacket and went over to his car. As he saw the police car pull away, he noticed he had no keys to his car, and he remembered he had placed the keys in the pocket of the policeman's jacket. He called the police office and informed them he needed the officer to bring his keys back. He started his car with the recovered key and decided the safest place for him that evening was home.

President John F. Kennedy Is Shot

I remember one of my fellow glee club members from Cleveland who will never forget the day John F. Kennedy was shot. This was during my sophomore year in college. All of the classes were dismissed, and I spent most of my time glued to the television and wondered how such a horrendous act could happen. Each of my fellow students had his own way of dealing with the national crisis. Wally Lutkus walked five miles home to deal with his deep sorrow of losing the President of the United States. Indeed, students at John Carroll along with other people of the United States exhibited terror, fear, and disbelief along with other emotions. Little did I know that terrorism would be developing by leaps and bounds in the years to come.

There were many classic pictures taken during this time, such as when Lyndon Johnson was to be sworn into office as President on Air Force One. It was such a privilege and felt eerie many years later when Kathy and I visited Air Force One at the Wright-Patterson Air Force Base in Dayton and stood in the exact spot where Lyndon Johnson took the oath of office as President of the United States. We discovered that this photograph was taken next to a cutout area where the slain president's body had been transported in John F. Kennedy's Air Force One plane. The photo of John-John saluting his father while Jackie stood in the background and the film of Lee Harvey Oswald being shot by Jack Ruby are other pictures that will be forever etched in my mind.

Some of my classmates immediately made plans to travel to Washington, D.C. to witness the happenings connected to the president's funeral and burial. At my 2011 class reunion at John Carroll, one of the group related his experiences in connection with President Kennedy's death. Among those traveling to D.C. were Dan Kush from Chicago and Mike Murray of Sandusky. The first big obstacle they faced was having permission from the university and their parents to travel to Washington, D.C. with little planning and no arrangements for lodging and food and little or no knowledge of the city itself.

With the needed approvals secured, the two set out for D.C. They had thought it wise to wear their ROTC Army uniforms, as this would be their best ticket into the many distinguished places they wished to visit. In fact, they found a place at Georgetown University to sleep and as they entered the line to view the president in the rotunda, Army personnel spotted them and put them to work directing people in the line to see the president. After several hours of directing traffic, they were given the chance to enter the line and the rotunda to view the president's casket. The line extended down East Capitol Drive almost twenty blocks to RFK Stadium. As they left the rotunda, they saw the most beautiful sunset they had ever seen.

The funeral was to be etched in each of these young men's minds forever. The sound of the drummers at the Capitol Building and the sight and footprints of the lone horse were lasting memories. Members of the group have said that if given the choice to again go on this trip, they would. The most common feedback is that this was an experience they would take advantage of in a heartbeat. As I reflect on my friends' experience, I wish I had taken the trip to see firsthand the funeral of my president. The word I have is that at least one gentleman, Dan Kush, was so impressed with

D.C. that he returned there in the employ of a newly elected Congressman in December of 1972.

Another classmate, John Morris, planned to make the trip to D.C.; however, he was the platoon sergeant for the Pershing Rifles drill team. A competition was scheduled for the evening of November 22 at Kent State University. Even after the assassination, the drill meet went on as scheduled. A moment of silence was observed prior to the competition. The John Carroll University drill team placed first in the competition for both platoon and squad categories. This team went on to become national champions for 1963-1964, defeating every school in the country. Upon returning to the campus, Morris organized a twenty-one-gun salute as the American flag was lowered to half staff.

Years later, I was to read about a number of acts of kindness to Jackie Kennedy in the form of letters. There were over 800,000 letters in the first seven weeks following the assassination sent to her. Two hundred thousand of the letters were sent to the John F. Kennedy Library in Boston. These letters remained there until Ellen Fitzpatrick decided to write *Letters to Jackie: Condolences from a Grieving Nation*. The book was released the week of March 1, 2000, and included 200 never-before-published letters.[28]

Several examples of our emotions at that time appeared in the book. One was Mary South, an eighth grader, who was just sitting down to play the organ at her Catholic school in Santa Clara, California, at the time of the tragedy. She said, "I tried to tell myself he would be all right, but somehow I knew he wouldn't. The tears wouldn't stop. The slightly damp keys were hard to play, but I offered it up that the president might live."

One of the shortest letters came from a student at the University of Massachusetts who wrote, "Dear Mrs. Kennedy: I haven't ever seen our football players cry . . . But today, they did."[29] If we look around, these acts of kindness are many places in our lives and deserve to be models for all of us.

Friend from Back Home

In my freshman year, I started out knowing no one on campus. In my sophomore year, Lenny Playko, a longtime family and personal friend, attended John Carroll. Lenny was the person I had hunted with in high school. We usually hunted rabbits, as they were plentiful at that time.

I remember one hunting trip with Lenny and his father at Eldred's farm, where I had been employed. We had been hunting around the river when a rabbit jumped up and just that fast went into a hole. Lenny had a beagle that was the best rabbit hunter around. His beagle immediately went into the rather large hole and went so deep we could not hear or see him. He was gone a good five minutes, and we were getting very concerned that he had gotten stuck in the hole. A few minutes later, his beagle came out of the hole, and after that, the rabbit came out of another hole near the first hole his dog had entered. Lenny was able to bag the rabbit, and all of us were to repeat this story several times in our lives.

Lenny and I saw each other at college several times, but since we were in different dorms and years, we each had our own friends.

Getting Married

Mail call was a big deal especially when a letter from a lady friend contained the words "I miss you" or when it's one from Mom or Dad with money in it, which showed up as a diagonal slit in the mailbox. On this particular day, there was a prank about to take place, but there were only a few people who knew what was going to happen. I was one who was not in the loop. As I entered the mail room, I noticed my friend Don Gresko reading and rereading a letter. I went over to him and asked if there was something wrong. He said he had gotten a letter from a girl he recently met, and she wrote him to tell him that she was pregnant. The rest of the story is that she was telling everyone he was the father. Don said, "I am not the father!" The more we talked, the more confusing the issue became.

After some more discussions, the suggestion was made for Don to go to a priest and seek guidance. Don decided that was the best route to take, so he started over to the chapel. Within a few minutes, the perpetrators of the letter began asking questions. I told them what had happened and that Don was going to see the priest. One of the perpetrators informed me that we had to stop Don from going to the priest, as the whole thing was a big joke. Now was not the time for us to talk but to take action.

We ran to the other side of the campus to catch Don before he talked to the priest. We arrived at the administration building and went to the chapel, and there we found Don. We guided Don out of the chapel and explained what had happened. Don was relieved it was over, and everyone else was happy we had stopped the prank before it got out of hand. It was a good lesson to keep away from pranks that can get bigger than planned.

Summer Job

The Summer after My Sophomore Year

At the beginning of the second year of summer employment for the college workers, it was decided that the head of the Pioneer Rubber Company would have a joint meeting with the parents and the college workers. I thought the meeting was kind of cool until the word got out that the summer help was in trouble. I didn't know what to expect since this was one of my first full-time summer jobs in business. I walked into the room and saw the official podium of the company at the head of the room. The college students were invited to take the seats with their parents behind them. All the parents and all the summer workers were present. I looked at my dad's face as he came into the room. He had a half smile on his face, and that helped me relax.

The president came into the room after everything was quiet and proceeded to tell us that summer employees needed to do a better job at their work and that horseplay would not be tolerated. I thought that the speech was a fair one, and the meeting was over as fast as it started. I noticed after the meeting that tasks were no longer accomplished the college students' way. This was done by the principle of divide and conquer. Rarely did all the students work together at one time. I also learned that when one works for a business, it, not the employees, call the shots.

Skyhook

I was working with another summer helper, Lenny Playko. Lenny and I were on a perpendicular moving platform attached to a skyhook, and we were assigned to paint a tall building with white paint. Above our heads, we could see the skyhooks holding on to the top of the building. Attached to skyhooks was a long rope, which was anchored to the ground on the other side of the building.

The afternoon sun was hot on this summer day. Lenny and I were painting about thirty feet in the air and minding our own business. We thought we heard a motor start, and soon a maintenance worker we knew came around the corner and mowed grass below us. We thought that it would help break up the afternoon if we could get his attention and see what he knew. One of us flipped a little spot of paint by the worker. He did not notice the paint. One more spot of paint was flipped near him, and he still didn't notice it. We decided that we were going to need a larger spot of paint much closer to the mower to get his attention. A larger spot of paint was put on the brush, and careful aim was taken to hit the ground on the right side of the worker. The paint was released from the paintbrush. At the same time, the wind kicked up to our right. As we watched the paint, it began to move where the worker was mowing, not to his right. My stomach sank as the paint hit him in the back of his shirt with the biggest part of the paint hitting his neck. He was not a happy camper.

Our original plan to talk to the mower had been turned around, and now it was looking like we were planning an attack on him. Lenny and I quickly pulled up the ropes that we used to lower and raise us on the skyhook. We did not want those ropes in anyone else's hands but ours. Despite the fact that the mower made sure we knew we had made a mistake, we got out of this one much better than we should have. I always wondered if the worker had ever forgotten it and forgiven us, as there was not much talk of the incident after that, and he did at least talk to us. Our good intentions had gone a bit sour.

---

[28] Anonymous, "Letters to Jackie," *Sentinel-Tribune*, March 12, 2010, 8, col. 1-2.
[29] Ibid., 8, col. 2.

Chapter 11

The Last Years at John Carroll University

Junior Year

First Semester

Business was my minor area of study. Since my father was an accountant, I wanted to see if I was attracted to, was interested in, and liked accounting. Mr. Francis J. McGurr ran an organized class with logical content. The material presented opened a new world of interest. However, the logic of entering accounts payable and accounts receivable was a constant point of misunderstanding for me. I, of course, worked hard on the class material and would tell my parents so every time I wrote or talked to them on the telephone. How would it look for me to do poorly in my father's area of expertise? I quickly decided that I would not follow in my father's footsteps. I waited until the end of the semester to tell my parents of my decision to go into the humanities. I knew that my initial employment was not accounting. I felt it would be some form of service to people, but I was not sure what it would be.

I began a new area of study in business and was excited about the course. The course was Principles of Economics. The book was one of the largest textbooks I had ever used. The professor in his easygoing manner was able to explain the principles so that the class could read and understand the material being presented in lectures and in the book. The principles were most useful since there was a relationship to everyday experiences in economics. The discussions on income and expenditures were fascinating. I believe that the professor knew the entire book by heart because I can't remember that there was ever a time he did not immediately have an answer to a question.

I was to have three psychology-related classes, Experimental Psychology, Psychology of Learning, and Social Psychology. I also had a course in the Philosophy of Man. My interest in psychology continued to grow as it did in philosophy. Philosophy continued to be the study of thought and is related to our actions. It is said to be at the base of all knowledge and reality. With the complexity of this broad area of knowledge, it made the process of understanding it difficult and, at times, near impossible.

Second Semester, Junior Year

I must admit that I was beginning to get a little excited. After this semester, I would be at the pinnacle of my undergraduate college years—a senior. This semester was more of the first semester. I continued and finished my courses in Principles of Accounting and Principles of Economics. The Philosophy of Infinite Being course turned out to be very informative since the infinite being is the source of everything, according to my Catholic religion. I registered for three psychology courses, Psychology of Personality, Tests and Measurements, and Abnormal Psychology. The instructor continually proved his knowledge in the area of personality.

The Tests and Measurements course was interesting, but the course which I would rate number one in terms of my interest was Abnormal Psychology taught by Dr. Glenn F. Williams, SJ. I remember well the field trip to a facility housing persons with mental illness. I was fascinated then and am still with the many syndromes that some people have to live with the majority of their lives. I have never understood the waste of human resources that comes from long-term mental illness. Medication has provided many people the chance to live productively in society. There are still many others who may be living in society, but they are not living productively.

Near the end one of my psychology classes, a number of us decided to do a skit on one of the early masters of counseling, Sigmund Freud. I played Sigmund Freud, and the others were either patients or stage hands. In playing the world famous psychoanalyst, I used his theories based on id, super ego, and ego. I remember the wig of white hair I wore to make me appear older. It wasn't a perfect skit, but it was the best we could do.

One psychology student who had a very interesting life lived in Cleveland and therefore was a "day hop." A day hop was a person who did not live on campus but commuted from his home. Therefore, the day hop was only there during the day, and then would hop home. This colorful person worked full time near the ships. At times, he would share stories about a world of work that I never knew existed. The workers on the docks are for the most part pretty tough people. One had to be able to protect himself, or he could perish. As we were talking about how he protected himself, my friend told us about a pair of shoes he would wear to work, and when he hit the shoes a certain way, knife blades would appear out of the front of either shoe. He provided many hours of interesting stories about his true world and the people who worked on the docks. I wonder where he might be today.

Extracurricular

Band

The band gave excitement to the home football rallies and also to the game. As the JCU Blue Streaks came on the field, the band played "Onward, on John Carroll." The band tried a yuletide sing-along in Kulas Auditorium and in the student center a swinging Sunday social. The glee club and the band welcomed Barat College to a formal concert. St. Xavier College Chorus came in May for a pop concert. A concert at the New York World's Fair in the U.S. Pavilion was a fitting event to get out JCU's name.

Mock Republican National Convention

It was the time to pick, ultimately, a president and vice president. What better way to know the political process than by doing it! The organizing of the mock convention received help from Oberlin University. There were 1,300 student delegates from fifty states who simulated national realities in their composing and adopting a party platform by manipulating and staging floor demonstrations that culminated in not only the nomination but also the election of the two top administrative positions in the government of the United States of America. It was a grand old time with a bonfire rally on Friday night. An inspiring speech set the tone of the day on Saturday morning. The afternoon saw the tests of strength forming the platform. The votes from the floor produced presidential and vice presidential candidates for the Republican Party and was the apex of the convention. After all was said and done, Barry Goldwater was the Republican nominee who was defeated by President Johnson by a two-thirds majority in the mock election. I saved some of the political buttons from the convention. Maybe I should visit the Antique Road Show and explain the origin of these buttons.

Glee Club

The first two concerts this season were at home and included Barat and Xavier Colleges of Chicago. On the road, we sang at Seton Hill and Mount Mercy of Pittsburgh, St. Mary's of Columbus, and ended with a trip to Trinity College in Washington, D.C. While on the road, we had just left a restaurant and were in the middle of pulling together a party when an officer of the law pulled over both buses. I began to feel sorry for the bus driver because I thought he may have just lost a large portion of his wages. I was wrong; we were not pulled over because of speed. We were pulled over because someone on one of the buses lifted the two-foot-long salt and pepper shakers from the last restaurant as a memento of the trip.

There was to be a quick solution for the possessor of the salt and pepper shakers. One of the officers of the glee club came up with a brilliant solution to finding them. It was that he would walk the aisle with closed eyes and an open hand. As soon as the salt and pepper shakers were in the hands of the law, we could enjoy our party. We did enjoy our party, and we decided that nobody on either of our buses really wanted the salt and pepper shakers after all was said and done.

Sodality

The sodality continued to provide spiritual guidance to its members. The sodality aims to heighten and intensify the Christian-based view of the world. The everyday application of the spiritual guidelines, the annual retreat, and the involvement in social problems offered a worthwhile direction to our lives. Social responsibility is an awareness fostered in each member. Studying the race issue, social work, and tutoring became central.

The summer between my junior and senior year was when I was scheduled to attend a retreat in Chicago at Xavier. The retreat was canceled, but I never received the notification. Since I was in Chicago, I stayed a few days in the dorm and hung around with some students, played some cards, and then came home. I was offered reimbursement for my transportation to and from Chicago. I took the payment but later found that I would have been more respected if I had refused it.

Sports

With the loss of all but one of the previous year's "Wolfpack" defense, a concentration on the offense was born. While the final football record was 4–4, this team was said to never give up. Classmates Steve Chamberlain and Jim Fineran finished the season as being very important to the team.

The basketball team was to go down to the wire on the decision for the PAC championship. All the marbles were at stake in the last game of the season as JCU took on Wayne State. The game was decided in the final thirty seconds, but the score favored Wayne State by one with JCU losing 51–50.

Entertainment

The seventh season of the University Series featured the renowned jazz musician Al Hirt, "In White America," the Bihari Ballet, Roger Wagner's chorale and orchestra, "Spoon River Anthology," Emlyn Williams, the Don Shirley Trio, and others. The University Series continued to provide excellent performers, many of whom were nationally known.

Additional big name performers were the Kingston Trio, the Chad Mitchell Trio and Sam Donahue, and the Tommy Dorsey Orchestra.

Dorm Life

Roommates

This was the year I lived in the newest dorm at that time, Murphy Hall. The rooms were set up so there were four persons sharing a living room in the middle area. I shared my room with Denny Doyle. Denny was a St. Ignatius High School graduate. One day, Denny picked up a mandolin and a banjo and without formal instruction began to play them. He became proficient with both instruments and played for others, as well as himself. Denny was a "fun" person to be around who always had a smile and something positive to say about everyone.

Nudist camp

At the end of my sophomore year, a classmate brought an article to me from the classified section of a Cleveland newspaper and said, "Read this."

I said, "Read what?"

He said, "Read about the contest to name a nudist camp." It seems a nudist camp was under construction in Cleveland, and the owners were looking for a name. The prize was a tour of the facilities, a free meal, being the guest of honor at the banquet, and a new sports jacket.

I asked him the name he was going to propose. He told me, "A name that will win."

The semester ended. I went home for the summer to work, and I returned the next year for classes. My friend came in on the first day back, and he said, "I won."

I asked him what he had won.

He said, "The name-the-nudist-camp contest, and I want you to go to the banquet with me." You know, I wasn't sure about going to a nudist camp being the prude I think I am, so I said that I couldn't go with him. He had a great time at the banquet; he gave a short speech, he got his sports jacket, he has named a nudist camp, and he knows what a nudist camp looks like firsthand. I missed out on this onetime experience. I must admit that I have at times wished that I had gone to that banquet.

Kiss—A New Approach

Everyone in their lives has times of unique music, dress, favorite cars, and preferred language to name a few. The words "cool" and "cool cat" are words familiar from my school days. In my college years, there was one word and one person I associate with the word "kiss." The meaning of this word was varied. The delivery of the word was as vivid a memory to me as the word itself. Denny Doyle was to me the all-time kisser. He credits another classmate for the institution of this practice. His delivery is what made him unique in the fine art of kissing. The word *kiss* meant a number of things depending on the setting. If someone said something to him he did not agree with, he might say, "Kiss." Someone could make him a little upset, and "kiss" could be his response. The word *kiss* could emphasize his feelings in a number of ways, making it a very brief and versatile exclamation.

When Denny gave a kiss, you knew you had been kissed. Denny's approach consisted of a look straight into your eyes, a raised pointer finger aimed at your head, and a loud, sharp cry of the word *kiss* with a simultaneous shaking of the hand and the upper torso. If you can imagine this combination, you are aware of the art of successful kissing. What I would give for one of Denny's kisses today!

Smoke in Your Eyes

Murphy Hall was equipped with a trash burner or incinerator. I never completely understood how the trash burner worked, except that when I had trash in my wastebasket, I carried it to a central point on the floor and emptied the contents of it into a chute. When the door leading to the chute was pushed back to its original position, the trash would go to the basement floor by gravity. Somehow the paper would catch fire and burn up the waste.

It was three o'clock in the morning when the fire alarm summoned all the pajama-clad residents of Murphy Hall to a meeting outside the front entrance. Not only was it the middle of the night but it also was frigid cold that winter morning in early 1965. Word spread fast that someone had emptied a large amount of newspapers into the incinerator, allowed the papers to start burning, and then emptied at least one wastebasket full of water down the paper chute and to the newspapers. Water on fire creates smoke, which in turn set off the fire alarm. I don't remember how many times the smoke alarm was set off by the incinerator, but one time was too much.

Janie, Very Nice But . . .

I was very aware that I only had a few years to find a young lady that I could live with the rest of my life. Most of my dating was done during the summer, as I did not have any studies to master. I worked harder at studying than dating during the school year. While at John Carroll, I was able to meet some girls, but the unfortunate thing was that I only went out one night a week. I had no car and not much time to spend with a person of the opposite sex.

The summer before my junior year, curiosity got the best of me, and I listed all the girls I had dated. I was curious how much energy I had put into dating. The list grew to around 100 different ladies that I had dated at least one time. A few of them were from Cleveland, and many were from my hometown or the surrounding area. I felt lucky that I had a pretty broad exposure to many eligible young ladies.

I remember one young lady that I dated from Cleveland named Janie. She lived close to John Carroll; that was a plus since I didn't have a car. From the first date, I thought she was the one. I was very infatuated with Janie. She was close to my age, we had similar interests, and we enjoyed being with each other. I used to go over to her house. She introduced me to champagne, and I have never lost my taste for this drink. Champagne was to become one of my most appreciated homemade wines.

My parents came to visit me, and we had decided to go out to dinner. Actually, I had pretty much decided to go out to eat, as I had asked Janie to go with us so everyone could meet. As the four of us stepped into the car, my dad asked where we were going to eat. The only places I knew where to eat in this neighborhood was Manner's Big Boy and the Cross Roads Tavern, both of which were inappropriate for the type of sit-down dinner we wanted. Janie said that she knew of a nice place a few blocks away.

We pulled up to the restaurant, and they had valet parking. That was fairly common in Cleveland. We walked into the restaurant and immediately suspected that we had chosen one of the most exclusive restaurants in this area. Everything looked expensive on the walls, the place settings, and the dainty outfits of the waitresses. The chef was wearing one of the tall white hats and was talking to the patrons about the food. As we were seated and given our menus, we knew we were in a very expensive restaurant. We ordered, had dinner, and had a pleasant conversation. I never did see the bill, but I saw my father asking my mother for some large bills. I knew my father always carried a few large bills on him, and he did not have enough money. Mom and Janie went to the ladies' room, and Dad looked at me and said, "I came real close to having to use my credit card." My mother and father had credit cards, but they were not used except for emergencies. I felt bad about Dad and Mom having to spend all that money on supper. I would have felt worse if there would have been no supper at all.

Unfortunately, I was in my junior year and needed study time. Janie wanted to have a boyfriend who was more accessible. This was one of several times that I could not spend time on a relationship because of my studies, and the relationship died. I was glad we parted because two years later, the love of my life, Kathy, and I began to date.

Hitchhiking

A common practice when I was in college was to put my thumb into the air pointed behind me as I stood on the side of what was usually a major highway. I tried to have a sign telling drivers my destination. I had both positive and negative experiences with it. I was not very experienced in hitchhiking, as I often used the bus. I had one negative experience trying to catch a ride with a person who lived near Willard where I was left behind. I never did figure out how that happened. I saw the driver who was giving me a ride inside Pacelli Hall and confirmed with him that he was taking me home. He said that he was and was getting the car at that time. He told me to wait at a nearby entrance to the building. I went to the exit and waited and waited and waited. I checked his room to see if he had been detained and found out that he had left. I never did figure that one out because the driver later told me he had come to the exit to take me home, and I wasn't there.

My first time hitchhiking was with Lenny Playko, also from Willard. The day of the big hitchhike, Lenny and I had received a ride from a student at JCU to the turnpike exit on Route 8. We tried to find a ride for about an hour on the entrance ramp, but no one stopped. It is important to note that hitchhikers are not allowed on the turnpike but were then allowed to wait for a car on the entrance ramp.

I was just about to give up. It would have been rather difficult for me to give up because at that point, we had no available ride anywhere. The person who dropped us off was on his way to Youngstown. At this time, a car pulled over and waited for us to get into it. Lenny taught me that you always run to the car so you are not holding up the driver, and they do not take off without us. We settled in the car, Lenny in the front and I in the backseat. It didn't take too long to realize that the driver had been drinking, as the inside of the car smelled like alcohol, and the smell got stronger the closer we were to the driver. The driver was talkative, and I was very concerned that the driver would be driving erratically. Fortunately, no questionable driving occurred on the trip. When we reached Norwalk, we were expecting to leave the car. The driver told us he was going to change his route and take us home to Willard.

When we arrived in Willard, Lenny made a cool move. He had the driver drop us off two blocks from either of our houses. When we left the car, the driver just sat there. Lenny said to me, "I am afraid this guy wants to know where we live. Let's go toward the house behind the car, and as we begin to go up the steps, we will bolt to the backyard and either hide or keep going." We did just that, and we looked back after we were in the backyard and saw the car take off. We each made it home in time to attend the football game at Willard High School.

I hitchhiked another time at the Route 8 exit of the Ohio Turnpike. Almost immediately, a driver stopped and began to tell me about himself. He was a medical doctor and belonged to Mensa, a society of persons who have an extremely high intelligence quotient. He dropped me off in Norwalk, which is about thirty minutes from Willard. I waited two hours for a ride, and not only did no cars stop but there also were only a few cars that came down the road. I called my parents, and they were able to pick me up in Norwalk. With these experiences that were not very reinforcing, I gave up on hitchhiking.

A Visit to a Friend

In my later years at John Carroll, I met a student named Tim, and we became friends. He was from the east side of Cleveland. His family had a business, and his father and brother worked in it. One weekend, I was invited to his house as a guest. When we arrived on Friday evening, his first move was toward some shrimp cocktail. I had never had much experience with shrimp cocktail, but he portrayed this delicacy as one of the best in the world. I didn't care for the shrimp that day but did acquire a taste for shrimp in later years. When his father arrived, I immediately could see that he would make a good salesperson. He was upbeat and very much a people person. My friend's mother made sure everyone was comfortable with their food and drinks. It was a great getaway weekend.

About a week after I had visited my friend, he visited my room. He saw a chessboard, which I hadn't put away. He asked if I would like to play a game. This was the first time I had played chess with my friend, so I toyed with the idea of using my three-step system to checkmate my opponent. Checkmate means placing my army in a position where the opponent cannot move his king. I would then capture his king and win the game. This play doesn't work all the time because the opponent must move certain players to certain squares to prevent this power play. I attempted the power play and beat my friend. He was speechless. He memorized the moves to checkmate and told me he had an acquaintance, a Mr. Home, he was going to beat with this play.

A few weeks went by, and Tim came into my dorm room very excited. He relayed to me that he had gone to the local establishment and played chess with Mr. Home. Mr. Home was pretty much the guru of chess in that nightclub. According to my friend, he was able to use the power play on Mr. Home. Mr. Home was impressed, to say the least, with my friend's moves on the chessboard. Mr. Home asked him where he had learned this great series of moves, and he gave him my nickname, the Emperor Jojo. Mr. Home wanted to meet me, but I never was able to hook up with this interesting person.

Mom's Fruit Salad

As I was about to finish my junior year in college, I received a copy of the *Willard Times*, my hometown newspaper. I opened the March 18, 1965, edition of the paper, and there, big as life, I saw a picture of my mother. The picture accompanied an article about my mother's fruit salads. I didn't need the recipes in the article because I had eaten the showcased three salads my whole life. In fact, I had helped my mother make the goodies on several occasions.

The first salad in the article was my mother's original fruit salad. It was made of apples, oranges, grapes, bananas, marshmallows, sugar, and a whipped topping. Red or white cherries and diced nuts were the other toppings. In the article, it was pointed out that during World War II, we raised purple grapes in the backyard and used them in the salad along with apples from our apple trees. The purple grapes became the identifying factor for the family after the fruit salad article was published in the paper. Whenever Mom's fruit salad was served, one of the family would recognize the fact that purple grapes from the backyard were served during World War II. As I reflected on this fruit salad, I began to think how many times I had eaten this tasty treat. I couldn't begin to count the times I had eaten it, but it was easy to remember when I did not like it—never.

In addition to this very tasty dessert, there were two other delicacies my mother made frequently. One was pineapple salad made from Philadelphia cream cheese, crushed pineapple, and marshmallows with whipped cream, all chilled in the refrigerator. The final special salad was a box marshmallow pineapple salad made with a graham crackers base, which was filled with marshmallows, scalded milk, and crushed pineapple covered with ground graham crackers and chilled in the refrigerator.[30] I always loved these two salads, but the fruit salad was always numero uno.

Another thought hit me, and that was how nice it would be to enjoy some of Mom's cooking now. Some of us can, but for the rest of us, how wonderful it would be if only Mom was here to bake us some cookies. For those of us who do not have a living mother, all we can do is to get out her recipe box and draw on the written instructions that our mothers gave us years ago. I bet we all are a bit hungrier now.

Summer Job

Willard City Streets, Sewer, and Cemetery Department

Working on the Willard City Streets, Sewer, and Cemetery Department was some of the most carefree working days of my life. These experiences happened during the summer after my junior year in college or in 1965. The superintendent of the department was my neighbor, Butch Rothschild Sr. Big Butch always treated me and others fairly, but if our performance was not up to expectation, he was right on us and expected us not to make the same mistake twice. Big Butch was also a master craftsman in all trades. I was always amazed at how Big Butch could give you a job to do, explain to you how it was to be done, and follow up to see it was done right. He was a great manager.

Cleaning Catch Basins

One of the first assigned jobs to be done in the early summer was cleaning catch basins. Catch basins are holding tanks located deep in the ground into which water and waste are drained from the streets to prevent flooding. Fall produced many leaves, and many of them were washed into the catch basins with the dirt from the winter water drain. Our job was to take a twelve-inch horizontal flat scoop attached to a long handle and scoop out the catch basins so they would be clean and ready for the summer rains. Without this cleaning, the sanitary sewer pipes would be susceptible to clogging. The scoop would hold enough waste to make it difficult to lift old leaves and other waste out of the basins several feet deep. After the waste reached the surface, we would place it on the street so that we could load it on the dump truck when it arrived. Several crews could be cleaning the many catch basins at one time using only one dump truck to haul the waste.

One of the difficulties of this job was that occasionally we dug too deeply into the waste, and it became impossible to lift as it was too heavy. This meant that we would need to dump the heavy waste and take a new scoopful with less waste. Being the kind of college kid that I was, this second try at taking out the waste would have shown poor judgment on my part and muddied up the water unnecessarily.

Years later, I was in Pemberville and saw a friend, Landry Sheets near a catch basin. I pulled over and asked him what he was doing. He explained that he was cleaning catch basins. At that time, a truck with a large tank on it was sitting nearby. My friend told me how the process worked. A pipe is placed into the catch basin and hooked up to the tank on the truck. Simply put, the vacuum on the truck sucks out the waste. This would have been a much easier process than what we did forty-five years earlier.

Hammering Cement

Another experience with the Willard City Streets, Sewer, and Cemetery Department was replacing a section of a pavement. Running a jackhammer was a new experience for the college student summer helpers. Big Butch had one of the experienced workers instruct us on the correct operation of the jackhammer. After receiving the proper instruction, each of the summer workers was to have his day with that machine. One of my first recollections about the jackhammer was that it was very, very heavy. Transporting it to the work area could only be accomplished by dragging this piece of equipment by the two handles and trailing the cutting portion of it to the work site. As I began to pull the lever on one of the handles to activate the hammer, I noticed that as the jackhammer began to bounce on the concrete, my muscles immediately began to bounce from the jumping motion. After I had cut out a small section of the concrete pavement, it was someone else's turn to use this piece of equipment. Since the piece of concrete pavement to be removed was large, Big Butch wanted each of us to take our turn and not have any adverse reactions to the motion of that monster.

It was at about halfway through the project that the air line that ran the jackhammer suddenly came loose. Since the hose was full of air under pressure, the line whipped around like a large snake, and yes, it could bite. At one point, the end of the hose began to hit my fellow workers. It was obvious that damage to the body and even a broken bone were possible options. It didn't take too long to realize that the best place to be was out of the path of this wild hose. One of the more experienced workers trapped the hose with his foot, and another shut down the air compressor so that there would be no more air produced, and the workers would be safe rather than sorry. After inspecting the jackhammer, it was found that the attachment connected to the hose had worked its way loose. It could have been a much more serious and dangerous event than it was.

Hot Asphalt

If we are not talking about concrete pavement, we could be talking of asphalt paving. On probably the hottest day of summer, we were repairing patches in some Willard streets. There had been a delay at or from the asphalt plant, and the city worker who picked up the asphalt in the city dump truck to be delivered to the repair crew was very late. With all the delays, it was discovered that the asphalt was beginning to set in the truck. Asphalt setting in the truck could be compared to concrete setting in the round tumbler on a cement truck.

Big Butch told me and one other worker to get in the back of the asphalt truck and start shoving it out so other workers could spread it before it had set. We jumped in the truck bed with our shovels. I always wore tennis shoes to work, as it usually worked well with the jobs we were to complete that day. Standing in an asphalt truck in tennis shoes with the dump section of the truck raised was not a pleasant experience. In the first place, portions of the truck floor were exposed. The bare spots were covered with oil that coats the asphalt. The truck bed floor was a slippery mess, and any quick movement meant that we could fall or slide on the asphalt and cover our clothing and parts of our body with a hot, dark-colored, sticky, and smelly oily solution. My hands could easily be covered with this oily solution because if we fell, we would break our fall with our hands, and our hands would come in contact with the truck floor. What a mess this was, as we did fall.

The worst part of the day was that the weather was very humid, and the temperature was well in excess of 100 degrees. The faster we shoveled, the hotter it became. The hotter it became, the harder it was to shovel and the more we would sweat. At one point, the sweating became so severe that we could hardly see anything. Wiping our eyes to clear the sweat only caused more blurry vision as our hands were covered with sweat and oil. Our bodies were becoming extremely tired. Leaving the truck was impossible, as the asphalt needed to be shoveled from the bed of the truck immediately.

Did I say that the box that contained the asphalt was at least ten degrees hotter than the air temperature, and the four metal sides of the truck bed created an inferno? We did chip all of the asphalt loose. Our final job was to use a solution that could cut the sticky surface that bonded together the remaining asphalt and to clean the bed of the truck. Because the hot asphalt was already out, the temperature in the truck bed had come down about ten degrees, so we could then almost see through our sweaty eyes. Our clothes were wet the rest of the day, and we wasted no time in taking a shower immediately after work. That was the last truckload of asphalt we had to unload in this manner.

Cemetery Duty

To be a successful worker in the Willard Cemetery, there were several steps to learn. The first step was to learn how to dig a grave. Once a notice was received that someone had died, the correct cemetery plot was to be located. If there was more than one burial plot open in the lot, the correct spot needed to be located. I would not want to dig the grave more than one time, and I would not want to dig up a burial plot that had already been used. Double checking correct burial plot was always helpful, and at times, the family needed to be consulted if more than one burial site in the plot was open.

Once the burial plot is identified, a prod (a long rod used to penetrate the soil) is used to locate any adjoining vaults, if they did in fact exist. After the adjoining vaults to the new burial plot were identified, the outline of the new vault was to be marked on the ground with four pieces of metal strips that formed a rectangle a bit larger than the size of the vault. The grave was to be dug either by hand or by machine. If there were tombstones close to the grave that could be marred by a backhoe, the grave must be dug by hand. If a backhoe could dig the grave without harming other tombstones, it was to be used. The burial hole usually is finished by hand.

While I was digging by hand once, I had less than a foot of dirt to move to finish the grave. As I continued to dig, one of the workers shouted, "Look out!" I jumped to the side of the unfinished grave and saw a wall of dirt from the adjacent grave fall into the new grave. Exposed from the next grave was the side of a vault. As I looked closer, I saw substances come out of the vault. I continued to dig out the grave until it was of the proper depth, height, length, and width. As I got out of the grave, I picked up the metal marker used on top of the ground to mark the size of the grave. One of the metal pieces was sharp, and as I handled the metal, I felt a piercing pain in my hand. I looked down, and blood was dripping from my right hand. I don't know if it was the incident with the vault or the cut that began to make me a bit sick to my stomach.

All of the dirt beside the grave was covered with a tarp, and the next event was the funeral. The base of the vault was put in place by the vault company before the funeral. The vault is placed near the grave but out of sight if possible.

We always were at the cemetery about a half hour before the procession entered. When the funeral procession came in the cemetery, our truck and tools were always hidden somewhere in the cemetery so that the family and friends of the deceased could not see them. Then we would wait for the service to conclude. Sometimes we would guide the funeral procession into the cemetery. After the last vehicle in the procession was out of site, we would then go to the grave. Before we would fill the grave with dirt, the undertaker had to certify that the vault was covering the casket and was properly sealed. There was one time when the vault wasn't directly on the casket, so it was moved to fit properly. The process was complete when the grave was filled with dirt. I always thanked God that I was not in the grave that day.

Another form of burial at the Willard Cemetery was in the mausoleum. I guess anyone could be buried in a mausoleum as long as it was public, not private. The difference between a regular burial and one in the mausoleum was that a regular burial was in the ground, and a mausoleum burial was above ground in a structure usually made of cement, granite, or marble. The inside of the vault was horizontal to the ground. Before the casket was placed in the vault, BBs were thrown on the floor of the vault so the casket would slide easily into it. A piece of formed concrete the size of the opening was used to seal the entrance to the vault. A piece of marble was then pushed up into the ceiling of the vault entrance and then dropped into a groove below the casket line so that no one could get into the double-sealed vault. I never buried anyone in the mausoleum but learned a lot about it from other experienced workers. I always felt it was easier burying someone I didn't know rather than someone who I was acquainted with.

Waterline Leaks

When a waterline is leaking, the best action one can take is to turn off the water valve. Locating a working turnoff valve is not always easy, as it may not exist. On one occasion, the city crew had been called out by a private construction contractor, as they wished to have the water shut off so he could proceed with his project. The lines were shut off, and the backhoe began to dig up the site. On the second pass of the shovel, a number of waterlines were dug up. The operator thought that all the water valves were turned off, so he pulled up the waterlines only to find water beginning to squirt out from them. As we looked closer, there was a spider line that was leaking. A spider line is one line that has several smaller lines running out of the end of this larger line. I did not know what to do, so I looked at some of the regular employees as if to say, "What are you going to do?" One of the senior workers, Abe Blankenship, ran to the utility truck and grabbed two large hammers. He ran back to the leaking lead or copper lines, and one by one, he began to hit them with one hammer on the top and one underneath the line. Within a few minutes, all the leaks were stopped, and everyone close to the break had wet clothes, especially Abe, the worker who hammered the lines together.

Another day, we were summoned to a new water leak on Woodbine Street about a block from downtown Willard. When we arrived, the water was rushing under the street, and the water pressure had literally pushed up large sections of asphalt. After checking, we found that it was a twelve-inch waterline, and there was no shutoff valve. Big Butch told the workers, "We will have to work this one wet." Within minutes, a backhoe was in place, and it proceeded to dig up the leak.

We put one large pump into the hole, and within minutes, a second pump was added to try to catch up with the leak. Water was coming out of the pipe; it seemed everywhere. One of the workers placed his hand under the leaking pipe to judge the size of the leak. It turned out to be a leak about ten feet long. A piece of twelve-inch pipe was cut, and two clamps were obtained. The large clamps were made out of rubber, which could overlap. On the rubber were screw-type latches to tighten the rubber around the old and new pipes to stop the water from leaking.

A pressure chain cutter severed one end of the pipe. This increased the water flow slightly. When the other end of the leaking pipe was cut, the water began to fill up the hole. A third pump was put into action, and slowly, water was drained enough for the new twelve-inch water pipe to be installed and the old pipe replaced. The rubber pads were wrapped around both ends of the new pipe, and the locking mechanisms were tightened until there was no leak. It was a great show of craftsmanship, as a large flow of water was brought under control.

Hauling Trash

Hauling trash was one of my more memorable jobs with the city of Willard. It was memorable because there were positives associated with this job; it was an easy job among all the very difficult jobs. Hauling trash proceeded in this fashion. On Friday mornings, two employees would start emptying the trash cans downtown. One person would drive the truck, and the other would empty the trash into the pickup. Sometimes there was nothing of worth in the trash containers; other times there would be several "goodies." The duties of the person taking the trash out of the containers were to empty the containers and to watch for any clean comic books or magazines. *Archie* and *Superman* were two of my favorite comic books. Reading was sometimes useful at the cemetery while waiting for the funeral procession to arrive. Sometimes we directed traffic into the correct section of the cemetery. Reading also might be helpful during the services as we waited for the burial.

Now that the downtown trash containers were clean, we would go to the Willard Area Hospital to pick up its trash. Since this was back in 1965, there were no such things as sharp containers to hold the hypodermic needles. Trash was handled carefully to avoid injuries.

Now it would be time to drive the pickup truck to the dump. In those days, a landfill was called a dump. Dirt would rise from the road in the dump as we drove on it. There was something like a fraternity among Willard city workers; they treated you good, and you treated them good. Another way to state it was that it was the fraternity of the "good old boys." The dump supervisor would come over to the pickup truck. After a little small talk, he would ask us what we had in it. Then he would tell us where to dump it. Usually, the dump looked pretty much the same anywhere we looked, but we would dump our trash where we were told. The man who ran the dump was interesting, and once in a while, we would find something useful that someone had thrown away. We would place any of these items in back of the seat for future use.

During and after the unloading process, there was usually a treat. The treat was rats running around in the junk. The rats were afraid of us, so we were never concerned about getting bit. I had heard that some people came out to the dump to shoot rats, but I do not remember seeing that happen. Once in a while, we would find a nice rock and would try to hit the rat as it ran in the junk. We came close to hitting a few rats, but I don't think we were ever successful. These rats were different than any rats I had ever seen. They usually had a dark-colored body, probably from the dirt and smoke in the dump, and they lacked a lot of hair. The lack of hair was probably because they had been close to a fire. When it was close to noon, we needed to get back to real work.

There is one other happening that was a favorite of the older college employees. It happened while driving a truck down the streets for the city of Willard. Your timing had to be just right to pull off this trick. With the driver in his seat and you in the shotgun seat beside him, you would wait until a young lady near the driver's age was walking on the same side of the street as the driver. She must be walking toward the driver. As the girl is a few feet in front of the truck, you would tell the driver to slow down. You would reach over and lay on the horn. The girl would naturally look up at the driver and you. You would yell, "He likes you," as you pointed to the driver. The girl would be looking while the driver, now in shock, could do nothing but stare at the girl. There was no comeback for the driver. Timing was everything. I still chuckle when I think of pulling off this trick. Maybe this would start up a relationship or maybe not.

The Dedication

Big Butch asked me and another worker if we were interested in working one weekend. A dedication of the boundaries of Firelands was to take place, and chairs were needed to be delivered before the ceremony and picked up after. Firelands was part of Western Reserve of the state of Connecticut. Lots were given to people who had homes that were burned by the British. Huron County, including Willard, was part of this territory. My pockets were seldom filled, so anytime I could earn money, I was there. We were to receive directions on how to set up the chairs from Sheriff John Borgia. I knew the sheriff, as I was an honorary deputy. I would occasionally ride around with a sheriff deputy, Doc Allingham, and help out when needed on his patrol. I figured that if the sheriff was going to be present, this was going to be a big event.

A coworker and I arrived on the assigned day at the dedication site on State Route 224 near the Richmond School. Route 224 is a truck route, and the large marker was located a few feet from the highway. The sheriff gave the directions for the set up and was carefully watching the traffic as it passed by.

As the ceremony was about to begin, a truck came by at a very high rate of speed, and the wind from the truck hit the participants with the force of a windstorm. The sheriff immediately waved his hand to a deputy who was sitting along the side of the road, and within a second, the lights on the sheriff car were on, and he was in rapid pursuit of the trucker. The relaxed mood at the dedication became tense when the trucker passed by us, but the fast action of the sheriff in taking the situation under his control restored the festive mood.

A short time later after the brief ceremony, the deputy sheriff reported back to the sheriff on his chase. The sheriff seemed pleased about the results. I was happy I was on the side of the law, as I was sure that my wages for the afternoon would not be close to the fine that the trucker probably incurred.

Water Leaks and the Man to Find Them

One afternoon in the summer of 1965, Big Butch Rothschild, the superintendent of streets, parks, and cemetery, asked the college workers if anyone was interested in working for a man who was going to check for leaks in the city waterlines. The work was going to be largely laying out and rolling up fire hoses. The catch was that we would be working all night and also all day the next day at our city job. Staying up half the night and going to work was nothing new to college kids. After all, there was always time to sleep after our day job was finished. I remember volunteering, and my memory tells me that Lenny Playko also volunteered. It was money, and it was to be a new adventure. We found that the person who was responsible to find the leaks was an interesting and intelligent person, and we shall call him Mr. Leaks. For example, he shared with us his business and his views on religion and marriage, to name a few. He seemed to have a happy marriage despite the fact that he was gone for long periods working in many different places in the world.

One of the things he shared with us was his trip to Saudi Arabia. Before discussing this jobsite, it is important to note that he worked with a medium-size red panel truck. In the truck were many dials, hookups to be used for the flow of liquids, and other related devices. The truck was essentially in the direct circuit or flow of whatever liquid was being tested for leaks. In the truck, the liquid could be measured by gallons; the water pressure and other variables also were monitored. All this information was fed into a formula that Mr. Leaks had developed to pinpoint leaks. It was easy to understand why he did not allow access to his special formulas.

In Saudi Arabia, it was essential that he pinpointed almost to the inch where the leaks of crude oil were present. I could picture our leaks specialist in the middle of the shifting sands trying to find the oil leak with his knowledge and his red panel truck's equipment. He was to find the leak location in the buried pipeline, which was located several feet in the sand. He calculated correctly where the leak was and did it within a foot of the leak. Finding that leak was very important to the Saudi Arabians, as the leaking oil was merely going back into the sandy ground with no means of recapturing it. As we talked to Mr. Leaks about how lucrative his business was, he shared with us that if one believes in God and works for God, God will provide for him.

For a short period, Lenny and I would lay out fire hoses and connect them to fire hydrants. The lines were then hooked up to the truck, forming a movement of water that could be measured. The reason we needed to do our work after midnight is that there was very little water being used at this time of the night, and if there were leaks in the section of the city where we were working, they could be detected by Mr. Leaks' formulas. It was always interesting to see who was having breakfast in the very early part of the morning when we finished our shift. It was also interesting to see Mr. Leaks explain the leakage in the water system in Willard.

After-Hours Summer Activities

At the end of my junior year, I had the privilege of knowing many young ladies who were home from college for the summer. As I have explained, I had time in the summer that I did not have when I was required to read books and, so to speak, kiss them good night when I'm done. At an all-men's school with no car and little money, there were not many chances to go out on a date. If the girl I was to date had access to a car, that would make the proposition of dating a bit easier. While traveling on the Cleveland Public Rapid Transit, it was possible to go on dates, but it was not the best situation. The best situation for dating was the summer when I was home, and I had access to my parents' car. Since I was working, I had some money to spend on dates.

There are times when people do something that is very foolish, and having three dates in one day was one of mine. I had thought that there would be some feelings of accomplishment if I were to have three dates in one day. I arranged for an afternoon date, a supper date, and an evening date. The afternoon date, which started at lunch, ended at 4:30 p.m. and was an activity that I cannot even remember other than lunch. The second date was during supper, and it was over at six thirty. I really had to hustle to complete the second date. I remember that it was not easy to leave a date after supper. The third date was not a lot other than riding around and talking. The first two dates were in Willard, and the third was in Norwalk. The only positive aspect of this experience is that I accomplished my goal. The negatives were that I had little money left after the dates, and I didn't enjoy the time with any of the ladies, as I was afraid they would find out that they were one of three dates that day. This was the first time I had multiple dates in one day, and it turned out to be the last. I went back to single dates that summer.

A Visit to the Ghost in the Graveyard

My parents attended college at the St. Francis Seminary in Carey. I was attending John Carroll University at that time. Also in attendance in this class were two young sisters from a surrounding city. My parents were always looking for a Catholic girl my age for obvious reasons. At one of the classes, my mother asked the girls if they would be interested in going out with me and a friend of mine. The girls must have thought a lot of my mother and father, as they said that should be fun.

Date and time was set, and my friend Dick Ellis and I located the girls' apartment in a city near Carey. The four of us hit it off, and we immediately began to carry out our plans of starting the evening with a big attraction, going to the cemetery to see the ghost embedded in the tombstone. On the way to the cemetery, I asked the sisters if they had seen the ghost in the tombstone. I had talked to one of the sisters about this subject when setting up the date, and now both of them admitted to having seen the ghost. Not only did they assure me that they had seen the ghost but they also knew exactly where the tombstone was and assured us that we were going to enjoy it. It was still light as we got to the cemetery, which was positioned on top of a large hill outside of town. As we parked the car and began to walk toward the back of the cemetery, I looked around and could see for miles. It was beautiful.

As we continued to walk toward the tombstone, I began to get a very uncomfortable feeling. The farther we walked, the more uneasy I felt. Finally, it hit me. The entire cemetery had been trashed; tombstones were pushed over, and some even looked as if they had been hit by a sledgehammer and broken into pieces. I began to stutter as I told the others about the damaged tombstones and the precarious position we would be in if we were caught in the cemetery. The rest of the group felt the same as I did. They did not want to get caught in the cemetery with all this damage near darkness. We could be blamed for the damages worth easily in the hundreds of thousands of dollars.

Things were about to get worse. I looked each direction up and down the road, and my heart sank as I looked toward the city. I could see the lights of a vehicle coming toward the cemetery at a very fast pace. We were all certain that it was a law enforcement agent who was thinking he had caught the criminals as they had returned to the scene of the crime. All we could think was that we needed to get out of here before we ended up in the local jail charged with a crime we didn't commit.

The four of us ran as fast as possible to the car, jumped in, and began our exit, faster than we had arrived. I looked in my rearview mirror and saw that a car was approaching us very rapidly. We didn't waste any time, and after a bit of a ride, we lost the other car.

The rest of the night was anticlimactic. None of us had so innocently been placed in such an unpleasant situation before. The sad part of the situation was that I never did see the famous ghost in the tombstone, and to this day, I do not even know if I could find that cemetery on the hill, let alone the ghostly tombstone.

Animals

When I was young, there were many kinds of animals around our house. We had the traditional dog; ours was named King. King was a smart dog and very well-mannered. He was a springer spaniel. He understood some commands, such as "stay," and he could perform a few tricks, such as "don't eat the piece of food on your nose." The frogs, toads, and turtles were usually transplants from the Willard Conservation League. We had no cats, but we did have parakeets.

It was at the end of my junior year when I inherited a pet white rat from a friend at John Carroll University. I obtained the pet as I was leaving for the summer, and he was packing for home. My friend had taken an experimental psychology course and now had to find a home for the white rat. I liked to have possessions that were unusual and attracted attention. I thought it was kind of cool to carry the rat around the neighborhood or on my shoulders and to have people come up to see it. I thought that it would be a great girl attractor; unfortunately, I was wrong. I was living in Willard, and people there loved to look at the rat, and a few liked to pet it.

Holding the rat was another story; it was impossible to convince most people, especially girls, to hold it. The conclusion I drew was that a white rat is a beautiful creature, but it still has the image of and is a rat.

A Burglar?

I always had an interest in law enforcement. I don't remember how it happened, but I grew to know a Huron County deputy sheriff, Doc Allingham. I never did know his real name because everyone called him "Doc." Doc was a big man, and I was always happy to be on his side when we had any activity. I had the pleasure of knowing his wife, Donna.

I learned that if I was to ride around in the sheriff's car, I needed to be an honorary deputy. John Borgia was the sheriff, and he made me an honorary deputy. When I was free to go on the rounds with Doc, I would contact him, and he would pick me up. As I think back, that might have looked rather funny to my neighbors to see me picked up by the deputy sheriff.

Every once in a while, there would be a suspicious car or a building with an unlocked door. One of these unlocked doors provided us with a very unusual experience. We were cruising through Celeryville, when we came to one of the large storage buildings used to process and store the vegetables that were grown in the rich black muckland. Doc's keen eye noticed a door that looked as if it was partially open. I was excited because I had never been in on a "burglar bust."

We parked the sheriff car and walked in the dark up to the door with our flashlights on. Sure enough, the door was unlocked and barely open. Doc had a bright light and began to look around the large building, which contained some machinery. Doc said he wanted to check out the upstairs. Since I didn't have a gun, he told me to stay downstairs with my light off and see if anything moved. It was spooky with this large warehouse, an unlocked door, and me with a flashlight to check out the ground floor.

It was very dark, and I felt nothing but my heartbeat. It was beating, and I hoped it stayed that way. Out of nowhere, I heard something moving across the floor, and it sounded like it was stepping on a piece of metal. I was scared. Someone or somebody was close, and all I had was a flashlight and my body for defense. I was told to watch out for anything strange. This was moving, and this was strange. I was half afraid to give up my position, but I had to take action. I turned on the light to find that there was a big piece of machinery in line with the sound I had heard. I got down on my knees to see under the machinery, and there it was. A dark-colored cat was staring at me and was sitting next to a piece of metal on the floor.

Doc came back and asked if I had seen anything. I said yes and shined my light on the cat. He said, "They can really scare you." I said, "I know." We locked up the building and notified the proper person of the open door. It was time for me to go home and enjoy my safe bedroom. I had learned that evening that everything is not what it seems to be. There was no burglar, and the cat didn't hurt me.

Senior Year Classes

First Semester, Senior Year

When my senior year rolled around, there was an air of confidence that we, the seniors, could possibly graduate from this extremely challenging university. This semester was to provide me with some new and exciting professors. The first was from the philosophy department. The course title was Principles of Moral Philosophy, and the teacher had a knack for making the topics interesting and helping me come up with a sound process of developing, identifying, modifying, and expressing my moral philosophy. His tests were fair and long. The entire test was essay. This fact raised two negative components for the teacher. One is he had to read page after page after page of writings of each of the several students in the class. The other was I possessed handwriting that is more like hieroglyphics than writing. The only factor in the definition of penmanship for me is the pen. Because of the poor quality of writing I possess, one of my grade school teachers would not grade me traditionally for penmanship, but she would give me the letter I. It stood for incomplete.

Somehow my professor did grade my papers, and somehow I received great grades. A major reason for my positive disposition about this course is that the subject matter was useful and could be applied to daily living.

The next class I enjoyed was Business Psychology, taught by Dr. John F. Michael, an active consultant in the field of business. He had worked in many different businesses and knew well the overall picture of business and the human behavior in it. The studies in human behavior that we were exposed to were interesting and significant. I was able to use the material from this class in my future administrative positions.

Social and Economic Reforms was an interesting and practical class. Mr. John R. Carpenter's knowledge base was second to none, and his distinctive voice kept me awake, so I heard all the interesting subject matters. Student learning was at the top of his priority list. He liked to keep in touch with the alumni.

My wife, Kathy, and I were at John Carroll for my 1991 or twenty-fifth class reunion. One of the tours offered was to the refurbished area in Cleveland called Ohio City. My former sociology teacher, Mr. Carpenter, was the tour guide. The drinks were gone when the tour wasn't half complete. He had a hard time believing that we were out of drinks, but he rebounded quickly by having the bus driver go to a certain bar. In no time, he had a few helpers replenishing our stock right way. The right way is that you don't run out of drinks, and we didn't.

Psychology of Adolescence was a course that offered useful material. The economics course of Money and Banking was dry at times, but the message of how this system works offered me many pieces of knowledge, which I am still able to apply to the world of banking. With the crisis of investments in 2008, concepts I learned in this course have been essential to my ability to understand these issues. Behavior Science in Business provided other needed information in dealing with people and business.

Second Semester, Senior Year

I finally reached this important point in my life, my last semester to complete, and I will have that sheet of paper that says I am a college graduate.

The Personnel Management course followed my teacher's previous class, Business Psychology, and he continued to be an outstanding instructor. Dr. Michael was interesting and informative and gave information that would help me succeed in my relationships with people in the workplace. The second course, Principles of Moral Philosophy, was my last philosophy course at JCU. The course Family was to be taught by a single person. At times, I have wondered how people can have an expertise without firsthand experience. This instructor knew, could teach, and confidently made the subject interesting and helpful.

I finished out my senior year with classes in Liturgical Theology and Human Growth and Development. The latter class on growth and development was well taught and beneficial.

Extracurricular

Government

We had a very dedicated junior and senior class president who made sure that everyone got a fair shake. Mike Murray, from Sandusky, listened to his class members and acted on their needs in an exemplary manner.

Louis Vitullo, a native of Riverside, Illinois, was elected the Carroll union president. Lou could be seen walking the quadrangle in the morning on his way to his office in the student union. He was a president who gave his all for his university.

Glee Club

This was to be my last year in glee club and my last year of formal singing. This was also to be my last road trip to girls' schools anywhere. We began the year in a newly renovated Kulas Auditorium. It was difficult to sing at first because there were no more barren walls and floors, and we had to sing louder to be heard. The first visiting ladies' schools were College of St. Mary of the Springs and Mundelein College.

After good reviews in Kulas, we were on our way to concerts at Siena Heights, Xavier, and Barat Colleges. Our vice president, John Minaudo, helped lead us as we ventured into the sunset of college and into the realities of life.

If my memory serves me right, when we were in Chicago, we stayed at the Palmer House. As I walked through the front doors, I saw a nice old structure with an impressive foyer.

That evening, there was a group of young men in the hotel, surely *not* John Carroll men, who did nothing but get into trouble all night. For example, I remember looking out the window and seeing a mattress fly by my window. So this is the big city! If that wasn't enough, I looked out my window and saw young men walking on the roof by the neon sign of the hotel. The sign was about three-fourths of the way up the hotel. With this being the Windy City, I wasn't sure why they were on the roof.

It didn't take long for the house detective to be on the scene. Something was going radically wrong at this point: *our* hotel room was targeted for an investigation. The detective knocked on our door and said, "Open the door." There was no "please" or "thank you" but an "open the door!" I made sure that the detectives were not going to rush the room by quietly putting the little chain with the sliding piece of metal in place. I slowly opened the door and said, "What do you want?"

The first words out of his mouth were "You can help me by taking that chain off the door and opening the door like I first asked you to do." We were asked many questions, but we did not know the answers because we were not the guilty party. Evidently, our room was located in the middle of the trouble, and we were presumed guilty by association. All of us in the room were cleared, and word had it that the bad guys were caught.

Sodality

The final year of the sodality was upon me, and next year, I would be at graduate school at a public university. I had concerns about the commitments I had made at JCU through the sodality to continue my spiritual self-improvements. My commitment next year would truly be a more personal one.

John Fox ably led the group as president. This was the year of the Model United Nations at JCU. The sodality represented a Jewish nation, and I was one of the delegates. The achievement of world peace and, if not peace, meaningful communication was our great hope for a safe and giving society. Another event was the spring games in which I was one of the representatives of the sodality.

There were several races and activities during the spring games, which happened near the Carroll gym. While the sponsoring organization slips my mind, the event I entered has not. It was a pie-eating contest, and the pie turned out to be a full-size cherry pie. It was a plus for me, as I love cherry pie.

The gun sounded, starting the contest. There were close to a dozen other participants. I started out strong, but soon my mouth was filled with pie, and I was not sure if I could keep it all down. I must have received some help either from God, my twin, or both because the pie began to disappear in my mouth. It seemed like fifteen minutes, and the game was still going. I took several large mouthfuls, cleaned the dish, and was proclaimed the first-place winner. My friend John Minaudo was a close second. I got the prize, and he had a full-page picture in the yearbook, the 1966 Carillon. I was surprised that I still was able to eat cherry pie after this experience.

Sports

Football that fall was to be a rebuilding year, as only thirteen returning lettermen were on the field. The first two games placed a damper on the possibility of winning a PAC championship for JCU.

But the team went on to win the remainder of the games and even beat Bethany, the already named PAC champs, by a 20–14 score. The fans from JCU felt that "we're number one" after the Bethany victory. The basketball team ended up in third place after a mixture of wins and losses.

The University Series

The University Series presented the play *Absence of a Cello*. The Don Shirley Trio provided piano and string music. Bramwell Fletcher played George Bernard Shaw in the *George Bernard Shaw Story*. A performance of *Les Feux Follets*, *The Subject Was Roses*, and *Trojan Women* was also a part of that year's presentations. As I thought of the many performances I had enjoyed at John Carroll, I hoped that my access to this type of culture would not end with my graduation.

Dorm Life

Bernet Hall

Bernet Hall has been the seniors' dorm as long as I could remember. The building looks like one of the originals. The person who watched over Bernet for ages as prefect was known affectionately as "the Duke," and his trademark was a cigar. Fr. D. Clayton Schario, SJ, was the prefect when I came into Bernet. Father Schario seemed like a friendly prefect and kept things in order.

While my friend and roommate from Youngstown Don Gresko and I were in that hall, there were two underclassmen acquaintances, Lenny and George, on campus. The attached picture shows

Some of my good friends

Don on the left; Lenny Playko, a good friend and hunting partner; my cousin and friend George Schlotterer now from Norwalk, and me. While I had many other friends, it was good to see that I no longer stood alone at John Carroll without hometown connections.

The Draft

On the advent of my twenty-first birthday, October 4, 1965, I received a present from the Selective Service Commission or the draft. The lottery, which at that time was the manner of selection for the Army draft, had chosen me to report for my physical and possibly active duty in the military.

I was to find the physical process to be one of the most adventuresome that I would ever experience in my life. I did not say that it was enjoyable in any manner, but it was adventuresome.

I was to report to the draft board in Norwalk near the downtown area. As I approached the lady with the clipboard on that Saturday morning, she asked for my name and the notice that had been mailed to me to attend this event. I was given a small Gideon Bible and told to board the bus. I was on the bus and wondered what was to happen next. I felt I was ready. I had brought with me a note from my doctor saying I had stomach ulcers and proof that I was in college, so I thought I might be eligible for a medical or student deferment. My major concern was that I would be allowed to finish my academic year so I would receive my bachelor's degree. I was to find out that the major purpose of the draft was to enroll any eligible young man into the military service.

As you may recall, draftees would probably be assigned to duty in the Vietnam War, a very unpopular war.

The bus pulled out of Norwalk on time, and we were on our way to Cleveland. When the bus arrived, everything worked like clockwork. The bus driver knew where to pull in; officials were there to meet us, and we were ushered into several examination areas. The examining personnel looked at every part of my body, including areas that were most private and most concealed. When the examinations of private areas were done, there was little privacy, as the examinations were done as rapidly as possible and often in front of many people. There were quotas in terms of numbers and time, and anyone who was to mess up the timetables was seen as non-cooperative.

I was seen as non-cooperative on my hearing test. When several people were given earphones, they had just enough time to put them on and take the test. Evidently, the person ahead of me had a large head because the earphones did not fit, and they allowed external noise to filter into my ear. I tried to adjust the earphones only to find out that the test had already started. I tried to obtain the attention of the drill sergeant who was overseeing the test. That proved to be a useless move on my part. I began to try to take the test by pressing a switch when I heard a sound. Well, I was hearing sounds out of the machine, sounds from other people in the room, and sounds from many places in that big building. Then the inevitable happened, the examiner was traveling around the room and checking the progress of the test results. The examiner was experienced. He could tell in one glance if the recruit was passing the test. When he came to me, he stopped dead in his tracks. My heart began to pound. He asked me, "What are you doing? Playing cat and mouse with me?"

I began to explain that I couldn't adjust the earphones. I learned real fast that the examination area was the domain of the examiner, and no excuses would be tolerated. He ripped my data answer sheet out of the machine and told me to go to the isolation booth. I thought, *Isolation booth? What did I do wrong?*

The isolation booth turned out to be a soundproof room in which all external sound was eliminated. I entered the room and put on the headphones, and the test began. To the delight of the examiner, I passed my hearing test in the isolation booth. I began to wonder if he was paid by the number of recruits who passed.

I was then directed to go to a special examination area to check on my ulcers. While I was waiting in line for a physician, I watched other persons talk to the MD. One young man was trying to convince the physician that he had a problem with his knees and couldn't put any pressure on the knees. I concluded that if he were to do an exercise, such as jumping off the examination table, that would be undue pressure. The doctor examined the knee and looked at the medical information that had been provided. Finally, he indicated that he would recommend a deferment. A big smile came on the recruit's face, and as the physician turned to go to the next person, he jumped off the examination table. The recruit had evidently forgotten that he could not put pressure on his knee.

I was examined. Ultimately, I remember having a IIS or student deferment, but I may have been given a medical deferment too. While going into the service was not an issue with me, going in at that time would have been a very poor time for me.

I had talked earlier in the year to a Marine recruiter about a commission. The recruiter was from my hometown, Willard. My brother had been a Marine, so it seemed logical for me to go into the Marines. This was not the time, however, as I was graduating from college, and I had enrolled in graduate school at Bowling Green State University. The military never did come up again as a serious discussion.

A Trip Home

Between the time I went to school in September and the semester break in December, I would usually make one trip home to see my family and friends. This trip home in October proved a bit special because my sister Ann was coming home as a freshman from St. Mary of the Springs

College in Columbus. She was bringing two of her new friends from the same school to find out what this town of Willard was like.

On Friday night, we went out to one of the few restaurants in town, Hartensteins, located on Route 224 east of town. The food and drinks were good as was the service, and Dad or Mom always paid.

After supper, we would sometimes go to our favorite country bar, Havana Tavern. Havana Tavern was not extravagant to look at from either the outside or the inside, but the rules in the bar were very permissive. In other words, as long as one did not get too rowdy or out of control, one could have a few drinks, have something to eat, and have a good time.

In those days, there were a number of different attractions. There was a jukebox in which many songs of the past and present were available. There was a pool table, which provided us with recreation. One of the seldom-seen games at that time was the shuffleboard. The playing field for the shuffleboard was very long wooden boards glued together and then sanded to a smooth surface. Silver pucks were slid to the other end by players. Each player tried to push the puck as far as possible without having the puck fall off the far end of the board.

At times, other games, such as pinball or baseball machines, would appear. One could always play the card game euchre if one felt both lucky and skillful, and other players were available.

On this particular evening, Ann and her friends were the life of the party at the tavern. The nice part of the party was that my dad and sometimes my mom would come. Later in the evening, there was talk about people from our group dancing on the tables, but I have not been able to this date to find out if anyone was brave enough to show off their dancing skills at that height.

A Broken Arm

One evening in my senior year, three friends and myself had just come back to campus after a hamburger and milk shake at Manner's Big Boy. As we approached the quadrangle (middle of the campus), one of our friends started to chase Don Gresko with an umbrella. As he came to the end of the sidewalk, he was unaware that there was an ankle-high wire next to the walk. He tripped on the wire, flew into the air, came down on the concrete, and broke his arm.

When I saw the inconveniences in terms of showering, dressing, and other movements, I vowed to work hard and try to avoid bone breaks. The vow must have been a poor one, as less than six months later, I had my right hand in a cast for several weeks as the result of an accident.

Deodorant Can Burn

The dorm rooms were constructed with a wall between them to share the plumbing for each room. There was a sink in our room and one that faced it in the next room. There was also an opening below the mirror in which discarded razor blades could be deposited. Over the years, one could see from one room to the other, as the divider between the two rooms on the razor blades slot had disappeared.

One day, I was shaving, and my neighbor in the next room was doing the same. He thought it would be cute to spray some deodorant through the razor blade hole into my room. I had my own cute idea, and I opened my window so that a draft would go back into his room. The next time he sprayed, which was real soon, his laugh turned into a scream because I had lit my Bic, and the deodorant spray immediately turned into a flame. The flame blew into my neighbor's room and gave him a scare.

After thinking through my actions, I felt lucky no one was injured.

Gas That Can Burn

College students are notorious for experimenting. One day, a friend told me that human gas would ignite if lit by a flame. Several men in my dorm room agreed with this theory but not everyone. Someone volunteered to have his human gas lit. The gas came, and it lit. Unfortunately, there were no pants between the gas and the flame. In fact, the gas lit so well that the hair and skin around the source of the gas were singed.

My friend walked around campus looking like a cowboy for several days after that burn. Everyone learned that the underwear stays on, or one will burn sensitive parts of one's body when human gas is lit.

SAGA Foods

SAGA Foods was the contracted agency that delivered food to all the participating students, who usually lived in the dorms. The quality of food was good, and it was better with a special diet. I had a special diet because I had stomach ulcers. As it was explained to me, I had a spastic stomach because I would transfer my stress to my stomach.

Today I would have been given antibiotics, as ulcers are diagnosed as a type of infection. I guess if I didn't have stress, my stomach would have been without the pain caused by excess acid.

It was to take me years to regulate my stomach condition. Until that time, abdominal pain was a frequent occurrence, and milk or Maalox was my best friend. Drinking beer was an experience for which I was to pay the price. The only positive factor about my stomach disorder was I was often given steak when the food was too spicy for me. I would receive some funny looks as I got my steak at the dining hall, and others were given the daily special. The selections were good for most meals, and there were seconds available.

I would like to share two food incidents, one concerning breakfast and the other involving a food riot.

One morning, I had just returned from my eight o'clock class and was going to eat breakfast. I remember picking up two very runny eggs, fruit, and juice. I had picked up an extra glass because I loved milk, and the self-serve milk was in the main dining room, located just around the corner from the main hallway. As I went from the main hallway to the milk dispenser, I slipped and fell on my back. As I looked up, I saw my tray and all my breakfast being dumped on my clean shirt and white pants. Loud laughs erupted from the several students in the dining hall. As I sat up, I saw two egg yolks running down the front of my shirt and the remainder of the food and drink on or beside me. I slowly began to stand up and noticed a third egg on the floor, which was the culprit in my undeserved fall. I cleaned myself up as best I could, ate my breakfast, washed out my clothes, took a shower, and dressed for the second time that morning before ten thirty.

There was a second unusual food experience. There had been tensions for some reason on the campus. I can't remember the reasons, but they didn't seem to affect me. One evening as I walked into the dining hall, the entire hall was very full. Usually, students would eat their supper, talk for a while, and begin their studies. I asked someone why there were so many people, and they told me, "Food riot." I found a place to eat with some friends by the side windows of the room. As I was nearing the end of my meal, I was watching for any sign of a food riot. I had never seen a food riot, and I was pretty curious about how the whole affair would roll out.

Everyone was waiting and looking for the sign that would start the riot. I can still see the first lone bun, one that was long and of medium width, come flying across the room. After that, I saw trays of food, glasses, drinks, and chairs flying everywhere. It was over as fast as it started. One of the main problems was that it was very unsafe to leave the dining hall, as food, glass, and broken furniture were everywhere. Since it was hard to distinguish who started and participated in the riot, I never heard of any disciplinary actions to any students. This was my first and last food riot.

Crossroads Tavern

Crossroads was a bar located within a short walk from John Carroll. The main drink specialty was beer, and the food specialty was a shaved-ham sandwich. In my days at John Carroll, this was one of the closest and most frequented bars. There was a jukebox, which played popular songs. One of the songs played was "Zorba the Greek." On occasions, patrons would start at each end of the room doing a Greek dance and end up in the middle with a bumping of the bellies. One person would be standing, and the other usually ended up on the ground.

An acquaintance was in Crossroads one evening when he issued a challenge to me on the Zorba dance, and I took it. He was at least seventy-five pounds over my weight and thus had a distinct advantage. For some reason, I felt lucky that evening. My energy level became much greater than normal, and I felt the energy coming from God, my twin, or some other force. We started at the opposite ends of the room and danced to the center. As I looked up to him, I said to myself, *I can take him*. We bumped, and to many people's amazement, I was still standing. I was able to produce a draw and almost a victory.

I then had to walk the return trip to my dorm. The properties surrounding John Carroll in University Heights are some of the finest homes and lawns. There was always talk among students that if one were to leave Crossroads and felt that the beer or food was making you tired, all you would need to do is lie down on one of the pampered grass lawns near John Carroll. The grass was just like a mattress and would be as good a place to sleep as your bed. But no, I did not sleep on the grass.

Lake Erie College

Lake Erie College was a girls' school located in Painesville, the northeast part of Ohio. On one occasion, I visited the town with the expressed purpose of checking out the girls from Lake Erie College. While in Painesville, I remember visiting two well-known bars, which had accommodations for dancing. It was normal to hear that girls at one location were supposed to be more attractive than the girls at the other location. When I visited the two bars, The Cove and The Deck, things were not that lively. I couldn't judge the girls from either location. The Lake Erie scene did very little to attract me to Painesville.

A friend of mine had the opposite luck with Lake Erie College. His fun may have been related to his Corvair car with the very large trunk in the front. The ritual was pretty simple. On Saturday afternoon, the trunk of the car was filled with beer cans, and ice was poured over the cans so that they were covered. In the evening, the group would take off with its container of cold beer. My friends knew where to go and who to see, and they returned very frequently to Painesville. While my friends had a good time in there, the old saying that the grass is always greener on the other side of the fence never worked out for me. The saying was usually a complete fallacy.

Mixers

The dances after the basketball games at JCU were called mixers. The crowd was there, so why not have another social event? The sodality sponsored them. I was very active in the sodality and at one time held an office. One of my duties in the sodality was to oversee the running of the mixers. That would mean checking on the availability of the gymnasium, seeing that there were people available to take the price of admission, making arrangements for the disc jockey, addressing any problem areas, and depositing the profits.

The persons who attended the mixers were men from John Carroll University and women from several colleges and nursing schools. High school senior females did sometimes gain admittance. The attendance was easily into the several hundreds.

One winter in 1965, I had just pulled some money from the admission gate, as we didn't like to keep all our eggs (money) in one basket. As I was walking through the downstairs halls, I noticed two young men randomly picking up some coats and immediately leaving the building. I followed the men outside into a very heavy snowstorm. I was concerned for both the safety of the monies and my personal security.

A not surprising fact was that both of the men were not as small as me. I followed the two men to their car, obtained their license number, and reported the theft to the police. The police said that they would follow up on the crime but told me not to expect much, as the car was registered in a tough part of Cleveland. When the individuals came to me to report their coats being stolen, they were given all the information we had. While the coats were probably not found, at least we did act on the theft as best we could. This fact was of some consolation to me.

"Say, Kids! What Time Is It?"

Stunt night was usually held in March, and each year, our class had tried to win the coveted first place. Our senior year turned out to be our year of laughs, as we gave our best and earned first place. As the opening line rang through the crowd, "Say kids! What time is it?" the peanut gallery along with much of the audience yelled, "It's Howdy Doody time." At that point, I knew it was a great night, as I felt the chills go up my spine.

Buffalo Bob, Howdy, Clarabell, the peanut gallery, and the entire cast acted like professionals. At the very beginning of the skit, I had the "pleasure" of leaving the peanut gallery with crossed legs for a date with the bathroom. The crowd loved my moves and went crazy with the actions of the rest of the cast. I bet every performer in this skit remembers his part and the great response of the crowd.

Train, Race Car, and Airplane Sounds on Campus

About eleven o'clock in the evening during finals week, several sounds came from, I believe, Bernet Hall. That was the time loud sounds could be heard on the JCU quadrangle. After the sounds of a train coming down the track, a car racing and an airplane coming in for a landing, the study-weary occupants of the other two dorms on the quadrangle would begin to yell for more.

I don't remember how many evenings the loud sounds graced the JCU campus, but I do know that whoever it was that was making the loud sounds had two qualities: they were good at it, and they got away with it.

My Future Contacts with JCU

Leaving John Carroll University was a bittersweet experience. The bitter part was leaving my friends of four years, a fairly secure environment, and a schedule that was, by semester, easy to follow. The sweet part was that I had a degree and was more on my own in the world, free to follow my own rules with the possibility of obtaining another degree at Bowling Green State University. After graduate school, I would need a job, and just maybe I would find that young lady I had dreamed of marrying.

There were a few ways after graduation in which I kept in contact with my undergraduate friends. Every five years after graduation, there were class reunions, and I tried to attend each one. It was always good to see the classmates who attended the reunions, and we missed the ones who were not able to attend. Interacting with the faculty was another treat. One such former teacher I had the privilege of seeing at the class of 1962 reunion was Fr. William Bichl, SJ, my logic teacher. Father Bichl made the world of logic come to life for me, and I was in debt to him for instilling the ability to organize my thoughts and my life. By the way, the SJ behind Father Bichl's name means Society of Jesus or that he was a member of the Jesuit order known for many areas, including teaching.

My other major contact with the university would be its periodic publication in which graduates were updated on the happenings of the university. Near the back of the publication was a report by class of happenings in classmates' lives. I would read this section religiously. Occasionally I would send in something about my life.

While writing this book, I became class-note friendly and e-mail friendly with our class correspondent, Dave Griffin. For years, Dave faithfully reported the class news by making it interesting and searching enough news to make a full column. He tried to keep up the interest of the class in my book through his column. Whenever there was an interesting e-mail, I would try to send it to Dave.

Prior to Dave being named class correspondent, Steve Chamberlain had a marathon stint over ten years of keeping the "class of 1966" news. Both Steve and Dave hail from Rochester, New York.

Summers

Willard City Pool 1966

Ice in the Shower

The summer after my junior year at JCU, I had a job as the manager of the Willard pool. The job was at times relaxed, but at other times, it was not an easy position. Whenever a child had to be pulled from the pool, it was challenging.

I remember the time when we had just cleaned the building before opening. It had taken the crew until the minute before opening this day to finish the cleaning job. One of the workers relayed to me that there was ice in the girls' shower room. I began to walk over to the building to inspect it as that did not sound right when a young girl came into the office with a very large cut in her foot.

We began treating the girl, and I asked her where it had happened. She said, "The shower." In a fraction of a second, I realized that the ice I was in the process of inspecting was actually glass. I ran to the girls' restroom to find glass in the shower and a few other girls with smaller cuts on their feet. The girls' side was immediately closed and recleaned. The boys' side was inspected with no sign of glass. To my knowledge, the girls were successfully treated, but I felt bad, and still do, that the glass was not discovered earlier. From that point on, no glass was allowed in the dressing rooms. I also made sure that closer inspections were completed.

To this day, every time I think of this incident, I get a chill and a pain in my stomach. As a result of this incident, I have had a special safety concern in every job in which I have been involved. I wish I could go back and somehow make it up to the little girls who were cut by the glass.

Unfortunately, we did not find the individuals responsible for this act, but it did not happen again during my job tenure.

The positive side is that when I was employed in Wood County in the future years, I was involved with various safety programs and was directly involved with the production of a safety video through the television station WBGU.

The Strangers

At about the same time as the incident with the glass, there was an event that had the staff at the pool concerned. It had to do with three young men of fairly good size (who were not from Willard) who began harassing one of my male lifeguards. On that day, one of them came to the office informing me of the visitors who were trying to pick a fight. Although no contact took place, I knew I needed to investigate. I asked the lifeguard for more details, and after that, I found the three young men and asked them to come to the office.

They were cooperative in doing so. As politely as possible, I questioned them about their actions with the lifeguard. There was a four-foot counter separating us, and I felt comfortable enough talking with them, even though one was larger than me, and there were three of them against me. My office was in a somewhat secluded spot. Seeing that I was getting nowhere with them and not sure that I had any violation of the law, I advised them to leave. I also informed them that the police would be coming soon to do their rounds at the park.

There was one significant happening before the three young men left. The person who took the money for pool admissions came to the office to place the money collected that day in the metal safe. As she put the money in the safe, mostly a big pile of dollar bills, I saw the young men observe her actions. It bothered me at the time.

As the young men began to leave the office, I called the Willard police and asked for a patrol car immediately, as the men were still on site, and I didn't trust them. I observed them as they walked from the building and went to the parking lot. I noted specific information about their car for the police. A patrol car was there within minutes and entered the parking lot as the three men were leaving.

I tried to calm my staff as best as I could because by the time the police came, stories were flying about the three visitors and their interaction with the lifeguard. A police report was taken, and the police were looking in town for the individuals in order to question them. The three visitors were not found anywhere. The police asked us to keep a lookout for them and to call if anything suspicious happened. They said they would be patrolling the grounds at more frequent intervals.

That evening, I went to bed before midnight and could not sleep. I continued to review the happenings of the afternoon, and within a few minutes, I sat up in bed. I remembered the three persons seeing the money being put in the safe, and I thought that I better go to the park and bring the money home. The safe had a padlock securing the money, which could be removed with a hacksaw. As I approached the parking lot at the park, I looked around to see if there were any strange cars or individuals. While there were lights at the Willard City Park, they were very dim, and I could not see well. The Willard pool was located near the edge of town, and while there were some homes near the park, it was composed of many acres of land, which were not well lit. There was, to my knowledge, nobody on the grounds except God and me.

I began to walk up the sidewalk next to the building and looked very closely for anyone in the tall bushes beside the sidewalk. When I opened the office door, I shut and locked it quickly. I opened the safe by removing the padlock and was happy to see the money in the safe. I took out the money and locked the safe. I became very alarmed as I began to leave the office. The door was a solid metal door, and there were no windows in the entire office that I could look out to see if anyone was around. But I opened the door and saw no one.

I began walking toward my car and again carefully looked at every large bush beside the walk. I don't know why, but I was sure at this point that sometime that night, the office would be robbed, and I didn't want to be there. I was sure of another fact. I should have asked for a police escort because I was terrified that someone might be on the grounds watching me. On the other hand, I really didn't think anyone was present despite my uneasy attitude. I knew the police were going to be around, and that was comforting. I opened my car door, sat down, and started out of the parking lot, realizing that leaving this place was a big relief. The incidents surrounding the three visitors had turned an average day into a very negative day. I now knew that the money was safe. I went home and went to bed a few minutes before midnight and slept well.

The next morning at opening time, I received a call from the head lifeguard. As soon as I heard her voice, I knew what she was going to say. She said that when she came into the office to open up for swim lessons, she noticed that someone had been in the office and had sawed off the lock of the padlock, and the money was gone. I told her that last night I couldn't sleep, so I came out and removed the money. It was safe at my house. I asked her to call the police and tell them what had happened, and I would be there shortly to deal with the situation.

As a closer investigation was begun, it turned out that there had been other objects taken from the safe. One of these objects was my portable radio.

Later that day, my radio was found on the inner park road. The antenna had been bent, it would not work properly, and it could not be fixed. The robbers were never caught, and it was circumstantial evidence that pointed to the three visitors. It was a scary experience for all employees. I was happy no one was hurt, and I reacted to my instincts.

A Management Issue

Another lesson I learned that summer was a management issue. The management issue had to do with dating employees. As a young man recently graduating from college, I was always on the lookout for an enjoyable time with an interesting lady. I confided in a friend that I was contemplating on dating one of my employees and wasn't sure if it was the right thing to do.

Immediately he filled me in on the faults of this type of dating. It could be seen by other employees as favoritism and could cause me to not be objective with the employee. I didn't date any employee.

I would see over the years how this practice has been the downfall of many administrators, married or not married. I was lucky to have a smart good friend and was glad he shared his knowledge with me.

After-Hours Summer Activities

The Boat

The summer weather allowed our family to spend many hours at Lake Erie. Before we had the family cottage in Huron, Ohio, we had a sixteen-foot fiberglass boat with a sixty-horsepower outboard motor. This allowed us to ski and fish in Sandusky Bay near Bay Bridge. From my high school days until the cottage days, "Fun in the sun" was the motto of our boat.

The downtime we experienced on the boat was usually caused by the malfunctioning of our motor. The mechanics from the nearby marina were frequent companions at our dock. The frequency was so great that my father had a tab with the mechanics. The next picture was the dock area where we kept our boat.

Near the end of my years at John Carroll, my parents built a cottage on the Huron River. The Huron River drains into Lake Erie. We had many good times at the cottage with family and friends. Late card games of euchre and fishing off the dock and in our boat gave us times we love to remember.

I enjoyed the sun and Lake Erie.

I spent much of the summer of 1966 preparing for graduate school. I was dating a few girls, but nothing exciting was happening, and I was beginning to get a little worried about finding a compatible mate. God had always listened to my prayers and answered them. The answer had not always been what I asked for, but they were answered. At times, I had not trusted God's actions enough, but He always had come through. I decided I needed to trust more and doubt less God's ability.

Unforgettable Person in My Life at This Time

Big Butch Rothschild

While I had known Big Butch before I attended college, it was not until I worked for him in the summer of 1964 that I really knew him. His name came to him as he had a son also named Butch, and he was, for years, larger than his son.

When it came to working with one's hands or head, Big Butch was a jack of all trades and a master of all. Anything that needed to be done around the house or on the job was something that he would be able to accomplish. In addition to his carpenter, plumbing, masonry, painting, welding, and machinery skills, he was a good cook.

Near the end of cleaning a mess of perch in Mildred and Big Butch's basement, he would leave the cleaning area and begin setting up to fry the fresh perch. By the time the last perch was cleaned, the first perch was ready to be eaten. There is nothing in the world like freshly fried Lake Erie perch, especially if they were prepared by Big Butch.

Big Butch had worked in almost every job related to construction. He was the superintendent of water, streets, cemetery, and many other departments for the city of Willard for many years starting in the early sixties. I had been around him, as his son Butch was a few years older than me, and I was always "hanging out" with Butch in his dad's garage on Clark Street. Big Butch also was the kind of person who would take time to explain to me how various tools and machines worked.

In the years before I worked with Big Butch for the city of Willard, there were many job skills I learned from him. He had a wooden boat he had made by hand. The boat, to my knowledge, never leaked, and the bottom needed to be sanded and painted frequently. I learned how to scrape, sand, fill holes, and paint a boat with him on those occasions.

Household appliances will break down. Big Butch was always careful to show how the electrical systems on these appliances worked and how to fix them when possible.

The Rothschild garden was known to be one of the best in the neighborhood. If vegetables were ever needed by neighbors, the weedless, well-fertilized, and bountiful crop of Mildred and Big Butch was available for others to use as the Rothschilds always had more than they could use.

The Rothschilds were not a family who sat around if there was work to be done. Their house inside and out was impeccable, and it was a credit to not only them but also the neighborhood.

As the superintendent of the Willard City Street, Sewer, and Cemetery, he was placed in many challenging situations. Fixing broken waterlines of at least twelve inches in diameter, operating a backhoe to make repairs on water or sewer systems, digging graves in the city cemetery, plowing snow, building wood or cement buildings, repairing city streets, cleaning out plugged sewer lines, and managing his crew were but a few of the jobs I learned how to do from Big Butch.

In later years as a young man, it was difficult for me to visit him in his living room as he sat in his La-Z-Boy chair dealing with his illness. Big Butch was strong to the end, and he never stopped trying to help other people to learn how to successfully deal with their environment. I will never forget Big Butch.

---

[30] Rio Brower, "Original Fruit Salad Is Double Duty Dessert," *The Willard Times*, March 18, 1965, 3.

Part V

Really on My Own

Chapter 12

Bowling Green State University and Kathy

During my senior year at John Carroll, I applied to a few graduate schools. I had majored in psychology in my undergraduate studies. I liked the area, and I didn't see any other discipline that was more appealing. Each application that was sent in cost around $50. I didn't have much money and thought I should know where I want to go before I started applying. I felt I didn't need to apply just to see if I was accepted. At Bowling Green State University, there were several areas of psychology, such as clinical, industrial, and school psychology. I decided school psychology at BGSU was best for me.

Classes

I made friends with a few of the students in my classes almost immediately, a married male and a single male. My new friend's wife was a teacher. They were exceptionally friendly people and fun to be around. I knew no one when I went to John Carroll, and now at Bowling Green, it was the same. I was very happy to come upon these new friends.

We three males had a regular ritual. Classes in psychology were all morning and afternoon. Lunch was at Union, where we played a little pool. For two semesters, that is what my weekdays looked like.

Weekends were mostly studying until Christmas when I met Kathy. Then it was home to see my honey as much as possible. This was the first time in my college days that a lady was to take some precedence over my studies.

First Semester

The first course I enrolled in was Introduction to Psychological Testing. I had taken a similar course at John Carroll, but I felt I should be exposed to more subject matter in the overall testing movement. I was wrong about this increased exposure. I should never have taken the class because I learned very little new material and could have enrolled in another more needed class.

My instructor in Developmental Psychology centered the course on the theory of learning by Dr. Jean Piaget. Dr. Piaget was French, and he was a genius in his theories of developmental psychology. There were many phases of learning that he identified for children of different ages. The area that interested me for children of different ages was called conservation of speed. One test for the conservation of speed utilized small play cars. Two cars would approach a tunnel together, but one would come out sooner and faster than the other. The question asked was why was one car ahead of the other car at the end of the tunnel when they came into the tunnel together. The answer would be that somehow the car furthest ahead had gained speed.

A year later, I was fascinated with the experimentation and developmental sequencing that would help me immensely in my physical development roles and thought processes in general. The instructor in Personality Theory was good, but it seemed I was always trying to catch up.

My research course on the other hand, aided me immensely. The different phases of organizing the subject matter, developing a hypothesis or what was to be proved or not proved, developing the methodology of research including the statistical analysis to be employed, identifying the subjects and the tests to be employed, and conducting the experiment and the analysis of the results gave one the information needed to write the report and make recommendations. This course was to give me a big advantage in completing my doctoral dissertation later in my profession.

The Boardinghouse

I found a boardinghouse to live in located about five blocks from the campus. The distance was not too great, unless my 1956 Pontiac would not start. The longer I had the car, the less likely it was to start. The standard routine if the car didn't start was taking off the air cleaner top and shooting starter fluid into the carburetor. The successful starting ratio was about 50 percent. If there was snow on the ground of any accumulation, I would need to keep the car moving or risk getting stuck. Why? I was running bald tires on my car, and the snow would become an ice rink.

My landlady was an extremely kind person. Her husband worked out of state and she had a daughter in college. Her son was an upperclassman at Bowling Green High School. The son was a good guitarist and would rock with one of his friends in the evening at the house.

I had my room and would use it or the library at BGSU to study. I prepared my own meals and cleaned my room.

I found out several years later that my room and the rest of the house were destroyed by an explosion. A garden now stands on the site instead of the house. I found graduate school much different than undergraduate school. In undergraduate school, there were always several other students around, and in graduate school, the number of students was radically reduced.

About Kathy

Dating the Girl I Wished to Marry

I finished my first semester at BGSU and found that many of the courses I took were not in a direction that I wished to pursue. Over the Christmas break, I worked as usual at the local clothing store Jump's. My elder brother, Walt, had worked there, and I had worked there for the Christmas vacation my entire undergraduate years. One of the benefits of working at Jump's was that I had always earned enough money to buy Christmas gifts for my family. With the discounts I received as an employee, I could buy even more gifts at either the Jump's clothing store or the Jump's clothing store for women.

I also had become proficient at wrapping gifts. I had been instructed when and how to put tissue paper in the boxes. I learned how to make attractive corners on boxes with the wrapping paper. I knew how to use enough but not too much wrapping paper and tape.

Another side benefit of working at Jump's was that as a single young person, I could wait on the single young ladies who would frequent the store to purchase something for their father, brother, or present boyfriend. I was on constant watch at the front entrance because any appropriate single girl was fair game for me. I learned many helpful practices in marketing and sales that helped me in my future profession. I enjoyed talking with the many interesting people who would shop in the store.

It was on December 31 of 1966 at around 1:30 p.m. that Kathy Long came into Jump's to buy a pair of gloves for a friend. We had known each other since I was in high school, as Kathy and my sister Ann were in the same class. At that time, they were freshmen, and I was a senior.

As I saw Kathy, I remembered an experience when she had been a passenger in the car I was driving after we had attended the World Day of Prayer Ceremony at one of the local churches while we had been given time off from high school. In Willard, the strip down Myrtle Avenue was the road from the downtown business area to Route 224. There was a turnaround at both ends of Myrtle Avenue. Around halfway down this street was Lee's Drive In, an ice cream and sandwich shop. Lee had great ice cream and tasty chicken sandwiches. Some of the Willard residents thought these sandwiches were the best anywhere.

On this day, I stopped at Lee's with a car loaded with young ladies. Kathy was one of the ladies who placed an order like the rest. After we had our order, I made the mistake of gunning the car as we went around the corner of the building to leave the parking lot. That was a big mistake, as Kathy spilled her milk shake on her blouse. I suppose she would have said it was a chocolate shake, and she was probably correct. She was not a happy camper. That should have been the end of the relationship. At any rate, it didn't help it.

Kathy and I did see each other a few times after the ice cream incident, but nothing serious developed. The reason we dated at this time was probably related to my persistent actions. The freshmen girls were top-notch when it came to attractive girls, and Kathy was a beauty. My father had always told me to not get serious with a girl until I was in the proper position. I knew I was in no position to get serious with a girl when I was a senior in high school. It was now five years later after the previous dating that Kathy walked into the door at Jump's.

Now it is back to Jump's the last day of 1966, and I was at her side. We had a nice talk that afternoon, and I asked her for a date that evening, which was New Year's Eve. I didn't have a date, so I figured she might not have a date. I was wrong, and once again, I earned no points with Kathy. She had a date that evening, and I could tell that she was a bit insulted by my thinking that she might not have a New Year's Eve date. Despite my thoughtless judgment, I convinced her to agree to a date the next night.

Little did I know that this date was to be the most important one of my life because it was the beginning of our life together. We went to Pullman Lanes, the only bowling alley near Willard. I was trying hard to bowl well, but I was much more interested in the lovely girl I was dating that evening. As fate would have it, Kathy beat me badly in bowling that first evening.

The morning after bowling, Kathy wasted no time in showing her interest in me. She came to my house to send me off to college. I was finding that she was the most attentive and affectionate girl I had ever dated. She also brought me a record titled *Georgy Girl*, the song that was very popular then and was applicable to the beginning of our relationship, as the words in the song talked about getting into a serious relationship. When I think of that morning, I think of one of the happiest mornings of my life. I knew I had found the love of my life, the woman of my dreams, and everything about it was an adventure with much happiness and excitement awaiting us.

Second Semester

I had to leave Kathy and get back to the university, as I was registered for classes. I was to find that some of my courses were a bit more interesting than those of the first semester. Psychology of Educational Counseling was taught by a relaxed teacher and exposed the class to different types of counseling techniques. Carl Rogers' techniques in counseling were very useful to me. In this type of counseling, information provided by the client is feedback to the client, so they better solve their problem by using input from themselves.

By far the most interesting and most time-consuming course was Psychometrics I. In this course, we traveled to different grade schools and conducted Wechsler and Stanford-Binet intelligence tests. With the results in hand, it was then time to score the test and come up with the IQ scores.

The Psychopathology course looked at various types of abnormal-type behaviors in society. It could be depression, criminal behaviors, personality disorders, or other behaviors in need of some type of help. I had been interested in this area because of experiences I had with persons with psychopathic behaviors. The last class I took in the spring of 1967 would be the final graduate course I took at Bowling Green State University until 1972 when I began working on my master's degree in special education.

Courtship, Wedding, and Honeymooning

As I came home on weekends to see Kathy, I viewed the future with much excitement and anticipation. I was to have a new family and friends. Kathy would be doing the same. Our lives were centering on each other, and each other's relatives and friends now were to mingle into one. With our limited resources, our recreation was visiting relatives, friends, and neighbors.

A courtship that started while we were miles apart soon grew into tolerating only a few minutes apart. The attraction we had for each other was almost instantaneous. I thought about Kathy and wanted to be with her every minute of my life.

I wanted a wedding the following January, and Kathy chose June of 1968. Unfortunately, a blizzard did occur in January on the same day as our wedding. We could have gone with Kathy's choice of date and had a nice day, but there would have been six months I would not have enjoyed Kathy's constant presence in my life. It was fast, it was exciting, and it produced a beautiful relationship that is still alive today.

Kathy's Past

I learned a lot about Kathy. I liked what I saw and heard! She was a hard worker. In her younger days, she was a babysitter for her neighbors—the Knolls, Shorty and Annie, and the Fries, Harold and Mary. The Knolls lived across the road from Kathy. Kathy's pay in those days was somewhere around 35¢ an hour. Bathing, snacking, and putting the kids to bed were her duties with the four Knoll children and the five Fries children.

Harold had a band that played at wedding receptions and other celebrations. Little did I know that Harold would be playing waltzes, polkas, and square dances at our wedding.

In later years, we visited Shorty and Annie, and I was to tease Annie on her ability to plant gardens. On one occasion, she planted two rows of peas, and instead of ending up parallel to each other, the rows ended up crossing each other.

Harold's band played another dance called schottische. This dance was a line dance in which the women usually would dance around the floor and kick up their heels the same way their mothers and grandmothers had done in their younger days and had taught them to do. By the time Kathy and I were married, we had enjoyed Harold's band on several evenings.

Kathy was very proud of her heritage and talked about her grandmother and grandfather Meyer who lived in their later years in the town of Monroeville. I never knew either of these grandparents, as they had both passed before we dated. I feel I have missed a great opportunity. Kathy would periodically ask me to drive by their home near the Faulhaber Plant in Monroeville. Her grandfather inspected the gas lines, and her grandmother was a housewife. The Faulhaber Company was the business where my future mother-in-law, Laetta, worked helping produce bicycle seats.

Kathy's paternal grandparents lived next door to her. She would visit her grandmother Loretta every day that she had time to walk to their house. Kathy's grandfather Ted Long worked as a butcher, a farmer, and eventually a railroader. Her grandmother had a small egg business and was a housekeeper. She was a wonderful cook and a pleasant person. Kathy's family and grandparents attended St. Sebastian Catholic Church in Bismark. Kathy's father, Albert, was a hard-working railroader who also helped out on his father's farm.

Kathy and her brother, Dave, were taught by the Franciscan nuns at St. Sebastian's School in Bismark. After eighth grade, they enrolled in Willard High School. I met her when she was in her freshman year. Kathy was to attend nurses' training at St. Joseph Hospital in Lorain, Ohio, and graduated in 1966.

Kathy's best longtime friend is Pat Elmlinger. Pat's family owned the only nearby grocery store in a town called Havana, and Pat was usually the cashier. If Elmlinger's Supermarket didn't have it, it did not exist.

I was to find out many other facts about Kathy as the years passed. Kathy was a contestant in the Miss Huron County beauty pageant. At the pageant, she met another contestant who would be a lifelong friend, Bonnie Still. I was always impressed with the fact that Kathy and Bonnie could perform in a pageant in front of all those people. We were to have many fun times with Bonnie and her husband, Jim Hicks.

Kathy has one sister and one brother, Agnes Balduff and Dave Long. I have always enjoyed a marvelous relationship with both of her siblings and families, and they became as true a family to me as my brothers and sisters became family to Kathy. Ag was the wife of a farmer and is the mother of four children. When her first husband, John Clayton, passed, Ag, living near North Monroeville devoted much of her time raising the children. They had three daughters, Amy Weisenberger, Beth Fritz, and Laurie Haughawout, and one son, John H. Clayton. She then worked at Midwest

Industries in Willard and ten years later married Lloyd Balduff, who was a railroad employee. They lived near Norwalk. Lloyd also has passed.

Amy is married to Dave Weisenberger. They have two daughters, Courtney Hipp and Jacqueline Weisenberger. Courtney is married to Drew Hipp. Beth is married to Rick Fritz. Their daughter is Brittany Fritz, and their son is Bryan Fritz. Laurie is married to Kim Haughawout, and their two sons are Andrew and Tyler Haughawout. John H. is married to Susan Clayton, and their son is John Steven Clayton.

Dave lives in Willard and married Diane Matteson. He worked at Midwest Industries as did Diane. They have a son, Eric Long, and a daughter, Hilary Crawford. Eric married Angela Long and has two daughters, Amber Lillo and Madelynn Long. Amber is married to Benn Lillo, and they have a daughter, Whitney Long, and a son, Brett. Hilary is married to Jim Crawford. They have two daughters, Cary and Caty Crawford, and one son, Cody Crawford.

Dave and Diane's house

After our December date, I was to continue graduate school until June of 1967. My relationship was growing with Kathy, and any weekend I could make it home to see her I did. At this time, Kathy was living with her brother, Dave, and sister-in-law, Diane, since it was closer to her place of employment. She was working as a nurse at Hillside Acres in Willard and, at this time, was working second shift. This worked out well for a late date. Dave would rise around three to four o'clock in the morning to get ready for work. This meant that they went to bed early, and Kathy and I had the exclusive use of the downstairs. Since I didn't have much money as a student, spending time at her brother's worked out well. We had the privacy we needed to get to know each other.

One evening when I was sitting next to Kathy, I felt the presence of another being. I looked to see who was in the room with us. I was actually rather startled and concerned because whoever was in the room had just brushed against my back. As I turned around further, I saw the outline of an animal. A closer look revealed a cat named Smokey. Smokey was roughly my age and was easy to distinguish from other cats, as he had lost an eye years earlier, and it was sewn shut. Every time I go to Dave and Diane's and sit in their parlor, I think back to the many evenings I spent with Kathy and Smokey.

Since I started dating Kathy in the winter, there were many times the snow was deep. With deep snow and bald tires, I was often stuck in Dave's driveway. Then I would ask Kathy to be the driver as I pushed the car out. We were a good team and worked together well despite the snowy circumstances.

The Show in Sandusky

Shortly after I had started to date Kathy, her brother and sister-in-law asked me to go to a show in Sandusky with them. You must understand that Sandusky is a very big city when one lives in Willard. Going to the big city was always a big deal, even though I had just spent four years in Cleveland and almost a year in Bowling Green.

At intermission, Dave and I went to the restroom. As we came out of the restroom, Dave asked, "What do you think of my sister?" I was taken aback by the question at first but thought, *He is being honest with me, and I will be honest with him.* Before I could answer the first question, he asked me another question about getting serious with Kathy. Knowing that he would probably feed my answer back to Kathy, I said that I liked Kathy a lot, and the relationship could become very serious. We enjoyed the movie.

Later, I was pleased with my answer to Dave, and after I thought about it, I was also very pleased that I was asked the question. I had never felt about any other girl the way I was feeling about her.

In later years, I asked Kathy if she had put Dave up to asking me those questions. All she would do is look at me and smile.

Blackbirds

As my first year at Bowling Green State University was flying by, a friend of mine, Bob Schodorf, invited me to go to the marshes around Lake Erie and see the blackbird project in which he was involved. His job was coming to an end. He explained that the job started when his adviser, the head of the biology department, had offered him a job to build fence traps and band certain birds. At this time, there was an overpopulation of blackbirds, and they were causing harm to many crops, especially corn. The blackbirds were so numerous that when a flock of them flew over, it was common for the birds to block the sunlight.

The day we were to see the blackbird project, the weather was overcast, and there was light rain. As we approached the first trap, I was very impressed with the size of the metal wire traps, which were fifty feet long and twenty feet wide. The height of the traps was six or seven feet. Upon walking into the bird trap, I was even more impressed by the entry points for the birds. In the middle were several four-by-four-inch openings, which ran about twenty feet made of turkey wire. The birds could pull in their wings and enter the trap to obtain the corn on the ground, but when they were ready to leave, their wings would be spread to fly out, and they couldn't go through the narrow opening created by the turkey wire.

Bob explained to me that he would start at the far end of the trap pushing the birds to the other end. When they flew to the other end, there was a large funnel that they drove the birds into, and as the funnel became smaller, the birds become more compact in the funnel. At a point, the funnel was blocked off, and the birds were run into a bag at the end of the funnel. Certain birds were tagged and released, and the others were handled in another manner. Bob explained the findings from the project and how the project was helping to control the blackbird population. The project that Bob worked on seemed to me to be a good use of government funds, and it gave Bob some experience in his field of biology. It was a very interesting and enjoyable day with my good friend.

The Willard Municipal Pool

My 1967 summer job was to co-manage the Willard Municipal Pool and Park with Dave Williams. Dave had recently graduated from Denison University and was enrolled in law school for the fall session. I had known Dave in high school and had previously enjoyed working with him as a summer employee at Pioneer Rubber Company. Summer employees at Pioneer were chosen from employee's offspring, and my dad and Dave's mother, Alice Williams, were two dedicated Pioneer employees.

Fourth of July

The idea of an old-fashioned Fourth of July celebration began to occupy my mind in the early summer as a great way for families to spend part of their day at the Willard City Park. Dave got behind the idea with me, and soon we were out canvassing the city merchants for prizes for our many games and activities. We organized various games: tennis for youth and older age groups, youth relay games, and adult games. The local radio station and the local paper helped get out the word on this event.

The ongoing Fourth of July softball tournament brought in many people and contestants for the games. Several awards were earned by deserving participants. The day ended with the well-established traditional fireworks, which Kathy and I enjoyed from the pool. The many people who worked to continue past practices and those who added some new ones all helped to make this day a success. Without participants, there would have been no games and activities.

The Flood

I was awakened on July 5, 1967, at seven o'clock by a bullhorn from a police car going down the street telling everyone not to drink the water from the tap, as it was contaminated and needed to be boiled. I soon found that as I had slept very soundly and late after the previous day's activities, Mother Nature had been busy. The cause of the drinking ban was a violent electrical storm and floods that had affected not only Willard but many other neighboring communities as well.

Later that day, my parents discovered that their lake cottage in Huron had several feet of water in the main floor. The reason the cottage flooded was that a large stone railroad bridge over the Huron River filled up with damaged boats and debris. A dam developed and caused the water to flood many areas upstream, including my parents' cottage.

Making matters worse at the cottage was that the cooking oil in the deep fryer had floated out of the appliance and settled on top of the water into all areas of the first floor. The cooking oil formed a ring about five feet up on all the downstairs walls. One part of the cleanup was fairly easy since almost everything in the lower floor needed to be discarded. Another part of the cleaning wasn't so easy because the walls all had to be washed several times to remove the dirt and oil that remained after the water receded.

The Grill

The well-known and popular restaurant and bar in downtown Willard was owned by Harlow Staff, and it was called "The Grill." In the 1960s, going out to eat was not as frequent an occasion as the present-day practice. In the summer of 1967, Kathy's mother and father invited Kathy and me to dinner at "The Grill." This was probably the first time I had been with Kathy's parents socially. I had grown fond of Kathy and wanted her and her parents to think highly of me. This dinner was a true test of all our relationships.

Before dinner was served, I heard someone being paged in the restaurant. The page was loud, but it was hard to hear the name of the person being called to the phone. People in the restaurant, including us, were looking around to see who was being called. As I looked around, I saw no important person going to the phone. Someone at the table next to us said the page was for me. I didn't believe them, but just to make sure it wasn't me, I thought I should go to the phone.

I excused myself from the table, still not sure the phone call was for me. About halfway to the phone, I thought, *If it is for me, I hope it is good news.* As I approached the archway between the dining area and the bar, I could see customers looking at me. One of the employees gave me the phone and said, "You can take the call here."

By now my heart was really pounding. I said, "Hello. This is Joe."

The voice at the other end said, "How is it going?" I knew immediately it was Dave Williams's voice. It was a relief hearing his voice and knowing that there was no problem at the pool.

I explained that things were going well. We had some small talk and said good-bye. I started back to my table. As I was going back to my table, I was convinced Dave purposely made me look pretty important in front of a restaurant full of people, including Kathy and her parents. As I sat down,

Kathy asked if everything was OK. I said that something had happened at work, and it was solved. I learned from this experience one more way of how to make someone look important. Thanks, Dave.

Now when I pass the pool, I think of the good old days when I was involved in managing it with Dave. My brother Mike eventually followed me as the manager. I know he enjoyed his management years of the pool, as well as teaching swimming lessons using his water safety instructor certification.

Good Times with Kathy

Corvair Rides

Kathy drove a white Chevy Corvair that her father gave her to use. When I was home during the summer of 1967, we would take rides to nowhere in particular. Yet these rides would turn out to be to everywhere because we were together. We thoroughly enjoyed each other's company.

One summer day when we were on a ride in the country near Kathy's house, she spotted an archer who was about to shoot an arrow at a target. The timing was perfect on Kathy's part because as the man drew back the bow, we were passing him. At the height of his draw, Kathy beeped the car horn. The man let go of the arrow, and we watched it go over top of the target. He was not as amused as we were.

Chicken Dinner

I was very excited to be invited to Kathy's grandparents for a Sunday dinner in the summer of 1967. Kathy had lived next to her grandparents her entire life. The family farm consisted of around seventy acres of which about five of these acres were used for housing and buildings. Facing the houses from the road, the home of Kathy's parents was to the right, and the home of Kathy's grandparents was to the left. Both properties had a house and a detached garage. The property of Kathy's grandparents also had five more outbuildings. Those buildings were a barn, a chicken coup, a granary, and two storage buildings.

This was the first time I had been invited to a meal at her grandparents, and I had been dating Kathy for several months. I was the type of person who saw what I wanted and went after it, so this was a chance to know the family better and hopefully to become better accepted. The idea of marriage had been proposed by me to Kathy's father, and he was concerned that I didn't have a full-time job. I wasn't worried about finding a job. I saw this meal as a kind of acceptance of me by Kathy's family.

Fried chicken was on the menu, and it is one of my favorite meals. As I came into the dining room and smelled the chicken, I asked where they had purchased the poultry. Immediately Kathy's grandmother, a very sweet lady, informed me that she had butchered the chicken the day before from one of the flock they had raised. I was impressed and shared how I had always been involved with the butchering over at the Eldred's farm where I had worked. I figured a little name-dropping identifying with farming was in order. I wanted everyone to know that this city slicker also was an experienced farmhand.

It was time to eat. The chicken, gravy, and vegetables were passed around. I took big enough helpings to show I thought it was going to be good but not so much that someone else would be cheated from his fair share. Actually, portions were not a problem, as there was more than enough to go around. The meal went fine, and I thanked everyone for the food.

After the meal, I went with the men to the front room to talk while the women cleaned up the table. I was a little uncomfortable about not helping with the dishes because in my family of eight, everyone took part in the meal process, including doing the dishes.

After the dishes were done and the table was cleared, I was asked if I wanted to play a card game called crazy eight. I am always up for a good game of cards and found that crazy eight was a very serious game in the Long family. Everyone brought out his jar of money and proceeded to put out the accepted fee of 15¢. I didn't have a jar, but I did have 15¢, so I was in the game. In crazy eight, each person received three cards and tried to get a high hand by drawing a card, matching the suit, and throwing away his worst card. When someone went out, the person with the lowest hand put a nickel in the pot. You can bet that everyone was looking as the losing party put in his nickel. No loser was going to get a free hand. This card game was to be a Sunday afternoon ritual for many Sundays to come.

Bill and Rachel

About two miles from Kathy's house was what I considered a Swiss Chalet–style house. When my family would take a ride in the country, one of the very eventful sights was to see the house that could "split a raindrop." The roof on this house has the sharpest pitch of any house I had seen. The house was very well landscaped with attractive bushes and trees. Little did I know that the occupants of that unusual house were very good friends of Kathy. In fact, after Kathy and I began to date, one of the first stops we made was to meet Bill and Rachel Daniels.

Within a split second of meeting Bill and Rachel, I found they impressed me as two of the most interesting and likeable people I had ever known. By design, the inside of the house was like the inside of a boat. In the middle of the living room was a modest fireplace, which heated the house in the winter. On the right side of the living room, there was a built-in sofa. To the left were a kitchen and a bar-type dining table capable of easily seating four people. On the backside of the fireplace were a bedroom and a bathroom. There were narrow steps located in the living room that led to the second floor where bedrooms were situated on both sides of the stairs.

One of the small yet most notable features of the house was located on the first floor near the center of the room where the kitchen was located. It was a window that overlooked the bird sanctuary in the backyard. It was here that Bill took pictures. It was also here that a large hole had been drilled in the frame of the window so that Bill could scare off undesirable birds and feed peanuts with his bare hand to the birds. Bill had pictures of the birds being fed by hand through this hole and a picture of the rifle coming out of the window with a bird sitting on the barrel of the rifle. You name it, and Bill usually had pictures of birds in action doing it.

Rachel, a pleasant lady in her seventies at the time, was known for her distinctive laugh and her three-foot-long white hair. She graduated from Oberlin College in Oberlin, Ohio, with a degree in ornithology. Their love of birds and the great outdoors was evident by the number of birds they fed in their backyard and the many pictures they had of nature.

Bill was raised in the middle of a swamp on Star Island in Old Woman's Creek in Erie County between Vermilion and Huron. He had been professionally trained at Orin R. Coile School of Photography and Journalism in Chicago. He had been the manager of a boat basin in Fort Lauderdale, Florida, for the Department of the Navy and had supervised 440 men who built $92 million worth of small vessels in 1942. He then moved around in the marina-managing business and finally took a job as one of two full-time photographers for the U.S. Forest Service. He traveled with Rachel as much as 50,000 miles a year across the United States. Bill was a pioneer in enlarging photographs with the copy usually being better than the original. Some of his work with the U.S. Forest Service has never been released to the general public.

After retirement from the forest service, he turned his attention to old photographs. He was the official photographer of the Willard Centennial Parade in 1974. I was honored to be one of Bill's photographers for that event, and I asked my brother Mike to work with me. Working with historic photographs, he produced 485 prints.

As has been mentioned, another of Bill and Rachel's loves is birds and bird pictures, with him photographing around 180 different species and painting the photocopies. Some of Bill's collection of bird photos was to be given to the Old Woman Creek Museum.

Kathy regularly rode her bike and visited Bill and Rachel's home as she was growing up. Throughout her grade and high school years and beyond, she would go to Bill and Rachel's home to talk about many subjects. I could see that I was an immediate member of their extended family the day I first walked into their house. Kathy and I spent many hours with them. We would talk, laugh, play cards, and eat with them. On occasion, we would accompany them on outings to photograph birds or wildlife. I remember one time when Bill knew of a towhee in a neighbor's woods. He invited me to go along, and he gave me the pleasure of photographing this bird.

There were many people who visited Bill and Rachel because of their similar interests. Their home and property were a haven for many people in the area. The cross section of people who frequented this setting amazed me. Bill and Rachel were people who valued their family, friends, and their life in the country surrounded by nature.

The wedding gift that we received from Bill and Rachel was all of our wedding pictures. Bill wanted to make sure he had taken every picture possible. Rachel was with Bill, as he photographed the wedding and helped him carrying and setting up the cameras, as well as keeping the cameras full of film. At the wedding, it was as if Bill and Rachel were the third set of parents for both the bride and the groom.

Bill's cameras were German, and as best as I can recall, his expensive cameras were hard to find and usually cost top dollar. Bill and Rachel were the photographers of persons with developmental disabilities that were used in several articles I had published in national journals on physical development.

Inexpensive Dating in Mansfield

Visiting relatives was a lot of fun and very inexpensive. One of the best times we had was babysitting for Judy and Walt's children in the summer of 1967 after they moved to Mansfield. There were always a few refreshments, and it was enjoyable to be around Kathy and the kids. On one occasion, Butch and Phyllis Rothschild and Kathy and I, all from Willard, went to visit Walt and Judy to play cards.

It was getting to be about one thirty in the morning, and Kathy thought I was looking in her hand. She gave me a poke in the cheek, and I fell off my chair to exaggerate the effect of the poke she gave me. I expected some sympathy from Kathy, but instead, she continued to falsely accuse me of cheating. We had a really late evening, or I should say an early morning, because when I dropped Kathy off at her brother's house, he was getting ready to go to work.

There were several relatives on both sides of the family we would visit to have an enjoyable evening. Our move away from our relatives made it difficult to see them on a regular basis, and even today when we visit the area, it is usually for more public events, such as weddings or graduations. The homey atmosphere of playing cards or games or just talking usually doesn't happen today.

Fire near Olena, Ohio

At this time, my sister Ann and Tom Herner also were dating, so it was usual for the four of us to go places together. Another inexpensive part of the dating was that Tom was buying a farm, and he had a farmhouse he was remodeling for their future home. On this particular evening, we left Willard in one car. We were going over to the farmhouse to play cards.

As we came within ten miles of Tom's house, we saw that the sky was very light in the north. An inquisitive part of all of our natures said, "Let's go see what it is!" As we got closer, we could see that it was a fire. We parked the car and walked toward the fire. There were many buildings between us and the fire, so it was dark behind these buildings that shielded us from the fire. As we turned a corner, we found that we were very close to the flames. The outbuilding was burning so furiously that it was beginning to engulf the main barn.

We looked to our left to see a fireman and a fire pumper unit. The fire pumper seemed to have water in it, yet water was barely running out of the hose. The fireman yelled to us and asked if we would blow air into the fuel tank and keep our mouth on the tank entrance so the air we blew in would not escape. The engine would be able to run, and he could hose down the 300-gallon gas tank next to the barn. Tom and I alternated blowing air into the tank so that this pressure would push the gas into the engine. It was not surprising that the fuel tank opening smelled and tasted like gasoline.

As we blew air and pressure into the fuel tank, the water pump worked, and water was spewing out of the hose. As the water found its way to the 300-gallon gasoline tank, the water turned into steam as soon as it made contact. The tank was so hot that it was probably close to blowing up. We stayed for around an hour until the fire was beginning to come under control. We left the fire, hoping that the 300-gallon tank would not rupture and cause an even bigger problem.

There was no card playing that night, nor was there much else happening, as we were pretty tired and smelly. We were sure that we had stopped the 300-gallon fuel tank from blowing up and causing more problems than they already had. As we left the fire, we all agreed that if it had been our fire, other people would have probably offered to help us as we had offered help this evening. There was no thought in our minds that a few years later, Ann and Tom's house would burn to the ground.

Cedar Point

I don't want to "come off" as one who never spent money on his girlfriend. One of the favorite recreational spots in this area, which was by no means inexpensive, was Cedar Point. Cedar Point is located on Lake Erie by Sandusky. There are many rides to enjoy, drinks and food to consume, and games to play. A favorite activity for young people who enjoy one another's company is to have their picture taken at a booth without a photographer. In this booth, a camera will take a series of pictures. When having one's picture taken, it is not known until the last second when the camera is going to take your picture.

Joe and Kathy at Cedar Point

Kathy and I were pretty proud of this pose, as we are both in the picture, facing the camera, and smiling with our eyes open.

Spoons in Olena

While euchre was a favorite card game, we also enjoyed a game called spoons. The amount of scrapes and scratches to one's body from the game depended on the aggressiveness of the players. Injuries were usually confined to the hands, but they could affect other parts of the body.

The rules of the game were simple. Each player sat around a table and started out with one spoon in his hand. Everyone placed his spoon in the middle of the table, and one spoon was taken out of play.

Since spoons is a card game, a look at the cards is needed. Each player receives four cards from a full deck. The first player picks a card off the deck and then throws away a card facedown to the next player. Each player picks up a card from the player to his right and discards a card to the player to the left. The object of the game is to match four cards. When the match happens, the person with the match picks up a spoon. All the other players then try to pick up a spoon. One player does not get a spoon, and he is out of the game. The game proceeds until there is one spoon left, and the player with that spoon is the winner.

The dangerous part of the game was when more than one player went after the spoon. Fingernails would often scratch other players' hands while securing the spoon in any way possible. It was common for a few drops of blood to be shed in the valiant attempts to get the spoon.

The most famous spoon snatching I know of happened at Olena, Ohio, at Tom and Ann's house. The game was at the point where everyone was picking up a spoon. Ann and Tom went after the same spoon. Tom pulled the spoon toward him. Ann also had a good hold on the spoon and did not let it go. As Tom pulled the spoon to his side, Ann held on to the spoon and leaped over the table landing on Tom and the spoon.

In the process, the table broke. I am sure the spoon was badly bent. The rest of the players in the spoon game immediately jumped back from

Tom and Ann. First, everyone wanted to see if Tom was breathing. After they saw Tom was OK, they watched the scuffle over the spoon. I believe Ann ended up with the spoon; both ended up with a few scratches but no broken bones.

The Stangs

While Kathy had known her uncle Norb and aunt Grace for many years, in 1967, I was to meet not only Grace and Norb but also the five boys, Richard, Leroy, Roger, Russell, and Tommy. Kathy had secretly planned this first get-together for me. None of the Stangs knew they were invited to this event.

They were to find out that evening that their windows were to "explode" when several handfuls of corn were thrown to celebrate the Halloween season. After hiding our car, we walked around the Stang house in the dark to find the best vantage point in which to throw the corn. After the corn was released, Kathy and I peered into a window to see the young Stang boys huddled in the middle of the room like a covey of quail.

After a few minutes of waiting, we knocked on the door and had a good laugh with Grace and Norb. The boys were not so sure they wanted to meet Kathy's new boyfriend, as they were still in shock from the corning. I likewise was not sure I wanted to meet this big guy called Norb, as I had just been involved in scaring the living tar out of his family.

We had a great time that evening and many others doing such activities as playing cards and even coloring eggs one Easter. The number of colors produced and the beauty of the eggs with their altered exteriors was truly amazing.

Halloween

One evening, Butch and Phyllis Rothschild, Kathy, and I decided that an evening of trick-or-treating would be fun. We knew several forms of tricking but were very selective. The common toilet papering of trees in the front yard was considered. After toilet papering the trees and bushes, it was fun to see people reacting to this prank. Since waiting usually meant waiting for several hours, we would not see the direct response to this prank, so we did not use this technique.

Rotten tomatoes were most often used in our prank. On this particular evening, we were throwing tomatoes at a vacant building. On one occasion, we had thrown several tomatoes at the window of our friend's building. We thought it was funny that they were not splattering when we threw the tomatoes at windows. The next morning, we found out why our tomatoes didn't splatter. The windows were open. What a mess!

Wreck Train

Kathy's father worked on the B&O Railroad out of Willard. He also helped her grandfather on the farm. In this picture of Albert J. Long and Laetta Long, we see their John Deere B antique tractor and the barn on the farm, which was previously owned by Ted and Loretta Long.

Whenever there was a major train wreck on the B&O lines, Albert was part of the wreck train

Albert J. and Laetta Long on their farm

crew. Albert operated the main piece of equipment on the wreck train, the big hook. I remember visiting Kathy when we were both in high school. At that time, her father was often gone on the wreck train. I always liked her father being on the wreck train because that meant that there was one less person around the house.

During our later courtship years, I was with Kathy and her mother when the news came that there was a large train wreck in Willard. It was not very often that Willard had a wreck train. Once we heard the news, we all decided that we were going to see Kathy's father in action. I was excited about seeing firsthand how that big hook worked. The three of us motored to Willard, and sure enough, there was a train wreck. Several cars and two engines were in the wreck. As we approached the trains, we noticed that the cable from the big hook was already attached to an engine. Kathy's dad was ready to pull the engine in a position to clear the tracks. He noticed the three of us as he went to work on the engine.

Albert had told me later that he didn't like having his family around when he was in a real challenging situation with the big hook, as he did not want anyone to see how dangerous his job on the wreck train could be. As I looked at all those huge cars and engines, I kept to myself how uncomfortable I felt about his safety. Albert surveyed the task at hand of moving the engine off the tracks. Cleaning the tracks so traffic could flow was a major concern of the wreck train crew.

Kathy's father began to slowly tighten the cable on the engine, and as the cable tightened, the crane began to lean toward the engine. A few minutes later, I heard a loud bang that sounded like metal hitting metal and saw that the cable line was not taut. I looked at the crane and saw it and the platform go back and forth several times. The crane did not tip, but it surely did "give a ride" to my future father-in-law in the cab.

Kathy and her mother were both very concerned about Albert being in that crane.

I understood why Albert didn't like his family to be around when there was a possibility of someone being hurt. As I had thought, Albert was very concerned that we had seen him in this dangerous situation.

Chapter 13

Engagement, Marriage, and our First Year

Engagement

Asking Kathy to Marry Me

One evening in the fall of 1967, I had a date with Kathy. I had asked her father the previous evening if he or his wife had any objection to me marrying his daughter. Since I had a job and loved his daughter, he gave me their approval. As I talked about the possibility of marriage with Kathy, I felt I needed to be open with her about some of my beliefs in life. I explained to her how important it was to me that having enough money to live on, not an excess, was a major concern of mine.

In later years, I found a biblical basis for my belief in having enough but not too much of anything. It was an eye-opener when I read 1 Timothy 6:8. St. Paul wrote, "If we have food and clothing, we shall be content with that."[31] There is no mention of an excess of either for contentment.

A little later, 1 Timothy 6:10 rewards us with the realization that Paul coined, the well-known phrase "For the love of money is the root of all evils."[32] I explained to Kathy that I had always striven for enough money to be comfortable and that I believed that the love of money is the root of all evil. The love of money would never be my goal.

Another understanding that has always been present and important in my family was how we spent our time. An area that was very hard to sort out was the amount of time to be spent on work. Without hard work, success on the job or around the home would be difficult. I resolved this issue by telling Kathy I would spend quality time with her and any children we might have.

I also told Kathy that with my high energy level and my need to be around people, involvement with community and organizations was important. My high energy level had produced an exciting life in my formative years, and I hoped that would continue. In other words, I didn't see that I would be a couch potato.

I also knew that family was very important to me. I felt the time together was very exciting and was something essential to my life. There were other related areas we talked about, but the important fact is that Kathy didn't have any objections to my stated needs.

Back to the proposal. We were in the living room of Kathy's house, and I pulled out a clean handkerchief, placed it on the floor, knelt on it, and asked her to marry me. I was pretty confident that she would accept, but it is never done until it is done. This statement about being done was to be a lesson that I would never forget, and I have applied it to my life.

The answer from Kathy was a very prompt "yes." I was happy, and she appeared happy. Now I needed to get an engagement ring.

The Engagement Ring

Our close friends Butch and Phyllis Rothschild lived in a large farmhouse with a few acres of land outside of Willard. It was located down the road from the Baltimore and Ohio Reservoir and the railroad yards. Butch was an engineer on the B&O Railroad, and Phyllis was a beautician. Kathy and I had gone to visit Butch and Phyllis one afternoon in the summer of 1967. The afternoon activities had led into the evening, and Butch and I decided to go into Willard and pick up pizza for supper. Both Phyllis and Butch knew that the pizza was to be an engagement pizza (containing an engagement ring), but Kathy was clueless.

The girls were talking about whether they should go to town with us, and finally, Phyllis convinced Kathy to stay at the farmhouse and catch up on the past. (That is what women do when they talk for a time; they catch up on things.) Driving back with the pizza was the only good chance I had to plant the ring in the right piece of pizza, the one Kathy was to consume. Butch and I conferred on exactly where to place the ring on the way to town. We thought the second bite should work just fine.

Butch and I picked up the pizza, and before we were out of the parking lot, I had the ring out and put it in the middle piece of pizza closest to the box opening. I knew I didn't want Butch or me to get the ring, and I certainly didn't want Phyllis to get it. As we pulled up to the farmhouse, I began to get a little nervous. I knew I loved Kathy and felt she loved me, but this was for a lifetime and what if she had changed her mind and said no. I began to talk to myself, and I said, *Take one step at a time. Make sure she gets the right piece. Make sure she doesn't swallow the ring.*

The time had run out. We were in the house, and I announced that we would serve the ladies. As I began to take Kathy's piece out of the box, she came into the kitchen. I was a little nervous since I didn't want her in the kitchen when I took her piece out of the box and placed it on the plate. I reminded her that Butch and I were serving them. She said she was in the kitchen to get a drink. I slowed down my cutting of the pizza and placement of her piece on the plate. When the women were seated, I served Kathy's piece, and Butch served Phyllis her piece. I didn't want to miss anything, so I quickly picked up my piece in the kitchen, and

Butch did likewise. As Kathy bit into the first piece and started to chew, I watched her as did Butch and Phyllis. Secretly I thought, *I don't know if this is a good idea.*

As Kathy bit into the second piece, I waited for her to discover the ring. She should find it in this piece. She finished the bite into the second piece, and she mumbled the word "hard." I asked, "What did you say?" She began to look at the pizza after she had bitten into it and then placed it on the plate. She said, "There is something hard in this pizza." I was holding my breath as I thought for sure she must have taken a smaller bite than we planned, and I hoped she didn't hurt her tooth. She pulled out the ring, which looked like a clump of tomato paste and melted cheese. As she began to clean it off, she shouted, "It's a ring, an engagement ring."

She was over to my chair in no time flat and said, "Yes, I will marry you." At that point, everything was cool. She assured me her teeth were fine, and she cleaned the ring and put it on her finger. The ring never leaves her hand unless she is having it cleaned, or she is doing some task that it would be dangerous to have it on her finger. I had waited a long time to have an unusual way to give Kathy the ring. It was risky, but it worked.

Planning the Wedding

We began all the necessary plans for the wedding. Kathy chose her friends for the bridal party, and I chose my friends for the groom's party. I had always been intrigued with suit coats that had tails, and that was my choice for me and for all the males in the party. My nephew Trace was the ring bearer, and he looked really cute in the tails at his young age of four.

Finding a hall for the reception was pretty easy, as the facility we wanted was not booked. Kathy chose all the flowers. There were many miscellaneous purchases, such as the pillow for the rings, matches, and cigars. The time-consuming task of picking out the wedding announcements, the reservation cards, the directions, and the envelopes was necessary. The real job was deciding who was to be invited and addressing all the envelopes. The illegibility of my writing made it imperative that Kathy would address the envelopes, and I assisted her by doing whatever she asked me to do to help.

Choosing the photographer was easy, as Bill and Rachel had volunteered for this position early in the process. Bill had promised to take many pictures, and that was exactly what he did. In my judgment, we had a shot of everything that happened, and we will treasure these pictures forever.

Then there was the task of taking marriage instructions from Kathy's priest, and it went much smoother than I had thought it would. To be truthful, we had no idea what this training was going to be like.

Kathy knew the hall, and she knew the ladies who were preparing the meal. My job was to agree that everything was well planned. I had no problem agreeing with all of Kathy's planning.

Bachelor Party

My bachelor party was the night before the wedding after our rehearsal. Several of my friends felt a bachelor party was in order. The evening was cold, and we did found a suitable place to talk, drink, and laugh.

Unfortunately, we went way beyond an acceptable hour to end our festivities. I was to pay for the late hour of frivolity the next day—our wedding day. I woke up tired the next morning. I saw that the world was covered with ice. The ice was so thick that it had coated and covered the cars. I rolled down the window of my car, and the ice was solid. I pushed my fist through the ice, and the only piece of ice that moved was where my fist had hit it. Since I wanted a January wedding and Kathy wanted a June wedding, I knew I was in trouble.

Marriage

The Wedding Day

Three priests from John Carroll University were lucky enough to make it to St. Sebastian Church in Bismark. The number of large buildings in this town could be counted on one hand. The Mass was to be concelebrated or performed by all three priests. Having three priests present made it sure that Kathy and I were married. The rain turned to ice and then to snow early in the day. It was a wonder how even some of the invited guests were able to brave the weather for the ceremony and the reception.

As the guests began to arrive in the near blizzard for the wedding, I was holding my breath and hoping that people were going to make it. Since it had been me, not Kathy, who wanted a January wedding, I tried to avoid the topic. Kathy's wish was to wait until June for a wedding, and I did not want to wait any longer to live without her. My decision-making ability was suffering a big blow with the continued snowfall and near impassable roads.

The snow was so thick that Kathy could not safely walk to the church from the car. Butch Rothschild had to carry her to the church. My groomsmen took their places as the ushers seated the people who had braved the terrible weather. I was happy to hear the music begin, as it told me that the organist had made it. The procession went well after the runner was put in place down the aisle. Kathy's father gave her hand to me, which said that I continued to have her parents' blessing. There were trips to the altar for different reasons, but the big trip was the actual wedding ceremony. As Kathy began to place the ring on my hand, I took a double take as I saw my ring for my first time. There were three diamonds carefully inlaid in it. I looked at the ring and said out loud, "Holy cow," as Kathy finished placing the ring on my finger. I was awed at the looks of my ring as I said my vows.

Later, we went back to our chairs and kneelers. I had the job of adjusting Kathy's dress and train. The movie being taken of our wedding was very graphic in showing me placing the wedding gown's train behind Kathy and then checking it at least twice to see that it was not in any way out of place.

The ceremony went well, which was more than what could be said for the progressively deteriorating weather. During the ceremony, the snow had gone from bad to worse. It was time for pictures, and we were ready for anyone or anything that was desired. Our wedding picture was all one could want.

As we tried to go to the hall for a luncheon, cars were sliding in every direction. When we reached the hall, I slowly began to leave the backseat of the car. At that moment, I realized that

Mr. and Mrs. Joseph B. Frederick

I had not flipped up my tuxedo tails, and I had sat on them. They were wrinkled. I tried unsuccessfully to straighten them out.

The luncheon went well for those who were able to make it. There was some time open between the luncheon and the reception. It continued to snow and blow throughout the afternoon and evening.

As people walked into the reception, the wind was blowing on a straight course into the entrance doors and into the hall. The hall had a good heating system, so the hall was warm all day despite the wind and weather.

It was time for the reception, and we were hoping that people would somehow be able to make it through the deep snow and wind. People began to arrive, and the band was playing. The band leader was Kathy's neighbor, Harold Fries. Kathy was not babysitting for the Fries tonight. She was enjoying the square, polka, and slow dances.

It was time to eat, and there was plenty of good food. A few friends and relatives were the bartenders, and they made sure there was plenty to drink.

The gift table was filled with presents and envelopes. Kathy and I thought that it would be a good idea to have some extra cash for the honeymoon, so we began to open some presents and then we opened a few envelopes containing cards and money. We ended up with plenty of money for our honeymoon. We stayed late at the reception and decided to leave when the time seemed right.

Honeymoon

Our honeymoon officially began as we left the wedding reception around eleven in the evening of Saturday, January 13, 1968. We exited the Knights of Columbus Hall in Monroeville and found the snow was much deeper than it had been earlier in the day. We were transported to our car, which was in the garage of Kathy's aunt Ruth and uncle Pete Wilhelm.

There had been threats by some of Kathy's relatives that they were going to put Limburger on our car's manifold. I have been told that when it is heated, it gives off an incredibly repugnant smell. I have never smelled burned Limburger and did not think that this was the time to start.

As we traveled to Kathy's house for her to change out of her wedding dress for clothing better suited for a honeymoon, the snow showed no sign of stopping. I didn't try to pull into Kathy's driveway because I was afraid I would get stuck and lose valuable time. The thought went through my mind that Kathy had already spent her last night as a single lady in her family house. Now she would be spending the nights and days with me as my wife. I had a hard time believing that the wedding had actually happened, and we were on our own. I had no time off from work, so I needed to take advantage of every minute we had.

Kathy began running toward the house and found the snow was over a foot deep and hard to cope with in a wedding dress. Eventually she made it to the house, changed, and made her way back to the road and our car. We were on our way. Travel was very slow, and the icy roads under the snow made it even more challenging. We made it to a major truck highway, U.S. Route 224, and while there was not much traffic, the wind from every truck we passed caused us to move to the right side of the road. The faster we went, the more we slid.

When we reached a gas station near Bloomville, Ohio, we pulled in and asked for a fill-up. While we didn't always have the money for a fill-up, we had raided enough envelopes at the reception to easily make it through our honeymoon. The attendant filled up our gas tank in what was still a mild blizzard. In those days, it was very rare for someone to fill up his own car as that was the job of the attendant. I handed him the money, and he said, "Have a nice honeymoon!"

I looked at Kathy, and she looked at me. I quickly asked the attendant how he knew we were just married and on our honeymoon.

He said, "A little birdie told me."

When I had proposed to Kathy, I made a few promises to her. I enjoyed different experiences in life, and I strived to have an interesting life. The gas station attendant had just provided us one of our first interesting experiences by knowing about our honeymoon. It took us about two months to solve the mystery of the little birdie. We were again having the car filled up in Mansfield. The attendant came up to my car window to collect his money and said, "Have a good honeymoon."

I quickly asked how he knew about our honeymoon, and he told me to come with him.

He opened the lid to the gas cap, and there was a note pasted on it that said, "Just married."

We settled into our honeymoon suite in Tiffin at the River View Inn on Route 224. The next morning, we awoke, and to our surprise, there were only a few other people staying at the large motel. After breakfast, the manager told us that the housekeepers were not able to make it to work because of the snowstorm, so they were going to move us down to the next clean room. Until the housekeepers could get to work, each morning, we would pick up our belongings and move to the next clean room.

When the housekeepers did come in, they would see Kathy and me and laugh for no apparent reason. As I later thought about the situation, they must have known that we were newlyweds because of something we were doing or saying.

My namesake Uncle Dr. Joe Schlotterer; his wife, Liz, and their children lived in Tiffin. Joe was the superintendent of schools in the New Riegel School District. As we traveled to their house in spite of the one- to two-foot snow accumulation, everything about life seemed beautiful to me, especially Kathy. The sun had come out, but it wasn't melting the snow. The world was starting to come out of its secure hiding place from the winter. We did some shopping and found a bargain on some records for mostly classical music: Mozart, Beethoven, and Bach.

Bargains were something I liked because it saved money. Kathy liked to save money too, but she didn't tolerate buying a year's supply of anything just to save cash.

We had been invited and traveled to Joe and Liz's house for drinks and supper for several nights on our honeymoon. We learned quite a bit about Liz on these visits. We learned that she was born and raised in Garrett, Indiana. Her family had moved to Willard for a short time. It was at this time that Liz became friends with two siblings, my aunt Theresa and my uncle Joe. Liz moved back to Garrett but did not end her relationship with Theresa. In fact, as a result of maintaining this relationship, Liz attended Theresa's wedding. Her attendance at the wedding sparked her reacquaintance with Joe. They began to date and eventually married.

Joe had decided that he was going to make our honeymoon even more of a success. Before we ate dinner, he served gin martinis. There are other types of martinis, but Joe favored only the gin variety. I remember having a martini and drinking it like I really knew what I was doing. To tell the truth, it was the first martini I ever had. In a few minutes, I came to realize how strong straight gin could be in a drink. I cut my drink to one as I waited for my head to clear. As I was having my drink, their seven children came down the steps to see the cousins that were just married. All the children were exceptionally well mannered and fun to meet.

The second night, we went out to dinner with Joe and Liz to a little restaurant in downtown Tiffin. Joe pointed out to me that a gentleman sitting a few tables over was the superintendent of Tiffin schools. I remember that when this superintendent and his wife left, Joe made a special effort to greet them by standing up and going over to the door as they were about to leave. I was impressed by my uncle's cordial words and actions. I tucked away this piece of knowledge for a future day. At the time, I had no idea that I would have positions in related areas where my title would be superintendent. I also had no idea about the responsibilities, stress, and uncertainty that these positions would hold for me and my family.

At the end of the week, our honeymoon was over, and we returned to our new home on Glenwood Boulevard. I discovered that weekend that the school I was working in had been shut down for the entire week while we were on our honeymoon. While I had taken the week off, I did not lose any pay from my job as physical education and recreation coordinator for the Richland County Board of Mental Retardation. We both were realizing that while our first honeymoon was over, the prospects of a new life with a new spouse was developing into a honeymoon for life. It was to be just that—a honeymoon for life.

We finished opening the cards and presents at the house of Kathy's parents the following weekend. People had been very generous with their gifts, and we didn't object one bit. One of the cards we received was from my summer job boss and his wife. This maintenance boss had many challenges from me and the other summer help. The card from my former boss and his wife was a sympathy card, sharing their sorrow with us on our marriage. The really cute part of the card was that he labeled me as his "ace painter." This was truly a compliment coming from my tolerant boss.

Our First Year Together

While we did not have much money, we had each other and a few possessions. Our couch came from my sister Mary Lu. We bought a new refrigerator, a new mattress and springs, a new black La-Z-Boy chair, and a ten-year-old four-door Chevrolet. I learned to ask Kathy what she wanted before I purchased items when the refrigerator had to be exchanged, as I had picked the wrong color.

Kathy was working as a nurse at the Mansfield Memorial Gardens Nursing Home, and I was at the

Physical education and recreation director at Richland County Newhope Center and Kathy

Richland Newhope Center. This picture shows my daily work outfit and Kathy.

Our New Life

I had found a house to rent a few months before Kathy and I had married. I had left my rental apartment and was living in and fixing up the house for us. My brother Walt was extremely handy with about any type of fix-up situation. He was very happy to help me with the various painting, floor upgrading, plumbing, and electrical modifications.

Those first few months I lived alone in our house were exciting knowing that Kathy would soon be there to share my life. After the wedding, it was very different to be moving into a new relationship with someone that I respected and loved. This was a new experience for both of us. For years, I had attended college and dreamed of finding a young lady who could minimize the loneliness that I had experienced in my single life. Now it was a new and real experience for both of us.

To say that there was not a period of adjustment for both of us would be to say that marriage is just a continuation of one's life before marriage. The excitement of a new relationship that we planned for the remainder of our lives was overpowering for me. Those early memories were enjoyable, and this new relationship will always be seen as some of the fondest years in my life.

I desired my life with Kathy to be as fulfilling as possible for both of us. A simple look into each other's eyes and a quick smile was a testimony to our love. I liked to express my love for Kathy by doing little tasks for her around the house, such as the dishes. Catching Kathy's look at me across the room was always exciting. Sharing our desire for children in years to come filled our lives with hope. I loved to give Kathy presents and see her eyes light up. Our first year of life together dictated that gifts were usually not large and could be something as small as a vanilla Bun candy bar.

Each of us came into this relationship with differences in opinions and preferences. Working through these differences showed us that we could both learn and in this process see our love become a relationship we both wanted in this marriage. Making up was fulfilling and ended a time of uncertainty. Relationships could suffer greatly because of disagreements, but we made a pact early on that we would always go to bed talking.

Thinking Back

As I began thinking back about our relationship, I went back to our high school days. I had known Kathy but had never been very serious about her nor her about me. I discovered some old pictures and started to go through them. As I came across her graduation picture, I had a thought. How could I not be attracted to this high school lady? She is nothing short of attractive.

Kathy's high school graduation picture

Our First Spat

It was bound to happen. A few weeks after Kathy and I were married, we had a small disagreement about something. Neither of us can remember the issue now.

I decided to take a ride to my brother's house. As I walked into his house, he asked, "Where is Kathy?" I said she was home. My tone of voice must have given away that something was wrong. He asked me, "Did you and Kathy have a disagreement?"

I said, "A small one."

Walt said, "You are not going to use our house as a place to hide out. You need to go back and get things straightened out."

I couldn't believe it; my own brother kicked me out of his house. That was to be the best thing that happened to me as a newly married person. I needed to talk things out with Kathy, and that's what we did on that occasion, and that's what we have done our entire married life.

Missy or Mistress Juliet de Glenwood

Shortly after our wedding, we were home talking and watching television in our newly rented home at 21 Glenwood Boulevard in Mansfield. There was a knock at the front door, and we discovered our good friends Butch and Phyllis Rothschild had come for a visit. During the course of the evening, we told them that we were thinking of buying a French poodle. This was all our dog enthusiast friends needed. We were in the car and headed toward Bellville, Ohio, to look at a miniature poodle that was advertised in the local paper.

It was an exciting time both to and from the location. We found the house where this miniature black poodle lived, and as we looked into its eyes, there was no doubt that it was going to be ours.

On the way back to our house, we discussed how we were going to care for the dog, which we named Missy, as we both worked and had no fenced area outdoors. Butch and Phyllis were as excited as we were and offered suggestions on how to handle our new situation. It was soon decided that when we left for work, we would barricade two doorways, so Missy could not leave the kitchen. The kitchen seemed like the best place for her, as there would be nothing other than a stove, cupboards, and barricades there.

Missy was at this time a very young puppy, and how much damage could a dog that small cause?

Butch and Phyllis left, and we were on our own to parent this beautiful small dog. The next day was a workday, and we were ready to leave for work. We went out the back door leading from the kitchen. As Kathy and I closed the door, we could hear this loud cry from Missy. We went back in to quiet her down, and each time we left, the cries became louder. Finally, we had to leave, or we would be late for work.

In the early evening, Kathy and I walked into the back door to greet Missy. She was there, but a large portion of our linoleum floor in the kitchen was not. It was chewed up. We knew immediately that our little French poodle might be little, but she surely was mighty. Luckily, there were a few pieces of the flooring in the basement, so I was able to patch the floor. Missy chewed the floor a few times after this first event, and each time, I had the job of completing the patching.

When Missy seemed to be doing better in the kitchen, it was decided that we would allow her the opportunity to have the run of the house as a result of her good behavior. We arrived home after Missy's first day with no restrictions on her movements in the home. I was pretty confident that Missy would not betray our trust and destroy anything else in the house.

As I opened the door, Missy was in the kitchen wagging her tail and trying to jump on my legs. I walked into the two front rooms and the dining room, and there was no sign of any misbehavior. I walked up the stairs and walked into our bedroom. The electric blanket was torn to shreds, so I immediately unplugged it to prevent any possible electrical shocks. As I looked at the foot of the bed, I could see teeth markings. I saw an old book of Kathy's that had also been chewed. Kathy walked into the room at this time and said, "Oh no, my antique Louisa May Alcott *Little Women* book."

Missy was nowhere to be found. She had heard the commotion upstairs, and she must have figured that there was someone in the house who did not appreciate her handiwork. Missy was eventually found behind a downstairs door huddled in the corner. We took Missy upstairs and made sure she knew that we were not happy with her handiwork. I wish I could say that this was the last time that Missy was to chew our belongings, but it wasn't. Today wire cages would have helped us prevent this young puppy behavior. Missy would be with us for thirteen years, and in that time, she was a wonderful dog and a great pet.

Olivesburg, Ohio

There was an Amish community north of Mansfield where Kathy and I enjoyed going to with our dog, Mistress Juliet de Glenwood. Yes, Missy was royalty, and a quick look at her lineage would prove it. Since neither Kathy nor I had ever had any association with the Amish, we were completely infatuated with their many different ways of living.

Olivesburg had a general store and another store, both of which catered to the special needs of the Amish. In one of the stores, they had groceries, which include Amish cheese. We could usually find $2 to buy a small chunk of Amish baby Swiss cheese. After looking at all the Amish supplies, we would decide that it was time for a ride in the country. A ride in the country would consist of going down the back roads and trying to find some Amish people riding in their buggies, plowing their fields, harvesting their crops, or hanging out their wash. Seeing any of these would allow the day to be considered a success in learning more about the Amish people. We were not always able to see Amish activities, but we were always on the lookout and sometimes had some good results.

Hoz and His Late-Night Visit

One evening early in our marriage, Kathy and I were watching TV in our front room. We heard noises on the front porch and saw someone looking around with a flashlight. I went to the front door and pushed the blinds aside. There I saw a face looking at me, and this face was illuminated by a flashlight. I immediately recognized my college friend Dr. John McMannis or Hoz. We opened the door, and we had a nice discussion and a few drinks. Hoz said he had to take off the next morning about nine o'clock. I said that I need to be to work at eight, so we bid our farewells before going to bed.

The next morning, Kathy fixed him a big breakfast, and as he loaded his suitcase in the car, he said to Kathy, "This looks kind of funny. No Joe around, and here I am loading my suitcase." As he said this, he looked around and asked, "Do you think anyone is looking? If there is, let's give them something to talk about." He planted a kiss on Kathy's cheek. If someone was watching, their curtains were surely shaking.

Our Mansfield Dentists

Kathy and I did not spend much time and money on an active social life when we first married; we simply couldn't afford it. A great accomplishment for us was after we paid our bills, we would try to save enough money so we could have a pizza and a few beers with my brother Walt and his wife, Judy.

Kathy and I were invited to a party for John Carroll graduates with some well-respected people in Mansfield. We knew few people in Mansfield, but we decided we could hold our own with these successful JCU graduates. Besides, it was free drinks and food. Kathy and I attended the party. At the party, we met many friendly people.

One of the people we met was a dentist who was to become our family dentist. He was the type of person who liked a good time. At a reunion at JCU in years to come, he attended and had the perseverance to stay up most of the night with his friends. He made a recommendation to both Kathy and me that we should have our wisdom teeth extracted, as they were not doing any good and might start causing some problems. He recommended another prominent oral surgeon. I believe he said that the oral surgeon was also a JCU graduate.

With little money but the knowledge that we really needed that procedure, Kathy was chosen to have her wisdom teeth out first. Kathy had to have her mouth X-rayed to see the position of the wisdom teeth. We discovered that our oral surgeon had a possession he was extremely proud of and would mince no words in telling us about it. It was an X-ray machine that took a 180-degree picture of the teeth and produced an X-ray on one sheet of X-ray film.

The date was set, and Kathy had her X-ray taken. I took off work to be with Kathy, and all was expected to go smoothly. The day came, and I drove Kathy to the office. She was taken into the office and prepared for the surgery. I stayed with her until she was to have her surgery. I then went to my assigned place in the waiting room. A reasonable amount of time went by as I was sharing the waiting room with two other people. Both of them were women and were there with their husbands who were also having surgery.

About an hour after the surgery, I heard a commotion near the room where the surgery was taking place. Someone was talking very loud. One of the ladies said, "I was afraid that my husband would have a reaction to the anesthetic, as this is not the first time this has happened."

I and the other lady began to comfort the woman whose husband seemed to be having trouble with the anesthetic. A few minutes later, the nurse came out and said, "Mr. Frederick, can you please come back to the surgery recovery area?" I didn't say anything to the ladies. I just went back to the surgery recovery area because I knew that Kathy must be having some difficulties, and they thought I could help. As I walked into the dimly lit room, I could tell that Kathy was having a tough time. I certainly wouldn't have thought she would be happy after major oral surgery.

I was seated for about two minutes, and Kathy seemed to be quieting down. Then the oral surgeon popped his head in the door and asked Kathy how she was doing. With that question, Kathy sat up straight in her bed and looked directly at the dentist, pointed her finger at him, and said, "You put atropine in my shot." Atropine is a solution used to dry up one's mouth, so there isn't too much saliva in the mouth. He said he had put the atropine in the shot to protect her. There was no more excitement around the office, so I took Kathy home, and she was feeling much better the next day.

I was scheduled for the surgery about a month after Kathy. I had one very big handicap going into the surgery. I saw how painful and trying the surgery was for Kathy. As I was sitting in the chair to be operated on, I saw the oral surgeon walk in. I said, "Are sure you know what you are doing?"

He looked at me and said, "I just finished reading the chapter in the book on how to do your operation, so I am ready." I knew he was kidding, but I was still a little concerned about it.

I came out of the operation losing all my wisdom teeth, and most of my wisdom teeth had been impacted. My mouth was very sore, but I went home and almost immediately took the prescription that the dentist had ordered. Kathy went out to buy some supplies I needed. I began to have the worst side effects of my life as a result of taking the pain medication.

For about an hour, the pain was excruciating. When Kathy came home, I told her what had happened with the pain medication. I asked her to throw it out. Both Kathy and I healed, and both of us have a good story about the experience.

Benny and the Pigeons

We had been in our house for a short period when we looked out our high window in the dining room and saw what looked like a pile of bird droppings. I walked outside to take a closer look, and sure enough, a bird had been sitting under the roof overhang on a piece of wood and was making a mess on the roof below the wood.

I decided to take my pellet gun out the next time and see if I could scare the bird by shooting air and making a loud noise. I didn't think I could shoot the gun in town with live ammunition, so this was the best alternative.

About a day later, I looked up, and there was a pigeon sitting beneath the roof on a piece of wood. I pumped up the gun and began to sneak around the corner when a man from next door was coming toward me.

We looked at each other, and he said, "I hope you can do something about that bird." I walked around the corner to where the bird was and took a couple of shots in the air. The pigeon flew away. We found a ladder and scraped the bird droppings off the roof.

We never saw that bird again, but as a result of this incident, Benny became best friends with Kathy and me. He was an acquaintance of a neighbor lady, and after he stopped in to see her, he would visit us when he had time. The funny thing about Benny was that he made good money at the local auto plant in Mansfield and was constantly giving us gifts.

Big Bear

In addition to my full-time job, I also worked at Big Bear Grocery Store as a stock and carryout person. I worked Friday evenings, Saturday mornings, and sometimes Monday evenings. Rounding out our income was Kathy who was working at the Mansfield Memorial Homes as a nurse in the adult living facility. My work was enjoyable, and meeting the public was usually a treat for me. In stocking shelves, there was no such thing as bar codes to rely on for pricing. Instead, there was a stamp in which the stocker needed to set the price of the product from a printout sheet developed by someone in central office. There were a couple of hazards needed to be dealt with in this job.

One hazard was if I was lifting a heavy box of canned goods, I needed to use my knees to lift them correctly. I remember at least one time when I lifted a heavy box with my back rather than my knees and legs. Working with a back out of place was very painful, and it became even more painful trying to sleep that evening and the next morning. The only fast cure for my back was by the chiropractor, Dr. Donny Ward.

Another negative with the job was that people shop and may not feel well. At the same time I was working at Big Bear, there was a Hong Kong flu outbreak. I was trying to avoid it. I wasn't sick when I came into work that day, but I was surprised to be able to finish my workday while having a most difficult time breathing.

Before I left Big Bear, the management was impressed with my work skills. They offered me a full-time job leading to a management position. Since this was not my chosen profession, I thanked them for the offer, but felt I needed to pursue my other profession.

A major reward I experienced on Friday evening was after working all week at the Newhope Center and Friday evening at Big Bear, Kathy and I would have a homemade Chef Boyardee pizza. The reason I was working at the store was that in 1967, I was making around $5,000 a year as a teacher. Those pizzas were the best, especially when eating them when watching the television show *Judd for the Defense* starring Raymond Burr. I also cannot forget our drink with the pizza, a cold Gold Label beer (a rather inexpensive brand of beer).

The Robin

It was the first spring of our life together and a reason to feel good about having each other. In 1968, we were marveling about the change of seasons and thought that God was generous for giving us the hope that comes with spring.

As Kathy was looking out the window of our back porch enjoying the pleasure of a free and sunny day, she called to me in a very excited voice. "I see the first robin of spring," she reported. I looked out the door and saw the robin bobbing along in our vacant lot. Anything that was enjoyable and free in those days was a welcome sight to two young newlyweds. Kathy thought it would be a great small newspaper article to announce to Mansfield that what we believed was the first robin of spring had been sighted in our yard.

We made a call to the local paper and asked who we should talk to about the first robin of spring. We were transferred to a department. We informed the reporter that we had observed the first robin of spring in our yard on Glenwood Boulevard. The reporter had some news for us. First, robins do not always leave our area for the winter, and second, there had been other people who had reported the first sighting of the year. We still enjoyed the thrill of *our* first robin of the year, even though the robin may have never left for the winter. We took comfort in the fact that there were probably several other Mansfield residents who did not know that the robin may stay in the area for the winter.

Singing

One of the very early discoveries that Kathy made about me was my love for music. I love to listen to records or the radio, and I love even more to memorize the words to popular songs. Two of my favorite singing groups are Frankie Valli and the Four Seasons and the Beach Boys. In years to come, we were to have the good fortune to see both groups in concert.

My favorite time to sing was while showering or taking a bath. There wasn't much else to do but wash up at that time, so singing songs from my favorite groups provided me with enjoyment, and I assumed Kathy was entertained, as I don't remember hearing any derogatory comments. Singing any time of the day and especially in the shower was a great joy to me at that time and would stay with me for my entire life.

Our First Wedding Anniversary

Kathy and I had many very enjoyable simple happenings in our first year of marriage. We would take rides in the country, visit our parents, and spend lots of evenings with my brother Walt, his wife, Judy, and their children, Trace, Jackie, Denise, and Peter. With both of us working and me working a second job, there was not a lot of free time. I was also taking a course to help complete my teaching certificate in special education.

It was January 13, 1969, and I drove into our driveway with a first wedding anniversary card for Kathy. I had a dozen red roses and thought I was doing pretty good. When I walked into the house, I didn't see Kathy. I asked, "Where are you?"

She said, "In the dining room." I walked into the dining room, and there was Kathy in her wedding dress. I couldn't believe it. She was prettier than the day I married her, and she had a card for me and my favorite meal prepared for supper. We had a lovely evening.

Kathy in her wedding gown for our first wedding anniversary

Conclusion and Link

This ends the book *People + Me* dealing with my life and the influence of people on me in the early years of my life.

I had prayed to God in my freshman year at John Carroll University to help me through the challenging studies, and I had some doubts that I was going to graduate. As my prayers were answered and I graduated from John Carroll, a whole new set of needs began to unfold.

It became evident that the world was a happy place yet challenging to me in my education, my profession, and my private life. As these challenges surfaced, I would again and again ask God for help. He would time and again help me, and this set the stage for the title to my second book, *God Keeps on Giving*. The end result of God's help in my education was to result in four college degrees ending in a PhD in educational administration and supervision.

God's help in my professional career resulted in forty-one years of service in the area of developmental disabilities starting as the physical education and recreation director at the Newhope Center in Mansfield.

My community service has been a great love of several organizations in which I have used my skills, many times as the leader.

God's greatest gift has been my private life. He has blessed me with a wonderful wife, Kathy; our two sons, Joe II and Mark; and Joe II's exceptional wife, Tara. We have been blessed with two very special grandsons, Zachary and Joshua.

Descendants of Joseph B. Frederick

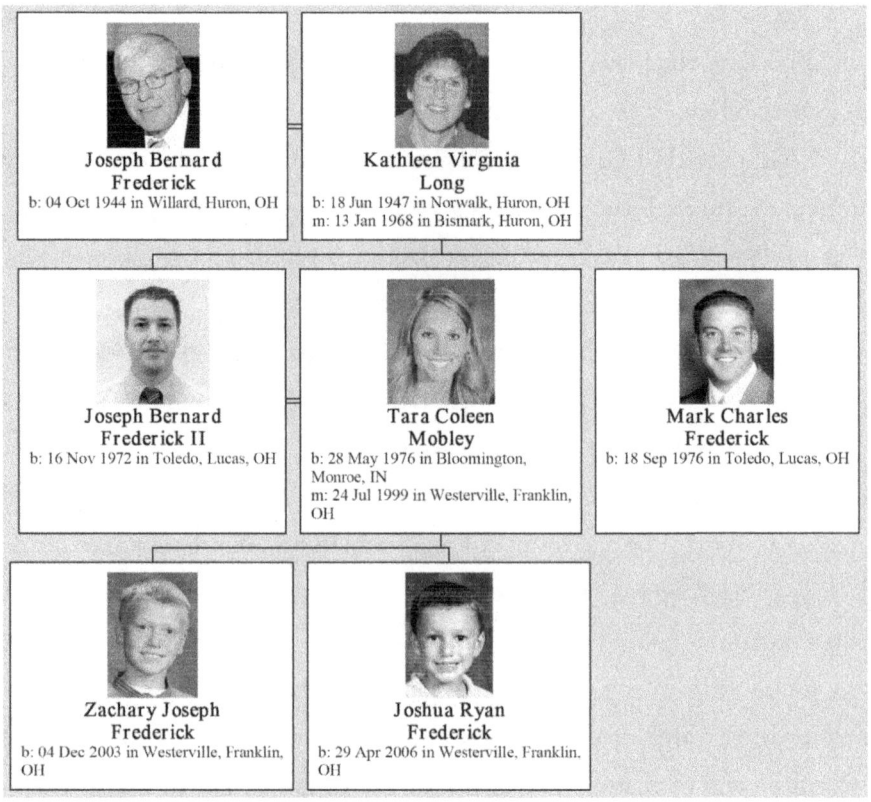

I believe God will keep on giving in a way that may not always be what I ask but what God sees as best. My family and I have adjusted to what God has given and have been satisfied. You are invited to take the next journey with me in my second book, *God Keeps on Giving*.

---

[31] Hickey, op. cit., 327.

[32] Ibid.

BIBLIOGRAPHY I

Albom, Mitch, *Tuesdays with Morrie*, New York: Broadway Books, 1997.

Anonymous, "I Eat My Peas with Honey," *Poetry Foundation*, Accessed 1/21/2013, http://www.poetryfoundation.org/poem/171639.

Anonymous, "Jesus, tender Shepherd, hear me," Accessed 4/10/2015, http://www.hymnary.org/text/jesus_tender_shepherd_hear_me.

Anonymous, "Jesus, tender Shepherd, hear me," Accessed 4/10/2015, http://www.hymntime.com/tch/htm/j/t/e/jtenders.htm.

Anonymous, "Letters to Jackie," *Sentinel-Tribune*, March 12, 2010.

Anonymous, *Novena to St. Francis*, New York: Gerffert-Hirten Publisher, 2005.

Brower, Rio, "Original Fruit Salad Is Double Duty Dessert," *The Willard Times*, March 18, 1965.

Fralick, Fr. J. B., *The History of Saint Francis Xavier Catholic Church*, Willard, Ohio, 1950's, updated by Larry Foran in 1975.

Hickey, James A., Imprimatur, *The New American Bible, Saint Joseph Edition, Revised Edition*, New Jersey Catholic Book Publishing Corp., New Testament, 1986.

Karban, Rev. Roger V., "Second Sunday of Easter: Acts 5:12-16, Revelation 1:9-11,12-13, 17-19, John 20:19-31," Commentary on the Sunday Readings, *The Messenger*, the Catholic newspaper of the Diocese of Belleville, (April 11, 2010).

Kelly, L.L.D., Right Rev. Msgr., William R. and others, *Living for Triumph, VII*, New York and others: Benzinger Brothers, Inc., 1949.

Larson McLaughlin, Jan, "Pemberville twins are very identical," *Sentinel-Tribune*, August 4, 2012.

O'Boyle, Patrick Cardinal, Imprimatur, *The New American Bible, Saint Joseph Edition*, New York, Catholic Book Publishing Co., Old Testament, 1970.

Rogers, Will, "I never met a man I didn't like," Accessed 4/10/2015, en.wikiquote.org/wiki/Will_Rogers.

Stuttaford, Thomas, Headline: "Ghost of the Missing Twin; Body and Mind," *The Times*, August 8, 1996.

Times Photo, "Explorers Become Air Minded for Fast Trip to Lake Camp Site," *The Willard Times*, date unknown in summer of 1960.

Weber, Fr. Herb, "Speech given at Blessed John XXIII Parish," Perrysburg, Ohio, February 5, 2011.

Weber, Fr. Herb, "Speech given at Blessed John XXIII Parish," Perrysburg, Ohio, June 2, 2013.

www.ingramcontent.com/pod-product-compliance
Lightning Source LLC
Jackson TN
JSHW082228090225
78635JS00001B/2